Ben Troke is a solicitor and a mediator with 25 years' experience working in health and social care, acting for the NHS and private sector providers all over the country. His particular interest is in decisions about mental capacity, medical treatment and deprivation of liberty, and he regularly deals with urgent applications to court in emergency situations.

Ben is independently rated as one of the leading practitioners in the country in the Court of Protection. He currently sits on the Law and Ethics Policy Unit of the Faculty of Intensive Care Medicine, and the Law Society's Mental Health and Disability Committee, and has a decade of experience of sitting on the ethics of clinical practice committee of a large acute NHS Trust.

Ben is a regular speaker at conferences nationwide and often provides training, in person and online.

Ben is also the author of 'A Practical Guide to the Law of Medical Treatment Decisions'.

A Practical Guide to the Law of Deprivation of Liberty

A Practical Guide to the Law of Deprivation of Liberty

Ben Troke, LLB, LLM
Solicitor and mediator

Law Brief Publishing

Published 2024 by Law Brief Publishing, an imprint of Law Brief Publishing Ltd
30 The Parks
Minehead
Somerset
TA24 8BT

www.lawbriefpublishing.com

Paperback: 978-1-913715-65-6

There's no place like home.

PREFACE

"*The law on deprivation of liberty*" may seem a bit dry, but this matters.

When arrangements for health and social care are made for someone, in their best interests, that could amount to a *deprivation of their liberty* – for example placing someone in a care home against their wishes – how does the law protect their rights?

This is the legal framework that protects us when other people, however well intentioned, start making decisions about where and how we live, often through to the end of our lives. I cannot think of anything more fundamental to our identity or our autonomy than that.

Each one of us could rely on others to make such significant decisions for us at some point in our lives. We will hope that the people involved in making or implementing those decisions, in a professional or personal capacity, will really understand what this involves and how important it is.

But we have managed to develop an overly complex, and poorly understood system that leaves tens of thousands of people without any meaningful safeguards, deprived of their liberty unlawfully; organisations exposed to potential liabilities; and huge amounts of time and money spent on a process that too often appears to yield little real benefit to those it is supposed to protect.

How on earth did we get here? Is this really what we want? And how do we make the best of it, and – perhaps – change it for the better?

Acknowledgements

The many mistakes and misjudgements in this are mine alone, but there would have been so many more without all the help I have been lucky enough to have.

I must acknowledge the influence of Lucy Series' work[*], particularly evident in the concluding chapters, and the inspiration I have taken from attending the wonderful Essex Autonomy Project summer schools, led by Professor Wayne Martin.

I am also grateful to a great many experts for sharing their wisdom so willingly and generously, including Alex Ruck Keene KC (Hon), Camilla Parker KC (Hon), Neil Allen, Julie Carr, Claire Webster, Rachel Griffiths and Lorraine Currie. Thank you to each of you for suggestions that have all significantly improved the book.

Special thanks must go to Mark Neary for sharing Steven's story so generously, and for kindly reassuring me that I was on the straight and narrow in presenting my own account of it.

I have also been lucky to have colleagues, past and present, who have made it possible to learn so much from them, and to have the opportunity to share it.

Finally, my love and my thanks to my family – Cathy, Emma and Genevieve. There really is no place like home.

Thank you all, and I hope that this is helpful.

Ben Troke
30 October 2023

[*] See the bibliography.

CONTENTS

APPENDICES

INTRODUCTION

The law in this vital area has long been a mess. In 2014, a parliamentary committee described the current legal framework – the "Deprivation of Liberty Safeguards" (DoLS) – as not fit for purpose, and that was before a Supreme Court judgment (*Cheshire West*) just a few days later meant that the system has since been overwhelmed with vastly more cases than it was built or resourced for.

In 2019, legislation was passed with the bare bones of a new system, the *Liberty Protection Safeguards* (LPS), to replace DoLS. But, despite a consultation in 2022 on a draft Code of Practice which added some detail, on 5 April 2023 the government announced that the LPS will not be implemented before the next general election (expected to be in late 2024). As the priorities of the next government are not to be taken for granted, LPS – at least in this form – may well now never be implemented at all.

Without long-awaited reform, we will still have to work with the current system, and all the problems that LPS was supposed to fix, notably:

- That DoLS does not apply beyond care homes and hospitals, and so anyone deprived of their liberty in other settings, such as their own family home, or supported living, can only have this authorised by a court order;
- Similarly, DoLS only applies over the age of 18, but this leaves a gap for 16–17 year-olds where, again, court orders are needed to authorise any deprivation of liberty, as the courts have only recognised parental consent to avoid a deprivation of liberty where the child is under 16; and
- Even where the DoLS system does apply, over 18 and in care homes and hospitals, there is a colossal mismatch between the system's resources and the workload, with an *average* delay of

around 5 months between referring a case into DoLS and it being processed.

When a High Court judge (Mr Justice Charles, no less, at the time the Vice President of the Court of Protection) describes dealing with the law around DoLS being "*as if you have been in a washing machine and spin dryer*"[1], we know we are in trouble.

As such, the issue of deprivation of liberty in the health and social care system can understandably cause confusion in practice, and certainly generates more heat than light.

Still, even without the prospect of reform anytime soon, a few things give me hope:

First, to get deprivation of liberty right, the most important thing is not actually found in the messy undergrowth of the law on DoLS, but rather in understanding the bigger picture of the Mental Capacity Act 2005 (MCA), a much more manageable and accessible bit of law. If anything good has come from the time and effort preparing for a reform that's been dropped, it is the increased focus on the importance of the MCA across health and social care.

Second, the focus should not be on the *deprivation of liberty* as if a bad thing, but always on the *safeguards* (the S of the DoLS) as a good thing. The system is better thought of as a spotlight than as a padlock, not enabling greater restrictions, but ensuring scrutiny of what is being done when it reaches a certain degree of intrusion and control over someone's life. It may be that we can take the lead from the rather more positive framing of the "*Liberty Protection Safeguards*", even if they never materialise.

Identifying something as a deprivation of liberty does not mean that the care involved is inappropriate, or the restrictions are excessive. It just

[1] Reference – House of Lords, post legislative scrutiny committee on the MCA House of Lords – Mental Capacity Act 2005: post-legislative scrutiny – Select Committee on the Mental Capacity Act 2005 (parliament.uk)

means that the effect of them is so intrusive in a person's life that – no matter that the person cannot make their own decision about them, and that they are in the person's best interests – there must be some additional safeguards, scrutiny and process to protect the person's rights.

Third, even without imminent reform, we are all on a learning curve, practitioners and service users, families, lawyers and judges alike, in an area of law that is still relatively raw and – in places – underdeveloped. Usually, the law develops over a long period, especially in a "common law" system like ours which depends on a case-by-case accumulation of judgments to add detail and interpretation to legislation, even where there is a core statute to begin with[2]. With or without LPS, the case law developed to date will remain, and we can build on it.

The fundamental problem we are tackling remains the same – how to protect the rights of people who are, in their best interests when they cannot make the relevant decisions for themselves, placed in care and accommodation which amounts to a deprivation of their liberty? And how to do it in a way that is efficient, effective and *cost effective*? An approach focused solely on the rights of the individuals is entirely legitimate, but the need to prioritise cannot be ignored when a system is asked to overreach the finite resources of the real world, as we will see.

Finally, the "near miss" of a reform abandoned may encourage a fresh look at the system we have, and how to make it work best in practice. While we all try to figure it all out, it will be up to the court to deal with challenges and resolve disputes. That is its role, and there is nothing wrong with finding our way together through the system, and – where we can – making it better – as long as we do not lose sight of "P", the patient or service user at the heart of the safeguards. That is the core of getting the Mental Capacity Act right, which is where we must start.

---

[2] Practice can take a while to adapt. I was giving training in 2018 when a psychiatrist in the audience put his hand up and asked something about the "*new* Mental Capacity Act", and I thought for a moment I might have missed a memo, before it became clear that he was in fact talking about the Mental Capacity Act 2005, which had been in force at that time for more than a decade.

Outline

So here's the plan: This book will look at:

Foundations:

1. Getting the MCA right.
2. How deprivation of liberty fits into the MCA context – s5 MCA, Article 5 of the European Convention on Human Rights, and *Bournewood.*
3. A case study: getting Steven home.

Defining a deprivation of liberty:

4. The road to *Cheshire West* – the domestic and European case law.
5. The Supreme Court case of *Cheshire West.*
6. At Home.
7. In Hospital.
8. "Eight C's" (conveyance, the clock, COVID, crisis, choice, constraints, covert medication and contact).
9. Consent and capacity.
10. Children and young people.
11. Imputability to the state.

What do we do about it? The safeguards and accountability:

12. The Deprivation of liberty Safeguards.
13. The interface with the Mental Health Act.
14. Safeguards beyond DoLS – the role of the court.

15. Accountability – Consequences and compensation for an unlawful deprivation of liberty.

Reform:

16. The impact of *Cheshire West* and the need for change
17. The Law Commission's review through to legislation.
18. The Liberty Protection Safeguards – what might have been.
19. What next? How things could yet change.

Conclusion:

20. What now? Making the best of the system we have for now.

I have also included some annexes:

1. Key statistics
2. A timeline to reform
3. A statutory definition?
4. Revised MCA s4B
5. Extract from Mark Neary's blog[3]
6. Schedule A1 essentials[4].

As "A Practical Guide", I considered including case studies of scenarios that might help to identify a deprivation of liberty. But as it happens, a document prepared by the Law Society in 2015[5] that does exactly that is being updated now, which I am pleased to be contributing to, and is due

---

[3] With Mark's kind agreement.

[4] Courtesy of Lorraine Currie and with thanks to her for sharing her work.

[5] https://www.lawsociety.org.uk/topics/private-client/deprivation-of-liberty-safeguards-a-practical-guide

for publication in early 2024. Rather than duplicate that, let me recommend that it is read alongside this.

Disclaimers

This book was commissioned (in late 2019!) as "*A Practical Guide to the Liberty Protection Safeguards*"! Repurposed as this now is, I hope that this can still be a useful exercise in taking stock of the law on deprivation of liberty under the current system and, in particular, *what we do now about all the problems that the LPS was supposed to address?!*

It may be helpful to look at how we got here, to understand the context. But for some readers, this may be your day job, and your focus may be on the present and how we use the tools we have now. Others might want to see a glimmer of hope for the future.

Some readers will be professionals at the frontline of health and social care, others expert lawyers in this field. Some may have the expertise of their experience in their own lives or those they care for. My own experience is entirely from advising the providers and commissioners of health and social care, and not from acting for individuals or families, which I appreciate would bring a very different perspective.

I will disappoint you all to some extent, no doubt, but I hope this is at least understood as well intentioned and balanced, and there is something useful for everyone.

This is limited to the law of England and Wales[6].

The law is correct as at 30 October 2023 but, of course, this does not constitute legal advice.

[6] The bulk of the case law comes from England, and around 95% of the use of DoLS are in England, so the text inevitably reflects that, but I would welcome feedback and input from those in Wales to make it more useful for you, in the event of a further edition.

PART ONE

FOUNDATIONS

CHAPTER ONE

GETTING THE MENTAL CAPACITY ACT RIGHT

Let's start with this: *the single most important thing about deprivation of liberty is getting the Mental Capacity Act (MCA) right*[7].

In my experience, when an organisation gets into trouble over a deprivation of liberty issue it is rarely due to some nicety or nuance of the law on deprivation of liberty. Instead, almost always, there has been a fundamental misunderstanding or misapplication of the MCA, though deprivation of liberty may well be the issue that has brought the problem to light.

To be clear: in depriving someone of their liberty in the health and social care context (as opposed to, say, criminal justice or immigration), the basis for this is that they cannot make the relevant decision for themselves (they "lack capacity") and that arrangements are made for their care or treatment in their best interests.

When those arrangements, even if the least restrictive to meet their best interests, may amount to a deprivation of liberty, there needs to be an extra layer of scrutiny and safeguards to protect the person's rights.

But any review and authorisation of the deprivation of liberty – however important a safeguard – does not in itself authorise the care or treatment involved, which must always be justified by proper use of the MCA. A

[7] This chapter assumes that we are dealing with over 16 year-olds, who lack capacity to make the relevant decisions, so within the scope of the MCA. Many of the points still hold good, by analogy, to children under 16, though of course there you are dealing with the Children Act 1989 rather than the MCA, see Chapter 10. There are also cases where there may be a deprivation of liberty for someone with capacity, using the inherent jurisdiction, see Chapter 14. But the great bulk of cases of deprivation of liberty for adults in health and social care are rooted in the MCA.

DoLS authorisation is not a substitute for using the MCA appropriately and asking the right questions:

- What care or treatment is appropriate / available?
- Can P make a decision for herself (with all reasonable help)?
- If not, what is in their best interests (taking into account her own wishes and feelings, values and beliefs, and the views of those caring for them?
- Is there is a less restrictive way to meet their best interests?

After that, if the care or treatment proposed may amount to a deprivation of liberty, then a further layer of scrutiny is needed as a check, given the gravity of the interference in someone's life, NOT as a substitute for that MCA framework and thinking.

To labour the point: if the care or treatment is lawful for P[8] it is because the MCA is used appropriately to do something in someone's best interests where they cannot make the relevant decisions for themselves. If it might amount to a deprivation of their liberty then this needs a Deprivation of Liberty Safeguards (DoLS) authorisation or a court order to make it a lawful deprivation of liberty, *but the lawfulness of the underlying care or treatment depends on the MCA*.

A DoLS authorisation is not in itself a green light, or a blank cheque, to do what you like for (or "to") a patient, no matter how intrusive or coercive, without due regard to the MCA.

[8] The MCA uses "P" to refer to the person who may lack capacity, and I'll do likewise, though I'll use a person's name for a bit more humanity where appropriate.

So, before I get to the issue of deprivation of liberty, I hope it will be useful to explain a few of things that most often go wrong with use of the MCA in this context[9]:

1. Misunderstanding "capacity" – Failing to recognise the assumption of capacity, treating it as a generic issue, instead of a focus on the specific decision that has to be made, and failure to identify the actual available options;

2. Over protectiveness: A natural concern to keep people safe leading to an inappropriately narrow view of best interests, unduly focussed on keeping people safe at all costs, or tempting us to find a lack of capacity too readily when a person is making a decision we feel is too risky; and

3. Best interests decision-making process: How to give proper weight to P's own views, and how to appropriately involve others such as their family.

Decisions, decisions

We cherish the idea of consent out of respect for the fundamental ethical principle of autonomy – i.e. that people's own lives should be determined by their own decisions as much as possible.[10]

But **autonomy** is only one ethical principle. A competing principle is of **beneficence**: doing good. We will often want to intervene in someone else's life and decisions because it will be better for them if we do (or so we think), and those driven towards the caring professions might well be at higher risk of finding it very difficult to let someone do something we

---

[9] I have written about this in greater detail in A Practical Guide to the Law of Medical Treatment Decisions, Law Brief Publishing, September 2020. If you happen to have read that already and can live without the recap, feel free to turn ahead to Chapter 2!

[10] I have a picture by my front door based on the Dr Seuss version of this, that you can choose your own path, thanks to the brains in your head and the feet in your shoes.

think will harm them. When the post legislative scrutiny committee looked at the MCA, it was critical of the aims to empower the patient being frustrated too often by risk aversion in social care and paternalism in healthcare.

The tension between autonomy and beneficence is a common thread through many of our challenges in health and social care: treatment without consent where it's what someone needs; or withholding something people want when we deem it bad for them.

At the core of the Mental Capacity Act 2005 (the MCA) are the questions of how we support people to make their own decisions where possible, how we make best interests decisions for people who cannot, and (crucially) how we tell the difference.

The MCA is a carefully crafted bit of work. There was a lot of thought and consultation, and a long period of implementation, and it is a great bit of law. It is well-written, coherent, and largely self-explanatory; we can readily see what it is trying to do, and how it goes about it; it has a clear code of practice[11], in plain English, with clear examples, albeit badly in need of updating[12].

The MCA provides a legal framework for making decisions about almost everything – from the vital, everyday trivia of what to wear, or eat, and management of our finances and property, through to some of the most important decisions of our life – where we live, who we have contact with, and whether or not we have risky medical treatment[13].

---

[11] https://assets.publishing.service.gov.uk/government/uploads/system/uploads/attachment_data/file/497253/Mental-capacity-act-code-of-practice.pdf published 2007.

[12] At the time of writing, the Ministry of Justice has committed to updating the MCA Code of Practice, but there is no sign of the timescale. An updated version of the update MCA Code that was subject to consultation in Spring 2022, but the document dealt with the LPS as well, which have since been dropped, for now at least. See Chapter 17.

[13] There are some significant exceptions, including capacity to contract, make gifts and retrospective assessment of capacity to make a will.

In fact, one thing that is entirely excluded from the MCA is the compulsory treatment of mental disorder without the patient's consent[14], which is the province of the Mental Health Act 1983 (as amended)[15].

So the one thing I do not like about the MCA is the title. I would not have called it the *Mental* Capacity Act (it started life as the Mental *Incapacity* Bill, which I think would have been even worse!). I think the word "mental" here is unhelpful and adds nothing, and can be misleading.

I have known clinicians treating physical health conditions flatly refuse to engage with the MCA, saying it is a matter for a psychiatrist.

That is just plain wrong. If a clinician or carer cannot give a view on P's capacity to make the decision about the treatment or care he proposes, then he cannot be confident that the patient has given valid consent. (I do appreciate that I will be jaundiced by disproportionate exposure to the clinicians who need support and advice about cases, either because they are less familiar with the legal framework, or because it is an especially sticky one. No one ever phones the lawyers to say everything's grand. But I have sometimes found that clinicians have got a stronger sense of the need for *consent* than they have of the niceties of the MCA, despite the

[14] MCA s28

[15] Other issues are sometimes described as "excluded" from the MCA – for instance decisions about marriage, sex or voting, but I think that is potentially misleading. The MCA still applies or those decisions to determine if P has the capacity to make that decision for themselves or not, but if they do lack capacity for that kind of decision then the MCA prohibits any best interests decision making. So if P lacks capacity for a decision about sex there is no such thing as "best interests sex", and any sexual activity without capacity, and therefore without consent, may be an offence under the Sexual Offences Act 2003. As you can imagine that is a proper can of worms, for instance, in cases of elderly couples married for many years still cohabiting and sleeping together, if dementia, for example, has undermined the capacity of one or both to consent to any sex. Or a young couple where one or both have a learning disability and they willingly have sex but one or both lack the capacity to consent for this to be lawful. This is not an entirely idle digression, since in those circumstances the authorities may feel obliged to intervene and impose restrictions on contact or time alone for the couple which can contribute to the possibility of a deprivation of liberty, which in turn needs authorisation.

obvious point that without capacity to make the decision there can be no valid consent).

There may be a useful role for a psychiatrist to give a view on a patient's mental condition, of course. But the treating clinician knows the information relevant to the treatment decision that needs to be made, has a responsibility to get consent, and (since there is no consent without capacity), cannot simply abdicate responsibility for assessing a patient's capacity entirely.

So, I love the MCA but I would drop the word "mental" from the title.

And if it were up to me, I would also drop the word "capacity"! My suggestion would be to call it instead the "Making *This* Decision Act", and I'll explain why.

The MCA is not about making *decisions in general*, and I think that the use of a fairly abstract noun like "capacity" lures us towards saying something meaningless (and dangerous) like "Doris lacks capacity".

"Capacity" in the MCA is defined as the ability to make the particular decision which needs to be made. So, to lack capacity for, say, a decision about where to live, or having an amputation, the person must be unable to make that decision. This is defined as being unable to understand, or retain, or weigh up and use the information relevant to that decision, or (and this is less common, given the scope of support that can be offered) unable to communicate a decision made. That's called the "functional test".

The inability to understand / retain / weigh up and use the information must be because of a (temporary or permanent) impairment or disturbance in the functioning of the mind or brain, sometimes called the "diagnostic test". The input of a psychiatrist might be helpful here to consider if there is such a condition and its impact on decision-making. But clearly the psychiatrist does not know as well as a surgeon, for example, the information relevant to the decision about an amputation (the risks and benefits, the options, and the consequences of refusing the treatment altogether), or a social worker, perhaps, about a decision where to live and the kind of care package available.

And this is why, if someone asks for your view about "capacity", you are best to reply "*for what decision*?". And why it is meaningless to say that someone "lacks capacity" without reference to the decision in question. Unless or until the decision, and the actual available options, are identified, it cannot be possible to assess whether or not the patient can understand or retain or weigh the information relevant to the decision, because you cannot know what the information is!

We all get casual at times, but it helps to have an alarm bell whenever you see or hear the word "capacity" followed by a full stop. It means nothing unless we are clear that we are looking at the patient's capacity to make a decision about this medication, or about that surgery, or about their admission to hospital or their residence on discharge. Each decision has different information which is relevant to it, and the fact that someone cannot make one decision does not mean that they cannot make any other. It is perfectly plausible that someone may lack the capacity to make a decision about complex chemotherapy options, for example, but be able to make a simpler decision about more straightforward issue, like who can be told about their treatment.

I think we do better to use the word "*decision*" much more often than the word "capacity". For starters, this unavoidably starts us off in the right starting place: what is the decision that needs to be made, and what are the actual options available, to identify the relevant information to meaningfully assess capacity?

Using "decision" also helps to avoid another huge bear trap by making sure we focus on the actual available options, and what is actually P's decision (as opposed to being the decision of the relevant public bodies, such as the NHS or the local authority, what options to offer). So, if Bob has a terrible disease and needs surgery, the surgeon may offer procedure A, or B. Each has risks and benefits, and Bob – if he has the capacity to make the decision for himself – can choose A, or B, or if he wishes can decline treatment altogether, for his own reasons, good, bad or indifferent.

Likewise, a local authority might offer to fund for Betty a certain domiciliary care package, or residential care in either the Oaks or the Willows, but not in the Firs (which is twice the cost).

Autonomy, and capacity, means choice among the options we actually have, not the power to command more than is possible.

But suppose Bob or Betty cannot make that decision for themself because his schizophrenia or her dementia means that they cannot understand or retain or weigh up the information relevant to the actual options (i.e. they each "lack capacity" for that decision). Then a "best interests decision" must be made.

But Bob's and Betty's options are the same regardless of their capacity.

It might be in Bob's best interests to have operation A or operation B, or perhaps to have no treatment at all. But you can't say (*as a matter of best interests*) that he should have operation C instead. The surgeon is not offering that to Bob, and the decision what treatment options to offer is the surgeon's decision, not Bob's. Bob can't make the surgeon offer something he is unwilling to do, whether because it is not clinically indicated, or because it is not available as a matter of practicality or funding or whatever. Bob's decision is to choose among the actual options made available to him by the clinician, and a best interests decision on his behalf is no different.

Likewise, the same goes for Betty's choice of the domiciliary care or the Oaks or the Willows residential care home. She has no "best interests" basis to insist on being *offered* something else, as opposed to choosing among the options actually available.

This seems trite, but (along with the role of, ahem, "next of kin", below) I cannot tell you how often this is the root of confusion and dispute.

"Best interests" does not trump resource allocation or professional decision-making about available options. It is not a queue jump card for stuff that would not have been available to the same person if he had capacity to make the treatment or care decision for himself[16]. Is it very important to make sure that someone does not get less because they lack capacity to make the relevant decision, but they cannot demand more.

Of course, there may be reasonable arguments about human rights on resource allocation, for example, which are beyond the scope of this book, and a judicial review can be brought to argue that other options ought to have been offered, but because *what to offer* is not the patient's own decision, it cannot be a matter of best interests or up to the Court of Protection.

But time and again cases are unnecessarily difficult because they start in the wrong place, asking what's in Bob's or Betty's best interests as if in the abstract, on a blank piece of paper or a blank cheque, without first properly identifying the decision or the available options.

Instead:

- Start with Bob's situation, and what does he need?
- What is to be made available to him, whether limited (reasonably, or else you may be challenged in judicial review) by resource allocation, or professional judgement?
- That identifies the options, and therefore the information relevant to the decision, and it is only at this stage that you can sensibly assess whether Bob or Betty has capacity to make this decision for themself, and if so to take their consent, if they give it.
- If they cannot make that decision for themself, as they cannot understand / retain / weigh up the information relevant to the

[16] See *MN v ACCG*, [2017] UKSC 22. The Supreme Court rejected an argument by a family of a young man with a learning disability that particular aspects of his care package should be changed as being in his best interests when in reality what they wanted was not practically or financially available.

> decision, then a best interests decision should be made for them, from among the same available options.

I strongly recommend using the word "decision" as much as possible, and am much more comfortable when I can see the word "decision" used in the paperwork far more frequently than the word "capacity".

Best interests and the protection imperative

Bob's best interests might well be to have the treatment that saves his life, or that gives him the best chance of the best medical outcome, but it is not as simple as that.

Equally, Betty may be *safer* in residential care than at home with a domiciliary care package, but that does not conclude the question of what is in her best interests. If best interests were simply whatever made someone "safer", then the MCA would say so. It doesn't. It says make the decision that is in their "*best interests*", taking into account a range of factors.

As we will see, the preservation of life at all costs is not necessarily in a person's best interests, as interpreted by the courts at least. And a view of best interests must be taken at a more holistic level:

> *"The most that can be said, therefore, is that in considering the best interests of this particular patient at this particular time, decision-makers must look at his welfare in the widest sense, not just medical but social and psychological; they must consider the nature of the medical treatment in question, what it involves and its prospects of success; they must consider what the outcome of that treatment for the patient is likely to be; they must try and put themselves in the place of the individual patient and ask what his attitude to the treatment is or would be likely to be; and they must consult others who are looking*

after him or interested in his welfare, in particular for their view of what his attitude would be"[17].

Those words are from the judgment of Lady Hale in *Aintree University Hospitals NHS Foundation Trust v James,* the first Supreme Court case to consider a medical treatment decision (withholding life-sustaining treatment) under the MCA.

In another context (a case under the inherent jurisdiction dealing with capacity for sexual relationships[18]) Munby J (later Lord Justice Munby) coined one of the most familiar phrases on this point, at the end of a passage I'll set out in full:

> *"The fact is that all life involves risk, and the young, the elderly and the vulnerable, are exposed to additional risks and to risks they are less well equipped than others to cope with. But just as wise parents resist the temptation to keep their children metaphorically wrapped up in cotton wool, so too we must avoid the temptation always to put the physical health and safety of the elderly and the vulnerable before everything else. Often it will be appropriate to do so, but not always. Physical health and safety can sometimes be bought at too high a price in happiness and emotional welfare. The emphasis must be on sensible risk appraisal, not striving to avoid all risk, whatever the price, but instead seeking a proper balance and being willing to tolerate manageable or acceptable risks as the price appropriately to be paid in order to achieve some other good – in particular to achieve the vital good of the elderly or vulnerable person's happiness. What good is it making someone safer if it merely makes them miserable?"*[19]

[17] [2013] UKSC 67, at paragraph 39 https://www.bailii.org/uk/cases/UKSC/2013/67.html

[18] *Local Authority X v MM* [2007] EWHC 2003 (Fam). The quote is at paragraph 120. https://www.bailii.org/ew/cases/EWHC/Fam/2007/2003.html

[19] Emphasis added, because that is a powerful quotation, often referred to in later cases.

A similar point has been made in judgments time and again. In a case about whether a 67 year-old lady must remain in residential care, or could return to her own home as she wished, Mr Justice Peter Jackson said:

> *"In the end, if M remains confined in a home she is entitled to ask "What for?" The only answer that could be provided at the moment is "To keep you alive as long as possible." In my view that is not a sufficient answer. The right to life and the state's obligation to protect it is not absolute and the court must surely have regard to the person's own assessment of her quality of life. In M's case there is little to be said for a solution that attempts, without any guarantee of success, to preserve for her a daily life without meaning or happiness and which she, with some justification, regards as insupportable".*[20]

It is easy to understand the anxiety in public bodies, and in the dedicated individual professionals working in health and social care, to keep people safe, and secure the best outcome for them within the scope of their expertise. At times this can incentivise a tendency to find a lack of capacity as a means to intervene and / or, having done so, to lean towards the best interests decision that tends towards the safest outcome. That needs to be treated with some care, and awareness of it is a good place to start.

Adapting a phrase previously used in the context of proceedings about the welfare of children, Mr Justice Baker called this the "*protection imperative*" to sum up this instinct in the case of *CC v KK*[21]. KK was an 82 year-old lady who had developed Parkinson's Disease and vascular dementia, on top of a paralysis of one side she had suffered since childhood. She lived alone in a rented bungalow supported by a social care package, which included provision of a "lifeline" system to call for

---

[20] *Re M (best interests: deprivation of liberty)* [2013] EWCOP 3456 https://www.bailii.org/ew/cases/EWHC/COP/2013/3456.html

[21] [2012] EWCOP 2136 KK v STCC [2012] EWCOP 2136 (26 July 2012) (bailii.org)

assistance, which she used no fewer that 1,097 times in a 6-month period, which I reckon to be about 6 times per day, on average.

She was placed, under a DoLS authorisation, into residential care with dehydration and a urinary tract infection. She challenged this, arguing that she was able to make her own decision to go back to her own home, which brought the case to court. I'll come back to the case in more detail in Chapter 9, dealing with the information that a person ought to have for their capacity to make decisions to be fairly assessed, but for now it is useful to mark Baker J's warning:

> *"...in cases of vulnerable adults, there is a risk that all professionals involved with treating and helping that person – including, of course, a judge in the Court of Protection – may feel drawn towards an outcome that is more protective of the adult and thus, in certain circumstances, fail to carry out an assessment of capacity that is detached and objective". ...*
>
> *"... in evaluating capacity the court must recognise that different individuals may give different weight to different factors. There is, I perceive, a danger that professionals, including judges, may objectively conflate a capacity assessment with a best interests analysis and conclude that the person under review should attach greater weight to the physical security and comfort of a residential home and less importance to the emotional security and comfort that the person derives from being in their own home. ... These considerations underpin the cardinal rule, enshrined in statute, that a person is not to be treated as unable to make a decision merely because she makes what is perceived as being an unwise one"....*
>
> *"In this case, I perceive a real danger that in assessing KK's capacity professionals and the court may consciously or subconsciously attach excessive weight to their own views of how her physical safety may be best protected and insufficient weight to her own views of how her emotional needs may best be met."*

The judge also quoted from a speech given by Lord Justice Munby[22] in very similar terms to his judgment in *MM* quoted above, but which adds, significantly:

> *"... The State must be careful to ensure that in rescuing a vulnerable adult from one type of abuse it does not expose her to the risk of treatment at the hands of the State which, however well intentioned, can itself end up being abusive of her dignity, her happiness and indeed of her human rights. What good is it making someone safer if it merely makes them miserable? None at all! And if this is where safeguarding takes us, then is it not, in truth, another form of abuse – and, moreover, abuse at the hands of the State?"*

In the case of Peggy Ross,[23] Cardiff City Council rushed off to court on a Friday seeking an order to prevent an 82 year-old lady who was resident in one of their care homes from going on a cruise holiday, which was due to depart the following Monday. She had been admitted to the care home due to her dementia around 3 months earlier. The local authority assessed Mrs Ross to lack capacity to make a decision about going on the cruise, as she "lacked insight [24]into her needs", and were concerned that it would not be safe for her to do so, because she was prone to wandering and might fall overboard.

The judge was critical of the assessment of capacity, saying that it was a comparatively simple decision for her to make, especially as she had been regularly going on cruise holidays with the same gentleman for the last 20 years. But, without time to really get into the evidence on this, he

---

[22] A lecture to the South Central Regional Branch of Solicitors for the Elderly, entitled "Safeguarding and Dignity: Protecting Liberties – When is Safeguarding Abuse?" (published in Brunswick Mental Health Care Review 2012 Vol 7 issue 18)

[23] *Cardiff City Council v Peggy Ross* (2011) COP 28/10/11 12063905 http://www.mentalhealthlaw.co.uk/media/Cardiff_Council_v_Peggy_Ross_%282011%29_COP_28-10-11_12063905.pdf. The case attracted significant media coverage.

[24] I have always been wary of use of "insight" as a substitute for the correct test of capacity. Very few of us would say that we are a below average driver.

concluded that it was in her best interests to go on the holiday in any event, even if she did lack the capacity to make the decision for herself.

With some sympathy for the concerns of the professionals involved, he said:

> *"My strong impression is that her social worker and the staff at the home want to do the right thing for her but are focussed on her safety and are acutely aware of things that might go wrong. Perhaps the prime example of this was the concern that Mrs Ross might 'wander' (as she undoubtedly has in the past when living alone) on the ship and go over the side. It was suggested, not without some force in my view, that this smacked of saying that her best interests were best served by taking every precaution to avoid any possible danger without carrying out the balancing exercise of considering the benefit to Mrs Ross of what, sadly, may be her last opportunity to enjoy such a holiday with Mr Davies. This led, in my view, to trying to find reasons why Mrs Ross should not go on this holiday rather than finding reasons why she should".*

What use is it making someone safer if it only makes them miserable, indeed.

Incapacitous autonomy

While lack of capacity for a particular decision may limit the exercise of your autonomy, it should not extinguish it.

In AB, Mrs Justice Lieven had agreed that the termination of pregnancy for a 24 year-old woman with a learning disability, against her wishes, was in her best interests, but the Court of Appeal reversed the decision; AB would go ahead to have the baby, even though it would be removed by the local authority. The Court of Appeal said that the decision had been rooted in the medical evidence, but that the failure to mention AB's wishes was a significant omission.

> *"Part of the underlying ethos of the Mental Capacity Act 2005 is that those making decisions for people who may be lacking capacity must*

> *respect and maximise that person's individuality and autonomy to the greatest possible extent. In order to achieve this aim, a person's wishes and feelings not only require consideration, but can be determinative, even if they lack capacity".*[25]
>
> ...
>
> *"The requirement is for the court to consider both wishes and feelings. The judge placed emphasis on the fact that AB's wishes were not clear and were not clearly expressed. She was entitled to do that but the fact remains that AB's feelings were, as for any person, learning disabled or not, uniquely her own and are not open to the same critique based upon cognitive or expressive ability. AB's feelings were important and should have been factored into the balancing exercise alongside consideration of her wishes".*

Even once capacity for a particular decision is lost, the MCA continues to respect the value of autonomy in many ways. Everything practicable should be done to help someone attain capacity[26]. Any decision that can reasonably be deferred until capacity is recovered should be so[27]. And in making a best interests decision, P should be not only permitted but encouraged and supported to participate as fully as possible[28]; and, crucially[29]:

> S4(6) … must consider, so far as is reasonably ascertainable—
>
> (a) the person's past and present wishes and feelings (and, in particular, any relevant written statement made by him when he had capacity),

---

[25] AB [2019] EWCA Civ 1215 at paragraph 71 and 76. https://www.bailii.org/ew/cases/EWCA/Civ/2019/1215.html

[26] MCA s1(3).

[27] MCA s4(3).

[28] MCA s4(4).

[29] MCA s4(6).

(b) the beliefs and values that would be likely to influence his decision if he had capacity, and

(c) the other factors that he would be likely to consider if he were able to do so.

I have seen cases in which a note has been made: "if Bob has capacity, ask him what he wants". No! Ask him anyway! *What he wants does not stop mattering, even if he does now lack capacity to simply make the decision for himself.*

Mr Justice Peter Jackson put it more eloquently[30]:

> *"… a conclusion that a person lacks decision-making capacity is not an 'off-switch' for his rights and freedoms. To state the obvious, the wishes and feelings, beliefs and values of people with a mental disability are as important to them as they are to anyone else, and may even be more important."*

That case, *Wye Valley NHS Trust v B*, is a prime example of the court's approach to best interests decisions, the individuality of the patient and respect for their wishes, even in incapacity.

Mr B was a 73 year-old with a long history of mental illness, diagnosed as paranoid schizophrenia, and poorly controlled type 2 diabetes, for which he had typically bounced between acute hospitals who struggled to deal with his mental health and mental health admissions which could not readily meet his physical health needs. For many years he had heard auditory hallucinations of the voices of angels directing his (non)compliance ("*If the Lord says it's no, it's no.*") and of the Virgin Mary, who was persuading him to become a Catholic[31].

---

[30] Wye Valley NHS Trust v B [2015] EWCOP 60 https://www.bailii.org/ew/cases/EWCOP/2015/60.html

[31] Although, in a line I love, he declined to join any organised religion because, he said, "I'm not fussy".

A chronic foot ulcer developed and became infected, for which he refused treatment other than allowing his dressings to be changed. When his bone became infected the treating trust applied to court. The medical evidence was that his infection would be fatal within days, but with successful amputation he would be expected to live for another 3 years.

Mr Justice Jackson found that Mr B lacked the capacity for the decision about the treatment, and so had a best interests decision to make. The judge went to meet him, and recorded that Mr B told him:

> *"I don't want an operation.*
>
> *I'm not afraid of dying, I know where I'm going. The angels have told me I am going to heaven. I have no regrets. It would be a better life than this.*
>
> *I don't want to go into a nursing home, [my partner] died there.*
>
> *I don't want my leg tampered with. I know the seriousness, I just want them to continue what they're doing.*
>
> *I don't want it. I'm not afraid of death. I don't want interference. Even if I'm going to die, I don't want the operation."*

The trust argued that little weight should be given to Mr B's wishes because he lacked capacity, which the judge accepted only to the extent that, of course, his wishes would have been entirely decisive if he had capacity. The judge refused to ignore the religious aspects of Mr B's beliefs, saying that they were

> *"...an inextricable part of the person that he is. In this situation, I do not find it helpful to see the person as if he were a person in good health who has been afflicted by illness. It is more real and more respectful to recognise him for who he is: a person with his own intrinsic beliefs and*

> *values. It is no more meaningful to think of Mr B without his illnesses and idiosyncratic beliefs than it is to speak of an unmusical Mozart.*[32]"

The Judge concluded, poignantly and eloquently, in a passage I respectfully quote in full:

> 42. *"Having considered all of the evidence and the parties' submissions, I have reached the clear conclusion that an enforced amputation would not be in Mr B's best interests.*
>
> 43. *Mr B has had a hard life. Through no fault of his own, he has suffered in his mental health for half a century. He is a sociable man who has experienced repeated losses so that he has become isolated. He has no next of kin*[33]*. No one has ever visited him in hospital and no one ever will. Yet he is a proud man who sees no reason to prefer the views of others to his own. His religious beliefs are deeply meaningful to him and do not deserve to be described as delusions: they are his faith and they are an intrinsic part of who he is. I would not define Mr B by reference to his mental illness or his religious beliefs. Rather, his core quality is his "fierce independence", and it is this that is now, as he sees it, under attack.*
>
> 44. *Mr B is on any view in the later stages of his life. His fortitude in the face of death, however he has come by it, would be the envy of many people in better mental health. He has gained the respect of those who are currently nursing him.*
>
> 45. *I am quite sure that it would not be in Mr B's best interests to take away his little remaining independence and dignity in order to replace it with a future for which he understandably has no appetite and which could only be achieved after a traumatic and uncertain struggle that he and no one else would have to endure.*

---

[32] But of course case law can often be found pointing the other way on the same issue, for example in *Manchester University NHS Foundation Trust v DE* [2019] EWCOP 19 at para 28 https://www.bailii.org/ew/cases/EWCOP/2019/19.html

[33] Used, no doubt, in the lay sense, but this is the one line of this judgment I would, with the greatest respect, quibble with, for reasons I'll explain shortly!

> *There is a difference between fighting on someone's behalf and just fighting them. Enforcing treatment in this case would surely be the latter.*
>
> *46. The application, which was rightly brought[34], is accordingly dismissed".*

I find this a very powerful and moving account of the weight to be put on Mr B's autonomy, notwithstanding his lack of capacity to make the decision for himself.

There are also some practicalities underneath this as well, of course. In reality, the prize here was another 3 years of life, which was attainable only with a good recovery and full co-operation with rehabilitation. With an unwilling and unco-operative patient, the real benefits may be much smaller or less likely, or both, and this must be taken into account in a *real world view* of the best interests of this patient, including how compliant he will be. If ever greater coercion is to be required to deliver treatment, where that's even feasible, we must question more stringently whether that is still in P's best interests, and (to the extent that it might constitute restraint or a deprivation of liberty) necessary and proportionate.

It is tempting to look at the recent trend of the case law and conclude that the "best interests" test is in fact coming ever closer to a "substituted judgement" test where P's wishes are effectively decisive.

There are certainly a number of those cases[35], and of course it is in keeping with our general social and cultural movement towards putting ever greater value on autonomy.

---

[34] This is worth noting. Though he rejected the trust's arguments that the amputation was in B's best interests, the judge said it was absolutely the right thing to do to bring it to court for a decision.

[35] See for example *Barnsley Hospital NHS Foundation Trust v MSP* [2020] EWCOP 26 https://www.bailii.org/ew/cases/EWCOP/2020/26.html

But there are still plenty of cases in which a medical treatment decision is made, in the face of P's indifference or opposition, to impose treatment including being brought into hospital coercively if need be, or to be placed or kept in residential care against their wishes, in their best interests[36].

For all the weight properly given to them in many recent judgments, there is no precedence accorded to P's wishes, and indeed no hierarchy at all, in the list of factors set out in MCA s4[37].

And the concept of respecting P's own wishes can itself become a bit slippery. For instance, the Act refers to P's "past and present wishes" but gives no guidance how to balance or prioritise. When they are not in line, should more weight be given to Bob's views prior to the loss of capacity, or his views now? Is our respect for autonomy owed more to the Bob who would have said "yes" before his accident, or to the Bob who is saying "no" now? What about the elderly man, a lifelong ethical vegetarian who, after a stroke or in dementia, now says that he wants a bacon sandwich?

And if we reach a view that our priority is toward the views of the person before they lost capacity, how can we make any sense of that for someone with a lifelong learning disability, for example? Can we conjure up the person's views absent their learning disability, any more readily than we can imagine an unmusical Mozart?

Putting the appropriate weight on P's own wishes, feelings, values and beliefs can be easier said than done. But you can be pretty sure that things will not go well (either for P, or the organisation when challenged about it later) if it is not a question that gets the appropriate thought and care.

---

[36] E.g. *NHS Foundation Trust v QZ* [2017] EWCOP 11 https://www.bailii.org/ew/cases/EWCOP/2017/11.html

[37] Though in 2017 the Law Commission did propose a reform to MCA to that effect, https://s3-eu-west-2.amazonaws.com/lawcom-prod-storage-11jsxou24uy7q/uploads/2017/03/lc372_mental_capacity.pdf recommendation 40, at para 14.2 onwards. See Chapter 17.

Who decides?

The starting point, of course, is that if you have capacity to make a particular decision (and we should assume that you do[38]), then it is yours to make. And that includes the authority to make a binding decision now for the future to refuse particular medical treatment in the event that capacity is lost. This is an Advance Decision to Refuse Treatment[39] (ADRT). Note that you cannot demand treatment in future, any more than you can demand treatment now, though of course anything you say about what you would like to happen in future will be helpful for best interests decision makers, and should be given proper weight in choosing among the actual available options.

You can also appoint someone to be the best interests decision maker for you, through a Lasting Power of Attorney.

There have been various forms of power of attorney in the past, focussed on managing property and money. Prior to the MCA, an Enduring Power of Attorney (EPA)[40] could be appointed for dealing with your finances.

But the MCA introduced new "Lasting Powers of Attorney" (LPA)[41], and provided for these to come in two flavours: property & affairs, or health & welfare.

A property and affairs LPA can run while the donor has capacity for those decisions, simply allowing the convenience of sub-contracting that work. Health & welfare LPAs only come into effect when the donor has lost capacity for the relevant decision themselves. Obviously, granting an LPA

38 MCA s1(2).

39 MCA s24-26, which includes the formal requirements that to refuse life-saving treatment in this way it must be explicit about that, and be in writing, signed and witnessed.

40 Enduring Powers of Attorney Act 1985

41 MCA s9-14.

to my partner does not entitle her to allow doctors to treat me against my wishes while I can still make that decision for myself!

The donor of an LPA must have capacity to make the LPA when it is made. Naturally, there is a limit to how far a professional faced with an LPA can be expected to play Poirot about the state of the patient's mind when the LPA was granted, potentially years ago, to assess if it is kosher. But you might reasonably raise an eyebrow when presented with an LPA purportedly granted by a patient who lacks capacity now for a care decision as a result of a profound and long-term learning disability.

And, of course, because making an LPA is simply someone bestowing certain decision-making authority onto their nominee, we can:

- Retract it at any time, while they still have capacity to do so
- Limit the scope of the decision-making authority – saying it applies to some decisions and not others (it will not confer the power for decisions about life-sustaining treatment unless it explicitly says so); and
- Impose any conditions or restrictions, including provisions that more than one attorney is appointed and if so whether they can make decisions individually, or only jointly.

When an attorney does become the decision-maker, they are still constrained by the legal framework of the MCA, i.e. they can only make a decision in the donor's best interests, and they are subject to all the duties of appropriate consultation (see below) to make a best interests decision as any other best interests decision-maker, including health or social care professionals. And so, though the legislation and court judgments talk of the LPA authorising the attorney to "give consent" to treatment, I really don't feel comfortable with that way of thinking about it.

"Consent" to me is all about the person themselves, and the ability to exercise autonomy fully and, at times, unwisely. An attorney can only make a best interests decision, and so I personally find it makes much more sense to speak of them as becoming the best interests decision-maker, not as someone giving "consent".

If you are unsure whether there is an LPA, or about the validity or scope of it, or whether the attorney is acting in the patient's best interests, it is the role of the Office of the Public Guardian[42] to police this.

So if you have a person before you and a best interests decision to make, and someone presents themselves as holding a power of attorney, that is the start of a discussion, not the end of it. You will want to see the document itself to check that:

- it is an LPA applicable to health & welfare decisions (not an EPA or an LPA for property & affairs)
- it has a stamp to show it has been registered with the OPG (otherwise it is not valid)
- the decision in question is within the scope of the LPA granted, including whether it explicitly includes life-sustaining treatment, if that is the issue
- whether it is a sole or joint attorney and any restrictions on their decision-making.

And while there being a valid and applicable LPA essentially makes the attorney the best interests decision maker, the best interests decision-making process is still required to be collaborative and inclusive (see below), just as it would be if there were no LPA. In my experience a lot of time and effort can be spent worrying about whether or not there is an LPA, or whether it is valid, and it doesn't really make a lot of difference in the end, for reasons I'll cover below.

Before that, though, let me get on my biggest hobby horse: the role of "next of kin" in best interests decision-making.

[42] https://www.gov.uk/government/organisations/office-of-the-public-guardian

"Next of Kin"

To illustrate this point when I am giving training, I often put up a picture of "the Simpsons" family tree and give the assembled health or social care professionals a moment to consider: "who is Homer's 'next of kin'"?

There will always be some who say his wife, Marge, fairly confidently, while a few tentatively go for his father, Abraham. Others, rightly, will sense a trap.

In English and Welsh law, *there is no such thing as "next of kin"*[43].

This comes as a surprise to most people, and this misconception is one of the biggest causes of difficulty and dispute in this context. There is no such thing as "next of kin". It is, in law, literally meaningless.

We tend to use the phrase to mean the person who gets your stuff if you die intestate (i.e. without a will), and so it feels like it works as a proxy for your nearest and dearest. Indeed, the Inheritance of Estates Act 1925 does set out in table form a hierarchy of family relationships who will inherit in case of intestacy. But it does not use the words, or define, "next of kin", and it has nothing to do with making decisions about your health or care.

Which begs the question why the phrase is used so widely and repeatedly throughout health and care, including in all kinds of official documentation?!

The reality is that it is used, understandably, as shorthand for a different, entirely appropriate set of questions – "Who would you like us to call? Who do you want us to share information with? Who do you want involved in decisions about your care?" I like much better the growing practice of recording "ICE" (in case of emergency) contact details, but

[43]Although, in fairness , in coming to write this down, I now realise that I owe an apology to anyone I did this with previously, since the Simpsons are *American*, and in the US there actually is a statutory definition of next of kin, unlike here. In future I'll use the royal family. Sorry.

our habitual reference to "next of kin" is deeply engrained and may take generations to shift.

But it is wholly wrong to think of anyone being "next of kin" as if thereby acquiring some form of decision-making authority over an adult who lacks capacity for decisions for themselves. Actually, it can be very damaging and harmful. An elderly patient should not be discharged from hospital to die in great pain at home with agonising pressure sores, on a "best interests" basis where she couldn't decide for herself, solely because that's what her son wanted and he was "next of kin".

I think it can also put an unfair and intolerable pressure onto the person who may identify themselves as "next of kin", if they feel that they bear sole responsibility for a grave decision about a family member's care or medical treatment.

Instead, coming to a best interests decision for an adult who lacks capacity to make a care or medical treatment decision is a collaborative process, and it remains so even if there happens to be an LPA that appoints a family member (whether or not they might consider themselves "next of kin") as an attorney for health & welfare.

MCA s4 sets out how best interests decisions should be made, and s4(7) mandates that the best interests decision-maker:

> "must take into account, <u>if it is practicable and appropriate to consult them</u>, the views of—
>
> (a) anyone named by the person as someone to be consulted on the matter in question or on matters of that kind,
>
> (b) <u>anyone engaged in caring for the person or interested in his welfare</u>,
>
> (c) any donee of a lasting power of attorney granted by the person, and
>
> (d) any deputy appointed for the person by the court,

as to what would be in the person's best interests and, in particular, as to the matters mentioned in subsection (6)".

Section 4(7) is massively important, and I'll pick a few key points out in turn.

In making a best interests decision, the decision maker **must** take into account the opinions of a list of specified groups of people, unless it is impracticable or inappropriate to do so.

It might be ***inappropriate*** to consult someone who would otherwise be on the list if, for example, the patient had said, or behaved in a way that showed, that they would not want a particular individual to be involved in such decisions. Bear in mind that asking for input into a care or medical treatment best interests decision involves telling someone a bit about the situation and options, necessarily breaching the patient's confidentiality.

A capacitous patient can consent to sharing information, of course. But sharing information can also be justified, in their best interests, where the patient lacks capacity for that decision.

And in some cases, Bob may still be able to make his own decisions about sharing information (since it is a different and perhaps simpler decision than the treatment decision for which he lacks capacity), and decide that he wants his son to be involved in decisions, but no confidential information should be shared with his daughter. That would be his right, and must be respected.

Anyone with an LPA or any deputy[44] should be consulted, and so to my mind it doesn't really matter for this purpose whether the attorney (or deputy) meets all the criteria to be the decision-maker themselves or not; they are entitled to be involved in the decision-making anyway.

---

[44] I have not included deputies here – essentially the same role and restrictions as an LPA, but appointed by the court – as they are extremely rare for health and welfare decisions.

And anyone who might have an LPA, even if invalid / inapplicable, is very likely to be in the crucial catch-all category – "those engaged in caring for P or interested in his welfare". Note that it does not say "family" and it does not, so help me, say "next of kin". It is deliberately wide, and it would equally include the neighbour who has known Bob for 40 years, or the guy who has a pint with him every day, as much as the estranged daughter. There's no "top trumps" and no exclusivity; the duty to consult (as far as practicable) includes anyone who can help the decision-making. You need not (as you might if trying to identify a singular "next of kin") worry whether the son in Australia trumps the cousin who lives next door. In many cases it may be perfectly reasonable to rely on one family member to speak for the family as a whole, but don't forget that friends, carers and others might know Bob just as well as anyone else, and in some cases better. The point is to make the right best interests decision for Bob, so the people who know him best are the ones to involve, which is not always the same as the closest family.

And don't forget that the professionals involved are also "those engaged in caring for P or interested in his welfare" and so, in my view, if a family member is the decision-maker by virtue of an LPA, for example, there is an equal obligation on them to consult with clinicians, social workers or carers, just as there is on professionals to consult with family and others if they are the decision-maker.

Knowing the individual is the key. You are not just asking someone what they think should be done for the best. The consultation duty in s4(7) is aimed "in particular as to the matters in subsection (6)", which is all about Bob himself, his own wishes and feelings, values and beliefs.

This consultation duty is all about helping the best interests decision-maker make the right decision for Bob, as an individual. Not for a typical patient with condition or care needs X and treatment / care options Y and Z. So, when it comes to the consultation duty under s4(7), the questions you should ask are "tell me about Bob", "what is important to him", "what do you think Bob would want in this situation?"

This should generate a collaborative approach and tone, and if there is any sense of either family or professionals being ridden roughshod over by the other then something is going badly wrong.

Given the duties of consultation on the decision-maker, I am not convinced that it makes an enormous difference whether the decision-maker is a professional with an obligation to consult the friends, family and others, or it is a family member (perhaps due to an LPA) with the same obligation to consult with other family and friends, as well as the professionals, carers and others.

Where there is an LPA, professionals should form their own view of P's best interests to stress test the position taken by the attorney, and then discuss any disagreement. It may well be that the attorney knows something about P that the professionals do not – that is why they are an attorney.

But in either case, LPA or not, any substantial dispute must be referred to the Court of Protection, and any concerns about whether an attorney is acting in the patient's best interests can be referred to the Office of the Public Guardian, especially if this is a pattern.

Key Points

- Before worrying about any issues of deprivation of liberty in this context, make sure that you are making the underlying decisions in the right way, per the MCA.
- Be especially careful:
    - not to be caught out treating capacity as if generic, losing sight of the particular decision/s that need to be made, and the actual available options;
    - not to be taking the safest option, or intervening too readily, simply from an instinct to protect;

  - and to be involving the right people in the decision-making process: those who know Bob best, and Bob himself, giving appropriate weight to his own wishes and feelings, values and beliefs.

- Making decisions in that way will feel collaborative and open minded; if your situation feels adversarial, entrenched or dogmatic, it may be helpful to take a step back, involve others, and to consider whether some form of mediation or an application to the Court of Protection is appropriate.

- Even without a dispute, the Court of Protection may be needed, for example to authorise a deprivation of liberty that falls outside the scope of DoLS, but in any case an application can and should be approached in a collaborative and non-adversarial way, and the key is to be getting the underlying MCA decision-making right.

- For this reason, by far the best preparation to deal with deprivation of liberty issues (including any potential reform) is first to focus on your MCA policy, regular training, and reflective practice.

We will see in Chapter 3 a case study of getting this badly wrong, and in Chapter 15 some of the liabilities that can bring.

Before that, let's move on to put the issue of deprivation of liberty into the wider context of the MCA.

CHAPTER TWO

SECTION 5 AND ARTICLE 5: FROM BOURNEWOOD TO DOLS

Proportionality, restraint and deprivation of liberty?

Deprivation of liberty is best understood simply: it is all about *proportionality*, *appropriate scrutiny* and *due process*.

If we have managed to avoid all the MCA beartraps set out in the last chapter, then we have a solid basis for making a best interests decision, and the MCA will protect us. There can still be liability, of course, if you are negligent in the care delivered, but the proper use of the MCA will avoid any liability you may have otherwise incurred for lack of the person's consent.

For instance, if I cut off someone's leg, I am likely to face years in prison for GBH. If a surgeon does the same thing, what stops it being a criminal offence is a combination of the clinical context and the patient's consent[45].

But if you have a patient *who cannot consent*, MCA s5 provides that no liability is incurred if you reasonably believe that a patient lacks capacity

[45] Note that you need both – the House of Lords has held that consent alone cannot avoid mutilating another person being potentially grievous bodily harm, in *R v Brown* [1993] UKHL 19, a case in which a group of sado-masochists unsuccessfully argued that their consent meant no laws were broken when they, among other things, stapled each others' genitals to bits of wood.

for a particular decision and you take a decision reasonably believing it to be in their best interests[46].

It is sometimes referred to in terms of a "general defence" or "a general authority". But this only goes so far.

MCA s6 clarifies that you are *restraining* P if you *"(a) use, or threaten to use, force to secure the doing of an act which P resists, or (b) restrict P's liberty of movement, whether or not P resists."*

And if what you intend to do amounts to restraint, then you need more justification, given the greater degree of interference in the person's life, however well intentioned. So the law requires not just the s5 criteria, but in addition that the step <u>is necessary to prevent harm and is proportionate to the likelihood and seriousness of that harm[47]</u>.

And the more we interfere in someone's life, beyond restraint and into something that amounts to a "deprivation of their liberty", we need a greater level of protection still. This is done in two ways: (1) a higher level of justification for the interference, and (2) a more robust process of scrutiny to ensure that any such power to interfere is being exercised properly.

Pausing here, we should recognise that the continuum of increasing degrees of interference in someone's life is, well, continuous, and though it is necessary for the purpose of triggering a step change in the legal safeguards to have a line drawn between mere "restraint" and "deprivation of liberty", this is inevitably a little arbitrary and subjective. Despite all the material to follow, it is best not to get too hung up on this, and to focus first and foremost on the fundamental principles of the MCA.

---

[46] Note the "reasonably"s in this and consider how much easier it will be for a lawyer defending you against any criticism if you have carefully documented your thinking, and not just your conclusions, on both capacity and best interests. We thank you.

[47] MCA s6.

However well intentioned, once our interference in someone's life, in their best interests, amounts to a deprivation of liberty (we'll come back to what that means), it is no longer enough to rely on MCA s5-6. Instead, a person can only lawfully be deprived of their liberty in this context[48] by:

- A court order; or
- An authorisation under the Deprivation of Liberty Safeguards (we'll come back to them); or
- To carry out life sustaining treatment or a "vital act", *while seeking a court order*.[49]

The need for greater safeguards when an intervention amounts to a deprivation of liberty comes from the individual's rights under Article 5 of the European Convention of Human Rights (ECHR) – the right to liberty:

Article 5 – Right to liberty and security

1. ***Everyone has the right to liberty and security of person. No one shall be deprived of his liberty save in the following cases and in accordance with a procedure prescribed by law:***

    a. *the lawful detention of a person after conviction by a competent court;*

    b. *the lawful arrest or detention of a person for non-compliance with the lawful order of a court or in order to secure the fulfilment of any obligation prescribed by law;*

[48] The law provides for lawful deprivation of liberty in many other context, of course, such as criminal justice and immigration control.

[49] MCA s4A and 4B. See Chapter 8 and Appendix 4 for the proposed amendments to this. And note that the "while seeking a court order" bit (pending the proposed amendments being implemented) is not optional. S4B gives no cover for life sustaining treatment or a vital act unless you are actually seeking a court order.

c. *the lawful arrest or detention of a person effected for the purpose of bringing him before the competent legal authority on reasonable suspicion of having committed an offence or when it is reasonably considered necessary to prevent his committing an offence or fleeing after having done so;*

d. *the detention of a minor by lawful order for the purpose of educational supervision or his lawful detention for the purpose of bringing him before the competent legal authority;*

e. ***the lawful detention of persons for the prevention of the spreading of infectious diseases, of persons of unsound mind, alcoholics or drug addicts or vagrants;***

f. *the lawful arrest or detention of a person to prevent his effecting an unauthorised entry into the country or of a person against whom action is being taken with a view to deportation or extradition.*

2. *Everyone who is arrested shall be informed promptly, in a language which he or she understands, of the reasons for his arrest and of any charge against him.*

3. ....

4. *Everyone who is deprived of his liberty by arrest or detention shall be entitled to take proceedings by which the lawfulness of his detention shall be decided speedily by a court and his release ordered if the detention is not lawful.*

5. *Everyone who has been the victim of arrest or detention in contravention of the provisions of this article shall have an enforceable right to compensation.*

This is from the Treaty of Rome, 1950. The British delegation were very prominently involved in drafting the ECHR, and the roots of this particular aspect might be found as far back as Magna Carta in 1215:

> *"Chapter 39 – No free man shall be seized or imprisoned or stripped of his rights or possessions … except by the lawful judgment of his equals or by the law of the land".*

In both Magna Carta and the ECHR, the focus is on the due legal process, and the essential qualities of the rule of law.

To be clear, the European Convention on Human Rights (ECHR) and the European Court of Human Rights (ECtHR) are, of course, wholly unrelated to European Union. As such, our position on this is unaffected by Brexit, though this distinction is sometimes wilfully or carelessly blurred. Withdrawal from the ECHR may yet be an election battleground.

For now, the ECHR (including Article 5) is incorporated into our domestic law by the Human Rights Act 1998, but if there ever were to be a move to leave the ECHR and replace it with a "British Bill of Rights", or to reform the Human Rights Act, it is surely inconceivable that there would not be an equivalent of the Article 5 included.

For all the talk of a British Bill of Rights in the febrile post-Brexit landscape, the consultation carried out in 2021/2022 on reform of the Human Rights Act 1998 was clear that all the ECHR rights we currently incorporate would still be protected, including Article 5[50].

Clearly, then, this is fundamental. But you will see that it is not an <u>unqualified</u> right, and liberty can lawfully be interfered with <u>if</u>:

- The person is in one of the specific categories (for this context the relevant one is – in the politically incorrect drafting of the 1950s – "persons of unsound mind", lumped together with alcoholics, drug addicts and vagrants[51]);

---

[50] https://consult.justice.gov.uk/human-rights/human-rights-act-reform/supporting_documents/humanrightsreformconsultation.pdf

[51] ECHR Article 5(1)(e). For children we may also be interested in Article 5(1)(d) which allows for detention of a minor for educational supervision. See Chapter 10.

- The deprivation of liberty is in accordance with a due process of law[52]; and
- The person has a right to challenge their deprivation of liberty, to be speedily decided by a court[53].

Remember the ECHR, in 1950, was drafted in the shadow of the Second World War. The focus is on *process*; there must be a due legal process by which you can be detained and, if detained, you must have a legal process available to you to challenge it. It must never be arbitrary, or beyond challenge.

These fairly abstract ideas were brought to life, and close to home, in the "*Bournewood* judgment"[54].

Bournewood

HL was autistic. He had been placed in Bournewood Hospital, in Surrey, from the age of 13, and lived there for more than 30 years.

In March 1994, aged 45, HL was "adopted" by a foster family, Mr & Mrs Enderby, and went to live with them at their home in Surrey, about 20 minutes drive away from the hospital. He became "one of the family", along with their children. He could not speak and had complex needs, requiring 24-hour care. He had no sense of danger, and could not safely go out without supervision and support.

He attended a Day Centre in nearby Woking once a week, and in the 3 years he was with the family, they had managed with "tantrums" once or twice a week, but had never had to call the police or seek admission to hospital.

---

52 ECHR Article 5(1)

53 ECHR Article 5(4)

54 *HL v United Kingdom* [2005] 40 E.H.R.R 32 – but which is, unusually, universally referred to by the name of the hospital rather than the patient.

On 22 July 1997, at the Day Centre, HL became "agitated". He was hyperventilating, pacing up and down, hitting himself on the head with his fists, and banging his head against the wall[55]. Mr & Mrs Enderby could not be contacted, so a local doctor was called, who attended and administered a sedative. Then, on the advice of a social worker who knew HL well, he was taken to the accident and emergency unit at Bournewood Hospital. The sedative had left him calm and relaxed, but in A&E he became more agitated again and was transferred to the "mental health behavioural unit" at the hospital.

Though the doctor at the hospital regarded the incident as "serious", he was "compliant" and had "not attempted to run away from the unit", and so the view was taken that it was appropriate to admit him as an "informal patient", rather than detain him under the Mental Health Act 1983 (the MHA).

Pausing here, the MHA 1983 is the core legal framework used for detention of patients for care and treatment for a mental disorder. It contains a number of safeguards to balance the protection of the individual's rights with the need, where appropriate, to intervene without their consent to provide treatment in their interests (and, occasionally, for public safety):

- There are certain thresholds that must be met before the powers of detention can be used, for example that the mental disorder is of a nature or degree which warrants the detention of the patient;
- the professional expertise or experience of those able to make such assessments are prescribed;
- there are strict time limits;
- certain treatment cannot be given without consent or a second opinion;

[55] According to the House of Lords judgment see below.

- rights to advocacy and a role for a "nearest relative"[56] who has certain powers to secure a discharge from detention;

- automatic rights to a due legal process for the patient to challenge the detention and have it considered promptly before a tribunal.

- And, after discharge from MHA detention, there is an entitlement to a holistic package of health and social care "aftercare"[57] aimed at preventing re-detention, in which the normally means-tested and charged for social care elements are also free of charge, like the NHS care element.

In short, you can see the safeguards in the MHA which meet the requirements of ECHR Article 5. Detention under the MHA is not arbitrary and, done properly, it is lawful.

Now, the MHA does still allow that patients can be voluntary, and "informal", ie the powers of detention under the MHA are not used. There is, even now, often perceived to be a certain stigma to being detained under the MHA, and not every inpatient admission demanded that those heavy handed processes be used, most obviously where a patient (with capacity to make the decision) consents to an admission for treatment of their mental health. Sometimes, with the best of intentions, clinicians avoid using powers (and safeguards) of the MHA, hoping to avoid unnecessary stigma[58].

But HL was neither detained under the MHA (with all the safeguards that would have followed from this) and nor was he truly a patient with capacity to consent who was agreeing to be there. He "had not attempted to run away" and was "*quite compliant*".

(It is worth noting the dangers of this perception. The case proceeded on the basis that HL was "*compliant*", but in fact other evidence suggested

---

[56] Not "next of kin".

[57] Mental Health Act 1983 s117.

[58] See Chapter 13 on MCA / DOLS and MHA overlap.

that this was misleading. His family described that he was frequently restrained by staff standing on his toes and holding his arms to his sides; they said that his toenails were black and fell out by the time he left hospital)[59].

And he was effectively detained – the clinicians' evidence was that if he had tried to leave he would "certainly" have been detained under the MHA, "*as I was firmly of the view that he required in-patient treatment*" – but without safeguards or due process.

There is no doubt that they thought they were doing what was best for HL. The key treating clinician had been looking after HL at Bournewood Hospital since 1977. But good intentions are no guarantee of respect for an individual's rights or their best interests, especially when imposed by authority entirely outside any legal process of scrutiny and effectively immune to challenge.

For example, it was thought best (by the clinicians) that Mr & Mrs Enderby's visits to HL should only take place when carefully managed and arranged, to avoid causing HL distress. Initially they told they family that it was "wise for you not to visit until staff feel it will be ok for you to do so… we do not want to face the scenario where, following your visit, he may expect to return with you".

Perhaps inevitably, relations between the hospital and the family became strained, and this meant that as at the end of October 1997 (when the case was heard in the Court of Appeal) HL had been in hospital for nearly 15 weeks without his family being allowed to see him at all[60].

His family brought legal proceedings to challenge his detention in hospital, relying (in the absence of the safeguards under the MHA) on judicial review and a writ of Habeas Corpus, a legal concept dating from

---

[59] Equality and Human Rights Commission Film: "The Bournewood Case". Available from https://www.equalityhumanrights.com/en/what-are-human-rights/human-rights-stories/bournewood-case accessed on 21 October 2023.

[60] We learn from the ECtHR judgment that the family were first allowed to visit HL on 2 November 1997.

the early 13th century[61]. To prevent unlawful detention, you can ask the court to order that the body (corpus) of a person be delivered to the court to determine whether their detention somewhere is lawful[62].

But on 9 October 1997, the Judge in the High Court, Mr Justice Owen, held that in fact HL had not been detained: no restraint had been used and "*there will be no restraint... until he has attempted to leave*". And even if HL was detained, he decided, it was not unlawful as the Mental Health Act 1983 had preserved the concept of an informal patient, admitted without formal detention, and so the hospital was entitled to rely on this and the common law[63] idea of "necessity".

The "doctrine of necessity" is the idea that it must be lawful to do what is reasonably required by particular circumstances, especially where they are extreme or unpredictable.[64]

Court of Appeal

The Enderbys appealed, and less than three weeks later, on 29 October 1997, in the Court of Appeal, the family won[65]. The three Court of Appeal judges unanimously held that HL had been detained in

---

[61] See Tom Bingham, The Rule of Law, Penguin 2011, p13.

[62] Habeas Corpus translates to "*that you have the body*".

[63] Common law means essentially built by judges in decisions in cases, rather than statute law, which has a basis in legislation which is then interpreted by the judges. Common law can be seen as flexible and responsive, or vague and uncertain, depending perhaps on whether the particular decision has gone your way.

[64] For example, in a famous case from 1884, some sailors who had killed and eaten the cabin boy when they were adrift and starving in lifeboat after a shipwreck, argued that they should have a defence to murder on the grounds of "necessity". Killing him did save their lives long enough to be rescued and stand trial, but they were convicted, and hanged (*R v Dudley & Stephens*, (1884) 14 QBD 273 DC). Conversely, using "necessity" in a medical context, in 2000 the Court of Appeal found it would not be murder to separate conjoined twins, where they would both inevitably die, but surgery to save Jodie would certainly kill Mary (*Re A* [2000] EWCA 254).

[65] [1997] EWCA Civ 2879, the written reasons for the decision were handed down on 2 December 1997.

Bournewood Hospital, and still was, and that it was unlawful. The only basis for detention of a patient for treatment of a mental disorder lay in use of the formal powers of the MHA, accompanied by its formal safeguards. The provisions relating to treatment of voluntary patients applied to those who consent, and "*HL was not even in the position of purporting to consent to the treatment. He had done nothing which could be construed as conferring authority on the hospital to retain him for that purpose*"[66].

The Court of Appeal were critical that the hospital had proceeded on

> "*...a false premise. It was based on the belief that they were entitled to treat L as an inpatient without his consent as long as he did not dissent. That was a wrong approach. They were only allowed to admit him for treatment if they complied with the [MHA] statutory requirements. On the evidence they would have undoubtedly complied with the statutory requirements but for their belief that this was not necessary*".

The court was also concerned that the misunderstanding of the law shown by the hospital in this case was widespread and reflected current practice affecting a very large number of patients.

Note that the Court of Appeal did not order that he must be released; it was open to the Trust to detain him lawfully by using its powers under the Mental Health Act, if the statutory criteria were met. HL's claim for false imprisonment, as he had been detained without lawful authority, was successful, but substantial compensation does not automatically follow in these circumstances (see Chapter 15) and the court awarded only nominal damages of £1, plus legal costs. The hospital appealed to the House of Lords.

---

[66] Per Woolf LJ, at para 44.

House of Lords

The House of Lords gave their judgment on 25 June 1998[67], and the 5 judges found for the hospital and largely reinstated the reasoning of the High Court[68]. From this judgment we learn that on 31 October 1997, 2 days after the Court of Appeal decision, the Trust "regularised the position" by detaining HL for up to 6 months using the Mental Health Act[69]. Under the MHA, an application for his discharge was made on 5 November 1997, and he was discharged from hospital, back to his family in early December 1997[70]. He had been detained for nearly 5 months.

The House of Lords were clearly conscious of the potential impact of the Court of Appeal judgment, had it stood, and the argument before them was joined by the Secretary of State for Health, the Mental Health Act Commission and the Registered Nursing Homes Association (RNHA) as interested parties. The Lords heard that the Court of Appeal approach would mean that another 22,000 patients, at least and possibly many more, would need to be detained under the MHA at any one time (on top of the usual figure of around 11,000) with "a substantial impact on available resources", prompting "deep concern" for the Royal Society of Psychiatrists, the Alzheimer's Society and others. The RNHA were concerned about whether care homes for the elderly, where patients may not be able to consent to their care and accommodation, might then need to be registered to enable them to use the detention powers of the MHA.

The Lords held that the provisions for a voluntary admission under the MHA were not limited to those who positively consented (ie including

[67] *In Re L* [1998] UKHL 24. The House of Lords was the highest domestic court until it was replaced by the Supreme Court in 2009.

[68] I would love to know, but have never found out, if the Trust paid HL his £1 awarded by the Court of Appeal and, if so, if he was made to give it back after the House of Lords' judgment.

[69] And from the later ECtHR judgment we learn that in fact on the day of the Court of Appeal decision he was detained under MHA s5(2) for up to 72 hours to allow the application for 6 months detention under s3 to be processed.

[70] Initially on s17 leave on 5 December 1997 and then discharged on 12 December 1997, as set out in the ECtHR judgment.

only those with capacity to do so) but extended to those who did not object. Lord Goff gave the leading judgment for the majority (three of the other five essentially just said that they agreed with him). Even after HL's move to the Enderby family, Lord Goff regarded him as still under the care of Bournewood Hospital and that consultant in particular, as she had known him for many years and had overseen his discharge into the community "on a trial basis", and so it was entirely appropriate that that hospital, and that doctor, should take the lead when a crisis arose. He felt it was clear that "all the steps in fact taken... were taken in the best interests of Mr L and, in so far as they might otherwise have constituted an invasion of his civil rights, were justified on the basis of the common law duty of necessity".

Lord Nolan, while agreeing with Lord Goff that the hospital did no wrong, relying on the common law doctrine of necessity, did explicitly agree with the Court of Appeal that HL had been detained. "*Mr L was closely monitored at all times so as to ensure that he came to no harm. It would have been wholly irresponsible for those monitoring him*" to do otherwise.

Lord Steyn went further. He acknowledged that healthcare professionals will "*almost always act in the best interests of the patient*", but in enacting the Mental Health Act, "*Parliament was not content in this complex and sensitive area to proceed on the paternalistic basis that the doctor is always right*". Reversing the Court of Appeal decision would strip the compliant incapacitated patients of virtually all the safeguards of the MHA, and "*the result would be an indefensible gap*[71] *in our mental health law*".

> "*...professionals are seldom enthusiastic about protective measures to guard against lapses by their members. And health care professionals are probably no different. But the law would be defective if it failed to afford adequate protective measures to a vulnerable group of incapacitated mental patients*".

[71] Yes – the origin of the reference to the "Bournewood gap" as the problem left by this case and the subsequent ECtHR judgment.

For these reasons, he said, he would have wished to uphold the Court of Appeal decision if possible, but found himself unable to do so.

The hospital's argument that HL had not been detained, he found, "*stretches credulity to breaking point.... The suggestion that "L" was free to go is a fairy tale*".

But he agreed that common law "necessity" could justify the admission of an informal patient, even if the MHA is not used, though he clearly deplored the consequences of this for the very vulnerable group then left without those protections:

> "*if considerations of financial resources are put to one side, there can be no justification for not giving to compliant incapacitated patients the same quality and degree of protection as is given to patients admitted under the [MHA]*"[72]

So, the Lords split 3:2 to decide by a majority that HL was actually <u>not</u> detained, but all five agreed that it was anyway lawful under the common law doctrine of necessity. Lord Steyn, though, was appalled that such a gap in the law should exist. The next step was for the family to appeal to the European Court of Human Rights in Strasbourg[73], whose judgment would lead to plugging that gap.

This was all, of course, before the Mental Capacity Act 2005 was introduced, but you'll notice that Article 5 of the ECHR (1950) doesn't get a mention in the domestic judgments so far either.

---

[72] One reason why these judgments are still worth detailed analysis now is that the same issues and questions arise time and again throughout the law and policy in this area. You might equally make the same observation as Lord Steyn's here about the disparity of protection that is afforded under DoLS where objection is a trigger for an appeal to court under MCA s21A, or as proposed by the Liberty Protection Safeguards to those who are "objecting" to their care arrangements, who are thereby entitled to the independent scrutiny of an AMCP, as against those "compliant incapacitated patients" who are not.

[73] They also went to the Ombudsman, who upheld their complaint about the care in November 2001.

European Court of Human Rights

It's not a quick road to Strasbourg. This was one of the reasons for the Human Rights Act 1998, which came into force in October 2000, bringing certain provisions of the European Convention of Human Rights (including Article 5, and Article 8, the right to private and family life) directly into the law of England and Wales, so that they could be given effect by domestic courts without having to go to the European Court of Human Rights.

Article 5, and the extent to which UK law was compatible with it, was the focus of the judgment of the ECtHR, handed down on 5 October 2004, in a case reframed as *HL v The UK*[74]. The seven judges[75] gave a single agreed judgment which reviewed the domestic legal framework, including the impending introduction of the Mental Capacity Act, as well as the history of the case and the factual background.

The UK government argued that HL was not detained from 22 July to 29 October 1997 (when the MHA was first used), and that finding otherwise would run counter to the policy that the informality and flexibility of a common law approach were preferable, with the statutory framework of the MHA to be used only were absolutely necessary.

The court was having none of it.

Providing more factual detail than previous judgments, the court noted that in the incident on 22 July 1997, HL was sedated before being brought to hospital, and then moved to another unit supported by 2 staff; his doctor said that if he tried to leave he would be detained under the MHA, and indeed he was formally detained under the MHA as soon as the Court of Appeal indicated that his claim would be allowed; the clinicians exercised strict control over his assessment, treatment, movement, contacts and residence; he would only be released to his family when those professionals thought appropriate; contact with his

[74] See note 10.

[75] Including the UK judge, Sir Nicholas Bratza.

family was directed and controlled by staff, and they were not permitted to visit him for more than 100 days.

The court agreed with Lord Steyn's description in the House of Lords that any suggestion he was not detained was a "*fairy tale*". It didn't matter whether the doors of the ward were in fact locked, lockable, or unlocked (which was in dispute). The concrete situation was that he was "*under continuous supervision and control and was not free to leave*"[76].

The question then, was whether the deprivation of his liberty was lawful under Article 5. He was of "unsound mind", but was the deprivation of his liberty in accordance with a procedure prescribed by law (Article 5(1))? And did he have appropriate recourse to appeal and challenge it (Article 5(4))?

To avoid "arbitrary" detention, the ECtHR held, the doctrine of "necessity" relied on in English law was not good enough. Contrasted with the formality and structure of the MHA, someone who is incapacitated but regarded as compliant, treated as an informal patient, had no effective safeguards:

> *"... as a result of the lack of procedural regulation and limits, the hospital's health care professionals assumed full control of the liberty and treatment of a vulnerable incapacitated individual solely on the basis of their own clinical assessments completed as and when they considered fit: as Lord Steyn remarked, this left "effective and unqualified control" in their hands. While the Court does not question the good faith of those professionals or that they acted in what they considered to be the applicant's best interests, the very purpose of procedural safeguards is to protect individuals against any "misjudgements and professional lapses".*

And on the issue of a right to challenge any deprivation of liberty, it was not enough that HL (or his family) were able to bring a judicial review and claim Habeas Corpus. There was no readily available and effective

[76] Another phrase we will come back to later...

way to challenge a clinician if they are permitted simply to rely on their own judgement of what is "necessary".

The UK was declared to be in breach of Articles 5(1) and 5(4) as our law (as the House of Lords had unanimously declared it to be) was not compatible with the patient's right to liberty.

But, again, a win in court did not necessarily lead to compensation. The ECtHR denied HL's claim for £10,000 in damages, and said that the declaration of the breach of his rights was "sufficient just satisfaction", though HL was awarded a little under 27,000 Euros for his legal costs[77].

Small beer, of course, compared to the true price of this judgment to the UK government, as they turned their attention to reforming the law to plug what had been identified as "the Bournewood Gap" – those patients who are not detained under the MHA, as they are not objecting, but who lacked capacity to consent to care that might otherwise amount to a deprivation of their liberty; Lord Steyn's "compliant incapacitated"; tens of thousands of them, potentially, who were left without proper safeguards of their Article 5 rights.

Our domestic law had been measured against the requirements of the European Convention of Human Rights and found wanting.

Plugging the Bournewood Gap – Introducing DoLS

Reform was necessary but, as Lady Hale would later observe[78], a vastly complex and bureaucratic scheme was not inevitable.

---

[77] See Chapter 15.

[78] In *Cheshire West* in the Supreme Court [2014] UKSC 19 at para 57: – the need for authorisation of a deprivation of liberty simply means that "*they need a periodic independent check on whether the arrangements made for them are in their best interests. Such checks need not be as elaborate as those currently provided for in the Court of Protection or in the Deprivation of Liberty Safeguards (which could in due course be simplified and extended to placements outside hospitals and care homes)*".

The government held tight to the view that the compliant incapacitated in the Bournewood gap should not all be pushed into the compulsory detention powers of the MHA. In a consultation on reform in March 2005[79], the government explained that:

> *"The Bournewood judgment raises complex issues to which there is no easy answer. The Government wishes to identify a way of delivering a workable system which gives to people of unsound mind who lack capacity appropriate safeguards against the unlawful deprivation of their liberty. The Government also wishes to secure the legislation required to address the findings of the ECtHR while maximising the scope for local discretion on implementation mechanisms".*

So we needed to establish a simple process to work alongside the MHA to comply with Article 5 ECHR; to ensure that anyone of unsound mind deprived of their liberty without use of the MHA had a clear legal framework to satisfy the requirement that it only be done by a "due process of law" (Article 5(1)); and that there was a clear and timely process by which any deprivation of liberty could be challenged (Article 5(4)).

What we got, instead, was the Deprivation of Liberty Safeguards, "DoLS".

In October 2004, Tony Blair had just announced his intention to resign as prime minister after the next general election, so he would not seek a fourth term, but his government were still busy. In particular, the law relating to mental capacity was approaching a landmark reform.

The Mental Capacity Bill was introduced into Parliament on 17 June 2004, and passed to become the Mental Capacity Act (MCA) on 7 April 2005. Its origins, though, lay as far back as the Law Commission report on Mental Incapacity in 1995, which was itself published after a long

[79] The "Bournewood consultation", 2005 – https://webarchive.nationalarchives.gov.uk/20120106092822/http://www.dh.gov.uk/prod_consum_dh/groups/dh_digitalassets/@dh/@en/documents/digitalasset/dh_4108641.pdf

consultation. That was followed by a further consultation and policy statement “Making Decisions”, in October 1999, followed by a draft Mental Incapacity Bill, which was subject to pre-legislative scrutiny by a joint committee of both houses of parliament, which then published a report in November 2003. A government response was published in February 2004, before the legislation was introduced.

There cannot be many bits of legislation that have had as much care and groundwork as the MCA, and I think it is reflected in a legal framework which is mostly clear, accessible and functional.

However, no part of this was addressed to the idea of detaining patients. MCA s6 made clear that any restraint needed to not only be in P’s best interests, but also necessary to prevent harm and proportionate to the likelihood and seriousness of that harm. But it did not contemplate depriving someone of their liberty.

The consultation in March 2005 estimated there were 100,000 adults in care homes and hospitals caught in the Bournewood gap, and the government suggested a scheme framed as “Protective Care”.

The consultation responses supported the decision not to extend the MHA to plug the gap, largely I think due to its perceived stigma, and the Deprivation of Liberty Safeguards were born.

As it was too late to use the Mental Capacity Act 2005, the Mental Health Act 2007 was used to add bits to the MCA later. This is why the DoLS parts of the MCA are all identifiable by the additional letter in the section number to show that they were added later and mucked up the initial numbering system – so look out, for example, for s4A and 4B, s21A, s39A to 39E, and Schedule A1 and Schedule 1A.

DoLS is essentially an administrative scheme. It applies to care homes and hospitals (but nowhere else – it did not seem to occur to anyone at the time that a deprivation of liberty could occur elsewhere), which are called “Managing Authorities”. They are empowered to grant themselves an “Urgent Authorisation” for a deprivation of liberty for up to 7 days (which can be extended “in exceptional circumstances” to 14 days), while they apply to the "Supervisory Bodies" for a Standard Authorisation, which can be valid for up to a year.

The Supervisory Bodies were initially the relevant Primary Care Trust (PCT) for DoLS in hospital, and the relevant local authority for DoLS in care homes. After the abolition of PCTs in the Lansley reforms which created Clinical Commissioning Groups in 2013, all Supervisory Body responsibilities rested with local authorities[80].

The six assessments required for a DoLS authorisation were that P:

1. is over 18 years of age;
2. That there are no valid refusals (this means for example no effective Advance Decision to Refuse Treatment that rules out the treatment proposed that would amount to a deprivation of liberty, or no-one with a valid health & welfare Lasting Power of Attorney who opposes it);
3. Has a mental disorder (using the definition of the MHA) – in effect establishing that P is of unsound mind (to get into the Article 5(1)(e) category who could be deprived of liberty);
4. Must be unable to make a decision for themselves "whether or not he should be accommodated in the relevant care home or hospital for the purpose of being given the relevant care or treatment" that amounts to the deprivation of liberty;
5. That P is not ineligible for use of DoLS by virtue of the MHA, ie either they are already detained, or the MHA is being used in a way incompatible with the proposed DoLS (the point of this is to plug the Bournewood gap, not to add duplication where the

[80] As with much NHS reform there was a certain circularity that the proposed Liberty Protection Safeguards reform would spread the responsibility of local authorities back out to CCGs and to hospitals for certain cases; and that, even before LPS could be implemented, CCGs had already been replaced by Integrated Care Boards, ICBs.

MHA already provides a legal framework, though this is notoriously complex – see Chapter 13); and

6. That the proposed or current deprivation of liberty is in P's best interests.

Two different assessors must carry out these six assessments between them – a Mental Health Assessor, and a "Best Interests Assessor" (BIA). The Mental Health Assessor and the BIA were distinct roles, with qualifications set by regulations.

The BIA must be independent of P's care, and – as you might expect – must complete the best interests assessment. The Mental Health Assessor must complete the mental health assessment, but other assessments can be carried out by either of them.

When under a DoLS authorisation, the P had a right to challenge this in the Court of Protection (s21A) and, equally crucially, such proceedings would attract non-means tested legal aid, paving the way (at least in principle) for easy access to the court.

We will go through the various safeguards of the DoLS process in more detail in Chapter 12.

The Mental Health Act 2007 received royal assent on 19 July 2007, and the parts of it establishing the DoLS came into force in April 2009.

It is fair to say that DoLS did not get the benefit of the same care and thought as had gone into the long gestation of the Mental Capacity Act 2005 itself. And it shows.

As Genevra Richardson notes[81]:

> "*the most persistent difficulties [with the DoLS] centre on three issues all of which were foreshadowed in Bournewood itself: resource burden*

[81] Bournewood 15 years on, in "Landmark Cases in Medical Law", Jonathan Herring and Jesse Wall eds, Hart Publishing 2015, at p136.

and administrative complexity; the relationship between DoLS and the MHA; and the definition of deprivation of liberty".

In addition, it later became clear that there were substantial numbers of deprivations of liberty which fell outside the scope of DoLS, whether in supported living, or P's own home for example, or in small group placements not registered as care homes, or because P was under 18 years old, which could only be made lawful by a court order.

So, the gap had been addressed, if not entirely filled.

But since deprivation of liberty is such an important issue, and the law is not always clear, it is, of course, a recipe for litigation.

Sure enough, there has been plenty of case law generated, especially about how we define a deprivation of liberty in different contexts. We will get to that, but for now let's start with a case that quickly put DoLS on the front pages, and contains so much to learn about how to use the safeguards (and how not to).

Key Points

- Deprivation of liberty is all about proportionality, appropriate scrutiny and due process.

- No matter how well intentioned, and no matter that they cannot make the decision for themselves and that it is in their best interests, the greater our interference with someone's life, the more it demands appropriate safeguards, scrutiny and a right to challenge it.

- At a certain point, our right to liberty under Article 5 of the ECHR is engaged. It is not an absolute right, but can only be infringed in certain situations (for example when the person is of "unsound mind"), by a due legal process, and with rights to challenge it.

- In the *Bournewood* case, in 2005, the European Court of Human Rights held that reliance on common law "necessity", heavily dependent on deference to clinical judgement and good intentions, was not enough to meet those Article 5 rights.

- Our law had to be reformed to plug "the Bournewood gap" – those patients who are deprived of their liberty, but not detained under the Mental Health Act because they are compliant.

- This led to the Deprivation of Liberty Safeguards, coming into effect in April 2009.

CHAPTER THREE

A CASE STUDY: GETTING STEVEN HOME

> *"In this case a local authority accepted a young man with disabilities into respite care for a few days at the request of his father and then kept him there for a year. The question is whether this was lawful"*[82].

Steven Neary loves music, swimming, Countdown and Mr Bean[83]. He was adopted by Mark and Julie Neary when he was 5 years old. After their split, Steven continued to live with his dad, with the support of a care package from their local authority, the London Borough of Hillingdon. He has childhood autism and a severe learning disability.

As Mark writes:

> *"routines are incredibly important to Steven as he attempts to make a threatening world feel manageable. His day is marked by routines, from the moment he opens his eyes ("Morning dad – Super Trouper")*

82 [2011] EWHC 1377 (COP) – Mr Justice Peter Jackson, handed down on 9 June 2011, determining whether Steven had been unlawfully deprived of his liberty and/or his Article 8 rights to family life had been breached by the local authority for all or some of the year he was kept away from his father. Before then there had been separate hearings and judgments to determine whether Steven should go home, and the extent to which the press should be allowed to report the case and identify the parties.

83 Where the descriptions of Steven and these events go beyond the published judgment, they are from the book written by Mark Neary, "Get Steven Home" (2011), available at https://www.lulu.com/en/gb/shop/mark-neary . It should be required reading for anyone dealing with deprivation of liberty, mental capacity and care planning. There is also a video about Steven and Mark as part of the Rightful Lives campaign exhibition available here: https://rightfullives.net/Stories/Steven-and-Mark.html

to the moment he drops off to sleep ("Night dad – don't drop the cherry cake")".

He explains that Abba is Steven's favourite band (followed by Take That and The Beautiful South), from which endless compilation tapes were produced, and the Cherry Cake refers to one of his favourite episodes of Mr Bean.

Steven finds disruption to his routine very difficult to manage, and so Christmas is always difficult, when things change, resources are closed, and even the TV schedules are unreliable, with Countdown off for 2 weeks. And in 2009, when Steven was 20 years old, Christmas was even tougher as Mark was feeling under the weather, which developed into flu and exhaustion from managing Steven's care as a single parent, and still working full time.

Steven had previously been for respite care one day a fortnight at a centre run by the local authority, and on 30 December 2009, Mark called them to see if they might offer a few extra days of respite care, which was agreed, and Steven went into respite that day.

Steven did not settle well into the respite placement that time, and after a "difficult night" in the words of the social worker, they suggested that he should be transferred from the familiar respite centre to a "positive behaviour unit". It was nearby, but he had never been before. It would only be for two weeks, to enable a proper assessment and a real break for Mark to recover, they said. Mark agreed. He later described that as "*the worst mistake I ever made*" and "*the start of a nightmare*".

Steven consistently said that he wanted to go home.

But by 15 January 2010, the local authority had taken a view that Steven should stay at the unit longer, as his disruptive behaviour there was thought likely to pose a risk at home. They were also concerned about his health and especially his weight, and how this was being managed at home. Mark was insistent that he just wanted Steven home. There was a series of meetings and correspondence in which, as the judge later put it:

> *"Hillingdon had by now decided that it would not let Steven go home, but had not revealed this to Mr Neary. Its approach was rather to manage his opposition. It is clear that Mr Neary never agreed to Steven remaining at the support unit for long term assessment, but that is what happened"*[84].

By 22 February 2010, the local authority's attitude to Mr Neary had hardened; an email from the social worker to the support unit included the remark that:

> *"There is always going to be something or other that Mr Neary will bring up and more often than not we are having to appease his needs rather than Steven's, however I want Steven to remain at the support unit"*[85].

Things continued like this until 11 April 2010. While staff were preparing a birthday party for another resident, Steven – unsupervised – left the property through the garden gate and went onto the road. He snatched the glasses off a passing vicar and threw them into the road, breaking them. He then walked towards the main road before being brought back by staff.

Until that point, Steven had largely been able to continue his routine of activities but these were all now suspended, pending risk assessments. Steven was now to be supervised at all times, and a keypad and alarm were fitted to the unit's front door.

On 15 April 2010, a new-fangled "Deprivation of Liberty Safeguards authorisation" was put in place, first an Urgent Authorisation granted by the unit itself, followed by a series of four Standard Authorisations which

---

[84] Para 54.

[85] This is quoted in the public judgment, and I imagine is deeply regretted by the individual who wrote it and by the local authority. The judge went on to note that the local authority accepted at the final hearing that Mr Neary had done nothing to deserve this disrespect. Mr Neary, though, seemed to take it almost as a badge of honour, titling his second book, about his experiences with the local authority and Steven's care more generally, "There's Always Something or Other with Mr Neary" There's Always Something or Other With Mr Neary (lulu.com).

purported to authorise Steven being deprived of his liberty at the unit for the rest of the year, the latest of which, on 19 November 2010, was granted for a further 5 months.

Mark's view was still that Steven should simply be allowed to go home, and by the middle of April 2010 it should have been clear that an application to the Court of Protection was necessary to resolve the dispute, in Steven's best interests. The local authority was talking about going to court at that stage, though only in terms that Mr Neary could make an application to challenge the local authority's decisions if he wished.

The local authority went through the motions of a transition plan for the possible return home, all the while having made a clear decision that it would not in fact allow Steven to go home, and nor should Mr Neary be told.

As this pretence became unsustainable, Mr Neary was told in early July that the local authority would not support Steven going home. Instead, plans were made for a long-term residential placement elsewhere, including the option of an admission under the Mental Health Act to a hospital in Wales.

In July 2010, Mr Neary mobilised his opposition, starting a Facebook campaign and attracting interest and coverage from the media, including the Uxbridge Gazette, Private Eye and, later, the Times, the Independent, BBC news and many others.

On 10 August 2010, the local authority assured Mark that it would issue court proceedings within a week. A psychologist reported on Steven's case and was critical of the lack of support for his autism at the unit. "*It is deplorable, and a clear sign of the adversarial approach being taken by Hillingdon, that this report was deliberately withheld from Mr Neary for at least 6 weeks*", the Judge later said[86].

[86] Para 114.

In fact, the local authority did not issue Court of Protection proceedings until 28 October 2010, after Steven had been at the unit for some 10 months. Even then, their application was framed not as a challenge to the DoLS authorisation, but rather asking for the local authority to be appointed as a health and welfare deputy for Steven, so it could make decisions about long term care and residence for him.

By that stage, Steven was increasingly agitated at the unit, and just a few days earlier he had absconded again, this time barefoot and in his pyjamas, crying and asking to go back to his dad's house.

On 23 December 2010, the case was first heard by a judge. Mr Justice Mostyn terminated the DoLS authorisation that was in place at that time and ordered that it was in Steven's best interests to go home, at least on an interim basis, subject to review. Steven has been at home with his dad since then.

In February 2011 a different High Court Judge, Mr Justice Peter Jackson, heard an application by five media organisations (the Independent, the Guardian, the Times, the BBC and the Press Association) for permission to report on the case, attend future hearings, and to identify Steven and Mark Neary and the London Borough of Hillingdon. By that stage the story had already been covered in the Uxbridge Gazette, Radio 4's "You and Yours", and on BBC London News, as well as featuring more than once in Private Eye. The facts and identities of those involved were already in the public domain to some extent. At that time, hearings in the Court of Protection were heard by default in private[87].

[87] "People should not routinely have their lives exposed to public gaze simply because their affairs come before the court as a result of their incapacity", para 15. Rare exceptions had been made – eg *Independent News and Media v A* – [2010] EWCA Civ 343, in which the media were allowed to attend a case about the affairs of an autistic savant musical prodigy, David Paravicini, who had already attracted considerable media attention for his musical abilities. Now they are routinely in public with a "transparency order", allowing the public to attend but restricting the identity of P being made public, in response to the negative perception of the Court of Protection as a secret court. See the significant work recently of the Open Justice project About

In this case, the judge allowed the media's application, noting that there was a real public interest in the work of the court being understood, and that there was no sign that Steven had been adversely affected by any of the extensive media coverage already.

This was to become the first Court of Protection case to be attended by the press and reported with all the parties identified, both individuals and public bodies[88]. This was unfortunate for Hillingdon, given the criticism they received in the ultimate judgment, when the case returned to Mr Justice Peter Jackson for a week at the end of May 2011 to consider whether the local authority had acted unlawfully.

He gave his judgment on 9 June 2011, and from the local authority's point of view it was brutal, vindicating Mark Neary on every substantial point. Given the earlier judgment on press involvement, it put the Court of Protection on the front pages of the newspapers the next day, for the first time, with the memorable headline in the Independent: "*The Right to Love*".

Peter Jackson J tries to be fair to Hillingdon. He notes that the local authority had provided high levels of support to Steven and his family; that they provide care to some 1,300 adults with disabilities and that it is no simple matter to provide care for people with complex needs. "*In the vast majority of cases, it is carried out without fuss, fanfare or public congratulation, but that can be forgotten when attention understandably turns to cases where things have gone wrong*".

Some "*tremendous results*" were achieved in the unit (notably a five stone loss in Steven's weight, which Mark was delighted about), and the family and local authority working together in future was essential to a successful package of support for Steven.

---

the Project – Promoting Open Justice in the Court of Protection (openjusticecourtofprotection.org).

[88] Later it would become the custom for public bodies to be named routinely in CoP proceedings unless there was good reason not to in order to protect P, though it is still unusual to name P themselves.

But that was as good as it got. The council was found to have breached Steven's rights under Article 8 of the ECHR (family life) and Article 5 (liberty), and to have unlawfully deprived him of his liberty throughout the year of 2010 from early January until he went home just before Christmas[89].

> *"[Hillingdon] acted as if it had the right to make decisions about Steven, and by a combination of turning a deaf ear and force majeure, it tried to wear down Mr Neary's resistance".*

> *"...far from being a safeguard, the way in which the DoL process was used masked the real deprivation of liberty, which was the refusal to allow Steven to go home".*

There are a great many lessons to learn from this case.

The road to hell is paved with good intentions, groupthink, and undue certainty

Hillingdon were not evil. Peter Jackson J said:

> *"I am satisfied that everybody concerned has genuinely worked to do the right thing by Steven at all times, and that a lot of hard work has been done to achieve this. The problems arose from misjudgement, not from lack of commitment"*[90].

And here lies the problem. People by and large do think that they are doing the right thing, and that they are motivated by good intentions, to help others. All the more so, perhaps, among people who dedicate themselves to a career in health and social care. But the need for safeguards is *precisely* because the goodness of intentions alone is not enough:

[89] Later the court approved a settlement of £35,000 in compensation for Steven (see Chapter 15).

[90] Para 16.

> *"The fact that it believed that it was acting for the best during that year is neither here nor there.*[91]"

And in many cases, certainty of the goodness of our intentions bleeds easily into undue certainty about the rightness of our position. This can lead to blinkered thinking, reliance on selective evidence, and an echo chamber of the like-minded, reinforcing rather than challenging their already settled decision. This was the "deaf ear" the judge referred to, and he continued that Hillingdon:

> *"relied on [Mr Neary] coming to see things its way, even though, as events have proved, he was right and they were wrong. In the meantime, it failed to activate the statutory safeguards that exist to prevent situations like this from arising"*[92].

Time and again, the judge finds, the local authority's approach was "one sided":

> *"...Hillingdon had never offered a compromise solution and ... in consequence the only outcome that it would have accepted from the series of meetings with Mr Neary was his agreement to its plan"*[93].

Now, it is important to be careful with the idea of *compromise* in this context.

Compromise is not a word that appears anywhere in the MCA Code of Practice. And in principle, where a person cannot make a particular decision for themselves, that decision must be made *in their best interests*, as if that is a single, objective reality. Establishing what is in Bob's best interests is a collaborative process, to be sure, as set out in Chapter 1 above. But it is wrong in principle to *compromise* on best interests, in the sense of knowingly doing something which is *not* in their best interests simply because it reflects a consensus between the various parties involved

---

[91] Para 27.

[92] Para 27.

[93] Para 112.

or, to put it less generously, placates someone who is objecting to something that should otherwise be done.

Determining best interests is not simply an exercise in compromise. Though I am a great believer in the potential value of mediation, including in the Court of Protection, as a way of addressing failures in relationships and communication in particular, this is one of the challenges with using mediation in this context.

Normally you can agree to compromise a dispute on any terms you like (including, if you wish, a terrible deal, or an "unwise decision"). You can shake hands to settle your multimillion pound claim for peanuts, where you have capacity to make that decision for yourself. But for a child, or an adult without capacity to manage litigation, such a settlement can only be agreed with the approval of the court, to protect a vulnerable litigant from such a bad deal being made on their behalf. And in the context of the Mental Capacity Act, what is *actually* in a person's best interests might not be whatever happens to have been agreed by the parties in dispute.

To this extent, a mediation cannot determine best interests in quite the same way as it can resolve a dispute between those able to compromise and reach their own agreement. Of course, it is likely to be compelling if there is consensus about best interests, but best interests are whatever they are (ie, ultimately, whatever the court thinks they are), and not necessarily whatever the parties agree.[94]

But that is not to say that an uncompromising attitude or rigid preconception of the outcome of the proper, collaborative decision-making process is right or OK.

And determination of best interests can be an iterative process – trying one approach or another to test whether risks are more imagined than real, for example. The MCA is about the art of the practical, and real

[94] Though this is all framed in terms of the Mental Capacity Act ie for people over the age of 16, the same issues clearly arise in the discussions and compromises between professional and parents in cases dealing with children.

experience should be embraced, and fairly considered, where this is appropriate. In this case, Hillingdon's mind was made up that Steven would not be allowed home permanently, and no amount of successful home visits as part of the purported transition plan (being used as cover while they found a residential placement out of area) was going to change that.

Start with Article 8

In *Neary* the local authority was found to have breached Steven's Article 8 rights, as well as Article 5. Note the emphasis that Peter Jackson J put on the right to family life issue.

> *"Decisions about incapacitated people must always be determined by their best interests, but the starting point is their right to respect for their family life where it exists. The burden is always on the state to show that an incapacitated person's welfare cannot be sustained by living with and being locked after by his or her family, with or without outside support"*[95].
>
> *"… it seems to me that the real issue relates to Steven's absence from his family home, rather than the deprivation of liberty to which he is to some degree or other necessarily subject wherever he lives"*[96].

As such, *"Article 8 represents the nub of the matter"*[97].

> *"In saying this, I do not imply that deprivation of liberty issues are unimportant in Steven's case. But by viewing the case primarily through the lens of Article 5 one risks repeating a central fallacy and conflating the secondary question of whether a person is lawfully*

[95] Para 24.

[96] Note how this contrasts with the idea elsewhere in this judgment that he would not have been deprived of his liberty if he had been at home with dad, which may need to have been revisited post *Cheshire West*. See Chapter 6.

[97] Para 151.

deprived of their liberty with the primary question of where he should be living"[98].

Dispute resolution, and timely application to court

Time and again, the judgment makes fundamental points (worth quoting at length) that it was not OK that the local authority thought it knew best, that it had the power to impose the relevant decisions and put the onus on Mr Neary to bring a challenge to court if he disagreed. The purpose of the Court of Protection is resolve such disputes; the local authority should have brought the case to court and done so much, much sooner than it did:

> *"the ordinary powers of the local authority are limited to investigating, providing support services and, where appropriate, referring the matter to the court. If a local authority seeks to regulate, control, compel, restrain, confine or coerce it must, except in an emergency, point to specific statutory authority for what it is doing, or else obtain the appropriate sanction of the court"*[99].

> *"Significant welfare issues that cannot be resolved by discussion should be placed before the Court of Protection, where decisions can be taken as a matter of urgency where necessary"*[100].

> *"it is disappointing that the meeting [on 30 April 2010] did not reach the obvious decision that an urgent application should be made to the court"*[101].

[98] Para 151.

[99] Para 22.

[100] Para 33.

[101] Para 90.

The letter from the social worker to Mr Neary on 27 May 2010 *"reverts to the misconception that the decision lay in the hands of the local authority"*[102].

> *"where a dilemma exists, the court provides an accessible forum. Often, parties will have a clear view of what they are proposing, but if a party needs more evidence or is uncertain about the best outcome of a difficult case, it is no shame to say so. Proceedings in the Court of Protection need not be adversarial. The fact that these have been is no more than the consequence of Hillingdon's stance. It is a great pity that it did not issue proceedings at least six months earlier, and regrettable that when it finally did so it did not share its internal doubts with others, instead pitching its case as high as it did".*[103]

> *"There are repeated references, particularly by the service manager, to the burden being on Mr Neary to take the matter to court if he wished to challenge what was happening. That approach cannot be right. I have already referred to the decision in Re S*[104]*, which rightly observes that the practical and evidential burden is on a local authority to demonstrate that its arrangements are better than those that can be achieved within the family. … Nor is it any answer to say, as Hillingdon has done, that Mr Neary could always have gone to court himself, and that it had told him so. It was Steven's rights, not those of his father, that were in issue. Moreover, local authorities have the advantage over individuals both in terms of experience and, even nowadays, depth of pocket. The fact that an individual does not bring a matter to court does not relieve the local authority of the obligation to act, it redoubles it"*[105] *(emphasis added).*

[102] Para 93.

[103] Para 142.

[104] [2002] EWHC 2278 (Fam) se below.

[105] Para 196.

Overstepping the role of the local authority

On this, the relevant extracts of Munby J's decision *Re S* [2002], referred to by Peter Jackson J in *Neary*, are worth reading in full as well:

> *"[115] I am not saying that there is in law any presumption that mentally incapacitated adults are better off with their families: often they will be; sometimes they will not be. But respect for our human condition, regard for the realities of our society and the common sense ..., surely indicate that the starting point should be the normal assumption that mentally incapacitated adults will be better off if they live with a family rather than in an institution – however benign and enlightened the institution may be, and however well integrated into the community – and that mentally incapacitated adults who have been looked after within their family will be better off if they continue to be looked after within the family rather than by the State.*
>
> *[116] We have to be conscious of the limited ability of public authorities to improve on nature. We need to be careful not to embark upon 'social engineering'. And we should not lightly interfere with family life. If the State – typically, as here, in the guise of a local authority – is to say that it is the more appropriate person to look after a mentally incapacitated adult than her own partner or family, it assumes, as it seems to me, the burden – not the legal burden but the practical and evidential burden – of establishing that this is indeed so. And common sense surely indicates that the longer a vulnerable adult's partner, family or carer have looked after her without the State having perceived the need for its intervention, the more carefully must any proposals for intervention be scrutinised and the more cautious the court should be before accepting too readily the assertion that the State can do better than the partner, family or carer.*
>
> *[117] At the end of the day, the simple point, surely, is this: the quality of public care must be at least as good as that from which the child or vulnerable adult has been rescued. Indeed that sets the requirement too low. If the State is to justify removing children from their parents or vulnerable adults from their relatives, partners, friends or carers it can*

> *only be on the basis that the State is going to provide a better quality of care than that which they have hitherto been receiving...".*

What goes in notes is not private or privileged

I suspect that there were some deep regrets about the way people had expressed themselves in places in the evidence that was put before the court, which found its way into the final published judgment or into the media.

It is a stark reminder to not document anything in health or social care records, minutes or correspondence which you would not be comfortable to hear read out in court or see in the papers.

Privilege over documents prepared for the purposes of litigation, and legal advice may be exceptions, of course, but that won't extend to what is simply part of P's health or social care file.

Transparency and good faith

It's ok to disagree about someone's best interests. And it's ok to be wrong from time to time, especially when we can get our heads round the fact that having good intentions does not always make us right.

In fact, I am vastly more comfortable with a client agonising over the right thing to do in complex circumstances, with good principles pulling in different directions (often the tension between paternalism and autonomy), than I am with an organisation or a health or social care professional who is unwavering in their certainty.

Often, these cases *should* feel difficult, because they *are* difficult. Perfectly reasonable people might disagree about what is in someone's best interests. That is why the MCA demands an open minded and consultative approach. My concern is redoubled when a client's position is clung to stubbornly when the facts seem to change around it. Or when there is a sense of evidence being cherry-picked to support a particular case and scrutiny being unwelcome or treated as hostile.

At the risk of stating the obvious, it is not steadfast, or commendable to dig a trench and defend it at all costs. Nor is it weakness to review, refine, or even reverse your position as evidence is tested and reconsidered, or as new evidence comes to light[106]. It may be, of course, human nature to want to be "right" at all costs – and let's face it, we lawyers carry our share of blame for this – but this can be where a critical friend can play a priceless role. And the very purpose of safeguards, like DoLS, is to protect people from the certainties of unchecked good intentions.

The Court of Protection is designed to resolve disputes and uncertainties. But – like the MCA generally – it is premised on the idea that people will be acting in good faith and, as such, will be open and transparent.

One of the more telling remarks among the barrage of criticism in Peter Jackson J's judgment was the line that, at every step, Hillingdon's behaviour had been "*calculated to prevent proper scrutiny of the situation it had created*".[107]

Hillingdon had decided in April 2010 that it would not let Steven go home, "*but had not revealed this to Mr Neary*", while its approach was to "*manage his opposition*".[108]

It was seen in the dismissive discourtesy that "*there is always going to be something or other that Mr Neary will bring up*", in the decision that Mr Neary was "*not to be informed*" of the decision made about his son's future[109], in deliberately withholding an expert report about his son from Mr Neary for 6 weeks or more[110] and in the judge finding offers of meetings to be mere "*window dressing*".[111]

---

[106] As is often attributed to John Maynard Keynes: "When the facts change, I change my mind. What do you do, sir?"

[107] Para 155(2).

[108] Para 54.

[109] Para 80.

[110] Para 114.

[111] Para 106.

And this lack of transparency did more than bring a needlessly adversarial approach both to planning Steven's care and to the eventual Court of Protection proceedings. By telling Mr Neary on 10 August 2010 that they were submitting an application to court to resolve the dispute, when in fact the local authority did not do this until 28 October 2010, the court's review of Steven's situation was delayed by months, when Mr Neary would have started the proceedings himself.

The role of advocacy

DoLS should also bring a safeguard in the provision of access to advocacy.

Mark Neary was appointed as Steven's Relevant Person's Representative (RPR), and where the RPR is not a paid professional, as here, and they request an IMCA to support them, then an Independent Mental Capacity Advocate (IMCA) must be appointed.[112]

In this case, Hillingdon rightly asked for an IMCA at the time the first DoLS authorisation was put in place and Mark asked for this, but they were told by the advocacy agency that he was not entitled to one. This was, apparently a misunderstanding on the part of the agency that sourced the IMCA service for the local authority, but, as Peter Jackson J put it, Hillingdon "*should have persisted*".

The positive contribution made by the IMCA when they were eventually involved six months later was praised by the judge and used to reinforce the point about their value.[113]

Misunderstanding DoLS

Though the judge put the focus on Article 8 (right to family life) and the more fundamental question of whether Steven was in the right place, this

[112] MCA s39D(2)

[113] Para 194.

is rightly seen as a seminal case about DoLS and their (mis)use, and they were plainly misunderstood as well as misapplied.

As Mr Neary put it, "*"Safeguards" seemed good – the reality didn't*".[114]

Peter Jackson J said:

> *"where stringent conditions are met [a DoLS authorisation] allows a managing authority to deprive a person of liberty at a particular place. It is not to be used by a local authority as a means of getting their own way on the question of whether it is in the person's best interests to be in the place at all. Using the DoL regime in that way turns the spirit of the MCA on its head, with a code designed to protect the liberty of vulnerable people being used instead as an instrument of confinement".*[115]

The local authority (as Supervisory Body) argued that they were not to be blamed for the failures of the Best Interests Assessors, three of whom had reviewed Steven's case in the course of recommending four Standard Authorisations over the year he was kept at the unit. The local authority argued that law is framed in terms that as supervisory body they "*must*" grant the standard authorisation when the appropriate recommendations are submitted[116].

The judge was having none of it. The local authority could not abdicate responsibility in this way, and it is not their role to be a "rubberstamp"[117].

> *"Where, as here, a supervisory body grants authorisations on the basis of perfunctory scrutiny of superficial best interests assessments, it cannot expect the authorisations to be legally valid".*[118]

[114] Para 145.

[115] Para 33(1).

[116] Schedule A1, para 50.

[117] Para 181.

[118] Para 33(3).

The supervisory body that receives the assessments must

> *"actively supervise the process by scrutinising the assessment with independence and with a degree of care that is appropriate to the seriousness of the decision and the circumstances of the individual case…".*[119]

The judge was critical of each of the four best interests assessments, which variously failed to take into account Steven's views, or his father's, were completed after "*cursory contact*" and "*in a hurry*", or failed to really consider the alternatives for Steven, in particular the possibility that he might return home[120]. He did not name any individual BIA, however, and noted that the first BIA involved was in fact completing her first ever assessment.[121]

But the upshot was that "*the decision about Steven was made on the basis of insufficient scrutiny of inadequate information*", and each of the purported DoLS authorisations were ineffective and unlawful.[122]

And a wider misconception about the function of the safeguards was evident not just in the case, but in the way that others discussed it. The Uxbridge Gazette, 21 July 2010, wrote:

> *"Steven … was served with a 'deprivation of liberty order' after he escaped from the care home in an incident where his father claims he was left unsupervised. The order, while it has no clear definition, means he must be under direct supervision and is not free to leave unsupervised"*[123].

But that is backwards.

---

[119] Para 175.

[120] See para 74, 95-96,

[121] Para 74.

[122] Para 184.

[123] Quoted at p82 of Mr Neary's book, above.

A DoLS authorisation does not demand that restrictions be placed on an individual. Rather, a DoLS authorisation is required where the restrictions which are imposed as part of a person's care plan, in their best interests, under the MCA, reach a degree of intrusion into that person's life that demands independent scrutiny as a safeguard.

The Deprivation of Liberty *Safeguards* are, well, *safeguards*.

They are not a mechanism by which someone *becomes* deprived of their liberty, but rather a layer of protective scrutiny brought into play when someone *is recognised as being* (or about to be) deprived of their liberty. The emphasis should be on the S in DoLS, not the D.

They are a spotlight and not a padlock.

The underlying care package, including any restrictions which impinge on a person's liberty must be justified under the MCA: the person must lack capacity to make those decisions, and they must be in his or her best interests, as well as – where they amount to restraint[124] – necessary to prevent harm and proportionate to the likelihood and seriousness of that harm.

Then a DoLS authorisation is appropriate as scrutiny where the arrangements might amount to a deprivation of that person's liberty. It is not an exercise which tightens any restrictions, but explicitly tests whether they can be loosened, while still meeting the person's best interests. This reflects the core principle in MCA that any best interests decision must be tested by asking whether their best interests can be achieved in a less restrictive way[125].

---

[124] MCA s6.

[125] "Before the act is done or the decision is made, regard must be had to whether the purpose for which it is needed can be as effectively achieved in a way that is less restrictive of the person's rights and freedom of action" MCA s1(6). Note that this is commonly misunderstood and misrepresented as saying that we must take the "least restrictive" option. That is not quite right, as the least restrictive option might not be in P's best interests. Best interests comes first, if P cannot make a decision for themselves, but we should test whether we can get there in a less restrictive way.

Where a care plan is restrictive enough that it could constitute a deprivation of a person's liberty as a matter of law, a referral to DoLS (or the Court of Protection where appropriate) does not create the restrictions or the deprivation of liberty; it recognises them and brings appropriate scrutiny accordingly.

Where a referral to DoLS or the court is not made in those circumstances, the result is not someone who is not deprived of their liberty, but rather someone who is *still deprived of their liberty, but without appropriate scrutiny*.

In this sense, the opposite of a DoLS authoristion is not *no* deprivation of liberty, but *an unlawful deprivation of liberty*.

I am sorry if it feels that I have laboured this point, but I cannot emphasise enough how important this is, and how easy, it seems, it is to lose sight of it.

Definition of DoL

Finally, though not at the definitive level we will see later in the *Cheshire West* judgment in the Supreme Court, the *Neary* judgment does have something useful to say about the definition of a deprivation of liberty which triggers the necessary safeguards.

In particular, Peter Jackson J rejected the local authority argument that the deprivation of Steven's liberty started only in April 2010, when the first DoLS authorisation was put in place. He agreed that the tightening of restrictions on Steven then, such as limiting the activities he had previously enjoyed, constituted "further deprivations of his liberty". But he found that Steven had in fact been deprived of his liberty since 5 January 2010 – ie essentially after the initial agreed period of very limited respite care ended. After that, the key features are

> *"[Steven's] objection to being at the support unit, the objection of his father, and the total effective control of Steven's every waking moment in an environment that was not his home".*[126]

The judge talked about

> *"Steven's essential experience of being away from home".*[127]

Though he didn't explicitly discuss it, there is a suggestion from this and a few other comments that there was no thought that Steven would be deprived of his liberty when he is at home with his dad. Referring to the local authority rejecting a return home, the judge says

> "*No reference is made to the possibility of a placement at home alleviating the need for a deprivation of liberty*".[128]

Likewise, referring to the third DoLS standard authorisation, the judge said

> *"the authorisation makes no reference to Steven's wishes or those of his father, nor to the possibility that deprivation of liberty would not be involved if he was at home".*[129]

Key Points

Whether a person could or should in fact be regarded as deprived of their liberty in their own home with their family would prove to be one of the more contentious aspects of the case law over the following years, as we will see.

---

[126] Paragraph 161.

[127] Paragraph 162.

[128] Para 96.

[129] Para 117.

For now, remember that so many of the most important lessons about the (mis)use of DoLS are there in one of the very first cases:

- The road to hell is paved with good intentions, groupthink and undue certainty;
- Start with the substance of the decision making about care and residence, and remember the Article 8 right to family life;
- Though *a compromise* is not necessarily the same thing as P's best interests, *an uncompromising attitude* is unlikely to help to resolve disputes, or to go down well with the court;
- Where an application to court is appropriate, the onus is on the public body not the family to do this, and delay is further damaging to P's rights – it is a rare dispute that will improve with keeping;
- If basic professionalism is not enough to keep discourtesy out of the approach and the documentation, remember that anything written in health or social care records may well end up in front of a judge or a journalist;
- In decision making, and in addressing any dispute, transparency and good faith is vital;
- Early and appropriate involvement of advocacy is always helpful;
- The role of DoLS is not to impose restrictions, but to recognise where there are restrictions that warrant independent scrutiny; DoLS as a spotlight, not a padlock.

Now, the crucial issue is how to define the point at which those safeguards should be triggered.

What does "deprivation of liberty" mean?!

PART TWO

DEFINING DEPRIVATION OF LIBERTY

CHAPTER FOUR

THE ROAD TO CHESHIRE WEST

With a process for scrutiny / authorisation that swings into action when there is a deprivation of liberty, there must surely be a clear definition, so we know when it is all triggered. Right?

In fact, a clear definition of a deprivation of liberty, and how to apply it in practice, has proven quite elusive.

We can of course look at the European Court of Human Rights (ECtHR) case law for their interpretation of Article 5 over the years, including prior to DoLS. We can look to the domestic case law, especially since the implementation of DoLS in 2009, and the Code of Practice that came with it. And since 2014, we have a Supreme Court judgment (*Cheshire West*) which sets out the definition of deprivation of liberty in fairly simple terms (the "acid test" – below).

But even since *Cheshire West*, there has been far from a consensus about how to apply that test in practice, especially in circumstances which can be very different from those in which that case arose. And if we are not to have a one size fits all approach, then where do we draw the line for where *Cheshire West* applies and when it does not?

So, let me start with a few words of comfort.

Firstly, if you are a little uncertain about it, then you are in good company. *Everyone* (lawyers and judges included) is still feeling their way towards where to find the edges of the concepts (this is, after all, a relatively new bit of law). And, I as I have said, I am always more reassured by a bit of healthy self-doubt than I am by undue certainty.

For example, when we look at the case of MiG and MeG shortly[130], you'll see that the Supreme Court held by a 4:3 majority that they were both deprived of their liberty. So *three judges of the Supreme Court* thought that they were not, and were "wrong"[131]. The Court of Appeal had *unanimously* held that they were not deprived of liberty either, so the three judges there turned out to be wrong as well, and so was the first instance judge, Mrs Justice Parker, who also held that they were not deprived of their liberty. In fact, that means that out of the 11 judges who heard the case across the High Court, Court of Appeal and Supreme Court, only four thought that the sisters' situation amounted to a deprivation of liberty, while seven did not. But some judges have more clout than others, and the system we have means that those four, being the majority when it got to the Supreme Court, determine how the law is interpreted (for now at least).

Equally, professional opinion can easily be split. Some research published in The Psychiatrist in 2011[132] used 12 real life case study vignettes, and asked groups of psychiatrists, Independent Mental Capacity Advocates (IMCAs), Best Interests Assessors (BIAs) and, ahem, "expert lawyers"[133] whether or not the scenario amounted to a deprivation of liberty. There is always, of course, a degree of subjectivity to this (at least until a judge tells us, subject to the point above!), but what's startling is the degree of inconsistency:

- There was total agreement about only one case out of the 12.
- On average, lawyers were most likely to identify a deprivation of liberty (three times as likely as a psychiatrist!), closely followed by

[130] See chapter 5.

[131] Well, in the minority in the Supreme Court at least, which amounts to much the same thing in our system, at least unless or until the law is changed by another Supreme Court judgment showing that they were right after all.

[132] Judgements about deprivation of liberty made by various professionals: comparison study, The Psychiatrist (2011), 35, 344-349

[133] Their phrase, and to be taken with a pinch of salt, as you'll see.

the IMCAs, who were twice as likely to discern a deprivation as a BIA.

- In one case, 50% of the lawyers thought it was a deprivation of liberty, though no other professional did.

- For some of the scenarios, 80% of the BIAs considered it to be a deprivation of liberty, against 67% of IMCAs and lawyers, and only 33% of psychiatrists. For another it was reversed, with 100% of IMCAs and 83% of lawyers seeing it as a deprivation of liberty, but only 60% of BIAs, and 50% of psychiatrists.

- Among professional groups, IMCAs were the most consistent, but even then only at a "fair" level of agreement.

- And if you ever feel intimidated by the "legal expertise" in any room, let me say that the research found that the level of agreement within professional groups was lowest among the lawyers, "suggesting their consistency of agreement was no better than chance"!

- The overall level of agreement across the board was statistically "slight" – better than tossing a coin, but not by much.

- The only certainty seemed to be that if even a psychiatrist thought it might be a deprivation of liberty then everyone else was likely to as well!

Of course, experience and expertise has evolved since 2011, as well as having the benefit of a greater body of case law as a point of reference. But the fundamental point is that this is an area where there is often a fairly subjective view taken, and it is more than possible to be reasonable but (later proven) wrong, which does make it all the more important to approach any undue sense of certainty with real caution.

And here is the vital second bit of comfort: for these purposes, it actually *does not matter whether we can be certain* that there is a deprivation of liberty.

The trigger for referral to DoLS (or the Court of Protection) is where the care "*might involve depriving the person of their liberty*"[134].

"*Might*".

The Introduction to the Code of Practice continues:

> "*This Code of Practice helps to explain how to identify when a person is, or is at risk of, being deprived of their liberty and how deprivation of liberty may be avoided*" (emphasis added).

And in paragraph 3.1 of the Code:

> "*A Managing Authority has responsibility for applying for authorisation of deprivation of liberty for any person who may come within the scope of the deprivation of liberty safeguards*" (emphasis added).

The flow charts at Annex 1 and 2 of the DoLS Code of Practice also put it in terms of identification of those who are "*at risk of being deprived of their liberty*" (emphasis added).

In the context of bringing applications to court about potential deprivations of liberty for children, Lord Justice Munby said:

> "*Need to apply to the court*
>
> *An application to the court should be made where the circumstances in which the child is, or will be, living constitute, at least arguably (taking a realistic rather than a fanciful view), a deprivation of liberty*"[135] (emphasis added).

[134] DoLS Code of Practice 2008, introduction, p1.

[135] *Re AF*, para 48.

And, in a case dealing with the interface between DoLS and the Mental Health Act[136], Charles J said that "... the DoLS regime ... applies when it appears that judged objectively *there is a risk that cannot sensibly be ignored* that the relevant circumstances amount to a deprivation of liberty".

It is not the role of the person referring the case to the scrutiny of the process (whether DoLS or the Court of Protection) to determine that there definitely <u>is</u> a deprivation of liberty. That is for the BIA (under DoLS) or the judge in the Court of Protection. Logically, the purpose of the safeguards is to involve independent expertise to consider whether there actually is a deprivation of liberty, and then to consider whether it should be authorised. Care should be taken not to set the bar too high, only referring clear or obvious cases of deprivation, and so denying meaningful safeguards to other, less clear cut cases.

Instead, the trigger for referral is a much easier question: *might* the person be deprived of their liberty? If so, a referral must be made.

The question whether P ***might be** deprived of liberty* is rather easier to answer than whether they *definitely are*, and this is actually the right question for the great majority of health and social care professionals (and lawyers) involved[137].

Still, reassuring as that perspective is, it would be a bit of a cop out to leave it there, and would not help those in the system who do have a role of determining the question of whether there is a deprivation of liberty. So we will have to go further, and we will look at the DoLS Code of Practice, and then the European and domestic case law.

Before we do, it is worth noting that a deprivation of liberty is not defined directly in the MCA or in DoLS itself. There is just a provision in the interpretation section of the MCA that "In this Act, references to

---

[136] AM v SLAM [2013] UKUT 0365 at paragraph 59 – see chapter 13.

[137] Those involved in The Psychiatrist research set out above might well have shown a great deal more consistency if the question was not whether P is deprived of their liberty, but whether they are *at risk of being deprived of liberty*?

deprivation of a person's liberty have the same meaning as in Article 5(1) of the Human Rights Convention"[138].

So let's start with some of the European case law.

European Court of Human Rights (ECtHR)

We have already seen the *Bournewood* judgment (*HL v UK, 2004*) in which the European Court of Human Rights identified a deprivation of liberty because HL was:

> *"...under continuous supervision and control and he was not free to leave".*

Earlier, in *Ashingdane v the UK*[139], the court dealt with a patient in a mental hospital and held that he could be regarded as "detained" even during a period when he was in an open hospital ward with regular unescorted access to unsecured hospital grounds, and the possibility of leave outside the hospital unaccompanied.

Coming just after *Bournewood*, in *Storck v Germany*[140] in 2005 the European Court of Human Rights set out a three-part test for identifying a deprivation of someone's liberty:

---

[138] MCA s64(5), which in turn defines the "Human Rights Convention" by reference to the meaning of that phrase "The Convention" in the Human Rights Act 1998, which is defined (HRA 1998 s21(1)) as "the Convention for the Protection of Human Rights and Fundamental Freedoms, agreed by the Council of Europe at Rome on 4 November 1950 as it has effect for the time being in relation to the United Kingdom". Quite why the MCA / DoLS couldn't directly just refer to the European Convention of Human Rights, I don't know.

[139] (1985) 7 EHRR 528.

[140] [2005] ECHR 406. Ms Storck was under continuous supervision and control in a psychiatric hospital, she was shackled to ensure her stay, and when she escaped she was brought back by the police. She was incapable of consenting because of the effects on her of the medication given to her for her mental disorder.

1. The objective element – "the person's confinement to a certain limited place for a not negligible length of time"; but also

2. The subjective element – absence of valid consent (this was the issue contested in the *Storck* case); and

3. Imputability to the state – the state must be responsible, in some way, for the circumstances of the DoL.

We will come back to the subjective element of absence of consent (Chapter 9) and the imputability to the state (Chapter 11).

It is fair to say that the focus tends to be on the issue of the first element, the *objective* bit (to such an extent that often the "definition" of deprivation of liberty is discussed in terms of this aspect alone, neglecting, or taking as read, the subjective and imputability aspects).

On the objective element, the case of *Guzzardi v Italy*[141] is often taken as the starting point. In this case, a Sicilian mafioso was convicted of involvement in kidnapping a businessman (who was released after a ransom was paid) and was sentenced to 18 years in prison. Prior to his conviction, though, while he was on remand he was transferred to Asinara, a tiny island off the coast of Sardinia, where he was placed under "special supervision" conditions.

These included that he must live there, follow a "law abiding life", and report to the authorities twice a day and at any other times on demand. He was also required to keep to a curfew between 10pm and 7am and not frequent any bars or nightclubs[142].

Signore Guzzardi argued that, taken altogether, this constituted a deprivation of his liberty, in breach of Article 5 of the ECHR.

---

[141] 7367/76 [1980] ECHR 5.

[142] Though that last part was probably academic, since Asinara is only approximately 20 square miles and virtually uninhabited. The 2001 census listed one man, though there is apparently a population of albino donkeys, from which the island may take its name.

Looking at the definition of deprivation of liberty for these purposes, the court noted that it must go beyond mere *restriction on his movement.* A different bit of the ECHR (Article 2 of Protocol 4) asserts the right to "freedom of movement", but note that neither Italy (then, in that case) nor the UK (now) has ratified or incorporated that part into domestic law.

Even so, it is worth setting out Article 2 to Protocol 4 in detail, for contrast to Article 5:

> *"Article 2 – Freedom of Movement*
>
> 1. *Everyone lawfully within the territory of a state shall, within that territory,* ***has the right to liberty of movement and freedom to choose his residence.***

So it must be that a deprivation of liberty for the purposes of Article 5, whatever it means, is something different from this.

In *Guzzardi*, the court said that Article 5

> *"is not concerned with mere restrictions on liberty of movement; such restrictions are governed by Article 2 of Protocol No. 4 which has not been ratified by Italy. In order to determine whether someone has been "deprived of his liberty" within the meaning of Article 5, the starting point must be his concrete situation and account must be taken of a whole range of criteria such as the type, duration, effects and manner of implementation of the measure in question"*[143] *(emphasis added).*

As such,

> *"The difference between deprivation of and restriction upon liberty is nonetheless merely one of degree or intensity, and not one of nature or substance" (emphasis added).*

That last phrase gets bandied about to the point of being a platitude about the blurriness of the line that needs to be drawn. It can feel like

[143] Para 92.

something of an abdication of the responsibility of asserting a view. The judgment in *Guzzardi* completed that paragraph with the less often quoted:

> *"Although the process of classification into one or other of these categories sometimes proves to be no easy task in that some borderline cases are a matter of pure opinion, the Court cannot avoid making the selection upon which the applicability or inapplicability of Article 5 depends"*[144].

The court then dealt with the issue of deprivation of liberty in a different context in the case of *Austen*[145]. On 1 May 2001, police responded to the anti-capitalism protests around Oxford Circus, in central London by "kettling" around 150 people in the area, and not permitting them to leave. One of them was Lois Austin, who had arrived at the protests at around 2pm. When she tried to leave at around 3.45pm so she could collect her daughter from a creche, she was stopped by police and was kept there until around 9.30pm. She sued the police for unlawful deprivation of her liberty[146].

The High Court[147] found that there had been a deprivation of liberty, but declared it to be lawful, justified as "necessary" by the circumstances the police faced.

The Court of Appeal[148] held that there was no deprivation of liberty at all, referring by comparison to the examples of a crowd at a football

---

[144] Para 93.

[145] *Austin v Commissioner of Police of the Metropolis* [2009] UKHL 5.

[146] Three other people who were not involved in the protests also sued, incidentally, including a man who was attempting to cross Oxford Circus to go into a bookshop and was caught up in the police cordon for around 7 hours, and two people who worked in the area and were out on their lunchbreaks, but were confined by the police at Oxford Circus late into the evening.

[147] [2005] EWHC 480, 23 March 2005

[148] [2007] EWCA Civ 989

match, or motorists unable to leave a motorway after police action in response to an incident.

The House of Lords agreed[149] that restrictions of that kind won't amount to a deprivation of liberty for Article 5 as long as they are proportionate and not arbitrary. (Though Lord Hope gave a powerful warning that "*...if confinement amounting to a deprivation of liberty ... is established, good intentions cannot make up for any deficiencies in [its] justification...*").

The European Court of Human Rights then heard a further appeal, and gave a judgment on 15 March 2012[150]. Great care was needed, it said, before using the "*purpose*" of any restrictions to define whether or not they amounted to a deprivation of liberty:

> "*...it is clear ... that an underlying public interest motive, for example to protect the community against a perceived threat emanating from an individual, has no bearing on whether that person has been deprived of his liberty, although it might be relevant to the subsequent enquiry whether the deprivation of liberty was justified under one of the paragraphs of Article 5(1)...*"

Pertinent to the health and social care setting, they continued:

> "*The same is true where the object is to protect, treat or care in some way for the person taken into confinement, unless that person has validly consented to what would otherwise be a deprivation of liberty*".

So good intentions and benevolence are not enough to say that restrictions cannot amount to a deprivation of liberty[151]. But the court went on to talk not of purpose but of "*context*":

149 [2009] UKHL 5

150 [2012] ECHR 459

151 Though these issues would come up again in the domestic case law, and especially on the road to the *Cheshire West* Supreme Court judgment, which came almost exactly two years later – see chapter 5.

> *"... the context in which action is taken is an important factor to be taken into account, since situations commonly occur in modern society where the public may be called on to endure restrictions on freedom of movement or liberty in the interests of the common good. As the judges in the Court of Appeal and House of Lords observed, members of the public generally accept that temporary restrictions may be placed on their freedom of movement in certain contexts, such as travel by public transport or on the motorway, or attendance at a football match .... The Court does not consider that such commonly occurring restrictions on movement, so long as they are rendered unavoidable as a result of circumstances beyond the control of the authorities and are necessary to avert a real risk of serious injury or damage, and are kept to the minimum required for that purpose, can properly be described as "deprivations of liberty" within the meaning of Article 5 § 1."*[152]

In this case, "*there was space within the cordon for people to walk about and there was no crushing, but conditions were uncomfortable, with no shelter, food, water or toilet facilities*". The coercive nature of the cordon "*points towards a deprivation of liberty*", but taking into account the type of restrictions, their manner of implementation and the *context*, the "*Court does not consider that those within the cordon can be said to have been deprived of their liberty within the meaning of Article 5*".

So, context is everything (but it is important not to conflate it with purpose, or good intentions – see chapter 5 and 6)[153].

Finally, for now, a significant case on the "freedom to leave" part of the test. In *Stanev v Bulgaria*[154] Mr Stanev had a diagnosis of schizophrenia, and was placed by the state against his wishes in an institution in a remote part of the country, 8k from the nearest village, when none of his family

---

152 Para 59.

153 And, later, when considering the impact of *Cheshire West* and its application for inpatient medical treatment, it was the ECtHR judgment in *Austin* that allowed Arden LJ in *Ferreira* to make the argument that the intensive care context justified a departure from the *Cheshire West* acid test. See chapter 7.

154 (2012) 55 EHRR 22.

were willing to act as a guardian. Conditions there were poor, with Mr Stanev sharing a small room with four other residents.

The European Court of Human Rights held that he was deprived of his liberty, and was not "free to leave" even though the institution itself was not locked, and he was able to go to the nearest village, where he sometimes worked in a restaurant; this was only done with the permission of the director of the institute, and if he did not return when expected, he would be sought by the police.

DoLS Code of Practice

So, when England and Wales came to introduce the DoLS system to address the gap identified in that *Bournewood* judgment, how did we tackle the vexed question of defining a deprivation of liberty to trigger those safeguards?

Well, the opening line of the DoLS Code of Practice (2008, introduced alongside the DoLS scheme) Chapter 2 ("What is a deprivation of liberty?") is:

> *"There is no simple definition of a deprivation of liberty".*

Well, thanks very much!

It goes on to pick out "*factors that can be relevant*" to identifying whether the situation goes beyond "mere" restraint and amount to a deprivation of liberty:

- "*Restraint is used, including sedation, to admit a person to an institution where that person is resisting admission.*
- *Staff exercise complete and effective control over the care and movement of a person for a significant period.*
- *Staff exercise control over assessments, treatment, contacts and residence.*

- *A decision has been taken by the institution that the person will not be released into the care of others, or permitted to live elsewhere, unless the staff in the institution consider it appropriate.*

- *A request by carers for a person to be discharged to their care is refused.*

- *The person is unable to maintain social contacts because of restrictions placed on their access to other people.*

- *The person loses autonomy because they are under continuous supervision and control*".

It is also worth looking at the MCA Code of Practice (2007)[155], which explains the effect of MCA s5 and 6:

> "*It is difficult to define the difference between actions that amount to a restriction of liberty and those that result in a deprivation of liberty. In recent legal cases, the European Court of Human Rights said that the difference was "one of degree or intensity, not one of nature or substance". There must be particular factors in the specific situation of the person concerned which provide the "degree" or "intensity" to result in a deprivation of liberty. In practice, this can relate to:*
>
> - *The type of care being provided*
> - *How long the situation lasts*
> - *Its effects, or*

[155] An updated Code of Practice for the MCA (long overdue) was issued for consultation in March 2022 as a single document combining the updated code for the MCA with the Code of Practice for the proposed LPS. While we are expecting an updated MCA Code of Practice, there is unlikely to be an updated DoLS Code of Practice anytime soon.

- *The way a particular situation came about.*"[156]

It then goes on to list the same factors as are set out above. These are red flags, it says, drawn from the body of case law, *but are not a checklist*[157].

It is important to be careful with any Code of Practice, as it cannot make law, and especially so where it has been significantly superseded by case law, as this has.

Domestic Case Law – Pre *Cheshire West*

The MCA came into force in April 2007, bringing into being the Court of Protection as we now know it, with the DoLS added to it by the Mental Health Act 2007, coming into force in April 2009.

Before that, the Court had to deal with questions of deprivation of liberty in the family division of the High Court, for example in *JE v DE and Surrey County Council*[158], in which Mr Justice Munby handed down his judgment between Christmas and New Year in 2006.

DE was 76 at the time of the judgment. A stroke had left him blind and with significant impairment of his short-term memory. The judge concluded that he lacked capacity to make his own decisions about his residence. The question was whether he had been deprived of his liberty by the local authority placing him into residential care in September 2005.

DE had been in a relationship with JE for many years, though only since August 2004 had he lived with her, and they had only married in June 2005. JE had mental health problems of her own, and apparently felt unable to care for him. On 4 September 2005, she put him in a chair on

---

[156] Para 6.52.

[157] And note that they are all about the material situation that P is in – the objective element of the deprivation of liberty, rather than worrying about the subjective element (lack of valid consent) or imputability to the state.

[158] [2006] EWHC 3459 (Fam).

the street in front of their house and called the police. There had been previous allegations of her neglect towards him, and she had stopped him from seeing his daughter by a previous relationship.

When the police attended they found him, a 75 year-old blind man, dressed only in pyjama bottoms a shirt and slippers, wandering down the road. He had no keys to the property and JE was refusing to let him in.

The local authority arranged his admission to a residential placement. Though DE was appreciative of the care he received, he continually said that he just wanted to return home to live with JE. The local authority would not allow this, though they would consider him going home if he did not live with her. They said that if JE attended and tried to take him home, the care home should call the police and should keep him there, under "the common law doctrine of necessity", though there were no restrictions on her visiting him, and very few restrictions on his everyday activities within the care home.

The judge acknowledged the extent of DE's freedom within the care home where he was placed, but rejected the local authority argument that this therefore amounted to no more than a restriction on his liberty. No, the judge held, he <u>was</u> deprived of his liberty.

It was not simply about a locked door:

> *"After all, a Category A prisoner detained in a maximum security prison and a Category C prisoner detained in an open prison are both equally deprived of their liberty, even though there is nothing more keeping the Category C prisoner in than a rule that he must not pass beyond a line drawn on a plan, a notice attached to a tree warning him that he must go no further and the threat of recapture if he leaves without permission".*

He was not "free to leave" and was, "in that sense, completely under the control of the local authority" because

> *"it was and is [the local authority] who decides the essential matters of where DE can live, whether he can leave and whether he can be with JE".*

Referring to the similarities with the *Bournewood* case:

> *"The simple reality is that DE will be permitted to leave the institution in which [the local authority] has placed him and be released into the care of JE only as and when – if ever, probably never – [the local authority] considers it appropriate. [The local authority's] motives may be of the purest, but in my judgment [it] has been and is continuing to deprive DE of his liberty".*

Note that this judgment does not go on to consider the lawfulness of that deprivation of his liberty, which was reserved for a further hearing (which – if it happened – was not, as far as I know, ever reported).

With the single question of whether or not DE *was* deprived of his liberty, this case puts a focus on being "free to leave" in the sense of choosing where to live. It does not obviously fit well with the analysis of the ECtHR which took a broader view of not only that aspect, but also the extent of the restrictions (supervision and control) under which the person lived in that setting.

There is not space here to cover every case dealing with the definition of deprivation of liberty on the way to the landmark decision in *Cheshire West*, but it is worth just pausing nearby, in Manchester[159].

This case was about E, a 19 year-old man who had a genetic condition (tuberous sclerosis) which had caused him a severe learning disability. Since the age of 9 he had been cared for full time by F in her own home, initially as a foster carer and then as an adult placement, where he was an integral part of the family.

---

159 Manchester City Council v G & E [2010] EWHC 621 (Fam).

At around the age of 14, he started attending a residential home for respite care, and also attended a special school.

The local authority had concerns about the care F was providing; in her application to continue his care as an adult she did not fully disclose criminal convictions as she should (three for theft and one for handling stolen property, the most recent of which was 25 years earlier); they were not sure she was managing his behaviour at home appropriately (E was heard to say "don't lock me in the cupboard" and to say that he'd been made to sleep in the wardrobe – though in fact there was no wardrobe in E's room); there was an incident on holiday in which E hit F.

Just after their return from that holiday, on 7 April 2009[160] the local authority (anonymised in the case to start with, but later revealed to be Manchester City Council[161]) removed E to a residential placement ("V unit"), and then moved him to a placement at "Z Road" in June 2009. He signed a purported tenancy[162] there, alongside which a separate package of domiciliary care was provided. It was, therefore, a supported living placement rather than meeting the definition of a care home[163], under which care and accommodation were provided together[164], and as such it was outside the scope of DoLS.

Indeed, when the local authority was challenged about the deprivation of E's liberty by his sister starting Court of Protection proceedings, the local authority solicitor wrote "*as E is not in [CQC] registered care the deprivation of liberty safeguards do not apply and therefore no authorisation is needed*".

---

160 Barely one week after the DoLS legislation came into force on 1 April 2009.

161 See Chapter 15 for the local authority being named and shamed.

162 There was no doubt that he also lacked capacity to make a decision about a tenancy, so the validity of that document is, at best, open to question.

163 s3 Care Standards Act 2000.

164 Though in fact it was the same company that provided both the "tenancy" and the care package, making the supported living set up look rather artificial, and E's lawyers argued that it should have been registered as a care home.

There was no question that E lacked capacity to make decisions about his care and residence for himself, and in the court proceedings the local authority accepted that he had been deprived of his liberty both in the initial residential unit and in the (purported) supported living placement at Z Road.

In his judgment in March 2010, Mr Justice Baker held:

> *"Mr. Y, the manager of [Z Road], did not accept that his organisation was depriving E of his liberty. He thought he was improving his quality of life, and he may well be right. In my judgment, however, the current care provision for E undoubtedly deprives him of his liberty. Staff at Z Road exercise what the Official Solicitor describes as complete control over E's care and movements, and over assessments, treatment, contacts and residence. As Mr. Allen [counsel for F] points out, the concrete situation is that E is currently confined to Z Road except when he is escorted to school or on visits or activities, and has no space or possession that is private or safe from interference or examination. Miss Street, counsel for the Official Solicitor, observed that E is unable to maintain social contacts because of restrictions placed on access to other people, including family members, and a decision has been made by the local authority that he will not be released into the care of others, or permitted to live elsewhere, unless such a move is considered appropriate. In assessing whether he is at liberty, it is also important to note that E has been prescribed Haloperidol, a neuroleptic medication, to reduce his agitation and more challenging behaviour. He has no control over the administration of that medication."*[165]

Finding that someone is derived of their liberty is not, in itself, a criticism, if this is done in keeping with the MCA and due legal process is followed to meet Article 5 and Article 8 rights. But here, again, the local authority was roundly criticised for the way it went about it in this case:

---

165 Para 78.

"The removal of E from F's care was an arbitrary act. There was no attempt to follow the legal procedure of urgent and standard authorisations which had become law only a few days earlier. All parties now agree that in the absence of any authorisation under Schedule A1 of the MCA [ie DoLS], or any order of the Court under that Act, E was unlawfully deprived of his liberty when placed at the V Unit and Z Road.

In particular, the local authority now accepts that significant mistakes were made in this matter. It failed to recognise that E's placement in the V Unit amounted to a deprivation of liberty to which the DoLS applied. Furthermore, it failed to recognise that the placement at Z Road constitutes a deprivation of liberty and that it should have sought approval from the Court under s.16 before it occurred.

It must be noted, however, that the local authority took a very long time to acknowledge these grievous errors. The solicitors' correspondence reveals that the authority was maintaining that DoLS did not apply in this case up to and beyond the start of these proceedings. I suspect that it was only when they read the analysis set out in Mr. Read's report [the independent social work expert] that they realised their mistake.

In fairness, I should record that little if any blame attaches to Miss T [the social worker]. In evidence, she told me about the paucity of training she had received on the MCA. Although she has requested training from her employers on the DoLS procedures, (which, it will be recalled, are set out in a schedule running to 188 paragraphs plus a Code of Practice), she has yet to receive it. The responsibility for the blatant errors that occurred in this case clearly lies higher up the line of management.

I therefore hold that by removing E from F's care, placing him at the V Unit and then moving him to Z Road without complying with the procedures laid down in the MCA, either the DoLS procedure in

> *Schedule A1 or an application to the court under ss 16 and 48, the local authority infringed E's rights under Article 5 ECHR".*[166]

As to the right to family life (Article 8):

> *"...I find that the removal from F's care, the failure to give any or any adequate consideration to his family life with F at the time of the removal or for many months thereafter, the failure adequately to involve F in the decision-making process about E's future, and the impediments to contact between E and F for several months after his removal constituted a serious breach of his Article 8 rights".*[167]

The local authority argued that since the care arrangements for E would be broadly the same, as his care needs would be the same, wherever he lived, on this approach he would be deprived of his liberty by the same token in a care package at home with F. F's lawyer disputed this, and the Official Solicitor, representing E, argued that it was unnecessary and undesirable for the court to give a view.

Baker J agreed, while holding out the possibility that in some cases there might be a deprivation of liberty in a family home, since he did not need to decide the issue in this case[168], and because "*I have been told that a judgment is "hotly awaited" from a senior judge which it is anticipated will address this issue after full argument*".

Nonetheless, the Judge did <u>not</u> order that E should return to F immediately, deferring that decision until psychiatric expert evidence on his best interests was available. He was keen to avoid the possibility of having to move him twice, and this shows that the unlawful way in which a placement is brought about does not necessarily determine that it is in P's best interests to be moved.

---

[166] Para 81-82.

[167] Para 90.

[168] See Chapter 6.

Doing the right thing and going about it in the right way are not one and the same. Equally, the court deals in reality and must address the best interests of P now, including the potential negative impact of moving P again, even if the situation he or she is in was wrongfully brought about. This, of course, can bring only cold comfort from a declaration of breach of rights in some cases, where the wrong can no longer be corrected.

That aspect of his decision was challenged by G, E's sister, though the Court of Appeal refused permission to appeal.

By May 2010, the evidence was available to reach a decision that E should return home to F, which was confirmed in a judgment given in July 2010[169], dealing with further issues, primarily an application by the press to lift the anonymity of the local authority[170].

As it happens, the "hotly awaited" case Baker J alluded to where a senior judge was already considering deprivation of liberty in a family home setting was *MiG and MeG* – the start of the final stretch on the road to *Cheshire West*, which we will look at next.

Key Points

- Defining a deprivation of liberty is often a matter of opinion, people can reasonably disagree.
- Crucially, the trigger for safeguards should be that there is a risk of a deprivation of liberty, not certainty.
- We know that there are three elements:

---

169 [2010] EWHC 2042 (Fam).

170 See Chapter 15. The judge also considered an application by F and G to be appointed as deputies for health and welfare decisions for E, which was rejected in a judgment handed down in October 2010 [2010] EWCOP 2512. For completeness, there was also a further Court of Appeal case dealing with the local authority's challenge to the order of costs against it, unsuccessfully, and simply incurring more costs.

   - Objective – confinement[171];
   - Subjective – lack of consent[172]; and
   - Imputability to the state[173].

- The early case law focussed on cases of people removed from their own homes and being placed into institutions, but we lacked a definitive judicial interpretation of the confinement element in particular.

---

[171] See chapters 5-8.

[172] See chapter 9-10.

[173] See chapter 11.

CHAPTER FIVE

THE "ACID TEST": CHESHIRE WEST

Part 1 – To the Court of Appeal

Though "*Cheshire West*" is universally used as the name of the landmark judgment we are just getting to, in fact the Supreme Court was considering an appeal which joined two separate cases:

- *P v Cheshire West and Chester Council* – which concerned the arrangements made by that local authority for the care and residence of a 39 year-old man; and

- *MIG and MEG v Surrey County Council* – which concerned arrangements made by Surrey for care and residence of two young sisters[174].

Each of these two cases, involving three individuals, was heard separately in the first instance, and then each was heard separately in the Court of Appeal, and only then, on further appeal from the Court of Appeal, were the two cases rolled up together so that the Supreme Court could hear them both together, as they raised similar issues.

MIG and MEG

The hearing in MIG and MEG's case was in October 2009, though the judgment was not handed down until 15 April 2010, just after Baker J

[174] How the ultimate judgment came to be known only as "*Cheshire West*" is, presumably, a tribute to the skills of the media team at Surrey County Council in keeping their heads down.

decided the *Manchester City Council* case, and this was the "hotly awaited" case he alluded to.

MIG and MEG were sisters. They both had substantial and permanent moderate / severe learning disabilities, and both lacked capacity to make their own decisions about their care arrangements and residence.

MIG (aged 18 at the time of the judgment) was moved to a family home with a devoted foster mother, had her own bedroom; she never attempted to leave home, but would have been stopped if she did try to do so.

MEG (aged 17) was one of four residents at a specialist residential home, which was not registered as a care home. She had her own bedroom, she occasionally suffered from outbursts and sometimes required physical restraint. She showed no wish to leave. She was on medication to control her anxiety.

In their respective placements, both MIG and MEG were under continuous supervision and control, in their best interests.

The case dealt with issues of contact and care, but also considered whether MIG and MEG were deprived of their liberty because, if they were, it would have to be authorised by the Court of Protection since both their placements would be outside the scope of DoLS (which only applies over 18 and in registered care homes or hospitals).

Parker J concluded that neither MIG nor MEG were deprived of liberty in their placements for a number of reasons:[175]

- "*each lacks freedom and autonomy dictated by their own disability, rather than because it is imposed on them by their carers. Each is under the continuous supervision and control of her carers … so as to meet her care needs rather than to restrain her in any way…*"

---

[175] Paras 230-234.

- "*No other arrangements less restrictive or invasive could be devised that would meet their care needs*"
- "*In neither of these homes are they principally there for the purpose of being 'treated or managed'. They are there to receive care*"
- They "*have no subjective sense of confinement*".

There is a thorough and helpful review of the domestic and ECtHR authorities about deprivation occurs, including in hospital and care homes, as well as other contexts including control orders for terrorism. Reviewing the police "kettling" case of *Austin*[176], Parker J emphasises that the context is key; in that case the police were maintaining public order, rather than deliberately detaining the crowd involved. She accepts that the fact it is not the detainer's *intention* to deprive someone of his liberty does not mean that no deprivation occurs. And whether there is a deprivation is a separate question to whether that deprivation is in the person's best interests.

Even so, the judgment is still rather ambivalent about this, and did not, perhaps, do much to clear up any confusion among practitioners required to assess whether or not a deprivation is occurring. Parker J referred at different times to "*intention*", "*purpose*", "*motivation*" and "*reasons*". She concludes that benign intentions are not relevant to the issue of whether or not someone is objectively being deprived of liberty, but goes on in the same paragraph[177] to say that it is permissible in this case to look at the "reasons" for MIG and MEG are each living where they are.

At the time, taken together with the judgment in *Re A and C* (also 2010)[178], this seemed to continue a dangerous conflation between the question of the existence of objective deprivation and the separate issue

---

[176] See chapter 4.

[177] Para 230.

[178] Re A (Adult) and Re C (Child); A Local Authority v A [2010] EWHC 978 (Fam) – see Chapter 6, where A and C were held not to be deprived of liberty, despite being locked in their bedrooms for 10-12 hours overnight, largely due to the context being a loving and supportive family home.

of justification of any deprivation by reference to the person's best interests.

At that stage, it was thought that part of the reason for the relative under-use of the DoLS system[179], in places, was the negative connotations of the phrase "deprivation of liberty" itself, making staff reluctant to see their (benevolent) care in those terms.

The strong impression given in this judgment was that it would need a regime to impose restraint and restrictions on P that go *above and beyond what is needed for P's own care and best interests,* before it could be considered a deprivation of liberty. But that cannot be the case, at least as regards a care home or hospital; the purpose of the MCA and DoLS is to protect people who lack capacity from well-intentioned intervention without due scrutiny or process, as was exactly the situation in the seminal case of *Bournewood.*

It is easy to see why the courts could be reluctant to hold that a "deprivation of liberty" is occurring in a family home, as the term itself is so pejorative. But holding that there is no deprivation occurring, by reference to good intentions, purpose, context, proportionality or even the person's best interests, however described, would only feed the confusion that care homes and hospitals need not invoke the DoLS safeguards, and due process at all, if care is reasonable and well intentioned.

MIG and MEG in the Court of Appeal

MIG and MEG's case went to the Court of Appeal, heard on 21 October 2010, with a judgment handed down on 28 February 2011. For no obvious reason, , in the Court of Appeal MIG and MEG were referred to as "P" and "Q" respectively.

The Court of Appeal (Wilson, Smith and Mummery LJJ) agreed with Parker J that neither P (MIG) nor Q (MEG) were being deprived of their

[179] At the time – see Chapter 16.

liberty, but for different reasons. Lord Justice Wilson gave the leading judgment[180], holding[181]:

1. A person's happiness is not relevant to whether he is being deprived of his liberty.

2. However, it is relevant to consider if a person *objects* to the confinement, because this is likely to lead to conflict and confrontation.

3. Use of medication is relevant, especially it may suppress a person's ability to express his wishes, and all the more if forced on the person.

4. It was, however, inappropriate to take into account that the "*purpose*" of the care package was to further the person's best interests, and Wilson LJ would "*dissociate himself from the terminology of that passage*" in which Parker J had referred to the "*reasons*" for the living arrangements as relevant.

5. On the other hand, the "*relative normality*" of the arrangements was very important to Wilson LJ: "*If the person is living with her parents, or other members of their natural family in their home, they are living – in that respect – the most normal life possible. Typically – but sadly not always – there will be no deprivation of liberty in such circumstances*".

Note that this list is not exhaustive, but simply reviews the factors that had been taken into account by Parker J in her judgment.

---

180 In the Court of Appeal there are usually three judges, and in the Supreme Court there are usually five, with decisions reached by a majority, if not unanimous. The individual judges' decisions are shared between them in draft, and so sometimes some of the judges simply say they agree with one of the others, rather than write out a full, reasoned judgment themselves. If there is more than one detailed judgment in the case, the leading judgment is the one regarded as the most influential, which the (the majority of) other judges refer to and support.

181 Paras 24-28.

Q (MEG) was closer to the "border" of deprivation of liberty (because she was not in a family home, was medicated and subject to occasional physical restraint), but on balance neither P (MIG) nor Q (MEG) were deprived of their liberty. It was significant that they both had good outside social contact and went out for trips and for education, giving them something like a "normal" daily balance between education and home.

Mummery LJ was "very attracted" by the idea that the local authority's intervention was to "rescue" them from "an abusive and neglectful environment", and therefore enhanced their lives and could not be regarded as a deprivation of liberty, but he accepted that this was a dangerous approach as "*it risks confusing matters which affect whether a deprivation of liberty is lawful with whether it exists at all*".

Lady Justice Smith's judgment explicitly rejects any such relativist approach – she says that a deprivation of liberty can exist whether or not a person's situation is better now than it had been before. Wilson LJ raised the issue but did not give an opinion.

Overall, in the Court of Appeal the main development is the move from "purpose" and "reasons" (per Parker J, leaning on the "contextual" approach in *Austen*) to an emphasis on issue of the "relative normality" of the placement (per Wilson LJ). This could be seen as a step in the right direction, avoiding some of the problems persuading people that there can be a deprivation of liberty despite their good intentions, so that the DoLS or Court of Protection process should be invoked where appropriate.

However, the idea that a care regime in the family home which allows "the most normal life possible" will usually not be a deprivation of liberty, could be just as problematic. This case was in the context of a family home or small (unregistered) residential home – i.e. outside the hospitals and (registered) care homes where the Deprivation of Liberty Safeguards would apply. But why couldn't it be argued that a regime in a care home or hospital which allows P "the most normal life possible" should, therefore, also be deemed not a deprivation of liberty. And what would we mean by "normal" anyway? "Normal" for P herself? "Normal" for people with P's disability? Or "normal" arrangements for people in the particular care home / other environment in question?

Leave was given to appeal to the Supreme Court, and since the appeal was heard alongside the *P v Cheshire West* case, it makes sense to pause MIG and MEG's story here and to introduce the "*Cheshire West*" P.

P v Cheshire West

P was a 39 year-old man with learning disabilities and autism, who lacked capacity to make decisions about his accommodation and care. He was placed, by Cheshire West and Chester Council, at a specialist residential unit, Z House, to meet his care needs. He also had pica, a disorder involving eating non-food including, in his case, his continence pads and their contents. As a result, alongside the other care provided to P, carers intervened at times to remove material from his mouth using a "finger sweep" (described in the judgment as "having his arms held by one member of staff whilst a second inserts a gloved finger into his mouth to forcibly remove any retained material"). And, to prevent him getting to his continence pads at all, he was put into a "body suit", which was zipped at the back.

His case went to court for review because, if it amounted to a deprivation of his liberty, it could only be made lawful, to meet his Article 5 rights, by the court as – like MEG's – his placement was not a registered care home where the DoLS system could be used.

In June 2011[182], Mr Justice Baker held that P was deprived of his liberty in his placement at Z House.

He acknowledged the recent Court of Appeal judgment in *MIG and MEG*, and recognised that there were reassuring, "normal" features of P's care:

---

182 [2011] EWCOP 1330

> *"…the local authority and those who work at Z House have taken very great care to ensure that P's life is as normal as possible. There are a number of features that, by themselves, might suggest that this is not a case where he was being deprived of his liberty. The type of accommodation is characteristic of the type identified by Wilson LJ in P and Q v Surrey CC as being not designed for compulsory detention. P has regular contact with his family. He attends a day centre five days a week, and enjoys a good social life with other residents and staff and in the community. All these features help to give his life a strong degree of normality."*

But:

> *"On the other hand, his life is completely under the control of members of staff at Z House. He cannot go anywhere or do anything without their support and assistance. More specifically, his occasionally aggressive behaviour, and his worrying habit of touching and eating his continence pads, require a range of measures, including at times physical restraint, and, when necessary, the intrusive procedure of inserting fingers into his mouth whilst he is being restrained.*
>
> *In my judgment, the steps required to deal with his challenging behaviour lead to a clear conclusion that, looked at overall, P is being deprived of his liberty."*

Mr Justice Baker made it clear that this finding was in no way a criticism of the care provided or the local authority:

> *"In my judgment, it is almost inevitable that, even after he has been supplied with a bodysuit, P will on occasions gain access to his pads and seek to ingest pieces of padding and faeces in a manner that will call for urgent and firm intervention. Those actions will be in his best interests and therefore justifiable, but they will, as a matter of concrete fact and legal principle, involve a deprivation of his liberty. The reason for attaching that label to those actions is not to stigmatise either P or his hard-working and dedicated carers, but so that all involved with his care recognise the implications of what is happening."*

So the judge recognised that the care amounted to a deprivation of P's liberty, and authorised it as being in P's best interests.

Perhaps emboldened by the Court of Appeal judgment in *MIG and MEG*, Cheshire West and Chester Council appealed against Baker J's judgment, arguing that it was no deprivation of liberty at all.

Cheshire West in the Court of Appeal

The Court of Appeal heard the *Cheshire West* case on 22 September 2011, with judgment given on 9 November 2011[183]. In the leading judgment, Lord Justice Munby, (with whom Lords Justice Pill and Lloyd simply agreed) doubled down on the relative normality reasoning of Wilson LJ in *MIG and MEG.*

He accepted that subjective good intentions do not render innocuous a situation that would otherwise be a deprivation of liberty[184]. But he distinguished this from *the objective issue of the aim of the restrictions*, put in terms of the "purpose" or "reasons", which he says must be relevant to whether or not a situation is a deprivation of liberty[185].

Like Wilson LJ in *MIG and MEG*, he said the key is to assess the "relative normality" of P's life, taking into account the particular care needs arising simply from his physical or mental condition. It is not appropriate to compare P with a healthy adult, who would clearly be deprived of his liberty in these circumstances. "*Some adults are inherently restricted by their circumstances*", and the Court of Protection is dealing with adults "*with significant physical and learning disabilities whose lives are dictated by their own cognitive and other limitations*".

183 [2011] EWCA Civ 1257

184 Though he does think that acting in bad faith could turn a situation into a deprivation of liberty – para 71.

185 Paras 75-76.

The appropriate contrast to draw, he said, is with "*the kind of lives that people like [P] would normally expect to lead*".[186]

In this case, he said, Baker J had failed to see that the restrictions and limits on his life at Z House were nothing more than "*the inevitable corollary of his various disabilities*"[187], and "*there was nothing to show the life he is living at Z House is significantly different from the kind of life that anyone with his concatenation of difficulties could normally expect to lead….*"

In particular, Munby LJ normalises and minimises the restrictions in the placement, describing them in terms which downplay them and treats P as a child, simply being given the care that is good for him.[188]

The reality, he decided, was that P was "*living a life which is as normal as it can be for someone in his situation*", and therefore he was not being deprived of his liberty.[189]

This was hugely significant, and seemed to raise a number of issues:

Since the introduction of the Deprivation of Liberty Safeguards, massive effort had been spent on education that a "deprivation of liberty" is not necessarily a bad thing, or inappropriate, but simply requires scrutiny and lawful authorisation (through DoLS or the court). Anecdotally, one of the reasons given for apparent underuse of DoLS was that professional staff understandably find "deprivation" a pejorative term, and were reluctant to recognise it in the care they provided which is, usually, assessed in good-faith to meet the needs of P's physical and mental condition. Munby LJ's judgment, perhaps, reinforced that (mis)perception: appropriate care could be no deprivation of liberty.

---

186 Paras 86, 97 and 102.

187 Para 110.

188 See chapter 10.

189 Para 110, 116.

If it were right that restrictions imposed simply to meet the needs of P's condition are *by definition* not a deprivation of liberty, it became difficult to imagine a situation that would be a deprivation that could nevertheless be lawful (whether by DoLS authorisation or by Court of Protection order) as being in P's best interests, necessary and proportionate, and the least restrictive option. It would seem that all the conditions that are required to make any deprivation *lawful* would, in effect, mean in most cases that there was *no deprivation at all.*

If there is no realistic alternative to his current placement and circumstances, then it seems there could be no deprivation of liberty.[190] Taken together with the then recent high-profile case of *Neary*[191], it seemed most likely that a deprivation of liberty will occur where a family and a public body offer competing proposals for care, and in particular where the state tries to assert some control over what would otherwise be family life, protected by Article 8 as much as Article 5. But a finding of a deprivation of liberty (and the safeguards being triggered as a result) seemed rather less likely in the absence of such a dispute.

Many worried about discrimination against those vulnerable people, lacking capacity for the relevant decisions, who may not have family offering alternative proposals, who may therefore be deemed not deprived of liberty, and denied any scrutiny of their care, either through DoLS or the court. Recent scandals and reports about care of the most vulnerable in society MIGHT suggest that more safeguards were required, rather than less.

Equally, there were those who found the language of judging X's care according to the life expected by "people like X"[192] uncomfortable, and ill-fitting with personalisation, or respect for the individual.

DoLS had been introduced because the European Court of Human Rights found that HL was deprived of his liberty at Bournewood mental

[190] Para 58.

[191] See chapter 3.

[192] Para 102.

hospital where he was detained as an informal patient, for which the common law doctrine of "necessity" was insufficient justification or safeguard. Lord Justice Munby observed that this is a far cry from cases in which someone is in a family or foster home, or small residential unit. However, Bournewood hospital was simply doing what it judged was in HL's best interests, as required by his physical and mental condition. That his foster carers wanted to bring him home seemed to be the only feature that would establish there was a deprivation of liberty in his case, following the Court of Appeal judgment in *Cheshire West.*

In the absence of family, or others, pressing for an alternative, the Court of Appeal reasoning in *Cheshire West* seemed to risk going full circle – back to before DoLS – re-establishing deference to a professional assessment; any restrictions put in place in good faith according to the physical and mental health needs being deemed not to be a deprivation of liberty, without significant scrutiny; perhaps not so very far, in practice, from the old common law idea of "necessity" criticised by the ECtHR in *Bournewood.*

Put another way – if the Court of Appeal approach in Cheshire West was right, *was there any point in "safeguards" that would only ever be triggered if a care provider felt that their own care was inappropriate?*

I have given quite a lot of detail about the first instance and Court of Appeal judgments in *MIG and MEG* and in *P v Cheshire West,* especially the reasoning of the Court of Appeal judgment by Lord Justice Munby, because this was the approach against which the pendulum swung back in the Supreme Court. If you think that the Supreme Court *Cheshire West* judgment went too far the other way, it may be best understood in this context, as a reaction against the potential implications of LJ Munby's approach.

Part 2 – The Supreme Court

Both MIG and MEG's and P's case were heard together by the Supreme Court in October 2013, and the much-anticipated judgment was handed down on 19 March 2014.

This was a big deal for nerds like myself, as the first case in which the Supreme Court had looked at DoLS, and in particular the definition of a deprivation of liberty.[193] And it is still (so far) the main event in terms of the case law on this.

Seven judges sat in the Supreme Court, rather than the usual five, reflecting case's significance, but the full judgment is a relatively trim 40 pages, of which the leading judgment of Lady Hale is about the first half. I also recommend watching the 5 minutes or so in which Lady Hale explains the judgment herself when the Supreme Court handed it down, which is still available on YouTube[194].

Think back to the DoLS Code of Practice (2008): "there is no simple definition of a deprivation of liberty". In Lady Hale's judgment, the "acid test" for a deprivation of liberty[195] is simply that that the person is:

> "***under continuous supervision and control and not free to leave***"[196].

Lady Hale comes to this formulation after a careful review of the case law of the European Court of Human Rights, and you'll recognise it as the

---

[193] And indeed only the second Supreme Court case considering the MCA at all, after *Aintree v James* on issues arising from the end of life care for David James [2013] UKSC 67.

[194] https://www.youtube.com/watch?v=Nq1G9C7hKWk&list=UUdkf93h71xVAl28v467Hk7w

[195] This is, of course, as regards the objective element – ie what it means to be confined – which must be in addition to the other essential elements that the person does not (or cannot) consent to it and it is, in some way, imputable to the state.

[196] Para 49.

same phrase used by the ECtHR in *Bournewood* and, in very similar terms, in a number of other cases.

To this extent, then, the definitive test settled on by Lady Hale, and accepted unanimously by the Supreme Court, didn't really pull up any trees. So why was it such a big deal?

For starters, it was a Supreme Court judgment, the highest domestic court in the country, and the first time the issues had been considered at that level.

But the most significant thing was the way in which Lady Hale explicitly rejected the reasoning of the Court of Appeal (in both cases, but especially the *P v Cheshire West* judgment) and made clear that a number of factors ought to be irrelevant which were, in fact, being widely relied on in practice at the time to say that there was no deprivation of liberty.

Arguably, then, the most significant thing about the Supreme Court judgment is not the positive definition that Lady Hale gives, which had been seen before, but the clear stripping away as irrelevant of other things which had been used to muddy the waters, especially:

- "Relative normality" – that the care arrangements are appropriate, or just reflect P's care needs.
- The good intentions or benign purpose behind the placement
- Compliance – that P is not trying to leave, so is acquiescent in some sense.

None of these matter when it comes to whether or not there is a deprivation of liberty that demands scrutiny (though of course they may be highly relevant to whether the arrangements are found to be lawful).

"Relative normality" is irrelevant[197]

The idea that identifying a deprivation of liberty depends on the nature and needs of the person on whom the restrictions are imposed was the core of the "relative normality" approach in the Court of Appeal (especially in *Cheshire West* but also, to some extent, in *MIG and MEG v Surrey*).

For many, the concern about this was that if living in circumstances that reflect P's care needs (the kind of life that "people like P" can expect, as a result of their disabilities) in itself indicated that there would be no deprivation of liberty, then only inappropriate care could be a deprivation, and therefore trigger the safeguards process as scrutiny. But which providers of care would readily identify a potential deprivation of liberty on that basis? And how could any such deprivation be justifiable or lawful, if care which is appropriate is no deprivation of liberty at all? It was also profoundly discriminatory, and Lady Hale was having none of it, as the opening paragraph of her judgment makes clear:

> *"This case is about the criteria for judging whether the living arrangements made for a mentally incapacitated person amount to a deprivation of liberty. If they do, then the deprivation has to be authorised, either by a court or by the procedures known as the deprivation of liberty safeguards, set out in the Mental Capacity Act 2005. If they do not, no independent check is made on whether those arrangements are in the best interests of the mentally incapacitated person, although of course the health or social care bodies who make the arrangements do so in the hope and belief that they are the best which can practicably be devised. It is no criticism of them if the safeguards are required. It is merely a recognition that human rights are for everyone, including the most disabled members of our community, and that those rights include the same right to liberty as has everyone else" (emphasis added).*

[197] For adults at least – see Chapter 10 for children.

And

> *"In my view, it is axiomatic that people with disabilities, both mental and physical, have the same human rights as the rest of the human race. It may be that those rights have sometimes to be limited or restricted because of their disabilities, but the starting point should be the same as that for everyone else. This flows inexorably from the universal character of human rights, founded on the inherent dignity of all human beings, and is confirmed in the United Nations Convention on the Rights of Persons with Disabilities. Far from disability entitling the state to deny such people human rights: rather it places upon the state (and upon others) the duty to make reasonable accommodation to cater for the special needs of those with disabilities.*
>
> *Those rights include the right to physical liberty, which is guaranteed by article 5 of the European Convention. This is not a right to do or to go where one pleases. It is a more focussed right, not to be deprived of that physical liberty. But, as it seems to me, what it means to be deprived of liberty must be the same for everyone, whether or not they have physical or mental disabilities. If it would be a deprivation of my liberty to be obliged to live in a particular place, subject to constant monitoring and control, only allowed out with close supervision, and unable to move away without permission even if such an opportunity became available, then it must also be a deprivation of the liberty of a disabled person. The fact that my living arrangements are comfortable, and indeed make my life as enjoyable as it could possibly be, should make no difference. A gilded cage is still a cage"*[198]*. (emphasis added).*

As she put it when handing down the judgment:

> *"The Supreme Court holds that people with mental disabilities have the same right to liberty as everyone else".*

[198] Para 44-45.

Benign purpose is irrelevant

Lady Hale said:

> *"People who lack the capacity to make (or implement) their own decisions about where to live may justifiably be deprived of their liberty in their own best interests. They may well be a good deal happier and better looked after if they are. But that does not mean that they have not been deprived of their liberty. We should not confuse the question of the quality of the arrangements which have been made with the question of whether these arrangements constitute a deprivation of liberty.*
>
> *.... We should not let the comparative benevolence of the living arrangements with which we are concerned blind us to their essential character if indeed that constitutes a deprivation of liberty."*[199]

And:

> *"In none of the more recent cases was the purpose of the confinement – which may well have been for the benefit of the person confined – considered relevant to whether or not there had been a deprivation of liberty. If the fact that the placement was designed to serve the best interests of the person concerned meant that there could be no deprivation of liberty, then the deprivation of liberty safeguards contained in the Mental Capacity Act would scarcely, if ever, be necessary. As Munby J himself put it in JE v DE [2007] 2 FLR 1150, para 46:*
>
>> *"I have great difficulty in seeing how the question of whether a particular measure amounts to a deprivation of liberty can depend upon whether it is intended to serve or actually serves the interests of the person concerned. For surely this is to confuse . . .*

[199] Paras 34-35.

two quite separate and distinct questions: Has there been a deprivation of liberty? And, if so, can it be justified?".[200]

In this, oddly perhaps, Lady Hale allows "Munby.2007" (in the High Court in *JE*) to show where "Munby.2011" went wrong (in the Court of Appeal in *Cheshire West*). As she puts it herself:

> *"It is very easy to focus upon the positive features of these placements for all three of the appellants. The local authorities who are responsible for them have no doubt done the best they could to make their lives as happy and fulfilled, as well as safe, as they possibly could be. But the purpose of Article 5 is to ensure that people are not deprived of their liberty without proper safeguards, safeguards which will secure that the legal justifications for the constraints which they are under are made out: in these cases, the law requires that they do indeed lack the capacity to decide for themselves where they should live and that the arrangements made for them are in their best interests. It is to set the cart before the horse to decide that because they do indeed lack capacity and the best possible arrangements have been made, they are not in need of those safeguards."*[201]

Compliance is irrelevant

This was dealt with simply, quoting from *HL v UK* (Bournewood):

> *"...the right to liberty is too important in a democratic society for a person to lose the benefit of Convention protection for the single reason that he may have given himself up to be taken into detention, especially when it is not disputed that that person is legally incapable of consenting to, or disagreeing with, the proposed action"*[202].

[200] Para 42.

[201] Para 56.

[202] para 90 of *HL*, quoted at para 7 of *Cheshire West*. The same point is made at para 119 of *Stanev v Bulgaria*, quoted at para 24, and elsewhere.

You need not be rattling bars and kicking doors to signify a deprivation of liberty.

> *"An unconscious or sleeping person may not know that he has been locked in a cell, but he has still been deprived of his liberty. A mentally disordered person who has been kept in a cupboard under the stairs (a not uncommon occurrence in days gone by) may not appreciate that there is any alternative way to live, but he has still been deprived of his liberty. We do not have any difficulty in recognising these situations as a deprivation of liberty."*[203]

Taken together, the effect was to end the line of argument that providing appropriate care, of good quality and with pure motives, won't thereby deprive the person of their liberty. The negativity and stigma of the phrase "deprivation of liberty" has no doubt played a part in this misapprehension, and it was given credibility by the Court of Appeal's approach in *Cheshire West* in particular. But after the Supreme Court judgment we have had to look a bit harder at the reality of the circumstances, and the impact on P, rather than take false reassurance from the quality of the care or the purity of the carer's motives.

And Lady Hale made clear that this was, explicitly, a matter of "policy", as she wrote under that heading:

> *"Because of the extreme vulnerability of people like P, MIG and MEG, I believe that <u>we should err on the side of caution in deciding what constitutes a deprivation of liberty</u> in their case. They need a periodic independent check on whether the arrangements made for them are in their best interests. Such checks need not be as elaborate as those currently provided for in the Court of Protection or in the Deprivation of Liberty Safeguards (which could in due course be simplified and extended to placements outside hospitals and care homes*[204]*). Nor should we regard the need for such checks as in any way stigmatising of*

---

[203] Para 35.

[204] Ha!

> *them or of their carers. Rather, they are a recognition of their equal dignity and status as human beings like the rest of us".*[205]

Interpreting the acid test

It is worth pausing here to reflect that it is important not to try to find reasons to characterise a situation as not a deprivation of liberty; *doing so does not lessen the restrictions P experiences in reality, but does lessen (or remove entirely) the safeguards that bring scrutiny to those restrictions and protect fundamental rights.*

For instance, the word "*control*" is a tempting focus. Following the Supreme Court judgment, I was often told by well-intentioned providers of care that they don't consider that the care arrangements "*control*" the individual, but rather "*support*" them. I often heard that the care plan *enables* and *empowers* the individual to make their own choices as much as possible (as it should). I was given examples of people who were allowed significant autonomy in their care and daily life, for instance when to get up, or what to have for breakfast, whether to come into a communal area or to stay in their room, or what to wear. Cases were put to me on the basis that if any decision in P's daily life could be identified which they were allowed to make for themselves, then this showed that there must be less than *continuous control* (I'll come back to "continuous"), and so there must be no deprivation of liberty.

But see how hard it is to describe that attitude without using words like "*allowing*" those choices, as if they are ours to allow.

Lack of capacity to make decisions about care and residence overall, to enable best interests decision making about a care plan that may amount to a deprivation of liberty, does not mean that P lacks capacity to make *every* decision for themselves. Of course they should be "*allowed*" to make decisions that they have capacity to make!

[205] Para 56.

Even setting that aside and assuming that we are only talking about decisions for which P does lack capacity, "control" is the *power* to interfere, determine, and prescribe, even if it is not constantly exercised. It is nonsense to say that P is not under continuous control because some (often small) aspect of the lives is left to their own autonomy, if the reality is that such autonomy would only be tolerated within certain limits. Being "*allowed*" to make some choices, but only if we approve of them, is no freedom from control. Ask yourself what would happen if someone "*allowed*" to make such a decision made a decision we didn't like?

Control that could be reasserted at any time that autonomy is exercised in a way we don't like is control that is constantly there.

An argument that care which is well-intentioned and person-centred is *enabling* not *controlling* is no better than an argument that good intentions or appropriate care can mean that there is no deprivation of liberty at all[206]. It only amounts to a device to avoid conceptualising care in a way which we MIGht be uncomfortable with, and which we feel is stigmatising. But this only has the effect of denying safeguards to those in our care, and the reasoning has been firmly rejected by the Supreme Court in this case.

I have recently come across the idea of the "*Burrito test*". This asks a simple question: "*would Bob be allowed to get up at 3am and microwave himself a burrito?*". It is intended to help to identify an institutional setting, as the lines blur between institutions and home, but I also think it could work quite well as a proxy for the extent to which Bob is under "continuous control".

We also need care with "*supervision*", especially in combination with "*continuous*". Looking at the case law, it cannot be the case that someone must be under 24 hours 1:1 care before they are considered to be deprived of their liberty. None of P, MIG or MEG would have met that test.

---

[206] See, for a recent example, *Re AEL* [2021] EWCOP 9, discussed in Chapter 6 about deprivation of liberty in the family home.

In fact, though "continuous" supervision and control is the conventional formulation of the acid test, in the *Cheshire West* judgment itself Lady Hale (including quoting other cases) uses the words "constant" and "complete" as often, and they need some caution.

Would we accept that someone might be deprived of their liberty if, among other things, they were watched by CCTV 24/7 – ie continuously, or constantly under supervision – but that it would cease to be a deprivation of their liberty if the cameras were turned off for an hour a day? A minute? A second?!

"Continuous", or "constant" cannot be interpreted too literally, to set too high a bar, and to deny people effective safeguards.

To avoid this trap, it might be better to think in terms of "*complete*" supervision and control, especially in the sense of having the opportunity and power to intervene, even if that power is not being *exercised* all the time.

Equally, taking the acid test at face value, and simplistically, on the "*free to leave*" limb, there were those who argued that care cannot amount to a deprivation of liberty unless someone is behind a locked door. It should be stating the obvious to say that this is not necessary[207], per the acid test.

MIG and MEG both went out regularly to an educational unit, as well as having other trips and holidays. P in the *Cheshire West* case "*went to a day centre four days a week and a hydrotherapy pool on the fifth. He also went out to a club, the pub and the shops, and saw his mother regularly at the house, the day centre and at her home*"[208]. During the year that Steven Neary was deprived of his liberty (unlawfully) by Hillingdon LBC, he largely continued his routine activities including swimming and the gym, at least for a time.

---

[207] See Munby J, as he was then, in JE v DE, se chapter 4.

[208] Para 17.

Remember that in *Stanev v Bulgaria*[209], Mr Stanev was held by ECtHR to have been deprived of liberty for the purposes of Article 5 though he walked down, unaccompanied, into nearest the village, 8 km from the institution into which he was placed, on a regular basis to work as a waiter, and as a handyman. This was with the *permission* of the director of the institute, and *steps would be taken if he didn't come back when expected and required.*

So "free to leave" is not about coming or going to a day centre, shopping or swimming. It is "*leaving in the sense of removing oneself permanently in order to live where and with whom he chooses*".[210]

Ask yourself, could they just pack their bags and go to live somewhere else? If the reality is that they would not be allowed to do so whenever they wanted to, then any suggestion that they are truly "free to leave" might be little more than a fairy tale, as Lord Steyn put it in the House of Lords in *Bournewood.*[211] (And if they are not "free to leave" in that sense, how is that being prevented if not by continuous supervision and control?).

We also need care with the tempting argument that "*she is not trying to leave*", which just falls back into the trap that compliance strips someone of their rights. HL was not actively trying to leave Bournewood hospital (and would have been detained under MHA if he had tried) but was clearly deprived of his liberty there. You should not need to rattling the doors trying to get out before consideration is given to whether you might be deprived of your liberty.

A close cousin to that mistake is: "he cannot leave anyway as a result of their condition or health / care needs". I've seen it argued that someone who cannot walk (by themselves or at all) therefore cannot be "not free

---

209 [2012] ECHR 46 (Application no. 36760/06). See Chapter 4.

210 Per Munby J, as he then was, in JE v DE, see chapter 4.

211 Thinking about it, I wonder if that – would describing P as "free to leave" feel like little more than "a fairy tale" – might also be considered a reasonably good proxy for the "acid test".

to leave", since their disability is stopping them, rather than any restriction being imposed. Again, if it needs saying, it is not OK to strip these important rights from people due to a disability.

A better way to consider the question is this – if a friend or family member tried to move them to live somewhere else, would we let them? If the answer to that is "no", or at least "not without a full best interests decision making process", then they may be seen as not free to leave, regardless of any inability to dance out the door by themselves.

You need both limbs

You do, though, need both elements of Lady Hale's acid test – it needs continuous (or constant or, perhaps better, "complete") supervision and control and being not free to leave.

Lady Hale's own judgment said:

> "[i]*t is possible to imagine certain situations in which a person is not free to leave but is not under such continuous supervision and control as to lead to the conclusion that he was deprived of his liberty.*"

I don't think that would offer me much comfort if I were locked in a cell and the guards wandered off. In reality, this has been rarely tested in the courts, and any argument that there is no deprivation of liberty, even though P is clearly not free to leave, or they are clearly under continuous supervision and control, but not both, might best only be constructed with the benefit of very careful legal advice.

A Local Authority v AB[212] involved a 36 year-old lady who was clearly "not free to leave" in that she had to reside at a particular property under the terms of a Guardianship order under MHA 1983 s7. As the judge, Sir Mark Hedley, described:

212 [2020] EWCOP 39.

> *"AB lives in a flat in supported accommodation where there is always support available at any time of the day and night. She is broadly at liberty to do as she pleases within her own flat. She is free to leave the accommodation but her leaving and returning will always be seen by a member of the supervisory staff simply because of the geography of the property. She is required to reside at that property and thus if she fails to return the police would ordinarily be notified. There is extensive support available to her but it is support for her to take up or not as she pleases. She has a long record of being unable to look after her own accommodation and accordingly staff will enter her flat for the purposes of inspecting, cleaning or repairing. Indeed they will often wait for her to leave in order to do that so as to cause the least possible distress to her. It follows that they have access to her property whenever they think fit."*

It was common ground that she lacked capacity to consent to these arrangements, and they were clearly imputable to the state. The only question for the court was whether they amounted to the objective element of the definition of a deprivation of liberty.

The Official Solicitor contended that they did, given the requirement to return to the property and the supervision she was under. The local authority emphasised the voluntary nature of the support and the freedom to come and go as she pleased (albeit not to go to live anywhere else), and the unsupervised time in the community when she was out.

The judge did recognise that for a deprivation of liberty there had to be both no freedom to leave (to live somewhere else) and continuous supervision and control. And that the "*continuous*" should apply to both the "*supervision*" and the "*control*". But even so, the court should be constrained by the "*policy of caution set out by the Supreme Court*":

> *"In the end, and only after very careful consideration, I have come to the conclusion that these arrangements do indeed amount to a deprivation of liberty. It seems to me that the question of supervision and control must be viewed in the context of the prescribed condition of residence. Thus whilst she may be free to leave the property as she chooses, she is always subject to state control requiring her return should*

she be otherwise unwilling to do so. The fact that she generally willingly returns does not of itself negate this point. Again whilst the supervision of her coming and going is not intrusive, it is the fact that all her movements are known and noted. Moreover, while she is free to do as she pleases in the community, there will inevitably be some obligation to restrain or control those movements should they become seriously detrimental to her welfare. That control could lawfully be implemented without recourse to the Court.

When considering a deprivation of liberty it is not sufficient just to see what actually happens in practice but to consider what the true powers of control actually are. Again the power to enter someone's private residence is a major intrusion on liberty however much, as it is here, it is to the benefit of the protected person for it to happen.

When looking at all these matters it is essential to consider them in the round and to ask whether in all the circumstances that actually prevail, or might reasonably come about, the arrangements amount to a deprivation of liberty. In my view they do here. In reaching that conclusion I have drawn upon the policy set out by Baroness Hale and that has, I should acknowledge, been a critical factor in my conclusion. However much these arrangements may be to the benefit of AB, and undoubtedly they are, one has to reflect on how they would be observed by an ordinary member of the public who, I strongly suspect, would regard them as a real deprivation of liberty. The policy that everyone should be treated the same leads me to the conclusion that I have set out." (emphasis added).

Applying the acid test to P in *Cheshire West*

Applying the acid test to P in the *Cheshire West* case was the easy bit; the Supreme Court was unanimous that P was deprived of his liberty. Mr Justice Peter Jackson had been right, and the Court of Appeal had got it wrong.

Lady Hale quoted Jackson J's judgment that *"[P's] life is completely under the control of members of staff at Z House. He cannot go anywhere or do anything without their assistance and support...*" and said that his conclusion that "*looked at overall, P is being deprived of his liberty*" should be restored.

On this, all seven Supreme Court judges agreed. No one criticised the care, but it was a deprivation of liberty that needed scrutiny and authorisation.

Applying the acid test to MIG and MEG

It was not so straightforward in the case of MIG and MEG; in relation to the sisters, the seven judges in the Supreme Court split 4:3, with the narrow majority (led by Lady Hale) finding that they were deprived of their liberty, applying her acid test.

Lady Hale recognised that it was a more controversial decision in their case than for P in *Cheshire West*. In the Court of Appeal, she noted, Lord Justice Wilson had found MEG's case very difficult, only reaching the conclusion that she was not deprived of her liberty after "protracted thought". He came to his view based on "*the small size of the adolescent home, her lack of objection to life there, her attendance at the educational unit, her good family contact, and her fairly active social life*".

However, as Lady Hale says, P in *Cheshire West* also enjoyed all those features. While MEG did not need the same sort of restraint P had as a result of his incontinence pads and pica, "*she did sometimes require physical restraint, and she received medication to relieve her anxiety*".

> "*Above all, the staff did exercise control over every aspect of her life. She would not be allowed out without supervision, or to see people whom they did not wish her to see or to do things they did not wish her to do*".[213]

MIG's case, perhaps, was harder still because, as well as going out to education and enjoying good family contact, "*she was living in an*

[213] Para 52.

ordinary family home".[214] Both Parker J and Wilson LJ had said that if these arrangements were a deprivation of liberty for which the state were responsible, then so would the placement HL enjoyed with his foster carers in *Bournewood* (apparently to benchmark that HL's care package and living arrangements with the Enderby family before that admission to hospital must – by definition – be *not* a deprivation of liberty).

Lady Hale deals with this only by saying that "*no-one has suggested this*" and that the court (in *Bournewood*) had not been called upon to confront that issue:

> *"The reality is that MIG's situation is otherwise the same as her sister's, in that her foster mother and others responsible for her care exercised complete control over every aspect of her life. She too would not be allowed out without supervision, or to see anyone whom they did not wish her to see, or to do things which they did not wish her to do."*
>
> *"If the acid test is whether a person is under the complete supervision and control of those caring for her and is not free to leave the place where she lives, then the truth is that both MIG and MEG are being deprived of their liberty. Furthermore, that deprivation is the responsibility of the state. Similar constraints would not necessarily amount to a deprivation of liberty for the purpose of article 5 if imposed by parents in the exercise of their ordinary parental responsibilities and outside the legal framework governing state intervention in the lives of children or people who lack the capacity to make their own decisions."*[215]

We will have to come back to the proper approach to children, as the case law on this has moved on a bit over subsequent years. For these purposes, the focus seems to be on whether being in a (foster) family home took MEG out of the scope of Article 5, and Lady Hale decided that it does not.

---

[214] For the impact of this reasoning, see Chapter 6.

[215] Para 53-54. For the family home see chapter 6; for children see chapter 10.

She raised a number of possible objections to MIG and MEG being regarded as deprived of their liberty, only to dismiss them in turn:

- Neither could survive without this level of control? True, but this just resurrects the comparison with others with their disabilities and thereby denies them the same right to liberty as everyone else.

- They are content with the placements and show no desire to leave? True, and Lady Hale described this as the most difficult aspect of the case, for her. *But compliance does not surrender your rights to proper scrutiny of restrictions.*

- They could express a "desire to leave", such that the local authority would start to look for another placement, if they were not happy where they were? True, but such a move would only be permitted after a formal best interests decision-making process, and *"In the end, none of these suggested distinctions is satisfactory. Nor, in my view, should they be"*

Joining the majority of the Supreme Court, finding MIG and MEG were both deprived of their liberty, Lord Sumption simply agreed with Lady Hale's judgment, while Lord Neuburger agreed with her in a separate judgment. Taking a key objection to MIG and MEG being regarded as deprived of their liberty, he said:

> *"it is a fair point that the Strasbourg Court has never had to consider a case in which a person was confined to what may be described as an ordinary home. However, I cannot see any good reason why the fact that a person is confined to a domestic home, as opposed to a hospital or other institution, should prevent her from contending that she has been deprived of her liberty".*[216]

He agrees with the minority, dissenting judges that

[216] Para 71.

> *"many people might react with surprise at simply being told that a person living in a domestic setting could complain of deprivation of liberty, but that is a point of little weight, particularly as such people may well retract the surprise when the consequences either way of Article 5 are explained".*[217]

To labour the point: the consequences of saying that some arrangement for care and residence of a vulnerable adult does not amount to a deprivation of liberty does not lessen the restrictions that person may endure; it lessens the scrutiny they are given and the safeguards that person enjoys to ensure that their rights are respected. He could add that a legal term of art, such as "deprivation of liberty", might well bear a meaning that's unexpected to the public.

Lord Neuberger goes on that in the case of "children living at home" (presumably, then, not adults?) restrictions that are imposed by parents in the ordinary exercise of parental responsibility are unlikely to transgress Article 5, along the same lines as Lady Hale.[218]

Lord Kerr is the final judge in the majority, agreeing with Lady Hale that MIG and MEG were deprived of their liberty, and also gives a separate judgment. He rules out benevolence as a factor in establishing a deprivation of liberty or not, and concludes:

> *"If deprivation of liberty is to be judged principally as an objective condition, then MIG, MEG and P are unquestionably subject to such deprivation, no matter how their situation MIGht be regarded by those "using ordinary language"".*[219]

[217] Para 71.

[218] Para 72, and see chapter 10 for more on children.

[219] Para 87.

The MIG and MEG Minority

The three Supreme Court judges who held that MIG and MEG were not deprived of their liberty (the "minority" judges, since they were outvoted on this) gave a variety of reasons. But it is probably fair to say that it boiled down to discomfort about finding a deprivation of liberty in a family home in particular, and the baggage of using that language in that context.

Lords Carnwath and Hodge gave a joint judgment, followed by a separate judgment from Lord Clarke, each politely disagreeing with Lady Hale about MIG and MEG.[220]

Lords Carnwath and Hodge recognised the value of safeguards for those who are identified as deprived of their liberty, but felt that there are legitimate concerns about bringing that bureaucracy into "*the sort of benevolent living arrangements which many might find difficult to characterise as a deprivation of liberty*" (in Lady Hale's own words). They were concerned that this judgment would go further than any European Court of Human Rights judgment to date, in finding a deprivation of liberty where:

- the person is not objecting[221],
- where the setting is not institutional, but as close as possible to normal family life, and
- where the court had initially authorised it as being in their best interests, and it is no more restrictive than is necessary to meet their needs.

The latter point has a familiar circularity: appropriate care is what you expect anyway; authorising it surely makes it a deprivation of liberty that

[220] Though, as I've said, they all agree on the "acid test" and how it applies to P in *Cheshire West*. Their only disagreement with Lady Hale and the majority was on how it applies to MIG and (especially) MEG.

[221] I'll come back to this in more detail in chapter 9.

is lawful, rather than no deprivation at all. And the idea that MIG or MEG's compliance negates any deprivation of liberty is also problematic for the reasons set out above.

But the central point is not so easily dismissed: Article 5 does seem to be most naturally concerned with institutional settings, and has been applied in that context. While the good intentions of the state in placing someone in an institution shouldn't mean the person gets no safeguards for their rights, the benevolence of the family home is something else entirely, and the heavy hand of "scrutiny and due process" sits much less easily there. This is precisely why gut instinct struggles against using the words "deprivation of liberty" to describe someone in a family home environment.

This, I think, is really why Lords Carnwath and Hodge recoil at the idea, and say that in the absence of clear authority from Strasbourg that Article 5 can and should stretch so far, "*we should be cautious about extending a concept as sensitive as deprivation of liberty beyond the meaning which it would be regarded as having in ordinary usage*":[222]

> "*We are concerned that nobody using ordinary language would describe people living happily in a domestic setting as being deprived of their liberty*". [223]

This may be more a question of terminology, or education: understanding that the exclusion from a definition of deprivation of liberty reduces the safeguards, not the restrictions. And it reflects the familiar instinct to downplay arrangements regarded as benevolent.

Commenting on the point that it had not been suggested that HL in *Bournewood* would still be deprived of his liberty on going back to the care of his foster family, they say this surely:

> "*...was because it had not occurred to anyone (including the court) that such a placement in an ordinary home environment would*

[222] Para 93.

[223] Para 99.

> *constitute a deprivation of liberty for the purpose of Article 5, even though the degree of control for practical purposes would be the same as before."*[224]

Lord Clarke was the final judge in the Supreme Court, you'll be pleased to know. Like all the others, he agreed that P in *Cheshire West* was deprived of his liberty, but he joined the minority in concluding that MIG and MEG were not. Like Lords Carnwath and Hodge, he said that:

> *"nobody using ordinary language would describe people living happily in a domestic setting as being deprived of their liberty".*

But whether or not that was true, the majority of the Supreme Court had made it clear that MIG and MEG were, in law, deprived of their liberty.

Crucially, though, just as with P in *Cheshire West*, no judge was critical of the care arrangements for MIG or MEG, even those who found that they amounted to a deprivation of liberty. It was appropriate, proportionate and in their best interests, and was authorised by the court.

<u>Key Points</u>

- The right to liberty is the same for everyone, regardless of disability;
- Neither the care providers' good intentions, nor P's compliance or contentment, are relevant to whether there is a deprivation of liberty; they are relevant to whether any deprivation of liberty is lawful, which is a separate question;
- The "acid test" for objective deprivation of liberty is that someone is "under continuous [or constant or complete] supervision and control and not free to leave";

---

224 Para 100.

- Do not set the bar too high – we should err on the side of caution to include people in the definition to ensure that their care is scrutinised; excluding people does not lessen the restrictions but lessens the safeguards;

- Do not deny what is really "control" by mischaracterising it as "support"; "continuous supervision" does not need to be 1:1 or 24/7; the focus should be on the impact on P, and the power of carers to intervene, even if not being used constantly.

- "Not free to leave" means P being unable to pack their bags and go to live where they want to; do not deny this by reference to an inability to exercise such freedom unaided, or lack of attempts to leave. Ask the hypothetical question, what would we do if they wanted to live somewhere else?

- It is clear that there can be a deprivation of liberty in any setting, including in the family home as well as in institutions, though the minority in the Supreme Court were reluctant to see a deprivation of liberty in a family home.

- How to apply the *Cheshire West* acid test in various settings would be tested in subsequent case law.

The immediate impact of *Cheshire West* was remarkable. It created roughly a tenfold increase in the number of DoLS referrals more or less overnight, as I'll describe in more detail in Chapter 16, prompting massive strain on the system and adding to existing pressure for reform.

Before getting to that though, it makes sense to look at:

- the way that the *Cheshire West* judgment has been interpreted in particular settings, in particular at the extremes of the family home (chapter 6) and in life-saving emergency medical treatment in hospital (chapter 7);

- some other factors relevant to the objective definition of deprivation of liberty (chapter 8);
- the other bits of the definition of deprivation of liberty that were not in issue in *Cheshire West*[225]: the subjective, lack of valid consent (chapter 9) and how that applies to children in particular (chapter 10); and the deprivation of liberty being imputable to the state (chapter 11).

[225] It was agreed that MIG and MEG lacked capacity to consent to the arrangements and they were imputable to the state, leaving *Cheshire West* only dealing with the confinement, the objective element of the definition of deprivation of liberty.

CHAPTER SIX

CHESHIRE WEST AT HOME

Let's be honest. When we think about "deprivation of liberty", we think of institutions – prisons, certainly, and hospitals, perhaps, where people are placed and cannot leave. Maybe a reluctant care home resident? But few people will readily conjure up an image of Steven Neary, living in his own home, making mix tapes with his devoted dad.

On a principled basis, people may have concerns about the state intruding, with administrative or judicial procedures, presuming to review and "authorise" what is happening in someone's own home. It might feel like the very opposite of the freedoms and liberties we think ought to be protected.

On a practical basis, of course, pending any reform[226], since DoLS only applies to care homes and hospitals, each deprivation of liberty identified outside those settings (for instance in supported living, or in their own home) could only be made lawful by an application to court. And however streamlined that process is made[227], it can feel like a waste of time and money, which families might feel ought to be better spent on the substance of the care package in question.

In both *Neary*[228] and *Manchester City Council v G and E*[229], Mr Justice Jackson and Mr Justice Baker respectively both implied that it would have been unlikely that it would have been considered a deprivation of

[226] See chapter 18 on the LPS.

[227] See chapter 14.

[228] See chapter 3.

[229] See chapter 4.

liberty if the person had been in their own home, even if under exactly the same restrictions.

In the *Manchester City Council* case:

> *"Common sense suggests that when considering deprivation of liberty there is a clear distinction between a placement at home, with family or an adult carer, and in a residential establishment. One can of course think of circumstances – those of the first Mrs. Rochester in "Jane Eyre", for example*[230] *– where someone might be deprived of their liberty although living at home. But in most cases the circumstances are more likely to fall into the category of a restriction, rather than a deprivation, of liberty".*[231]

Another case from around the same time addressed the extent to which the state should reach into someone's own home, to protect vulnerable adults and children who may be deprived of their liberty. There were two separate linked cases heard together, by Munby J (later Lord Justice Munby) in July 2009[232].

A was an 8-year-old girl, and C was a 20-year-old young woman. They were not related. They were both at particular risk at night, due to a genetic condition (Smith Magenis syndrome) associated with learning disability, disturbed sleep patterns and serious self-harming behaviour. They each lived at home with their family, and to keep A and C (and others) safe, each family had, as a last resort, taken to locking their daughter in her bedroom overnight. No one said that there was any real alternative.

The court had to consider whether this was a deprivation of liberty, to engage Article 5, despite being only an act of private individuals rather

---

[230] I don't want to spoil it for anyone, but if you don't know, Mrs Rochester is locked away in a secret attic room when she goes mad.

[231] Para 117.

[232] *Re A (adult) and Re C (a child); A local authority v A* [2010] EWHC 978, though it took nearly a year to hand down the judgment.

than the state, and what role the state, through the local authority, has in such cases.

Years before *Cheshire West* reached the Supreme Court, Munby J relied on the familiar three-part definition of a deprivation of liberty to engage Article 5:

1. Objective confinement: Whether A or C were being confined in a particular space for a not negligible period of time, sufficient to amount to an objective deprivation of liberty;

2. Subjective lack of consent: Whether A or C had not validly consented to this (it was agreed that neither A nor C had capacity to validly consent to the bedroom door being locked overnight); and

3. Imputability to the state[233].

On the question of an objective element, perhaps surprisingly, Munby J holds that neither A nor C was deprived of her liberty, despite being locked in a room for 10-12 hours at a stretch. *Context* was everything, in his mind (though there are those who consider that the judgment was just wrong!).

The judge quoted at length from the recent judgment of Parker J in *MiG & MeG*[234]. He also referred to the recent, then, House of Lords judgment in *Austin*[235], in which a person was kept "kettled" in a confined area with the May Day protestors in 2001 for up to seven hours, but the Lords held that she was not deprived of her liberty, at least partly because the police

[233] See chapter 11.

[234] [2010] EWHC 785 (Fam) see chapter 5.

[235] [2009] UKHL 5, the House of Lords judgment before it later went to the European Court of Human Rights. See chapter 4 for the ECtHR judgment, and chapter 7 for the judgment's use in (dis)applying *Cheshire West* to the medical treatment context.

had acted reasonably and proportionately to manage public order, and deprivation of liberty was not their intention.

Munby J accepted "that the question of intention in the sense of mental attitude is irrelevant to the question of whether someone is deprived of their liberty". Nonetheless, as Parker J did, Munby J talked about A and C not being deprived of liberty due to the "*context*" of the confinement – ie being in the family home.

Is it appropriate to have different standards as to what is a deprivation of liberty according to whether it occurs in someone's own home, or a more institutional setting? It seems likely that being locked in a room in a care home or hospital for 12 hours a day would be a deprivation of liberty for the purposes of Article 5.

This really does touch a nerve about the extent to which the state should reach into someone's own home; the tension between Article 5 and Article 8 (the right to private and family life).[236]

In *MiG and MeG*, Parker J had held that "*in my view it is possible for a person to be deprived of their liberty in a domestic setting*", referring to a passage from the Code of Practice[237]:

> "*it will only be lawful to deprive someone of their liberty elsewhere (for example in supported living arrangements in their own home, or in a day centre) when following an order of the Court of Protection*".

But in MiG and MeG's case, Mrs Justice Parker did not think that they were deprived of their liberty. Nor did Lord Justice Mummery, Lord Justice Wilson, or Lady Justice Smith, three judges of the Court of Appeal. And nor did Lords Carnwath, Hodge and Clarke, Justices of the

---

[236] We see it in other contexts, of course, for example in whether the parents of a child should have the last word about their proposed medical treatment, or if it is appropriate for this to fall to a judge determining their best interests – see the Charlie Gard and Alfie Evans cases, and the recent Nuffield Council on Bioethics paper. https://www.nuffieldbioethics.org/topics/beginning-of-life/disagreements-in-the-care-of-critically-ill-children

[237] Paragraph 1.20.

Supreme Court. As I have said, of the eleven judges who heard that case it was only four (albeit, timing their run well, enough for a 4:3 majority in the Supreme Court, where it really counted) who thought that they were deprived of their liberty, so as to trigger the safeguards to protect their Article 5 rights.

So it should be no surprise that after that Supreme Court judgment, there were plenty of people who felt that it had gone too far in bringing the spectre of deprivation of liberty and its due process into the privacy of someone's own home, and no surprise that some judges would be among them.

***

In February 2015, Mr Justice Bodey dealt with the case of "Mrs L", a 93 year-old lady with a diagnosis of severe dementia who was still living alone in her own home, as she had since she was widowed nearly 40 years earlier. Her daughters agreed between them various arrangements to help keep Mrs L safe, which were stepped up after an incident in 2013 when she "*became disorientated and wandered away from her home very unsuitably clothed into the local town*" and was returned by the police. After that, the family enclosed Mrs L's garden with a fence, and with gates to the street which Mrs L could not easily open, though she would still have access from the house to the garden itself. Sensors on her door at night would alert the family if she were to leave the property by herself.

The local authority applied to court for authorisation of her arrangements as a deprivation of her liberty, and Mr Justice Bodey noted that "*the fact that Cheshire West was heard by seven supreme court justices and that the decision was by a majority of 4:3 demonstrates the difficulty of the topic*".

He held that she was not in fact deprived of her liberty at all[238]. He described her as being exactly where she wanted to be, contented, "*at*

[238] Accepting arguments made by one of Mrs L's daughters, acting as her litigation friend; I suspect that if it had been the Official Solicitor acting as litigation friend, his

home" and not in "*a placement*", and said that being in her own home must be a relevant consideration. She had three visits a day from carers, but these were the minimum necessary to meet her needs, and she had "*ample time to spend as she wishes*". Though "*finely balanced*", he came to the view that she was not deprived of her liberty (ie on the objective aspect).

He protested that:

> *"This is not per se because Mrs L is in her own home; nor because she wishes to be there. Those features alone would not necessarily stop particular arrangements amounting to a deprivation of liberty. Rather it is a finely balanced decision taken on all the facts of the particular case".*

But very clearly, he would have seen identical restrictions in an institutional setting in a very different light.

He also bolstered his position by saying that if he was wrong about the objective aspect, then he would find that it was anyway not imputable to the state:

> *"This is a shared arrangement set up by agreement with a caring and pro-active family: and the responsibility of the State is, it seems to me, diluted by the strong role which the family has played and continues to play."*

We will look a bit more at imputability in chapter 11[239]. On the application of the *Cheshire West* test, I am not entirely sure that this judgment stands up to scrutiny, and seems to put weight on the very factors that the majority of the supreme court had rejected.

---

position would have been that there was a deprivation of liberty, though it is not clear whether that would have changed the outcome.

[239] Including more recent case law showing the Bodey J was, with respect, quite wrong on that point.

The Rochdale Saga

A more explicit one-man crusade against *Cheshire West* was fought, but ultimately unsuccessfully, by another High Court Judge, Mr Justice Mostyn, which played out in the saga of *KW v Rochdale MBC*[240].

Perhaps because I have two young daughters myself, I find KW's situation desperately poignant. Known in the judgment as "Katherine", she was 52 at the time of the proceedings, but had been disabled by brain damage she suffered while undergoing surgery around 18 years earlier. At that time she had three small children, and the effect of the brain damage was to stop her sense of the passage of time. Though her now adult children had left home, each day she felt that she has lost her small children, and so anxiously searched for them, wandering the streets with her walking frame looking for them, if allowed to do so.

She now lived with 24/7 support (paid for roughly 2/3 by the local authority and 1/3 by the NHS) largely to stop her wandering, as well as helping her with other physical health needs.

Just 8 months after the Supreme Court judgment in *Cheshire West*, her case was brought to court on the basis that her care package clearly amounted to a deprivation of her liberty, in light of that judgment, and therefore just needed review by the court, as she was in her own home and outside the scope of DoLS. That was uncontentious, with the same view being taken by Katherine's lawyers and by the lawyers for the local authority. Both counsel just asked the court to authorise the undoubted deprivation of liberty as being in her best interests.

But they did not reckon with the judge, Mr Justice Mostyn:

> *"Notwithstanding their excellent arguments, and with great respect, I do not agree. I find it impossible to conceive that the best interests arrangement for Katherine, <u>in her own home</u>, provided by an independent contractor, but devised and paid for by Rochdale [Borough Council] and CCG, amounts to a deprivation of liberty*

[240] [2014] EWCOP 45

> *within Article 5. If her family had money and had devised and paid for the very same arrangement this could not be a situation of deprivation of liberty*[241]*. But because they are devised and paid for by organs of the state they are said so to be, and the whole panoply of authorisation and review required by Article 5 (and its explications) is brought into play. In my opinion this is arbitrary, arguably irrational, and a league away from the intentions of the framers of the Convention.*
>
> *It has been said that a consequence of the Supreme Court decision is that there will be tens, if not hundreds, of thousands of similar cases requiring Court of Protection authorisation and periodic reviews. This is not surprising as the facts of this case are unremarkable."*[242] *(emphasis in the original)*

Mostyn J clearly had one eye on the resource implications, opening the judgment with:

> *"If it does amount to a deprivation of liberty then my order will have to provide for periodic reviews by this court. Such reviews plainly have significant resource implications for this hard pressed local authority. Every pound spent on such reviews is a pound less for other vitally necessary projects."*[243]

But his objections were certainly principled as well as pragmatic. He put Article 5 in its context, the ECHR being drafted in the shadow of the gulags after the Second World War, and being concerned with protecting individuals from the state, and with Article 5 (the detention of people of unsound mind, or alcoholics, drug addicts, vagrants, or people with infectious diseases) as obviously contemplating an institutional setting.

---

[241] This raises an issue about imputability to the state, see chapter 10 and, with great respect, I am not sure it is correct in light of other case law.

[242] Para 7-8.

[243] Para 1.

As the minority in the Supreme Court had, he noted that no ECtHR judgment had ever identified a deprivation of liberty in a domestic home.

Philosophically, he asked what "liberty" for Katherine means, and referred to John Stuart Mill's account of liberty as essentially freedom from interference, unless to protect others, saying:

> *"...this doctrine is meant to apply only to human beings in the maturity of their faculties ... Those who are still in a state to require being taken care of by others, must be protected against their own actions as well as against external injury."*

For Mill, he says, the idea that Katherine's care package in her own home infringed her liberty would be "*utterly impossible*".

This approach has deep roots. In a prosecution in 1855, a judge directed a jury that a "lunatic" who had been kept in a darkened room for many years, emaciated, dirty and doubly incontinent, no longer able to walk due to broken shinbones, had not been falsely imprisoned because "the lunatic is a prisoner by nature"[244].

A guide to the Mental Deficiency Act 1913 wrote:

> *"The mentally defective almost more than any other class of afflicted persons need care and protection rather than liberty".*[245]

Like those forebears, Mr Justice Mostyn's approach could not be more different from Lady Hale's emphasis on the universality of human rights, regardless of disability; he has obvious echoes of the Court of Appeal judgment in *Cheshire West*, seeing any restrictions on Katherine as caused by her disability and not by her care package.

---

[244] The Huxtable Prosecution, see "*Inconvenient People: Lunacy, Liberty and the Mad Doctors in Victorian England*" by Sarah Wise, 2013, p193.

[245] Wormald and Wormald, "*A Guide to the Mental Deficiency Act 1913*", 1914.

He quotes with approval Lord Kerr, from the *Cheshire West* dissenting minority, but then accepts (the judicial hierarchy being what it is[246]) that

> *"The opinions of the majority are binding on me and I must loyally follow them even if I personally agree with the view of Parker J and the Court of Appeal in MIG and MEG; with the Court of Appeal in Cheshire West; and with the minority in the Supreme Court".*

But then he finds a way to "distinguish" Katherine's case – ie to identify a difference between the cases significant enough to say that the precedent of the higher court is not binding on him in this case.

Looking at the Supreme Court's "acid test" (under continuous supervision and control and not free to leave) and applying it to the "so-called constraints" on Katherine, he decided that in fact she was <u>not</u> "not free to leave" (if you'll forgive the double negative). He found, as a mater of fact, that:

> *"Katherine's ambulatory functions are very poor and are deteriorating. Soon she may not have the motor skills to walk even with her frame. If she becomes house-bound or bed-ridden it must follow that her deprivation of liberty just dissolves. It is often said that one stress-tests a proposition with some more extreme facts. Imagine a man in hospital in a coma. Imagine that such a man has no relations demanding to take him away. Literally, he is not "free to leave". Literally, he is under continuous supervision. Is he in a situation of deprivation of liberty? Surely not[247]. So if Katherine cannot realistically leave in the sense described above then it must follow that the second part of the acid test is not satisfied.*

[246] This is the system of precedent, in which a lower court must follow the relevant judgments of higher courts (the Supreme Court being the highest domestic court).

[247] See my comments on conflating freedom to leave with physical ability to leave in chapter 5. We will come back to this in chapter 7.

By contrast MIG was a young woman with full motor functions, notwithstanding her problems with her sight and hearing. She had the physical capacity to leave in the sense described.

In my judgment there is a very great difference between the underlying facts of MIG's case and of this case notwithstanding that in both cases the protected person lives at home.

It is my primary factual finding that in Katherine's case the second part of the acid test is not satisfied. She is not in any realistic way being constrained from exercising the freedom to leave, in the required sense, for the essential reason that she does not have the physical or mental ability to exercise that freedom".[248]

He goes on to protest (too much?) that he would not rule out the possibility of a deprivation of liberty in someone's own home in all circumstances, referring for example to house arrest / bail conditions in the criminal law context. But:

"... I am of the view that for the plenitude of cases such as this, where a person, often elderly, who is both physically and mentally disabled to a severe extent, is being looked after in her own home, and where the arrangements happen to be made, and paid for, by a local authority, rather than by the person's own family and paid for from her own funds, or from funds provided by members of her family, Article 5 is simply not engaged".[249]

Bearing in mind that a High Court judge sits two judicial layers below the Supreme Court, it takes some chops to continue:

"I am of the view that the matter should be reconsidered by the Supreme Court."[250]

248 Para 22-25.

249 Para 26.

250 Para 27.

And the case concluded with some confusion over whether or not he could grant leave to appeal directly to the Supreme Court without having to go to the Court of Appeal first. He couldn't, it turned out, and so it was to the Court of Appeal that the case went.

Before that appeal, Mostyn J gave a judgment in another case, *Tower Hamlets v TB*[251], in December 2014, which was mainly concerned with TB's capacity to make decisions about sex and contact, but which was nonetheless taken as an opportunity to add a few paragraphs to "*amplify my reasoning*" as his judgment in KW had come in for "*a certain amount of criticism*".

He argued that it would really be discrimination to treat a disabled person as just the same as an able-bodied person, since their circumstances are very different. The disability gives rise to an obligation to intervene to support a disabled person and help to meet their needs:

> *"But to characterise those measures as state detention is to my mind unreal. I referred to the historical context in which Article 5 of the ECHR 1950 came to be formulated. It followed the Universal Declaration of Human Rights of 10 December 1948 which in its preamble referred to "the disregard and contempt for human rights [which] have resulted in barbarous acts which have outraged the conscience of mankind"; which in article 3 guaranteed liberty; and which in article 9 proscribed "arbitrary arrest, detention or exile." It was aimed at the midnight knock on the door; the sudden disappearance; the prolonged detention. Article 5 was not aimed at Katherine, seriously physically and mentally disabled, who is living in her own home and cared for round the clock by carers paid for by an organ of the state.*
>
> *In this case TB will not be cared for at a place which she understands to be her home. Further, she has the motor functions to achieve a departure in a meaningful sense. She will be monitored round the clock and were she to leave to try to go "home" she would be brought back.*

[251] [2014] EWCOP 53

> *Her situation is therefore very different to Katherine's, and the acid test is met. Although I personally cannot see that her situation amounts to state detention in any sense other than by reference to the term of art devised by the majority in the Supreme Court, I must loyally*[252] *follow that decision. I therefore declare that TB's care regime does involve detention under Article 5. Accordingly there must be at least six-monthly reviews*[253] *by this Court, no doubt at some considerable expense to the public purse.*
>
> *At paragraph 1 of my decision in Rochdale Metropolitan Borough Council v KW I referred to the very serious resource implications to local authorities and the state generally if periodical court reviews are required in such cases. Notwithstanding the arrival of the streamlined procedure recently promulgated by the Court of Protection Practice Direction 10AA*[254] *there will still be tens if not hundreds of thousands of such cases and hundreds of thousands if not millions of documents to be processed. The streamlined procedure itself requires the deployment of much man and womanpower in order to identify, monitor and process the cases. Plainly all this will cost huge sums, sums which I would respectfully suggest are better spent on the front line rather than on lawyers".*

Given these views on the public purse, you might have thought that he would have seen the advantages when the two day Court of Appeal hearing of Katherine's case, due to be heard in early February 2015, was vacated[255]. The local authority and Katherine's lawyers agreed that Mostyn J's judgment had been wrong, and that an Order should be substituted instead that Katherine was clearly deprived of liberty in her

---

252 ?!

253 Actually, the court would typically review any court ordered deprivation of liberty in the same way as DoLS, which is limited to a 12 month authorisation.

254 This is the *Re X* streamlined process for applications to the Court of Protection for cases of deprivation of liberty in the community outside the scope of DoLS, which I will explain in chapter 15 among the other impacts of the *Cheshire West* Supreme Court judgment.

255 Ie the hearing was cancelled.

care package and that this was authorised, and would therefore need ongoing review.

Instead, Mostyn J ordered that the case should come back before him for a further hearing, which took place on 2 March 2015[256].

Mr Justice Mostyn was clearly annoyed by the approach taken by the parties and the Court of Appeal, which he described as "*procedurally impermissible*", going into some detail about the powers of the Court of Appeal to overturn a decision in this way. He came to an interpretation of the Court of Appeal's order (which, I think it is fair to say, was not shared by the parties) that the Court of Appeal had not in fact decided that Katherine was deprived of her liberty, but had just directed a further hearing at which he, Mostyn J, could decide if she was. And she wasn't, he said, unless

> "*the restrictive changes proposed amount to bodily restraint comparable to that which obtained in P v Cheshire West and Chester Council. Any restrictions short of that will amount to no more than arrangements for her care in her own home and would not, consistently with my previous judgments, amount to state detention. Therefore, in such circumstances there would be nothing to review [as a deprivation of liberty].*
>
> *It will be apparent from what I have written above that in the absence of a reasoned judgment from the Court of Appeal explaining why I was wrong I maintain firmly the correctness of my jurisprudential analysis in my principal decision as augmented in my Tower Hamlets decision. In this difficult and sensitive area, where people are being looked after in their own homes at the state's expense, the law is now in a state of serious confusion*".

Essentially, then, he demanded that the Court of Appeal should spell out exactly why he was wrong. So they did.

---

[256] [2015] EWCOP 13.

The Court of Appeal[257] explained that it had, clearly, agreed that KW <u>was</u> deprived of her liberty, and it was wrong to interpret their order in any other way. And that Mostyn J was wrong to say that the Court of Appeal approach to this was beyond its powers. They said that, with respect, the law on deprivation of liberty had clearly, and recently, been resolved in the Supreme Court, and concluded:

> *"This litigation has an unfortunate history. The judge has twice made decisions which have been the subject of an appeal to this court. On both occasions, the parties have agreed that the appeal must be allowed. This has led to considerable unnecessary costs to the public purse and unnecessary use of court time. We regret to say that it is the judge's tenacious adherence to his jurisprudential analysis leading to his conclusion that Cheshire West was wrongly decided that has been at the root of this. He says at para 26 of the second judgment that "the law is now in a state of serious confusion". Even if Cheshire West is wrong, there is nothing confusing about it.*
>
> *In our view, the judge's passionate view that the legal analysis of the majority in Cheshire West is wrong is in danger of distorting his approach to these cases. In the light of the unfortunate history, we are of the opinion that the review should be conducted by a different judge…".*

Ouch.

But Mr Justice Mostyn remained "tenacious", and he was not about to back down from his trenchant view that *Cheshire West* should not be applied in the person's own home, despite being relieved of his duties to review Katherine's ongoing case.

In *CD*[258], a couple of weeks later, dealing with the superficially unrelated question of whether a lady with paranoid schizophrenia should have a hysterectomy, Mostyn J took the opportunity to say:

---

[257] [2015] EWCA Civ 1054, on 15 October 2015.

[258] [2015] EWCOP 74

> *"... the Court of Appeal stated "even if Cheshire West is wrong, there is nothing confusing about it". It may seem that way from the lofty heights of the Court of Appeal; and of course the literal words of the Supreme Court's test are perfectly easy to understand. But for we hoplites*[259] *who have to administer it at first instance the scope and ramifications of the test are, with respect, extremely confusing. As Mr Matthewson, instructed by the Official Solicitor for CD, rightly stated "anyone who deals with this day by day knows this is confusing". What of the situation where, as here, the protected person actively and fervently expresses the wish to undergo the procedure that is said to amount to a deprivation of liberty? What of the situation, as was the case in Bournemouth Borough Council v PS & Anor [2015] EWCOP 39, where the protected person shows no inclination whatsoever to leave the home where he is cared for round the clock? What of the situation where the protected person is seriously disabled, perhaps bedridden, perhaps in a coma, and is thus physically incapable of exercising the freedom to leave? The answers I received from the Bar when discussing these scenarios belie the blithe suggestion that "there is nothing confusing" about the test. I do not accept the criticism that my approach to these cases is "distorted" by my "passionate" and "tenacious" belief that Cheshire West is wrong. Rather, it is a loyal*[260] *approach which tries to apply literally and purposively the Supreme Court's test while at the same time pointing out how confusing and curious it is, to say nothing of the cost it causes to the public purse".*

I have told this story in some detail partly because many people will instinctively sympathise with Mostyn J (and the Supreme Court minority in *Cheshire West*) that a person's own home <u>is</u> different, and should be treated differently, from an institutional setting[261]. And also, honestly, because of the compelling rarity of such a soap opera of a very senior

[259] Hoplites were the ancient Greek foot soldiers, fighting on the front line. I'll admit I had to look this up.

[260] ?!

[261] See chapter 19.

judge and the Court of Appeal being so openly disdainful, even if framed in terms that require a "classical education" to understand.

Most of all, it shows how far we have come in applying the *Cheshire West* Supreme Court Judgment to the private home, despite Mostyn J's "loyal" attempts to scupper it. However tenacious, his uprising got nowhere, and we are left with the Court of Appeal judgment that *Cheshire West* is clear, and applies in our own homes, whether Mr Justice Mostyn liked it or not[262].

Case law since *Rochdale*

Perhaps with more sympathy for Mostyn J than the Court of Appeal had, in 2017 NHS Dorset Clinical Commissioning Group issued proceedings in the Court of Protection seeking declarations that four people they were supporting through Continuing Healthcare packages were not being deprived of their liberty, despite meeting the *Cheshire West* acid test, on the basis that they were in their own homes. They were intended to be test cases, it said, as the law was not clear and the outcome would affect more than 100 other patients for whom this one CCG would have to apply to court for authorisation if they were deprived of their liberty.

In the event, we never got a judgment on that. The CCG withdrew the proceedings because it rethought its position once it saw a response drafted by the Official Solicitor; difficulties with funding the lawyers for the individual patients meant that the value as a test case would be limited; and (ironically) the Law Commission had just published its report on proposed reforms, both weakening the argument that there was no deprivation in someone's own home, and reducing the need for the test case about it, if we were soon to get a more efficient process to authorise them.

---

[262] To be fair to Mr Justice Mostyn, remember that he was the judge who decided that Steven Neary should go home, when he heard the case just before Christmas 2010 – see chapter 3.

We only know about this because the Official Solicitor would not let the CCG drop the cases without an argument over the legal costs that had already been incurred in preparing to fight the point, which is the reported judgment[263].

A more recent case shows how well established it is now that *Cheshire West* reaches into the family home (while also showing well the reasons it can be tough to swallow).

Re AEL[264] was the first judgment handed down in 2021. It involved a 31 year-old woman who lived at home with her parents. There was no suggestion at all that this should change. But if the care package amounted to a deprivation of her liberty, then it needed the appropriate periodic, independent review to meet her Article 5 rights, which had to be done by the court as she was outside the scope of DoLS, being not in a care home or hospital.

There had been an argument for years about whether or not she was deprived of liberty. The local authority considered that she plainly was. AEL had

> *"a rare chromosomal condition leading to a number of physical and mental disabilities. She has severe learning disability, significant visual impairment and profound deafness. She suffers from asthma, eczema and severe allergies. She is non-verbal and can only walk short distances. She does not have a regular sleep pattern. At times, she may behave in a way which causes herself injury".*

As a result, funded by the local authority by direct payments to her family, she needs

> *"24-hour care and supervision, with 2:1 support for some activities in the community. In addition to her parents, two private carers have*

263 NHS Dorset CCG v LB and others [2018] EWCOP 7, in which Baker J decided the CCG should not have to pay the Official Solicitor's claim for £15,000 wasted costs, as the application, and the decision to withdraw it, had both been reasonable.

264 [2021] EWCOP 9.

> *been consistently involved in AEL's care for some time, but she does not require sedation or restraint, and no assistive technology is used in her care arrangements. If the current level of care was not provided, AEL would be a danger to herself and others because she has no concept of road safety, is unable to alert others to her needs, and unable to manage her own nourishment or hygiene".*

Her father was her primary carer and clearly, rightly, took great pride in the quality of care provided for her which was the principal reason why she was one of the oldest living patients with her rare condition in the world. He did not accept that she was deprived of her liberty and made the familiar points that the care she received was no more restrictive than necessary to meet her needs; that his approach was to "support" (not "control") and be responsive to her wishes, such that "*AEL decides what she wants to do and when she wants to do it excepting if her safety could be compromised*"; and to describe this, in her own home, cared for by her family, as a deprivation of liberty was "*palpably nonsense*", only leading to an unnecessary process that was "*a complete waste of everyone's time including the court's and a complete waste of public money.*"

There are obvious echoes of the (ultimately unsuccessful) arguments in the Court of Appeal and the minority Supreme Court judges in *Cheshire West*, and I suspect that Mr Justice Mostyn, for one, would have had some sympathy with the father.

But Her Honour Judge Hilder was very clear:

> *"The law is now settled, and the facts of AEL's care arrangements are not in dispute. Viewed objectively, the key aspects of AEL's experience are that:*
>
> *a. she requires, and is given, 24-hour care and supervision – she is never "left to her own devices" but is accompanied by carers at all times; and*
>
> *b. although she is regularly given the opportunity to make choices, and carers generally strive to facilitate realisation of her choices, there is an acknowledged limit to AEL's ability to do what she wants – ultimately,*

all the activities she undertakes are risk assessed by AEL's parents and/or carers and "the principle" of such assessment is that they may decide not to allow her to do anything which they consider could compromise her safety.

In my judgment, these two aspects of AEL's living arrangements clearly amount to "continuous supervision and control." Even if carers are available and willing to take AEL to McDonald's at whatever hour she wishes, she is not "free to leave" their care. The reality of her disabilities is that AEL's safety is permanently at risk unless she has support. Therefore, she has 24-hour support and she is thereby under continuous control in the sense that her freedom may be interfered with at any moment. The intention may be benevolent; the arrangements may indeed ensure that she has a much happier, healthier and longer life than she would otherwise have; but "a gilded cage is still a cage." The 'acid test' of deprivation of liberty is made out".

She went on:

"Looking at AEL's circumstances "in the round", I have regard to the "underlying principle" of Cheshire West – what it means to be deprived of liberty must be the same for everyone. Although I have not asked him, rhetorically I invite [the father] to consider how he would categorise AEL's living arrangements … if they were applied to him. I strongly suspect that he, and ordinary members of the public, would consider such arrangements to deprive them of their liberty.

Finally, like Sir Mark Hedley in A Local Authority v. AB[265]*, I have regard to the "policy" of Cheshire West. However benevolent AEL's carers, however much all relevant parties consider that the current arrangements for her care are in her best interests, AEL's disabilities make her vulnerable. If there is any room for doubt as to whether or not AEL's living arrangements are a deprivation of her liberty (which in my judgment there is not), as Baroness Hale identified, we should err on the side of caution. AEL should have the benefit of a periodic,*

265 [2020] EWCOP 39. See chapter 5.

> *independent check that arrangements continue to be in her best interests. Such requirement is not to stigmatise her or her loving family, but quite the opposite – to ensure recognition of her equal dignity and status as a human being."*

The judge concluded:

> *"All in all, I am in no doubt that AEL's current care arrangements amount to a deprivation of her liberty. I do not regard that as in any way a criticism of [her father] or her other carers."*

That last point is important, and it is easy to sympathise with the parent or carer in the family home who rails against being told that the care they are providing is "depriving" their loved one "of their liberty". Or who feels that the costs of the process of review and authorisation of the deprivation of liberty might better be spent on the substance of the care package itself.

But there you go – as the Court of Appeal in *Rochdale* had it, the law is now clear and simple, whether you like it or not.

The fact that many tens of thousands of cases outside the scope of DoLS (ie not in care homes and hospitals) might now be identified as a deprivation of liberty that required authorisations was one of the most significant consequences of *Cheshire West*, and led to the development of a dedicated process for deprivation of liberty in the community cases (see chapter 14).

Whether that is the way the law *should be*, we will come back to.

<u>**Key Points**</u>

- The law is clear that there can be a deprivation of liberty in a person's own home, applying the *Cheshire West* test;
- But this has been controversial, and resisted by many, including some judges;

- It is likely to remain a fault line in any reforms – do we want our own homes to be treated in the same way as a care home or hospital? And if not, why? And is it always easy to define what we mean by a "home" with the lines between this and an institutional setting increasingly blurred[266]?

Before we get to that though, we need to explain one of the ironies of *Cheshire West*: while the battle against it being applied universally, as one size fits all, raged loudest in the private home, the only place where a bite has successfully been taken out of it to date was at the very opposite end of the spectrum: in a hospital intensive care unit.

[266] See chapter 19.

CHAPTER SEVEN

CHESHIRE WEST IN HOSPITAL

After all the (unsuccessful, so far) effort to establish the family home as an exception to the *Cheshire West* acid test, there is an irony that the only setting in which the tide has turned against it could not be further away: intensive care in hospital.

At the time of the *Cheshire West* judgment, very little case law had tackled deprivation of liberty in the context of hospital inpatient treatment, and especially in terms of physical rather than mental health.

The Supreme Court judgment did not appear to limit itself to any particular context, dealing as it did in very strong, broad principles, such as the universality of human rights; though the three individuals were in long term residential / domiciliary placements, the acid test was expressed in a way that appeared to be quite generic.

But it is fair to say that custom and practice was <u>not</u> to refer large numbers of hospital inpatients to DoLS or to the Court of Protection, and in the necessary prioritisation of any referrals made by acute hospital trusts have tended to be towards the bottom of the triage process[267].

It would be bad enough if everyone in ICU needed a DoLS authorisation, but it may be worse. A "*Dear Colleagues*" letter from the Department of Health after *Cheshire West* said:

> *"The Department has stated that it does not consider a state of unconsciousness in itself as being a mental disorder for the purposes of*

[267] Anecdotally, I repeatedly hear that around 90-95% of hospital inpatient cases referred to DoLS are not processed before the patient dies / is discharged / recovers capacity.

> *DoLS. The implications are that an individual who is unconscious under anaesthetic but does not have a mental disorder is not eligible for DoLS"*[268].

This implies that anyone sedated into unconsciousness would need any deprivation of their liberty to be reviewed by a court, if DoLs cannot be used, though I am not aware that this has been tested in any case.

There is also an issue over any deprivation of liberty that takes place in the Emergency Department at hospital since DoLS cannot be used to authorise this – P needs to be a detained resident, which is only the case once a patient had been admitted to hospital[269].

Understandably, this adds to the importance of identifying any deprivation of liberty appropriately.

Re FG

The first case after *Cheshire West* to confirm its application in the acute hospital setting was *FG*, heard by Mr Justice Keehan in late May 2014[270]. FG was a 24 year-old woman, in the very late stages of pregnancy, with an expected delivery date around a week after the hearing. She was known to have schizoaffective disorder, and had been detained under the Mental Health Act. Her persecutory delusions led her to believe that mental health services would murder her and her unborn child. The treating clinicians applied to court for an order allowing a plan for her obstetric care that would include very significant coercion and restraint, if need be, to secure the safe delivery of her child in the event that she was non-compliant with care and treatment in labour.

---

268 https://www.mentalcapacitylawandpolicy.org.uk/wp-content/uploads/2015/10/DH-Letter-to-MCA-DoLS-Leads-Oct-2015-FINAL.pdf – para 23.

269 See chapter 14.

270 [2014] EWHC 2262 (Fam) and [2014] EWCOP 30.

Keehan J was clear that the starting point is the presumption of capacity for pregnant women, like any other patient, to make their own decisions and that this remained the case for those who are diagnosed with a mental health problem. However, in this case he was satisfied that FG lacked capacity to make the relevant decisions, and that the proposed interventions in her best interests were such that they should be considered by the court.

As to whether the proposals would amount to a deprivation of FG's liberty, he explicitly applied the *Cheshire West* acid test:

> "*It will commonly be the case that when at the acute hospital P:*
>
> *i) will have obstetric and midwifery staff constantly present throughout her labour and delivery;*
>
> ii) *will be under the continuous control of obstetric and midwifery staff who, because she lacks capacity to make decisions about her medical case, will take decisions on her behalf in her best interests;*
>
> iii) *will often not be permitted to leave the delivery suite.*
>
> *Those factors may, when applying the acid test, lead to a conclusion that P is or will suffer a deprivation of her liberty when at the acute hospital. If the Trusts are to deprive P of her liberty, they have a duty not to do so unlawfully.*"[271]

The judgment went on to provide important guidance on the circumstances in which an application to court must be made, and guidance on obstetric cases in particular. For our purposes, though, the crucial thing is the simple application of the *Cheshire West* acid test to determine if there was a deprivation of liberty in a hospital setting, albeit that the authorisation of the deprivation of liberty incidental to consideration of the proposed medical treatment.

---

[271] Para 96.

Ferreira

In November 2013 (between the Supreme Court hearing the *Cheshire West* case and handing down its judgment, as it happened) Maria Ferreira was admitted to King's College Hospital in London with breathing difficulties. Maria was 45 years old. She had Down's Syndrome and learning difficulties. She was confined to a wheelchair and lived at home with her sister, Luisa, and their parents. Maria did not like hospitals.

She got worse in the next few days, and was transferred to intensive care, where she was sedated and intubated. A mitt was placed on one hand to prevent her removing her breathing tube, but it was not enough to stop her doing it, and this caused a cardiac arrest which was fatal. She died on 7 December 2013.

An inquest into her death was opened by the Coroner of Inner South London. The question was the *kind* of inquest that would be held.

Ordinarily, an inquest is heard by a coroner alone, but in certain categories of case, thought to warrant greater scrutiny, there should also be a jury, for example where the death was caused by the police. Another such category was where the deceased died "*in state detention*"[272].

Now, Maria had not been referred for a DoLS authorisation when she was in hospital. Very few such patients were. But Maria's family wanted a jury inquest, and they argued that she should have been under a DoLS authorisation, and was effectively in state detention because she met the *Cheshire West* acid test criteria for a deprivation of liberty, which amounted to the same thing.

---

[272] Coroners and Justice Act 2009 s7. NB this was changed by the Policing and Crime Act 2017, which came into force on 3 April 2017, to make clear that the definition of "state detention" for the purpose of the Coroners and Justice Act 2009 should not include those under a DoLS authorisation, so removing the prospect that every death under a DoLS authorisation needed a jury inquest, but of course that came after the court had to decide Ferreira.

At face value it was hard to imagine someone more "*under continuous supervision and control and not free to leave*" than those who are in intensive care units, often unconscious, or sedated into unconsciousness.

So when the coroner refused the family's request for a jury inquest, the family's judicial review against the coroner became, in effect, a case on whether or not the *Cheshire West* acid test applied to ICU. If so, every patient in those circumstances, without a DoLS authorisation or a Court of Protection order, would be unlawfully deprived of their liberty.

The case was heard by Lord Justice Gross and Mr Justice Charles, sitting as judges in the Divisional Court, who handed down a judgment on 29 October 2015[273]. King's College Hospital did not take an active role in the case, and so this was a dispute between a family and a coroner, with no voice for the NHS in the proceedings, despite the potential implications.

Unhelpfully, while both judges agreed that Maria was not in state detention, so as to require a jury inquest, they gave contradictory reasons. Charles J argued that the answer lay in the wording of the Coroners and Justice Act 2009 which defined "*state detention*" as meaning "*compulsorily detained by the state*"[274]. He felt it was possible to be deprived of liberty (per the *Cheshire West* acid test) but it to not be a "*compulsory detention*", and that there was no "*compulsion*" in Maria's case.

Gross LJ found no real distinction between "*compulsory detention*" and "*deprivation of liberty*" but thought it would be an inappropriate extension of *Cheshire West* from its context of long-term social care to apply it in this setting.

The family appealed to the Court of Appeal and at this stage, mindful of the potential impact on the NHS, an application to intervene[275] in

---

[273] [2015] EWHC 2990 (Admin).

[274] s48.

[275] An organisation may be allowed by the court to intervene in a case if it can show that it is sufficiently affected by it, even if it is not directly involved in the dispute.

proceedings was made both by the Secretary of State for Health and Social Care and on behalf of the intensive care community, through the Faculty of Intensive Care Medicine and Intensive Care Society acting jointly[276]. The intervening parties joined the coroner in arguing that the *Cheshire West* acid test should not be applied literally in an ICU setting, that Maria was not deprived of liberty, and provided evidence on the practical implications if the court were to find that she was.

The Court of Appeal decision[277] in January 2017 has the great benefit of being a single judgment, given by Lady Justice Arden, with whom the other two appeal judges simply say "I agree". Even so, it is a lengthy judgment, and the reasoning is not straightforward or uncontroversial. The implications are still being chewed over years later, but at first blush it seemed to be built on 4 key planks:

1. **Context** – Arden LJ says that the context of the cases in *Cheshire West* was very different, and so the case can be "*distinguished*" – ie the Court of Appeal do not have to follow it. In particular, leaning on the European Court of Human Rights judgment in *Austin v UK*[278], she says that there are some contexts in which movement is restricted – regardless of capacity – in which Article 5 is not engaged, eg motorway travel, public transport or football crowds. The "*urgent or intensive care*" context, she says, is also such a case.

Under a striking sub-heading *"life saving treatment: in general no deprivation of liberty"* she says:

> *"…**any deprivation of liberty resulting from the administration of life-saving treatment to a person falls outside Article 5(1) …** so long as [it is] rendered unavoidable as a result of circumstances beyond the control of the authorities and is necessary to avert a real risk of serious*

276 Full disclosure, together with Alex Ruck Keene, counsel, I acted *pro bono* for the FICM and ICS in this case in the Court of Appeal.

277 [2017] EWCA Civ 31, 26 January 2017.

278 The case of police kettling May Day protesters – see chapter 4.

injury or damage, and [is] kept to the minimum required for that purpose".[279]

She then explains that:

> "*... what these qualifications mean is in essence that the acute condition of the patient must not have been the result of action which the state wrongly chose to inflict on him and that the administration of the treatment cannot in general include treatment that could not properly be given to a person of sound mind in her condition according to the medical evidence*".

She says that, in policy terms, the need for scrutiny of long term residence and care package in *Cheshire West* does not demand the same approach in acute medical treatment:

> "*... the policy reasons for finding a violation in Cheshire West do not apply in this case. There is in general no need in the case of physical illness for a person of unsound mind to have the benefit of safeguards against the deprivation of liberty where the treatment is given in good faith and is materially the same treatment as would be given to a person of sound mind with the same physical illness*".[280]

2. Non–discrimination – As that shows, a key part of her reasoning is, essentially, "*non discrimination*", and Arden LJ repeats that it is important that P's medical treatment is not materially different from another patient who is not of unsound mind.

> "*The purpose of Article 5(1)(e) is to protect persons of unsound mind. This does not apply where a person of unsound mind is receiving materially the same medical treatment as a person of sound mind. Article 5(1)(e) is* ***thus not concerned with the treatment of the physical illness of a person of unsound mind.***"[281] (emphasis added).

---

[279] Para 89, emphasis added.

[280] Para 93.

[281] Para 95.

3. Free to leave – As a fall back, Arden LJ concludes that even if she is wrong about the non-engagement of Article 5 altogether, Maria Ferreira would not have met the *Cheshire West* acid test anyway, as she was not "*not free to leave*".

As a matter of fact, there was some dispute about whether the Trust would have allowed her to leave, if her sister had tried to remove her, but crucially Arden LJ said that this test does not depend on that hypothetical question. Instead it must be P herself who wants to leave, and she must be prevented by the state from leaving, rather than their physical inability to leave.

> "*In the case of a patient in intensive care, the true cause of their not being free to leave is their underlying illness, which was the reason why they were taken into intensive care. The person may have been rendered unresponsive by reason of treatment they have received, such as sedation, but, while that treatment is an immediate cause, it is not the real cause. The real cause is their illness, a matter for which (in the absence of special circumstances) the state is not responsible. It is quite different in the case of living arrangements for a person of unsound mind. If she is prevented from leaving her placement it is because of steps taken to prevent her because of her mental disorder.*"[282]

Respectfully, this line is difficult to reconcile with other case law, including *Cheshire West* itself.

4. Resources – Finally, though Arden LJ echoes the consensus among the lawyers involved that resources alone cannot justify a distortion of the legal framework, she clearly finds it comforting that she has been able to

[282] Para 99, emphasis added. Mostyn J would be likely to agree with this echo of his approach in *KW v Rochdale* (see chapter 6). But in that case, the Court of Appeal rubbished this approach in October 2015. And the idea that someone cannot be deprived of their liberty if they are physically unable to try to leave does not seem easy to reconcile with the Supreme Court judgment. It is best not to rely on this aspect of the judgment too heavily, I think.

avoid the huge impact on resources that would have followed from a different decision.

To assist the Court of Appeal, the Intensive Care Society and Faculty of Intensive Care Medicine jointly filed a witness statement by Dr Daniele Bryden (ICU Consultant in Sheffield Teaching Hospitals, and currently Dean of the FICM) and written submissions by counsel to ensure that the court was well informed of the practical implications of its judgment. Dr Bryden explained the reality of life in ICU, the time it takes to deal with a DoLS authorisation, and the impact on relationships with patients and families.

Clearly this had a real impact on the court because, unusually, Lady Justice Arden quotes extensively from Dr Bryden's statement as an appendix to the judgment, ending with Dr Bryden's eloquent conclusion about the commitment of resources to dealing with identification and authorisation of deprivations of liberty in ICU:

> "*Ultimately, this all detracts from the real priorities for ICU staff; the investigation and treatment of critically unwell patients, their recovery and rehabilitation, and the safe and effective delivery of patient care*".

Arden LJ referred to the *FG* case[283] above as an example of proposed treatment which would still engage Article 5, and therefore needs court authorisation of the deprivation of liberty. Significant restrictions were to be imposed on FG as a result of her mental disorder, rather than her physical health needs. It was certainly not the same treatment as anyone with her physical health need – pregnancy – could expect, and so it would still be regarded as engaging Article 5 to ensure appropriate protection from discrimination.

The *Ferreira* reasoning enables providers of inpatient physical healthcare to say that treatment of physical health will <u>not</u> in itself constitute a deprivation of liberty, where it is materially the same treatment that would be given to any patient, regardless of their capacity. But it is not

283 [2014] EWCOP 30, dealing with obstetric care.

clear whether this is restricted to "*life-saving medical treatment*" (or exactly what this means), or reaches to any "*treatment of the physical illness of a person of unsound mind*", or somewhere in between (where?).

Note that the Supreme Court refused permission to appeal further, with three justices (including Lady Hale herself) saying simply that there was no arguable point of law to consider as the Court of Appeal "*were right for each of the reasons they gave*"[284].

Case law since *Ferreira*

The courts next got a chance to apply the *Ferreira* judgment in a case called *Briggs*.

Paul Briggs was a police motorcyclist who was catastrophically injured in a traffic accident on his way to work on 3 July 2015, leaving him (by the time of the court proceedings, nearly 18 months later) in a minimally conscious state in a neurological rehabilitation placement, and dependent on artificial nutrition and hydration to survive.

The substantive issue for the court was a disagreement whether or not it was in his best interests for that treatment to be continued (unusually, perhaps, with the family arguing for withdrawal of treatment, against the judgement of the clinicians), which is rather beyond the scope of this book[285]. But the case led to a discussion about the law on deprivation of liberty in the context of acute medical treatment for a very pragmatic reason: a challenge to a DoLS authorisation (under s21A of MCA) attracts non-means tested legal aid[286]. A welfare decision being made by the court under MCA s15/16, for example about medical treatment, only gets access to legal aid if extremely stringent means test criteria are met. This makes the world of difference to the prospects of obtaining legal

[284] 26 May 2017.

[285] If you're interested in this sort of thing, I recommend A Practical Guide to the Law of Medical Treatment Decisions!

[286] See chapter 12 on the safeguards.

representation, given the brutal level at which the means testing bar is set, leaving a great many people outside the scope of means tested legal aid, but far away from being able to pay privately.

For Mr Briggs, there was a DoLS authorisation in place[287], which was ostensibly challenged as a vehicle to get the case before the Court under MCA s21A with the benefit of non-means tested legal aid, and a bit of judicial leeway was given to allow the case to proceed on that basis. But the reality of case was that it was a dispute about serious medical treatment, rather than about any deprivation of liberty that may have been entailed.

The case was heard by Mr Justice Charles, and a decision handed down in December 2016[288], agreeing with Mr Briggs' family that continuing his artificial nutrition and hydration was not in his best interests.

The Secretaries of State for Health and Justice, and the Director of the Legal Aid Agency had all been joined to the proceedings for the argument about the proper scope of s21A, and whether it could stretch to cover disputes about medical treatment for a patient under a DoLS authorisation, as Charles J had allowed. Permission to appeal against that approach was allowed and it went up to the Court of Appeal, as it was of practical importance, despite the fact that Mr Briggs himself had died early in 2017.

The Court of Appeal heard the *Briggs* case in July 2017[289], by which time they had the benefit of the *Ferreira* Court of Appeal judgment from January that year. Though they deplored the lack of true access to representation in such cases, in the absence of non-means tested legal aid, the court held that s21A proceedings should not be stretched to cover

---

287 Unusually, perhaps, in an acute medical treatment scenario and, perhaps, deliberately to allow these proceedings.

288 [2016] EWCOP 48.

289 *Director of Legal Aid Casework v Briggs* [2017] EWCA Civ 1169.

issues (like continuation of serious medical treatment) which were effectively unrelated to the DoLS authorisation.

For our purposes, though, it is of most interest that, commenting on the *Ferreira* judgment, Lady Justice King said:

> *"In my view, Ferreira confirms what I myself would regard as an obvious point, namely that the question of deprivation of liberty does not arise where a person* ***who lacks capacity is so unwell that they are at risk of dying if they were anywhere other than in hospital*** *and therefore, by virtue of their physical condition, they are unable to leave the hospital". (Emphasis added).*

This spin on *Ferreira*, focussed on the extent of the patient's illness ("so unwell…"), perhaps goes a little further than *Ferreira* itself, which focussed on the ("life-saving") nature of the treatment.

Similarly, in September 2017, Peter Jackson J dealt with a case[290] in which a family and treating clinicians both sought a declaration to allow withdrawal of artificial nutrition and hydration (CANH) from a 50 year-old female patient, in her best interests, though this was, in his words, "*dressed up*" as a s21A challenge to DoLS authorisation. He said:

> *"As was the case in Briggs, the proceedings were brought as a deprivation of liberty challenge under s.21A. In doing so, Mrs B explicitly acknowledged that the central issue was not M's deprivation of liberty but the withdrawal of CANH. She cannot be blamed for taking this course in the light of the law as it then stood. However, the Court of Appeal decisions in Ferreira … and now in Briggs have swept away two fictions. The first was the idea that* ***a person without any real awareness was being deprived of liberty by virtue of receiving life-sustaining treatment: the court will never again be faced with absurd applications for a deprivation of liberty authorisation …*** *The second fiction was the use, for reasons of funding, of s.21A applications instead of best interests applications under ss.15-17.*

[290] *M v A Hospital NHS Trust* [2017] EWCOP 19

> *Where such serious decisions are concerned, any distortion of the legal framework is surely particularly inappropriate"*[291]. *(emphasis added).*

This new gloss – that it would be "*absurd*" to consider someone to be deprived of their liberty when receiving life sustaining treatment "*without any real awareness*" – should be treated with a little caution, since plenty of other case law makes clear that someone can be deprived of liberty without being aware of the restrictions[292].

In *PL v Sutton CCG*[293], Cobb J was considering an application about withdrawal of artificial nutrition and hydration for a 79 year-old lady who was resident in a nursing home. To effect the planned withdrawal, she would first be moved to hospital, and the court considered whether she might be deprived of her liberty there. The judge said that she would not, relying on *Ferreira* to say that the real cause of her not being free to leave is her illness, not her care: she would be "*in a state of very low cognition and possibly unconscious, receiving palliative care, as her life ebbs away*". (If so, it seems difficult to describe this as "*life-saving medical treatment*", if that were truly the line where the *Ferreira* exception kicks in).

In 2017 – 2018 there was a flurry of litigation surrounding the short life of Charlie Gard, and then of Alfie Evans. The issue of deprivation of liberty came up when the court refused an application by the parents in each case to allow them to remove their son from hospital and take him somewhere else, after the court had decided that this was not in his best interests.

---

291 Para 39.

292 Not least, of course, in *Cheshire West* itself at paragraph 35 per Lady Hale, quoted in chapter 4.

293 [2017] EWCOP 22.

In *Gard*, the argument that he was being deprived of his liberty appears to have been first raised in the European Court of Human Rights, which said that "*this aspect of the claim is manifestly ill-founded*".[294]

The Evans family made an argument in terms of habeas corpus[295] and deprivation of liberty, which they said were distinct from the court's finding on his best interests. The Court of Appeal[296] gave this very short shrift, saying that he was clearly <u>not</u> deprived of his liberty, following the judgment in *Ferreira*, and that in any case any deprivation of liberty would have been lawful as authorised by the court, in his best interests. But their explanation of *Ferreira* is interesting, especially as the Court of Appeal in *Evans* included Lady Justice King (who had applied it in *Briggs*), saying:

> *"In Ferreira the Court of Appeal decided that a person is not being deprived of their liberty where they are receiving treatment and are physically restricted by their physical infirmities and by the treatment they are receiving ... Arden LJ concluded ... that <u>restrictions resulting from the administration of treatment</u>, because they are the "well-known consequences of a person's condition, when such treatment is required", <u>do not amount to a deprivation of liberty</u>".*[297]

Again, if the reality was that treatment was being withdrawn for Alfie, it would seem odd to say it could be no deprivation of liberty for him to be kept in hospital against his parents' wishes if "*life-saving treatment*" is the test.

---

[294] Application no. 39793/17, Charles GARD and Others against the United Kingdom https://hudoc.echr.coe.int/eng#{%22itemid%22:[%22001-175359%22]}

[295] Like the Enderbys' attempt to get HL home from Bournewood hospital – see chapter 2.

[296] [2018] EWCA Civ 805.

[297] Para 60-61, emphasis added.

A similar point was argued, and lost, in another case about withdrawal of treatment for a desperately ill child in *Raqeeb*[298], in which Mr Justice MacDonald said:

> *"I am not persuaded that the decision of the Trust deprived Tafida of her liberty for the purposes of Article 5 of the ECHR. The Court of Appeal [In Alfie Evans] has made clear that a person is not being deprived of their liberty where they are receiving treatment and are restricted physically by their infirmities and by the treatment they are receiving."*

When the court later came to consider issues around the legal costs of the proceedings[299], Mr Justice MacDonald said that, given the Court of Appeal authority to the contrary, the argument that she was deprived of her liberty "*was always bound to fail and time should not have been taken up with it...*"

The *Evans* Court of Appeal judgment is not often referred to in interpretation of *Ferreira*, perhaps as a result of the urgency with which each of the hearings in the *Evans* case took place. "R*estrictions resulting from the administration of treatment*" being no deprivation of liberty should not be taken out of that context, and perhaps, respectfully, goes a bit further than the court might have intended, or would have said with more time for reflection.

It would, though, fit with Arden LJ's broader comment that (barring situations of discriminatory treatment) Article 5(1)(e) "***is not concerned with the treatment of the physical illness of a person of unsound mind***".

In September 2019, Lady Arden herself (now part of the Supreme Court) referred to her decision in *Ferreira* when she was part of the court in *Re D*[300] (which mainly dealt with the scope of parental consent to negate

298 [2019] EWHC 2531 (Admin).

299 [2019] EWHC 3322 (Fam).

300 See chapter 10.

what would otherwise be a deprivation of liberty for a child), explaining that:

> *"It follows that there will be cases where a person loses their liberty but the acid test in Cheshire West, as Lady Hale describes it, does not apply. That conclusion is shown by observing that D's case is about living arrangements. It is not about a child, or anyone else,* ***needing life-saving emergency medical treatment****. For the reasons which the Court of Appeal (McFarlane LJ, Sir Ross Cranston and myself) gave in R (Ferreira) v Inner South London Senior Coroner [2018] QB 487, the situation* ***where a person is taken into*** *(in that case)* ***an intensive care unit for the purpose of life-saving treatment*** *and is unable to give their consent to their consequent loss of liberty, does not result in a deprivation of liberty for article 5 purposes so long as the loss of liberty is due to* ***the need to provide care for them on an urgent basis because of their serious medical condition****, is necessary and unavoidable, and results from circumstances beyond the state's control"*[301]

That takes us back to the context in which Ferreira arose, but she did not take the chance to disapprove any of the subsequent cases that seemed to have seen it more broadly.

Interpreting and applying *Ferreira* has not been straightforward[302], but the Faculty of Intensive Care Medicine prepared some guidance for the intensive care setting[303] in its Midnight Law series, which concludes:

- The courts have emphasised that the primary concern in relation to patients in intensive care is to ensure that care is being

---

301 [2019] UKSC 42, paragraph 120, emphasis added.

302 In August 2018 the CQC published guidance purporting to explain *Ferreira*, but which was quickly withdrawn when challenged by the Faculty of Intensive Care Medicine as being inaccurate and misleading.

303 https://ficm.ac.uk/sites/ficm/files/documents/2021-10/midnight_law_deprivation_of_liberty_in_icu_july_2021.pdf co-written by Alex Ruck Keene and myself.

delivered in the best interests of the patient. Deprivation of liberty will only relatively rarely be a relevant issue.

- Where the patient's circumstances do amount to a deprivation of their liberty, then steps should be taken to obtain formal authority. Whilst those steps are taken, the priority should continue to be to deliver care in the best interests of the patient.

The "*Ferreira* Line"

Many will agree that a literal application of the *Cheshire West* acid test everywhere, including throughout the acute medical inpatient context up to and including intensive care, would have been inappropriate, unwarranted, and would have caused enormous practical problems for the NHS in particular. But once we step away from the one size fits all, universal test applying everywhere, we create a new question: where exactly does the *Ferreira* exception stop, and the *Cheshire West* acid test start to apply again? Where is the "*Ferreira* line"?

Taken together, these judgments are the best material we have, to date. From them, we must try to pick out some principles.

Intensive care was the scenario in which *Ferreira* arose, of course, but the reasoning and language in the Court of Appeal did not explicitly limit it to that setting.

Arden LJ referred to "*life-saving medical treatment*" as "*in general no deprivation of liberty*"; her following subheading says there is no policy need to apply the *Cheshire West* acid test to "*urgent medical care*", which seems rather broader.

Jackson J (in *M*) had referred to "*life-sustaining treatment*" for someone "*without any real awareness*".

Lady Justice King (in *Briggs*) referred to someone who "*is so unwell that they are at risk of dying if they were anywhere other than in hospital and therefore, by virtue of their physical condition, they are unable to leave the hospital*".

Back to Lady Arden herself, after her elevation to the Supreme Court and in *Re D* she talked, again, about "*life saving medical treatment*", but also about care "*on an urgent basis because of their serious medical condition*".

Each of those quotes refers to the facts of the particular case before the court, which have typically involved examples of serious, urgent treatment.

The broader statements of principle come from Lady Justice King, in the Alfie Evans case, of "*restrictions resulting from the administration of treatment*" being no deprivation of liberty.

And Lady Justice Arden in *Ferreira* itself that (subject to being materially the same treatment as for anyone) "*Article 5(1)(e) is not concerned with the treatment of the physical illness of a person of unsound mind*" which seems broadest of all.

It seems to me likely we can say that *Ferreira* applies well beyond intensive care. The seriousness and urgency of the treatment are common themes in judicial reasoning, and it seems reasonable to assume that *Ferreira* becomes harder to rely on as time passes[304] and/or the patient recovers.

As King LJ said in *Briggs*:

> "*It may be the case … that as the treatment progresses and P's physical condition improves, his or her ongoing care becomes a deprivation of liberty and, at that stage, a standard authorisation [i.e. DoLS] or court order will be required if the continued retention of P on the ward is not to become unlawful*".

---

304 See chapter 8 for the relevance of duration for the definition of deprivation of liberty.

If we take "life-saving treatment" as the line, say, then there may come a point in a patient's journey of recovery at which it becomes a bit of stretch to apply this. Is it still life-saving on a general ward? Or in rehabilitation? Or once they are deemed to be medically fit for discharge, especially if their discharge is delayed by lack of social care arrangement for a suitable placement, and in the meantime, they would not be allowed to go home?

We will see in chapter 15 the case of *Esegbona,* in which compensation was ordered against an NHS trust where the patient wanted to go home but was not allowed to do so for around 4 months while arrangements were made for her to go to a care home against her wishes, and without consulting her family. She was given a tracheostomy[305] in that admission, but if it was argued in that case that Article 5 did not apply because it involved medical treatment in hospital, then it was unsuccessful.

The basis for disapplying the *Cheshire West* acid test in (some) acute inpatient medical treatment is the difference in the <u>context</u> from that case, which dealt with long-term living arrangements.

Few inpatients would regard themselves as *living* in hospital, which is why – if *Cheshire West* does apply – the focus tends to be more on the "*continuous supervision and control*" element, and the "*not free to leave*" bit is adapted to consider the prospects of discharge home, or transfer to another hospital.

As an admission to hospital drags on, and as they get further away from having to be in hospital because they could not survive anywhere else, the harder it may be to argue that the context is so very different from the individuals in *Cheshire West.*

We also know, of course, that treatment for a physical illness which is *materially different* as a result of the patient's mental disorder is not protected from the proper scrutiny of Article 5 by the *Ferreira* exception.

In *Ferreira* itself, the court gave the example of the *FG* case, described at the start of this chapter, in which the very restrictive plan for dealing with

[305] A tube inserted through an incision in her neck to help her breathe.

FG's labour reflected her schizoaffective disorder, not simply her pregnancy. This was clearly a plan, and a degree of restriction, born not solely of the medical need but of provision for her non-compliance as a result of being of unsound mind. The judge at the time expressly recognised it as being a deprivation of her liberty that warranted separate scrutiny and authorisation, alongside authorisation of the care and treatment plan itself. Post *Ferreira,* it should still be regarded as a deprivation of her liberty, bringing the protection of Article 5.

The case law references to "*life-saving*" or "*life-sustaining treatment*" arguably poses a particular challenge for palliative care settings, where it may not feel apt to frame the care in those terms; and if there is little guidance on what amounts to a deprivation of liberty in hospital, there is next to nothing on the hospice setting.[306]

A particularly wide interpretation of *Ferreira* was taken by the government during the COVID pandemic, when emergency guidance was issued in April 2020 (and only withdrawn on 10 August 2021), which I'll deal with in the next chapter.

For now, remember that, in practice, where a patient needs to be given treatment or brought into hospital against their wishes, for example, in general a court will need to consider the substance of the treatment plan itself, and those proceedings will typically also deal with the deprivation of liberty, if any, which would be involved in putting the plan into effect. That can often include the problem of conveyance (see next chapter).

In that situation, do not discount the possibility of a deprivation of liberty because the proposed restrictions may only be short-lived. There

---

306 In *Briggs* [2016] EWCOP 48, at the first instance hearing, Charles J seemed to accept the argument that if Mr Briggs was deprived of his liberty in hospital, then so he would equally be if he were moved to a hospice after withdrawal of CANH, because "during the period after the cessation of the CANH leading up to his death his physical liberty would not change even if (as is at least likely) he moves from the hospital to a hospice". I am not aware of any other reported judgment dealing with a substantive question of deprivation of liberty in a hospice. I will tackle this a little more in chapter 9 on consent. See also the Law Society guidance (2023) in which there will be a chapter dedicated to hospice settings.

are certainly cases, especially in the medical treatment context, where the courts have found a deprivation of liberty measured in minutes or hours (see next chapter).

Equally, the pressures on the whole system are now such that attendances at the Emergency Department may now be counted in days than in minutes, perhaps raising more issues about when it might amount to a deprivation of liberty.

There can also be extra complication where treatment of physical health is necessary for a patient already detained under the MHA, which I will come back to in chapter 13.

This is an area where any undue certainty should be treated with suspicion, and you should have a low bar for seeking urgent legal advice. We are all still trying to find the landmarks around this bit of the map.

Just as I have emphasised that a situation being a potential deprivation of liberty ought to trigger some scrutiny and safeguards, so we should err on the side of caution if we are not sure that the *Ferreira* exception applies.

And, above all, vital medical treatment should never be compromised or delayed by anxiety about a potential deprivation of liberty issue. It is generally better to explain ourselves to a judge than a coroner.

Key Points

- *Ferreira* (Court of Appeal) held that – because the *context* is different from *Cheshire West* – Article 5 is not engaged in at least some situations of treatment of physical health, if the treatment is the same as it would be for anyone.

- It is unclear how far that exception goes, but certainly it is not limited to intensive care only, though that was the scenario *Ferreira* itself arose in; and it is unlikely to extend to all inpatient treatment regardless of seriousness or urgency. Until we get clearer guidance from the court, we have to draw the line case by case, and err on the side of caution in securing scrutiny and safeguards for people who may need them.

- With appropriate legal advice, it is useful for hospital trusts to adopt their own reasonable interpretation of *Ferreira,* within their policy on deprivation of liberty, and ensure that this is applied consistently and confidently.

- Focus on the question *whether the treatment is materially the same for any patient.* (It is quite easy to think of a scenario where there is a deprivation of liberty because the treatment is more restrictive than it would be for other patients, as a result of the person's mental disorder. It is quite hard to think of a scenario where a court would find that the restrictions amount to a deprivation of liberty, despite the treatment being just the same as it would be for any other patient, because it is insufficiently "*life-saving*").

- In many cases of disputed medical treatment, the whole care plan needs court approval, time permitting, including consideration whether there is any deprivation of liberty. Urgent legal advice should be available to clinicians 24/7.

- Never delay any vital treatment out of concern about any potential deprivation of liberty[307].

It might be helpful now to work through a few more factors we have not really covered yet, which may be relevant to identifying a deprivation of liberty, in hospital and elsewhere ,which I will (though admittedly slightly contrived) list as 8 Cs:

- Conveyance – when is a journey a deprivation of liberty?

---

307 See Part Three of Chapter 14 for how to authorise any deprivation of liberty in the Emergency Department in particular.

- The Clock – myths around duration of the restrictions to be a deprivation of liberty
- COVID – interpretation of deprivation of liberty during the COVID pandemic;
- Crisis – how to deal with emergencies, and the use of s4B of the MCA;
- (no) Choice – does the lack of an available option affect whether or not someone is deprived of their liberty?
- Constraint – are there particular restrictions (cot sides on a bed? A lock on a door?) that necessarily amount to a deprivation of liberty?;
- Covert medication; and
- Contact – what if someone is restricted from having contact with others?

CHAPTER EIGHT

EIGHT C ISSUES

There are a few more issues that can bear on how we recognise an objective deprivation of liberty, which I have contrived to collect under a list of "8 Cs":

- Conveyance – when is a journey a deprivation of liberty?
- The Clock – myths around duration of the restrictions to be a deprivation of liberty
- COVID – interpretation of deprivation of liberty during the COVID pandemic; and
- Crisis – how to deal with emergencies, and the use of s4B of the MCA;
- (no) choice – does the lack of available option affect whether or not someone is deprived of their liberty?
- Constraint – are there particular restrictions (cot sides on a bed? A lock on a door?) that necessarily amount to a deprivation of liberty?
- Covert medication; and
- Contact – what impact does it have if someone is restricted from having contact with others?

Conveyance

It is a quirk of the system that though a DoLS authorisation can (and, strictly, should) be obtained where possible in advance of the person arriving in that hospital or care home setting (so that the scrutiny is effective before taking them there, rather than presenting the assessors with a "done deal"), the authorisation only comes into effect on arrival[308], and it confers no authority to take the patient there in the first place.

As such, conveyance has often proven to be a thorny issue. What if taking someone to a placement may involve more coercion than is comfortably permitted by relying on MCA s4 (best interests), s5 (the general defence of acting reasonably in P's best interests) and s6 (restraint is permissible only if necessary to prevent harm and proportionate to the likelihood and seriousness of that harm)?

Often the answer is an instinct to regard the conveyance in itself as no deprivation of liberty. This is reinforced by the DoLS Code of Practice:

> *"Taking someone to a hospital or a care home*
>
> *2.14 Transporting a person who lacks capacity from their home, or another location, to a hospital or care home will not usually amount to a deprivation of liberty (for example, to take them to hospital by ambulance in an emergency.) Even where there is an expectation that the person will be deprived of liberty within the care home or hospital, it is unlikely that the journey itself will constitute a deprivation of liberty so that an authorisation[309] is needed before the journey commences. In almost all cases, it is likely that a person can be lawfully taken to a hospital or a care home under the wider provisions of the*

---

308 "The new provisions in the MCA do not cover taking a person to a care home or a hospital. But they can be given before the relevant person arrives there so that they take effect on arrival (see for example paragraph 52 of Schedule A1 to the MCA)." – per Charles J in *GJ v the Foundation NHS Trust* [2009] EWHC 2972 (Fam) at para 9.

309 And of course such an authorisation would need to be by the court, since DoLS can only authorise a deprivation of liberty in a care home or hospital, and not in a vehicle.

Act, as long as it is considered that being in the hospital or care home will be in their best interests.

2.15 In a very few cases, there may be exceptional circumstances where taking a person to a hospital or a care home amounts to a deprivation of liberty, for example where it is necessary to do more than persuade or restrain the person for the purpose of transportation, or where the journey is exceptionally long. In such cases, it may be necessary to seek an order from the Court of Protection to ensure that the journey is taken on a lawful basis". (emphasis added)

In many cases where the substantive care or treatment proposed itself needs court authorisation, the court will want to see a comprehensive care plan including how P will be brought to / from hospital, for example, such that any deprivation of liberty involved will be dealt with in the court's order.

However, the court has not always been very accommodating where conveyance alone is in issue.

In *DCC v KH*[310] the local authority (DCC) applied to court urgently because KH, a young man living at a residential care home under a DoLS authorisation, was evidently very reluctant to return to that placement after a session of supervised contact with his family, some 100 miles away. The local authority was not comfortable that it could rely on the DoLS authorisation at the care home to authorise the use of force to bring him back there.

The Official Solicitor, on behalf of KH, complained bitterly that the application had been brought at short notice, and resisted the order sought on the basis that it was unnecessary, as the DoLS authorisation in place included the authority to *return* KH to the placement. It cannot have been Parliament's intention that care homes would have to apply to

[310] Unreported, (2009) COP 11729380, summarised on https://www.mentalhealthlaw.co.uk/DCC_v_KH_(2009)_COP_11729380

court every time someone who is under a DoLS authorisation manages to leave without authority or refuse to return.

The judge agreed with the Official Solicitor, and going further than is usual in these cases, even where an application is rejected, she ordered the local authority to pay the other parties' wasted legal costs for having brought the application unnecessarily.

This conclusion was reinforced by Mr Justice Mostyn in a case in 2010[311]:

> *"It would be little short of absurd if the local authority and [the care home] had powers to restrain him from leaving but not to compel him to return: the greater power must include the lesser. I will therefore declare that this power is implicit in the current and any future standard authorisation."*

These cases, then, are good authority that a DoLS authorisation, once in effect, includes the authority to fetch someone back to their placement[312]. But it remains the case that the DoLS authorisation does not come into effect until P arrives at the placement, and so it cannot be relied on as conferring the power to take them there in the first place.

This is a gap which would have been filled by the LPS[313], though the question whether or not a conveyance amounts to a deprivation of liberty, like every other aspect of the definition, may still have been contentious.

---

[311] *Re ADE (Scope of Schedule A1)* (2010) COP 11821802, also unreported, but summarised here https://www.mentalhealthlaw.co.uk/Re_ADE_(Scope_of_Schedule_A1)_(2010)_COP_11821802

[312] This remains the case though there are some who think that they are wrongly decided, Mostyn J not having been fully addressed on the differences between DoLS and the MHA as regards absence without leave. It may also be difficult to reconcile this implicit power with the idea of DoLS as a spotlight rather than a padlock. Perhaps it is better to rely on MCA s5/6 as authority to fetch someone back to a place where it has been decided that it is in their best interests to be.

[313] See chapter 18.

In practical terms, where coercion is likely to be required, for example to bring a patient into hospital for proposed medical treatment against their wishes, or to discharge them to residential care when they only want to return to their own home, it is likely to be proper that an application to the court is made to consider the merits of the substantive course of action, the concrete proposals for putting the plan into effect, and any proposed conveyance. A detailed plan, including any proposals for use of physical restraint or sedation for conveyance, can often be the central focus of a court application before a proposed course of treatment, or discharge, and this could be authorised by the court[314].

The circumstances in which conveyance can amount to a deprivation of liberty in itself is another issue where more guidance would be welcome.

On the clock – the role of duration

One related argument often heard is that a journey cannot really in itself amount to a deprivation of liberty, since the objective element of the test for a deprivation of liberty requires confinement in a particular place for a "*non-negligible period of time*"[315], and the duration of all but the most extreme journeys may be considered, relatively, negligible. But this is an argument that should be treated with some caution, whether in conveyance, in acute medical treatment, or elsewhere.

The case of *ZH*[316] is good authority, upheld by the Court of Appeal[317], for finding a deprivation of liberty for the purposes of Article 5 in a situation which only lasted for 40 minutes in total.

---

[314] Sometimes, perhaps, "*to the extent that those arrangements amount to a deprivation of liberty*", if there is any doubt about whether or not they are a deprivation of liberty and the court does not wish to determine that.

[315] *Storck*, see chapter 4.

[316] [2012] EWHC 604 (QB)

[317] [2013] EWCA Civ 69

ZH was 16 years old and on a day trip with his special school to the local swimming pool in Acton, West London, on 23 September 2008. He was one of five students, with three carers. ZH has severe autism and epilepsy, suffers from learning disabilities and cannot communicate by speech. He cannot swim, but was there as a familiarisation visit. ZH left the group and was standing by the side of the pool, transfixed by the water; his carers kept their distance, knowing that, with his aversion to being touched, he would be likely to react badly to any intervention.

The manager of the pool was apparently less understanding and, concerned at his behaviour, called the police, who duly attended when ZH had been standing by the pool, staring at the water for around 40 minutes. When two police officers arrived they approached ZH directly. One said "Hello, I'm Hayley" and gently placed a hand on ZH. He promptly jumped into the pool, fully clothed. Unable to swim, he was shepherded towards the shallow end by a combination of two lifeguards and the police, and then things went from bad to worse:

> *"Once the officers lifted ZH from the water, he was immediately placed on his back and restrained by several officers applying force to his body, holding him down and shouting loud commands which ZH did not understand. The judge was not satisfied that any attempt was made to calm him down before he was restrained. Neither ZH nor any of the officers suffered any physical injury. As the judge said … this suggested that the restraint was applied without excessive force and that ZH's struggling was effectively restrained, or that he was not violent in his struggling. The carers tried to calm ZH down by showing him a banana and a lollipop, but the police told them to move away. They urged the police not to restrain him in this way, saying that he was autistic and epileptic. PS Wallace and PC Murray arrived and assisted in maintaining the physical restraint. It was only when handcuffs and leg restraints were placed on ZH that the application of force ceased. During the course of the restraint, ZH lost control of his bowels. <u>This period of restraint lasted about 15 minutes</u>.*
>
> *ZH was then taken out of the building to a police van which was parked in the car park. He was placed alone in the cage in the rear of*

> *the van, still in handcuffs and leg restraints. He was soaking wet, very agitated and distressed. While he was in the police van, another carer, Ms Harley, arrived at the scene. She was not allowed to get into the caged area of the van, but was able to calm ZH by speaking to him through the open rear door. At about 16.20 hrs, the police removed the handcuffs and leg restraints. After he had been examined by the London Ambulance Service, he was permitted to leave with his carers. He remained highly distressed and was too upset to change his clothes. He had been in the van for about 25 minutes"*[318]*. (emphasis added)*

Proceedings were brought against the police, alleging that they had acted unlawfully – essentially overreacting, being heavy handed and without due regard for the MCA. The first instance judge found that they had breached his Article 5 rights, as he was deprived of his liberty unlawfully, as well as Article 3 rights (not to suffer "inhuman and degrading treatment") and awarded substantial compensation. Despite the fact that the total period of restraint was around 40 minutes, the Court of Appeal upheld the judge's findings entirely:

> *"...the restraint of ZH was closely analogous to the classic or paradigm case of detention in prison or a police cell. In particular, it is difficult to see any difference in kind between being detained in the caged area at the back of a police van and being detained in a police cell. In fact, ZH was deprived of movement throughout the entire period of the restraint. The restraint was intense in nature and lasted for approximately 40 minutes and its effects on ZH were serious".*[319]

Clearly, this is a very different context to the provision of health and social care, but it is best to be really careful about reliance on certain timescales before triggering the safeguards of Article 5. There is no "free pass" to deprive someone of their liberty for a short period only, if the restrictions do amount to a deprivation of liberty.

---

318 Taken from the Court of Appeal judgment, at paragraph 19-20.

319 Para 83.

In *Cheshire West* in the Court of Appeal, Lord Justice Munby said

> *"If, perish the thought, [one of the barristers in the case] were to find himself locked in a police cell for three hours, he would indubitably be deprived of his liberty".* [320]

The potential restrictions in her obstetric care in *FG* might have only been over a matter of hours, but was seen as a potential deprivation of liberty.

Similarly, in *Re P (paracetamol overdose)*[321] the judgment refers to authorising not only the medical treatment (around 21 hours of giving medication against P's wishes) but also the consequential deprivation of liberty. That case predates *Ferreira*, so it might well now be argued that there is no deprivation of liberty in giving life-saving medical treatment (such as an antidote for a paracetamol overdose), perhaps, but it certainly wasn't argued that a duration measured in hours meant it couldn't be a deprivation of liberty at all.

In the medical treatment context, I have sometimes heard of a "rule of thumb" that anything less than 7 days either doesn't amount to a deprivation of liberty or that it doesn't warrant referral to DoLS or the court in any case.

The origin of this dangerous myth may be that a DoLS urgent authorisation can be given by the care home or hospital covering a deprivation of liberty of up to 7 days (extendable if there are "exceptional reasons" to 14 days) to allow time for a Standard Authorization application to be processed. And the DoLS process requires that a standard authorisation referral is made at the same time as an urgent authorisation is granted, and so, perhaps, the "logic" runs that if you won't need more than 7 days to be authorised, you won't need a standard and so shouldn't bother doing an urgent authorisation.

---

320 [2011] EWCA Civ 1257 at para 42.

321 [2014] EWHC 1650 (Fam), and see chapter 10 as the case involved a 17 year-old.

Paragraphs 6.3-6.4 of the DoLS Code of Practice says:

> *"...an urgent authorisation should not be used where there is no expectation that a standard deprivation of liberty authorisation will be needed. Where, for example:*
>
> - *a person who lacks capacity to make decisions about their care and treatment has developed a mental disorder as a result of a physical illness, and*
> - *the physical illness requires treatment in hospital in circumstances that amount to a deprivation of liberty, and*
> - *the treatment of that physical illness is expected to lead to rapid resolution of the mental disorder such that a standard deprivation of liberty authorisation would not be required,*
>
> *it would not be appropriate to give an urgent authorisation simply to legitimise the short-term deprivation of liberty.*
>
> *Similarly, an urgent deprivation of liberty authorisation should not be given when a person is, for example, in an accident and emergency unit or a care home, and it is anticipated that within a matter of a few hours or a few days the person will no longer be in that environment".*

But this cannot be good authority for the idea that any period under 7 days cannot be a deprivation of liberty. It just leaves open the question of exactly what legal framework legitimises it if it is (see the section on dealing with emergency situations below).

In the Court of Appeal in *Ferreira*, the intervening intensive care community asked the court to give an indication of any period that could reliably be disregarded for the purposes of Article 5. Though the court helpfully (from our perspective) probably went further in disapplying Article 5 in that context than might have been expected[322], they flatly

[322] See chapter 7.

refused this invitation to couch this in terms of duration of the restrictions caused by the care being provided.

In *Sessay*[323], a 23 year-old, sued a mental health trust and the police for unlawful detention after being taken from her home to hospital and held there for 13 hours, without using the powers that might have been available under s135-136 of the Mental Health Act. The hospital policy provided a target of 4 hours to process patient admissions and put the proper legal framework in place, with a long stop of 8 hours. The court rejected the argument that the hospital could rely on common law necessity in the meantime, but also rejected Ms Sessay's argument that the maximum time of 8 hours waiting for processing and formal detention was in itself unlawful:

> *"Plainly whether there is false imprisonment or deprivation of liberty for the purposes of Article 5(1) will depend on the facts of the particular case".*

In *HJ v Norfolk and Suffolk NHS Foundation Trust*[324] the treatment in question was relief of HJ's chronic constipation by occasional enemas which, without her compliance, involved restraint by 4-5 staff, lasting 3-5 minutes each time. Though the court found that it was not a deprivation of liberty that needed authorisation for other reasons, covered in detail at the end of Chapter 13, it was not suggested that the short duration of the intervention meant that deprivation of liberty should not be considered.

Any argument that a particular period of time is necessarily too short to possibly be a deprivation of liberty needs to be treated with some caution, and there is certainly no obvious basis for saying that a period of restrictions of less than 7 days cannot amount to a deprivation of liberty for that reason alone.

---

323 *Sessay v SLAM and the Metropolitan Police* [2011] EWHC 2617.

324 [2023] EWFC 92.

When I have seen this argued, it has often been on a very parochial basis – for instance based on a median intensive care stay of 3-5 days – but forgetting that the overall duration of stay under conditions that impose very significant restrictions would be very much longer, once any subsequent inpatient care is included and taken as a whole. It can be easy to lose sight of the total time P has been restricted as they progress from one clinical team to another, but Article 5 would not segment restrictions based on them being imposed in fragmented, smaller chunks of time in different administrative units of the same hospital, for example.

Often, significant restrictions measured in hours which are planned may be part of serious medical treatment which itself warrants an application to court. Unplanned restrictions more often take place in the context of dealing with emergencies or a crisis, which we will look at below. But we should be very careful of any false reassurance that there can be no deprivation of liberty due to a relatively short timescale.

Covid: The "*Ferreira* Stretch"

Next, in this part, before we get to dealing with emergency situations generally, let's consider the experience of COVID.

In guidance, regularly updated throughout the pandemic[325], and only withdrawn on 10 August 2021, the Department of Health and Social Care offered this rather creative interpretation of *Ferreira*:

> ***"Delivering life-saving treatment: application of the Ferreira judgment***
>
> *Where life-saving treatment is being provided in care homes or hospitals, including for the treatment of COVID-19, then this will not amount to a deprivation of liberty, as long as the treatment is the same as would normally be given to any patient without a mental disorder.*

[325] https://www.gov.uk/government/publications/coronavirus-covid-19-looking-after-people-who-lack-mental-capacity/the-mental-capacity-act-2005-mca-and-deprivation-of-liberty-safeguards-dols-during-the-coronavirus-covid-19-pandemic#paragraph-8

> *This includes treatment to prevent the deterioration of a person with COVID-19. During the pandemic, it is likely that such life-saving treatment will be delivered in care homes as well as hospitals, and it is therefore reasonable to apply this principle in both care homes and hospitals. The DoLS process will therefore not apply to the vast majority of patients who need life-saving treatment who lack the mental capacity to consent to that treatment, including treatment to prevent the deterioration of a person with COVID-19.*
>
> *This means that, for example, a person who is unconscious, semi-conscious or with acute delirium, and needs life-saving treatment (for COVID-19 infection or anything else), is highly unlikely to be deprived of liberty. They must be treated based on a best interests decision. (The exception to this is people described above. [this refers to a passage on Advance Decisions to Refuse Treatment])*
>
> *If additional measures are being put in place for a person who lacks the relevant mental capacity when they are receiving life-saving treatment, for example to stop them from leaving the place of treatment, then the 'acid test' set out in Cheshire West … should be considered. If the acid test is not met, then the person is not deprived of their liberty and the DoLS will not be necessary."*

The logic was that treatment for COVID is life-saving treatment, and therefore the *Ferreira* exception for life-saving treatment applies to take any such care, however restrictive, outside the scope of Article 5, even if it is delivered in care homes, rather than hospitals.[326]

Of course, the government's interpretation had more than one eye on the practical implications of adding to the already swamped DoLS system in the context of a pandemic, and such guidance does not establish or change the law.

Perhaps any stretch is understandable in the circumstances, but I wonder whether Lady Justice Arden would recognise it as in keeping with her

[326] This is still, of course, subject to the caveat that the treatment must be the same as it would be for anyone, regardless of their mental disorder.

judgment in *Ferreira*, and I am not aware of this having been directly tested in the courts.

In stretching the application of *Ferreira* not only past ICU but beyond hospitals and into residential care in this way, it is not clear exactly what "treatment" it is envisaged care homes would be providing, nor whether that was imagined to include restrictions such as social distancing or isolating individuals to reduce risk of infection with or transmission of the virus.

The Joint Committee on Human Rights was critical of the way in which restrictions on liberty were imposed throughout the pandemic, often with little understanding of the proper legal basis for this, an unduly blanket approach, or a disproportionate impact on the elderly, the disabled, and the lonely[327].

And on this, we must recognise the point made powerfully by Hayden J in a letter to the Directors of Adult Social Care, dated 4 May 2020[328], giving guidance on the approach to MCA / DoLS and the Court of Protection during the pandemic:

> *"It was expressed to me … that there appear to be some who believe that careful adherence to proper legal process and appropriate authorisation may now, at times, be required to give way to other pressing welfare priorities. I understand how this view might take hold in establishments battling to bring calm and reassurance to intensely distressed people, both in the Care Homes and within their wider families. It is important, however, that I signal that whilst I am sympathetic to the pressures, I am very clear that any such view is entirely misconceived.* ***The deprivation of the liberty of any individual in a democratic society, holding fast to the rule of law, will always require appropriate authorisation. Nothing has***

[327] Protecting Human Rights in Care Settings – Report of the Fourth Session of 2022-23, https://publications.parliament.uk/pa/jt5803/jtselect/jtrights/216/report.html

[328] Available here https://courtofprotectionhandbook.files.wordpress.com/2020/05/letter-vp-to-adass-4-may-2020.pdf

> ***changed. The Mental Capacity Act 2005, the Court of Protection Rules and the fundamental rights and freedoms which underpin them are indispensable safeguards to the frail and vulnerable."*** *(emphasis in the original)*

Writing in late 2023, I can hope, perhaps, that this can be regarded as of more historic interest, though the government's approach to this can be seen again in the LPS Code of Practice guidance on the interpretation of the *Cheshire West / Ferreira* definition, see chapter 18.

Emergencies and the modification of MCA s4B

MCA s4A makes clear that the MCA does not authorise any deprivation of liberty unless:

- It is giving effect to a court order;
- Or a there is a DoLS authorisation[329];
- Or under MCA s4B.

MCA s4B is the provision that deals with emergencies, and said [emphasis added]:

> *(1) If the following conditions are met, D is authorised to deprive P of his liberty while a decision as respects any relevant issue is sought from the court.*
>
> *(2) The first condition is that there is a question about whether D is authorised to deprive P of his liberty under section 4A.*
>
> *(3) The second condition is that the deprivation of liberty—*
>
> *(a) is wholly or partly for the purpose of—*

[329] Added by the MHA 2007, amending the MCA to bring in the DoLS.

(i) giving P life-sustaining treatment, or

(ii) doing any vital act, or

(b) consists wholly or partly of—

(i) giving P life-sustaining treatment, or

(ii) doing any vital act.

(4) The third condition is that the deprivation of liberty is necessary in order to—

(a) give the life-sustaining treatment, or

(b) do the vital act.

(5) A vital act is any act which the person doing it reasonably believes to be necessary to prevent a serious deterioration in P's condition.

This is sometimes described as a statutory codification of the old common law idea of necessity, which we discussed in relation to the *Bournewood* case. The policy has never been to paralyse or hinder the delivery of appropriate, urgent care, of course.

As much as we rightly fear paternalistic overreach, and must respect people's rights, sometimes there is other stuff to worry about, including keeping the person in your care alive for long enough to think about these things a bit more carefully. The fear of doing the wrong thing, or liability that may follow, is a terrible reason to allow a patient to come to avoidable harm[330].

Without wishing to be glib about it, it is tempting to think that it is better to explain yourself to a judge than to a coroner.

[330] See death by indifference, a report in 2007 by Mencap on the increased mortality for patients with a learning disability from treatable conditions, and its various follow up reports.

MCA s4B would have been amended significantly under the LPS proposals, which I will summarise in chapter 18 as those changes have never been brought into force. Note that under MCA s4B as originally drafted, and still in force, giving "life-sustaining treatment" or carrying out a "vital act" is lawful, even if it amounts to a deprivation of liberty, but only *while a decision is sought from the Court*. And so, in principle even if not always in practice, an application to court must be made (bearing in mind that there is 24/7 access to the court if need be[331]) for it to be properly relied on.

And also note that this legislation sees life-sustaining treatment in emergency circumstances as something that can be a done, while seeking court approval, even if it is a deprivation of liberty. Of course, we now have the question whether any treatment in a real emergency can amount to a deprivation of liberty at all, after *Ferreira*, as long as it is the same treatment as anyone would get for their physical heath in that situation.

For patients already admitted to hospital who try to leave, there are also certain "holding powers" that may be available under the Mental Health Act, which are beyond the scope of this book, but broadly include:

- Section 5(2) – Power to detain for 72 hours if a doctor thinks an application under the MHA ought to be made.
- Sectio 5(4) – Power to detain for 6 hours if a nurse thinks the patient ought to be detained under the MHA but it is not practicable to immediately get a doctor to make the recommendation necessary to use section 5(2).

See Part Three of Chapter 14 for authorisation of deprivation of liberty in the hospital Emergency Department in particular.

[331] Ask your lawyers how this can be accessed if need be; many specialist health and care law firms provide for 24/7 advice on call.

(No) choice?

Is there no deprivation of your liberty if you have nowhere else to go?

There may be a bit of this in the idea that it is not a deprivation of liberty to be kept in hospital if you are so sick that you could not be anywhere else (and live). But it also feeds into the sense that it is only really a deprivation of liberty if you are taken away (to an institution), or kept away, from your own home, with the emphasis of Article 5 seen as about where someone lives (away from "home") rather than on the restrictions on them there.

In the Court of Appeal in *Cheshire West*, Munby LJ said that "*matters are of course very different where a person has somewhere else to go and wants to live there but is prevented from doing so by a coercive exercise of public authority*"[332] and gave examples of *Bournewood, Neary* and *JE.*

Citing this, in *C v Blackburn with Darwen Borough Council*[333], Mr Justice Peter Jackson, who had been so sympathetic to the family in the *Neary* case, decided that Mr C, a man with an acquired brain injury, was not deprived of his liberty by being kept in a care home against his wishes, despite them having had to call the police when he kicked down a door trying to escape, *because he had nowhere else to go*:

> *"In the present case Mr C undoubtedly wants to live somewhere else, but this is a reflection of his unhappiness with the care home. He would like to be able to live an unconfined life in the community, but this is not realistically possible due to the extent of his difficulties. I distinguish his situation from those where a person has been removed from a home that is still realistically available."*

But be careful before relying on this to say that there must be a viable alternative before someone is to be regarded as deprived of their liberty. Jackson J was dealing with this after the Court of Appeal in *Cheshire West*, but before the Supreme Court decision, and the (un)availability of an

332 At para 58.

333 [2011] EWHC 3321 (COP)

alternative seems very close to the argument that P is just in the appropriate place to meet their needs, which was strongly rejected by the Supreme Court.

Even with the temptation to frame deprivation of liberty in terms of removal from *a home*, and therefore the logic that *there is a home to go to*, it would seem pretty arbitrary to deploy or deny safeguards on such a basis. Imagine two people identically restricted in care homes, but one of them has lost their tenancy during the admission, while the other has their own house still. Is only one of them deprived of their liberty? Does someone lose their Article 5 rights to challenge a care home placement if their family manage to sell their house quickly? Is someone in a police cell deprived of their liberty, or not, according to whether they happen to be homeless?

On this approach, "*for those without a claim to another place or person, liberty has no meaning*"[334].

This seems to me to be a dangerous route to go down, for all the frustration of a procedural challenge in which it might be argued that there is no alternative.

And even in some cases where the court is told that there is no alternative (for instance where a child or young person is being held in hospital for want of an available social care package able to support them) there are times that the court has not just accepted that it is therefore necessarily in their best interests[335].

The European Court of Human Rights agree that it is not necessary for there to be an alternative placement or home before someone can be considered to be deprived of their liberty[336].

---

334 Lucy Series – Deprivation of Liberty in the Shadow of the Institution, 2022, p163.

335 See chapter 10 and 14. I've not seen a case in which it was argued that the absence of an alternative in itself means that there cannot be a deprivation of liberty.

336 See Stanev v Bulgaria [2012] ECHR 46 (Application no. 36760/06). Mr Stanev was held to be deprived of his liberty, though he had nowhere else to go.

Constraint?

Lady Hale in her *Cheshire West* Supreme Court judgment emphasised that "*in the end, it is the constraints that matter*", by way of keeping the focus on the reality experienced by P. But it does not follow that every constraint, even those commonly seen as real red flags, in itself means that there is a deprivation of liberty.

As a jobbing lawyer in this field, perhaps the most common question from health and care providers is: we have just put cot sides on the bed, so is he now deprived of his liberty?

Or the same question triggered by a door being locked, or secured by a code that the patient does not know.

To be sure, those are properly seen as among the red flags, to prompt a long hard think about whether P is *at risk of*[337] being deprived of his liberty, alongside, for example, use of physical restraint, covert medication, or restrictions on contact with others.

But we know that none of those – in isolation – is necessarily a deprivation of liberty; it is the cumulative impact of all the restrictions that need to be considered. It is just too simplistic to say that a locked door = deprived of liberty, or use of cot sides does. We know that the person must be "*not free to leave*" and "*under continuous supervision and control*".

A locked door does not necessarily mean that I am not free to leave (in the sense of going to live somewhere else), still less that I am under continuous supervision and control.

But such particular constraints should certainly raise questions whether they are warranted – are they necessary and proportionate? Is there a less restrictive way to meet P's best interests? And kept under review – has anything changed that allows such constraints to be eased?

[337] See the introduction to chapter 4.

And let me take the chance to repeat an important point – if the falls risk makes consideration of use of cot sides on someone's bed appropriate, for example, then it should be discussed with them for them to decide for themselves, if they have capacity to make that decision, and a best interests decision appropriately made for them if they do not, per MCA s5.

If the intervention proposed amounts to a restraint on P then it is lawful under the MCA if, in addition to being in their best interests, it is necessary to prevent harm and proportionate to the likelihood and seriousness of that harm.

Concern about the intervention being a deprivation of liberty is no good reason to delay or not to put it in place at all where otherwise appropriate; if need be, advice can be sought about getting appropriate authorisation if it might be a deprivation of liberty.

Covert medication

As we will see in chapter 12[338], the use of covert medication can be a significant "red flag". The DoLS Code of Practice highlighted the use of "sedation" as a factor, bearing in mind that it might supress the patient's expression of their opposition to their care and residence; all the more so if the medication is given covertly.

In *AG*[339] the court was considering a challenge to a DoLS authorisation, and it became clear that AG, a 92 year-old woman, was being given strong, sedative medication covertly by her care home. District Judge Bellamy noted that this was not only an interference with her Article 8 rights, but also:

[338] On the issue of the duration for which a deprivation of liberty should be authorised.

[339] [2016] EWCOP 37.

> "*medication without consent and covert medication are aspects of continuous supervision and control that are relevant to the existence of a deprivation of liberty*".

He held that convert medication must only be used in "exceptional circumstances", and gave some guidance:

- Use of covert medication must be subject to full consideration with healthcare professionals and the family.

- Any covert medication must be clearly identified within the assessment and any DoLS authorisation.

- He recommends that a care plan with covert medication is not authorised as a deprivation of liberty for longer than 6 months, but if it is this should include clear provision for regular, possibly monthly reviews, including the family, the RPR and professionals, and there should be a review each time the medication given covertly is changed.

In any case where covert medication is being used, you would do well to seek early legal advice if this is not regarded as part of a deprivation of liberty and explicitly authorised as such.

Contact

Restrictions on P's contact with others is also a serious matter. It is another red flag for consideration whether the situation overall may amount to a deprivation of liberty. No doubt it was an aggravating factor that HL was denied visits from his foster family when he was detained at Bournewood Hospital, for example.

In some cases, the restriction on contact is the central issue; perhaps P has been determined to lack capacity to make decisions about who he has contact with, and a decision is made that it is not in their best interests to have contact with a particular person, perhaps an estranged family member, or an abusive partner. Or sometimes, P is assessed to lack capacity to make decisions about a sexual relationship, and so may need to be restricted from unsupervised contact with anyone with whom sexual activity might take place, to prevent what would otherwise be potentially a criminal offence[340]. These (additional) restrictions can then mean that someone becomes deprived of their liberty where they may not previously have been.

Like a locked door or cot sides, or covert medication, denial of P's contact with someone needs careful justification, and robust decision making under the MCA, but it does not follow that it is necessarily a deprivation of their liberty.

If anything, it may raise issues of ECHR Article 8 (right to private and family life) rather than Article 5 (right to liberty).

The same point has recently been made in terms of that most modern of intolerable restrictions on contact – removing someone's mobile phone. In *Manchester City Council v CP*[341], Mr Justice MacDonald had to consider an application by the local authority to authorise the deprivation of liberty of a 16 year-old girl[342].

P had ADHD and was assessed to be "*working at the level of a 7 year-old*". She was also described as "*a funny, likeable, and kind young person with skills in creative arts, including making TikTok videos, and a love of animals.*" After being taken into care, various acts of severe self-harm left the children's home unable to cope, and she was assessed not to warrant detention under the Mental Health Act.

She was confined to a placement which she lacked capacity to consent to, and subject to 3:1 supervision and various restrictions. There was no

---

340 Sexual Offences Act 2003, since sex without consent is an offence, and without capacity there can be no valid consent. This can mean that even long term married couples may need to be separated and supervised closely in care settings where one or both loses capacity to make decisions about sex. I'll leave that particular can of worms there, for these purposes.

341 [2023] EWHC 133 (Fam).

342 See chapter 14 for an account why such cases need court approval.

doubt there was a deprivation liberty, and the court authorised it.

The question was whether restrictions on her access to her phone / tablet / laptop – to prevent her putting herself at risk, including of sexual exploitation – should be considered and authorised by the court as part of that deprivation of liberty.

The judge held that, however important access to phone / laptop is to a typical 16 year-old's sense of liberty, ECHR Article 5 is all about ***physical*** liberty. The "*continuous supervision and control*" bit of the *Cheshire West* acid test should be focussed on physical liberty and not stretched further.

Restrictions on her access to her phone etc are more suited to Article 8 (right to private and family life) than Article 5, and in some ways this offers her greater protection.

The local authority could restrict her access using its parental responsibility under Children Act s33 by virtue of the Care Order. If force were needed to restrict her access, then an application could be made to court for a separate order about this; it was not appropriate to roll it into the authorisation of the deprivation of liberty.

It is a really interesting judgment, and may be reassuring in some ways. *Not every restriction must be seen as a "deprivation of liberty issue"*. And as the judge said, there may be greater protection for some rights that are distinguished in this way – eg Article 8(2).

But this may mean a more nuanced approach to restrictive care plans is needed, distinguishing bits that are relevant to deprivation of liberty, and bits that are not, with a separate legal basis / authorisation needed for the restrictions that are not, rather than the court (or DoLS) authorising everything in one go. (Equally, then, it is important that BIAs are not "signing off" restrictions on contact / social media etc where this might give a provider false reassurance that this is legitimised by a DoLS authorisation when in fact they raise different Article 8 issues, and without a court order addressing those issues we may only be reliant on MCA s5).

As I have found from trying to end my daughters' screen time, restrictions on access to devices and the internet may *feel* like a deprivation of liberty, especially to "kids these days", but should not, perhaps, in itself be treated as a deprivation of liberty in law.

Which brings me to two more problematic Cs – consent, and children – which demand chapters of their own.

Key Points

This is where the European and domestic case law get to on defining deprivation of liberty:

- The *Cheshire West* acid test – that P is under continuous supervision and control and is not free to leave (to go and live somewhere else) – defines the objective element of the DoL;

- There is definitely no exception to the *Cheshire West* for cases in the family home or any other domestic setting (see the *Rochdale* saga);

- But (after *Ferreira*), *Cheshire West* should not be applied to certain medical treatment situations, at least in "*life-saving medical treatment*"[343] and potentially to medical treatment much more widely, unless the treatment is materially different than would be given to any patient, regardless of their mental disorder.

- In addition, of course, to establish a deprivation of liberty for Article 5 purposes

    - P must not validly consent to the restrictions (ie, in this context, he lacks capacity to consent to make the relevant

[343] Which the government seems to interpret to include any "treatment" at all for Covid.

decisions and arrangements are being made in their best interests), and

- the situation must be imputable to the state.

CHAPTER NINE

CONSENT AND CAPACITY

Like imputability to the state[344], the "subjective" element of the *Storck*[345] three-part test for a deprivation of liberty can feel like a bit of a backwater, a sideshow to the main event of the test of confinement for the objective element.

But it is fundamental in making any best interests decision for someone, never mind going so far as to deprive them of their liberty in their best interests, that the person lacks the capacity to make the relevant decisions for themselves.

In much of the work of the Court of Protection, for instance in dealing with property and affairs, or in medical treatment or disputes about care, disputes about whether or not someone has capacity to make the relevant decision for themselves are commonplace.

But in reported cases about deprivation of liberty it is relatively rare that the focus is on P's capacity; far more often the arguments turn on whether the circumstances amount to a deprivation of liberty and, if so, whether they are in P's best interests.

So the case law on this aspect is relatively limited, but it should never be taken for granted. And there is an argument, which I'll get to below, that actually the issue of consent should get a lot more attention, and might offer a principled way out of some of the problems caused by *Cheshire West*[346].

---

344 See chapter 11, and how brief it is compared to the attention paid to the objective element in chapters 4-8!,

345 See chapter 4.

346 See chapter 19.

Let's start with the basics[347].

An adult[348] with capacity to make their own decision can consent to or refuse treatment or care, or choose among options which are being offered or made available to them.

This means that an adult, with capacity to do so, can consent to any care package or offer of residential placement, no matter how restrictive, and it will be no deprivation of their liberty.

And such consent *means that they can change their minds* – and if their consent is withdrawn then either the restrictions must be stopped or justified within an appropriate legal framework.

There can be no *consent* without the *capacity* to make the relevant decision[349]:

> *"The [European Court of Human Rights] takes the view that a person's consent to admission to a mental health facility for in-patient treatment can be regarded as valid for the purpose of the Convention only where there is sufficient and reliable evidence suggesting that the person's mental ability to consent and comprehend the consequences thereof has been objectively established in the course of a fair and proper procedure and that all the necessary information concerning placement and intended treatment has been adequately provided to him"*[350].

---

347 I cover this in more detail in "*A Practical Guide to the Law of Medical Treatment Decisions*" (2020).

348 For these purposes, over the age of 18, though the Mental Capacity Act 2005 applies from the age of 16, see chapter 9.

349 Subject, perhaps to a gloss that can be put on this, which we will consider in the conclusion.

350 *M v Ukraine* [2012] ECHR 732.

The framework of the MCA / DoLS[351] will only be available if the person lacks capacity to make the relevant decisions about their care and residence.

Without wanting to repeat the ground already covered in chapter 1, remember that:

- Capacity means the ability to make the decision that needs to be made, at the time it needs to be made.

- Being able to make the decision means being able to understand the information relevant to the decision; retain the information relevant to the decision; and being able to use or weigh it up to reach a decision[352].

- In rare cases, given all that can be done in practice to enable and support communication, a person might also lack capacity for the relevant decisions if they are able to make but unable to communicate their decision.

- If they are unable to make a decision, in the sense above, it must be because of an impairment or disturbance in the functioning of the mind or brain ("the diagnostic test")[353].

- It should be assumed that a person has capacity for any decision unless it is established otherwise[354] and they should not be treated as unable to make a decision unless all reasonable support has been given to enable the person to make the decision for themselves[355].

---

351 LPS would have been just the same. Other frameworks, such as the Mental Health Act 1983 – see chapter 13 – may still be available.

352 MCA 2005 s3.

353 MCA 2005 s2.

354 MCA s1(2).

355 MCA s1(3).

- An "unwise" decision does not establish that a person lacks capacity for the relevant decisions[356] (though it may well trigger professional duties to assess carefully whether they do).

This is all about the balance between autonomy (enabling and respecting individual choice about our own lives) and paternalism (protecting the vulnerable). This plays out not only in the threshold for establishing in/capacity, but also in the way that best interests decisions are to be made for someone once lack of capacity for that decision is established:

- Any best interests decision should be deferred until P has regained capacity to make it, if possible;

- Lack of capacity notwithstanding, P must be involved in the decision-making as much as possible;

- P's wishes, values, feelings and beliefs, now and in the past, must be taken into account appropriately[357];

- Those who know P well should be consulted — anyone P has said should be consulted, anyone with a Lasting Power of Attorney or Deputyship, and those engaged in caring for P or interested in their welfare[358].

If someone has capacity for the relevant decisions, then their decision is final regardless of what anyone else thinks. In best interests decision-making where a person lacks capacity for the relevant decision, the consultation process is wide ranging and not necessarily restricted to family only, and still less to any nominated individual.

If P had capacity to do so in the past, then they could have appointed a Lasting Power of Attorney (LPA). An attorney, properly appointed and

---

356 MCA s1(4).

357 MCA s4(6).

358 MCA s4(7).

registered with the Office of the Public Guardian, can be given decision-making power over either property & finances, or over health & welfare.

But an LPA does not give the attorney a "blank cheque" even over decisions within their remit; they can be restricted by any provisions of the LPA itself; they still have to abide by the MCA ie decisions on health & welfare can only be made once P has lost capacity for those decisions, they can only be made by the attorney in P's best interests and, in making those decisions, the attorney has the same duties of consultation (including with those engaged in caring for P or interested in their welfare – ie including professional carers / NHS / social workers etc, as well as other friends and family) as any other decision-maker.

In any case, an attorney has no power to authorise something that would otherwise amount to a deprivation of liberty[359].

The same goes for a Deputy, which is similar to an LPA but appointed by the court (far more often for property & finances; only very rarely for health & welfare decisions).

Two issues needs a little more unpicking: the information that is relevant for a person to need to understand / retain / use or weigh up; and (which I'll take first) the nature of the metal disorder there must be.

Mental disorder / unsound mind

Though the MCA is framed in terms of "an impairment of, or disturbance in, the functioning of the mind or brain"[360], Article 5 of the European Convention of Human Rights only provides for deprivation of someone's liberty in this context, and subject to there being a due legal

[359] Though MCA s11 provides that an attorney may "restrain" P, only if P is reasonably thought to lack capacity for the relevant decisions, it is reasonably believed to be necessary to prevent harm, and to be proportionate to the likelihood and seriousness of that harm.

[360] MCA s2(1).

process and a right to challenge any deprivation of liberty, if they are of "*unsound mind*".

For DoLS to be used, a person must lack capacity to make the relevant decisions about their care and residence, and they must also be "*suffering from a mental disorder within the meaning of the Mental Health Act 1983, but disregarding any exclusion for persons with learning disability*"[361].

In turn, this builds in the MHA definition of mental disorder, ie:

> "*any disorder or disability of the mind*"[362]

The exclusion for learning disability (ie that it only counts as a mental disorder for the purposes of the MHA if it is "associated with abnormally aggressive or seriously irresponsible conduct"[363]) is disregarded for the purposes of DoLS, so any learning disability can meet the criteria without that extra requirement.

"Unsound mind" is, perhaps, a broader term and is not defined with precision in the domestic law. The ECtHR case of *Winterwerp*[364] is the best place to start:

> "*The Convention does not state what is to be understood by the words "persons of unsound mind". This term is not one that can be given a definitive interpretation: ... it is a term whose meaning is continually evolving as research in psychiatry progresses, an increasing flexibility in treatment is developing and society's attitude to mental illness changes, in particular so that a greater understanding of the problems of mental patients is becoming more wide-spread.*"

---

361 MCA Schedule A1 para 14(1).

362 MHA s1(2).

363 MHA s1(2A), though this may change in proposed reforms to the MHA.

364 WINTERWERP v. THE NETHERLANDS – 6301/73 [1979] ECHR 4 (24 October 1979) *http://www.bailii.org/eu/cases/ECHR/1979/4.html*

But it certainly involves more than simply behaviour or beliefs that deviate from the norms of a particular society. As such,

> *"...no one may be confined as "a person of unsound mind" in the absence of medical evidence establishing that his mental state is such as to justify his compulsory hospitalisation...*
>
> *"... except in emergency cases, the individual concerned should not be deprived of his liberty unless he has been reliably shown to be of "unsound mind". The very nature of what has to be established before the competent national authority – that is, a true mental disorder – calls for objective medical expertise. Further, the mental disorder must be of a kind or degree warranting compulsory confinement. What is more, the validity of continued confinement depends upon the persistence of such a disorder..."* (emphasis added).

The wording of Article 5(1)(e) in referring to "unsound mind", and the *Winterwerp* judgment explaining this in terms of a "true mental disorder" established by medical evidence, are reflected in our domestic law.

So DoLS[365] requires a mental disorder, defined by reference to the MHA, as well as lack of capacity for the relevant decisions. They are not one and the same. For instance, sedation into unconsciousness in intensive care (or in alcohol) can be the basis for a lack of capacity for certain decisions, but would not meet the criteria for a mental disorder (which is why DoLS might not be available in situations where the only impairment or disturbance in the functioning of the kind or brain is chemically induced, rather than due to a mental disorder).

Subject to there being a "mental disorder", for our purposes, to bring any case within Article 5(1)(e)'s definition of unsound mind, we can turn to the question of capacity to make the relevant decisions.

---

365 Similarly, it was proposed that for the LPS to apply there must be a "mental disorder", by reference to the MHA s1(2). This is the basis for the three proposed LPS assessments including both an assessment that P lacks capacity for the relevant decisions, and a "medical assessment" that there is a mental disorder.

For DoLS[366], capacity means

> *"... capacity in relation to the question whether or not he should be accommodated in the relevant hospital or care home for the purpose of being given the relevant care or treatment"*[367].

The relevant information

So what is the relevant information for a decision about being accommodated for the purpose of being given the relevant care or treatment?

An important point first: it is not necessary to understand every little detail of the information to constitute capacity to make the decision, a broad overview is enough[368]. And the information must actually be available to P before it can really be said that their understanding etc has properly been tested.

Remember KK from chapter 1, the 82 year-old lady who suffered from Parkinson's and vascular dementia, who had used the "lifeline" emergency call service nearly 1,100 times over 7 months before she was admitted to a nursing home. KK consistently objected to staying there and said that she wanted to go home, so the case came to court to determine if she lacked capacity to make that decision for herself, as the professionals thought, and if so whether it was in her best interests to stay in the nursing home, against her wishes.

The judge, Mr Justice Baker, found that she had capacity to make the decision for herself. It appears to have made a difference that he heard oral evidence from KK herself, rather than relying on written evidence about her. He described her as "*clear and articulate*" and "*betraying relatively few signs of the dementia which ... afflicts her*". She was realistic

366 For LPS, this would have changed to lacking capacity to "consent to the arrangements" which will amount to a deprivation of liberty.

367 MCA Schedule A1 paragraph 15.

368 *CC v KK* [2012] EWCOP 2136, as mentioned in chapter 1.

about her care needs and accepted that she needed some support. She may not have been able to weigh every detail, but she understood in broad terms, and that was enough. We should be wary of what he called "*the protection imperative*".

Crucially, the judge was very critical of the fact that the local authority making the application had not really considered what support would be available for her if she went home, and on this basis the judge felt that she couldn't really be said to have failed to understand, retain or weigh up the information relevant to the decision. She hadn't been given the information relevant to the decision because, in honesty, the local authority had decided that she ought to stay in residential care and not explored any alternative, never mind tested her understanding of the options.

The same judge came back to the question of what is the relevant information that needs to be understood / retained / weighed or used to make a decision in this context in *LDV*[369].

Baker J had to consider whether a 33 year-old woman (L) with a learning disability could consent to her admission to a psychiatric hospital (WH), such that she could be an informal patient, without using the MHA, and it would not amount to a deprivation of her liberty, no matter how restrictive. The hearing pre-dated the Supreme Court judgment in *Cheshire West*, and so the judge refers to the issues raised in the Court of Appeal – relative normality, and context, but even then the restrictions were thought to be a deprivation of her liberty.

For our purposes, though, the most relevant part is the judge's consideration of her ability to consent to any confinement, and the specific information that she would have to be able to understand / retain / use or weigh, which he held was:

---

[369] *A Primary Care Trust v LDV & Ors* [2013] EWHC 272 (Fam) (18 February 2013) *http://www.bailii.org/ew/cases/EWHC/Fam/2013/272.html*

(1) that she is in hospital to receive care and treatment for a mental disorder;

(2) that the care and treatment will include varying levels of supervision (including supervision in the community), use of physical restraint and the prescription and administration of medication to control her mood;

(3) that staff at the hospital will be entitled to carry out property and personal searches;

(4) that she must seek permission of the nursing staff to leave the hospital, and, until the staff at the hospital decide otherwise, will only be allowed to leave under supervision;

(5) that if she left the hospital without permission and without supervision, the staff would take steps to find and return her, including contacting the police.

Crucially, this tells us that the *question of confinement* is central to the assessment of capacity. The nature, extent and enforcement of the restrictions are a core part of the information that P must be able to understand / retain / weigh up to make their decision if they are to consent to the arrangements. It cannot only be about the care and accommodation itself, though that is what the legislation focussed on.

In *LBX*[370], Mrs Justice Theis determined the relevant information for a 29 year-old man with a diagnosis of a learning disability to make a decision for himself about his residential placement:

"(1) what the two options are, including information about what they are, what sort of property they are and what sort of facilities they have;

[370] *LBX v K & Ors* [2013] EWHC 3230 (Fam) (19 June 2013) *http://www.bailii.org/ew/cases/EWHC/Fam/2013/3230.html*

(2) in broad terms, what sort of area the properties are in (and any specific known risks beyond the usual risks faced by people living in an area if any such specific risks exist);

(3) the difference between living somewhere and visiting it;

(4) what activities he would be able to do if he lived in each place;

(5) whether and how he would be able to see his family and friends if he lived in each place;

(6) in relation to the proposed placement, that he would need to pay money to live there, which would be dealt with by his appointee, that he would need to pay bills, which would be dealt with by his appointee, and that there is an agreement that he has to comply with the relevant lists of "do's and "don'ts", otherwise he will not be able to remain living at the placement;

(7) who he would be living with at each placement;

(8) what sort of care he would receive in each placement in broad terms, in other words, that he would receive similar support in the proposed placement to the support he currently receives, and any differences if he were to live at home; and

(9) the risk that his father might not want to see him if he chooses to live in the new placement."

The judge also specifically excluded, as setting the bar for capacity too high, a number of issues:

"... firstly, the cost of the placements and the value of money[371]*; secondly, the legal nature of the tenancy agreement or licence; and, thirdly, what his relationship with his father might be in 10 or 20*

[371] Note that neither being placed somewhere in your best interests in itself, nor being put under a DoLS authorisation there, relieves you of the obligation to pay for the care and residence, even if you don't want it – see *DM v Doncaster MBC* [2011] EWHC 3652.

years' time if he chooses to live independently now. To include them would result in surprising results, for example, such that he could be said to have capacity to decide to live somewhere where there was not a tenancy agreement, and the position in relation to the long-term consequences is again setting the bar too high. The Act in s.3(4) makes it clear it is the "reasonably foreseeable consequences" only".

Consent for children and young people is addressed in the next chapter.

Advance Consent

I don't like the phrase "advance consent" (as opposed to what?! It is hardly "*consent*" to ask a patient afterwards). But it has come into usage enough to need to be addressed[372].

Consent from a patient can be relied on to negate what might otherwise be a deprivation of their liberty where it is fairly short term, and fairly predictable. For example, there is no question of a deprivation of liberty needing authorisation where a patient consents on the way into surgery, and this consent also covers the expected post operative recovery, perhaps a few days in ICU, before capacity to make further decisions for yourself is likely to be recovered.

The same principle, surely, could reasonably apply to someone with capacity consenting to care in a hospice, even if their capacity is then lost.

But it becomes harder to rely on that consent the longer into the future we go, and the more things change from what was actually discussed and consented to while P was able to make the decision. "Advance consent"

---

[372] In the White Paper leading to the current draft Mental Health Bill, the government asserted that "advance consent" is already a feature of the law, even allowing for a confinement in a psychiatric hospital to be treated as voluntary on that basis. This has been firmly challenged by many, including the Law Society, as not reflecting the law as it stands; and if it is to become the law it should be fully and openly debated and put on a statutory footing, rather than brought in by asserting that it is already the law.

should be seen as giving a blank cheque to any restrictions at all in the future, without independent scrutiny or safeguards[373].

Anyone seeking to rely in advance consent to say that there is no deprivation of liberty, would want to have good evidence of P's capacity at the time the consent was taken, and that the care plan is entirely in line with the specific restrictions that were consented to. It might, perhaps, be less onerous in some cases, as well as more protective for P's rights, to recognise that there may be a deprivation of liberty now and have it scrutinised / authorised in the usual way.

Capability

One important point: *capacity in the sense of the legal term of art should not be confused with a layman's use of capability or ability.*

It is routine, in the context of a potential discharge from hospital back to a family home, to assess a patient's ability to carry out certain tasks to look after themselves, or activities of daily living. I sometimes see an assessment whether a patient is able to use stairs safely, or one described as "the kettle test", simply whether the patient can safely make a hot drink for themselves.

Where such tests don't go well for a patient, it must not find its way into the notes that "*patient lacks capacity to live at home*". *Capacity* is the ability to make a particular decision ***not*** the ability to carry out a specific task.

It does not follow from the fact that Doris cannot safely make a cup of tea for herself that she lacks capacity to make decisions about her care and residence. Her capacity for that decision needs to be assessed, if there is reason to do so rather than rely on the statutory MCA assumption that she has capacity.

---

[373] The draft Code of Practice for the Liberty Protection Safeguards seeks to put greater weight on the possibility of "advance consent", and stretch the concept further, in excluding certain situations that might otherwise be regarded as a deprivation of liberty at the moment.

You are on much safer ground to stick to "ability" or "capability" when discussing physical tasks, and keep "capacity" for decision making (or, perhaps better, use "able to make a decision" or "able to do a task", for the reasons set out in chapter 1).

Compliance / objection / assent?

Compliance with care or residence arrangements does not stop them being confinement, to meet the objective element of the definition of deprivation of liberty, as we saw in *Bournewood* in ECtHR, and in *Cheshire West* in the Supreme Court. To mistake compliance for "consent", to avoid recognising there may be a deprivation of liberty, would repeat the mistakes made by the lower courts in those cases, and deny the appropriate safeguards to those who may need them most.

It is not necessary to be resisting the restrictions for there to be a deprivation of liberty.

But conversely, the idea of "objection" can still play a significant role, not least in the question of P's access to the safeguards that follow from recognising a deprivation of liberty[374].

As we have seen, though, the judiciary often struggle with the idea of a deprivation of liberty where P is "happy" or has "no subjective sense of confinement" (see the Court of Appeal and the minority of the Supreme Court in *MiG & MeG / Cheshire West*).

In *Cheshire West,* Lady Hale said the most difficult aspect of the case was why it cannot be said that P, MiG and MeG were giving tacit consent to placements where they were manifesting contentment[375]. Lord Neuburger said that there might be "rare" cases where an absence of

[374] See chapter 12 re DoLS, and if anything this would have been increased under LPS.

[375] Para 55.

objection might amount to a form of consent to meant that there is no deprivation of liberty for want of the subjective element.[376]

However, this line of thought was explored no further, and in *Cheshire West* it was simply agreed between the parties and accepted by the court that where P lacks capacity to make the relevant decisions about care and accommodation for themselves, then the subjective element of a deprivation of liberty is established, and (subject to imputability to the state) everything rests on the objective element / confinement, which was really the sole focus of the Supreme Court in that case.

I'll come back to whether the subjective element warrants a little more attention in chapter 19, and whether this might just offer a principled basis on which to roll the scope of the *Cheshire West* acid test back towards the original focus of Article 5, looking at institutional placements and contemplating an element of coercion.

However, the complexities of the subjective element – lack of valid consent – are already evident in the context of children and deprivation of liberty, which we will turn to next.

Key Points

- If P has capacity to make the decision and consents to the arrangements for their care then there is no deprivation of liberty.
- That consent can stretch into the future beyond the loss of capacity, for example with pre-operative consent to post-operative care, or on admission to a hospice.
- Reliance on such "advance consent" becomes more problematic the more time passes, and – especially – as the restrictions depart from what was discussed and consented to.

---

[376] Para 68.

- The relevant information for the decision about care and residence has been set out in case law, especially in *LDV* and *LBX*, above and crucially also includes the information about *the confinement*, if there is to be consent.

CHAPTER TEN

"KIDS"

In law, as in life, children[377] can cause trouble (and I say this with the sincerity of someone trying to write this book while my 7 and 10 year-old daughters "*will not*" go to bed).

This chapter will focus on identifying a deprivation of liberty for someone under 18. Being a child also affects the way in which a deprivation of liberty can be authorised, which I will come back to in chapter 14 where I will also, sadly, have to say a bit about the current state of resources and availability of suitable placements, and what the courts have had to say about this.

Two particular issues arise for identifying a deprivation of liberty for children:

- How is the bar set for the *objective* element (the confinement), if it is any different to an adult?
- And to satisfy the *subjective* element (the lack of valid consent), what role is played by those with parental responsibility?

Treating incapactous adults as children

Before we start though, we need to slay one dragon.

One interesting aspect of the *Cheshire West* Court of Appeal judgment, finding that P was not deprived of his liberty, was the tendency in the

[377] In this context, I mean anyone under 18 – see below.

language, and arguably therefore in the thinking, to *infantilise*, treating him (a 39 year-old man) as if he were a dependent child:

> *"The "body suit" that P wears is an 'all-in-one' garment, the essential feature of which is that the zip is at the back, rather than the front, so that P cannot access his continence pads. It is, as Ms Richards properly emphasised, nothing like a strait-jacket; it is more akin to a child's 'baby grow'. Reference is made to the fact that P is strapped into his wheelchair. But this is for his own safety. With all respect to those who may take a different view, one could just as well argue that a small child, because he has to live where his parents determine, is deprived of his liberty if, as a baby, he is strapped into a buggy or, as an older child, is strapped into a car seat. Nor can I attach the same weight as Baker J to the "finger sweep" of P's mouth to remove materials which, not least having regard to his own health and safety, ought not to be there. This is obviously intrusive, as Baker J says, but again it has to be looked at in context. It is little different from what any properly attentive parent would do if a young child was chewing or about to swallow something unpleasant or potentially harmful. The only difference is that with an adult like P two people are needed to do what one could manage alone if dealing with a smaller child."*[378]

Is that really ok? Surely the difference is not only that two people are needed for the intervention as P is bigger, but that *he is an adult*!

More recently, Hayden J in *TN v an ICB*[379], dealt with a dispute over covid vaccination for a 22 year-old man with a severe learning disability, in which his mother argued that her parental responsibility entitled her alone to make the decision where TN was a child and therefore also, despite his adulthood, where could not decide for himself. Hayden J disagreed.

> *"Children are not chattels of parents. Our domestic law emphasises responsibilities rather than rights. In most situations, a parent will*

[378] LJ Munby, para 114.

[379] [2022] EWCOP 53, para 27.

have ultimate responsibility for taking decisions concerning their children's health, education, and welfare. It is obviously right that this should be the case, but it is not ubiquitously true. Parents do not have absolute rights in respect of their children. Occasionally, for example, in the sphere of serious medical treatment, parents are sometimes ambushed by their own grief and distress which ill-equips them to identify where the best interests of their children lie. Thus, I reject [the mother's] primary proposition and, inevitably, therefore, the analogy [she] seeks to make with adults who lack capacity.

In any event, however, incapacitious adults are entitled to the same choices and opportunities as the rest of the adult population. These rights are more extensive than those available to children. They include rights to forge personal and sexual relationships, to marry etc. The Mental Capacity Act 2005 imposes an obligation actively to promote P's decision taking however limited the sphere might be in which it can be exercised. It also requires assessment of wishes and feelings, even where P lacks the ability to understand, weigh or evaluate the decision in focus. Thus, the law extends the freedoms of adulthood to all adults, which includes the incapacitious. Any other approach would be discriminatory".

Incapacitous adults are not just big children.

Lucy Series describes a public event at a barristers' chambers after the Court of Appeal judgment in *Cheshire West.* The philosopher AC Grayling was speaking about the nature of "liberty" for an incapacitous adult, comparing them to a four year-old, prompting the Official Solicitor, Alastair Pitblado, to retort from the audience: "*one can be flippant about little children if one wants, but these aren't children, they're adults*".[380]

Let's look at the law for actual children, starting with the objective question of confinement.

---

380 Series, "Deprivation of Liberty in the Shadows of the Institution", Bristol University Press, 2022, p167.

Actual children: confinement?

The starting point is that there is no minimum age for Article 5. It does not say on its face that it applies only to adults, any more than does the right to life (article 2) or the right not to be tortured (article 3).

Since the sisters placed by Surrey County Council (MiG and MeG in the *Cheshire West* Supreme Court judgment) were only teenagers at the time their cases were considered by the court, the judiciary did have to think a bit about the difference, if any, there might be between children and adults.

Per Lord Kerr:

> *"All children are (or should be) subject to some level of restraint. This adjusts with their maturation and change in circumstances. If MIG and MEG had the same freedom from constraint as would any child or young person of similar age, their liberty would not be restricted, whatever their level of disability. As a matter of objective fact, however, constraints beyond those which apply to young people of full ability are – and have to be – applied to them. There is therefore a restriction of liberty in their cases. Because the restriction of liberty is – and must remain – a constant feature of their lives, the restriction amounts to a deprivation of liberty.*
>
> *Very young children, of course, because of their youth and dependence on others, have – an objectively ascertainable – curtailment of their liberty but this is a condition common to all children of tender age. There is no question, therefore, of suggesting that infant children are deprived of their liberty in the normal family setting. A comparator for a young child is not a fully matured adult, or even a partly mature adolescent. While they were very young, therefore, MIG and MEG's liberty was not restricted. It is because they can – and must – now be compared to children of their own age and relative maturity who are free from disability and who have access (whether they have recourse to*

> *that or not) to a range of freedoms which MIG and MEG cannot have resort to that MIG and MEG are deprived of liberty"*[381].

So, for Lord Kerr, any five year-old say <u>should be</u> under continuous supervision and control and not free to leave due to their age and dependency, and so is not objectively deprived of their liberty for the purposes of Article 5.

Of course, that leaves us with grey areas, as the child grows up, though the law tends to prefer clear, bright lines where possible to provide certainty.

Lord Justice Munby himself came back to the issue in *Re AF* (2018)[382], in which he considered 7 children between 11 and 16 as test cases on the question of where Article 5 is engaged where children are in the care of a local authority. He concluded that, of course, each case must be considered on its merits, but gave a "rule of thumb" that:

> *"i) A child aged 10, even if under pretty constant supervision, is unlikely to be "confined" for the purpose of Storck component (a)[ie the objective element of the deprivation of liberty].*
>
> *ii) A child aged 11, if under constant supervision, may, in contrast be so "confined", though the court should be astute to avoid coming too readily to such a conclusion.*
>
> *iii) Once a child who is under constant supervision has reached the age of 12, the court will more readily come to that conclusion".*

He also usefully reminded us that, in this context as elsewhere, being "*free to leave*" for the purposes of the *Cheshire West* acid test did not mean going out for some trip or outing, but "*leaving in the sense of removing himself permanently in order to live where and with whom he chooses...*".

---

[381] para 78-79. Lord Kerr also wrote that MiG and MeG should also be compared to someone of the same "*station*", but I am not sure what that means, and it is seldom mentioned again.

[382] [2018] EWHC 138 (Fam)

As such, continuous supervision and control was likely to be the key part of the objective element for a child, as few children would be able to decide to go to live on their own, certainly under 16.

He also made clear that an element of restriction on movement may be an ordinary part of the exercise of parental discipline, without amounting to confinement, referring to the decision of the Court of Appeal in *In Re K (A Child)*[383], in which Judge LJ[384], as he then was, gave as examples of what were mere *restrictions* on liberty of movement:

> *"...the way in which parents restrict the movements of their children from time to time by, for example, putting young children into bed when they would rather be up, or "grounding" teenagers when they would prefer to be partying with their friends, or sending children to boarding schools..."*[385]

Very young children are not confined for the purposes of Article 5 where it simply reflects the needs of their age, as Irwin LJ said in *Re D* Court of Appeal[386]:

> *"...the question whether there is "confinement" should be approached in the careful way analysed by Lord Kerr in Cheshire West... A three year-old child must be restrained for her own safety if walking near a busy road, or playing near a bonfire. This restraint would be unlawful if exercised over an adult*[387]*. But it is lawful if exercised by any adult looking after the child. In my view, there is no need for an elaborate analysis of delegated parental responsibility to explain this. In such circumstances, restraint to keep the child safe lawfully could (and*

383 *In Re K (A Child) (Secure Accommodation Order: Right to Liberty)* [2001] Fam 377.

384 That's right – in a great example of nominative determinism, Igor Judge was a court of appeal judge at the time and later actually Lord Chief Justice, the head of the judiciary, from 2008 to 2013.

385 Para 99-101.

386 D (A Child) [2017] EWCA Civ 1695

387 Rightly, in my view, emphasising that adults who lack capacity for particular decisions are not big children – see above.

> *normally should) be exercised by any nearby adult. The true analysis is that explained by Lord Kerr. For all present purposes, "confinement" means not simply "confining" a young child to a playpen or by closing a door, but something more: an interruption or curtailment of the freedom of action normally to be ascribed to a child of that age and understanding. In most of the myriad instances in life where children are restrained in one way or another – by being compelled unwillingly to go to school, go to bed at a given time and so forth – there can be no question of their being "confined" so as to fulfil the first limb [the objective element] of the test in Storck."*[388]

That case went on to the Supreme Court, mostly about the subjective element of parental consent (see below), but Lady Hale also took the chance there to comment on the objective question of confinement, making clear that her own acid test (continuous supervision and control and not free to leave) needs modification for children[389]. She said:

> *"… the crux of the matter [is:] Do the restrictions fall within normal parental control for a child of this age or do they not? If they do, they will not fall within the scope of article 5".*

She goes on to say that the child's disability makes no difference:

> *"… a mentally disabled child who is subject to a level of control beyond that which is normal for a child of his age has been confined within the meaning of article 5 limb A [ie the objective element]".*[390]

So, the *Cheshire West* acid test does apply differently for kids, not only because "continuous supervision and control" may mean something different at different ages, but we also have Lady Hale's "crux of the

---

388 Para 158.

389 [2019] UKSC 42 https://www.supremecourt.uk/cases/docs/uksc-2018-0064-judgment.pdf

390 She goes on to say that the consent of a parent might mean that limb B – the subjective element of lack of valid consent – is not met. See below.

matter" question to crystalise this: are the restrictions within normal parental control" for a child of that age.

You would not regard a toddler as deprived of their liberty, to warrant Article 5 legal safeguards, because they are under continuous supervision and control and not free to leave. You would, of course, expect nothing less.

There is, then, a modified form of the "relative normality" approach taken by the Court of Appeal in *Cheshire West*, and rejected in the Supreme Court, but *based on age rather than disability*; Lady Hale's universalism is for grown ups; for children the test is being treated the same way as other children the same age, regardless of disability.

Restrictions which are not relatively normal for even a young child can still be a confinement, and so can give rise to a deprivation of their liberty, subject to the other elements of lack of valid consent and being imputable to the state.

There is a case of a court recognising and authorising a deprivation of liberty for a 10 year-old[391]. In that case, the parties agreed that the boy was objectively deprived of his liberty, since he was placed at a specialist children's home and was constantly supervised with physical restrictions used to prevent him leaving, due to his care needs arising from severe autistic disorder and severe learning disability. He was under a Care Order, and so it was not possible for his parents' consent (or the local authority's) to negate what might otherwise have been a deprivation of liberty, and a court order was required[392].

---

391 "*Daniel X*" [2016] EWFC B31
http://www.bailii.org/ew/cases/EWFC/OJ/2016/B31.html

392 See below. It is sensible, of course, for any local authority in that situation to seek that the court authorises the deprivation of liberty at the same time as dealing with the substance of any placement decision.

So now let's look at the subjective element – the extent to which consent (and whose consent?) can mean that there is no deprivation of liberty for the purpose of Article 5, even if the objective element is met.

A child's consent

In law, anyone under 18 is "a child" (according to the Children Act 1989). But try telling that to a 16 or 17 year-old! And they would have a point, wouldn't they, not least since the MCA 2005 treats anyone over the age of 16 as assumed to have capacity to make their own decisions[393]. And since the case of *Gillick* in 1986[394], the law has recognised that a child under 16 can have the competence (due to their understanding and maturity) to make a medical treatment decision for themselves (in that case, a girl under 16 deciding about the contraceptive pill) without involving their parents.

Where a child is over 16 and has capacity to make his or her own decision about care arrangements that would otherwise amount to a deprivation of their liberty, then their consent is enough to disapply Article 5. *Valid consent means that there is no deprivation of liberty at all.*

Likewise, for a child under 16 but *Gillick* competent to make the same decision, their consent means that there is no deprivation of liberty, so no need to apply to court. (It is important though to be cautious whether any such consent is genuine[395], and in any case to remember that restrictions which are lawful only in reliance on consent would have to be stopped if that consent were withdrawn.)

[393] Though of course there may be cases where we are not relying on the MCA, and the Supreme Court in Re D (below) rejected an argument that the MCA excludes all other legal frameworks once someone reaches 16.

[394] [1986] AC 112

[395] See *Re T* [2021] UKSC 35.

The harder question is the extent to which the consent of a parent[396] to an arrangement that would otherwise meet the "acid test", as modified for children, means that there is no deprivation of liberty at all, and so no trigger for any safeguards[397].

Parental consent

In the *Neilsen* case[398], a 12 year-old Danish boy was placed in a secure mental health setting for 5 months, but the European Court of Human Rights held that it was no deprivation of his liberty, as it was authorised by his mother, acting within the reasonable bounds of her parental responsibility.

This has long been widely regarded as a little controversial, and out of step with the rest of the case law. I would not advise anyone to be overconfident in relying on it today, and it was doubted in our own domestic series of judgments about a boy known as D.

D was a boy of 15 years, diagnosed with ADHD, Tourette's syndrome and Asperger's, as well as a mild learning disability. The judgment describes that:

> *"his parents struggled for many years to care for D in the family home. He had significant difficulties with social interactions. His behaviour was challenging; he was observed to be physically and verbally aggressive. D would urinate and defecate in inappropriate places. He presented with anxiety and paranoid behaviours. .... Medication had limited effects"*[399].

[396] Strictly, of course, any person with parental responsibility (ie excluding a local authority with a care order, see below) see Practical Guide to the Law of Medical Treatment, chapter 6, but I'll use "parent" as shorthand.

[397] Note the difference between court authorising a deprivation of liberty vs consent (whether from a child or parent) meaning that *there is no deprivation of liberty at all.*

[398] *Neilsen v. Denmark* [1988] EHRR 175.

[399] *Trust A v X* [2015] EWHC 922 (Fam) at para 13.

After a referral to Child and Adolescent Mental Health Services, D was admitted to a specialist hospital. He lived in a dedicated 6 bed unit in the hospital grounds, and attended a special school on site full time. The unit had a locked front door, and D did not leave the ward without staff accompanying him. Under general observations, he was checked on by staff every 30 minutes or so, though he sought out staff contact more regularly. When in the community he was supervised one to one.

D was not detainable under the Mental Health Act, and so if there was a deprivation of his liberty in this situation it had to be authorised by the court to meet his Article 5 rights since – under 18 – he would not be within the scope of DoLS.

Mr Justice Keehan held that it was:

> *"obvious that very young children will be under the 'complete supervision and control' of the parents and 'will not be free to leave' the family home without supervision. Such a state of affairs would certainly not amount to a deprivation of liberty".*[400]

But it would be wrong, he said, to go so far as counsel for the local authority in this case contended and accept that *Cheshire West* did not apply to cases of children under 16 years old:

> *"The protection of Article 5 of the Convention and the fundamental right to liberty applies to the whole of the human race; young or old and to those with disabilities as much as to those without. It may be those rights have sometimes to be limited or restricted because of the young age or disabilities of the individual, but 'the starting point should be the same as that for everyone else', per Baroness Hale: Cheshire West at para 45".*[401]
>
> ...

[400] Para 31.

[401] Para 42.

> *"... the acid test definitions of a deprivation of liberty apply as much to D as they did to the subjects of the appeals in Cheshire West".*

There was no great dispute that these arrangements amounted to an objective deprivation of liberty, if the modified *Cheshire West* acid test were applied, or that D himself lacked *Gillick* competence to consent to these arrangements, or that they were imputable to the state.

The only question, then, was whether what would otherwise have been a deprivation of liberty was *negated by the consent of his parents.*

The hospital trust which brought the application to court argued that the parents' consent was <u>not</u> enough to negate the existence of a deprivation of liberty (and therefore the need for court approval). D had been resident in locked psychiatric wards for 15 months, at the age of 15, and treating clinicians "*remain uneasy about caring for and depriving a child of his liberty, given the length of time and his age, with only authority provided by way of parental consent*".[402]

Keehan J disagreed.

Having held that he was "*wholly satisfied that D lives in conditions that amount to a deprivation of his liberty*" (ie as the objective element) [403], Keehan J went on to consider the proper scope of the exercise of parental responsibility[404]:

> *"The decisions which might be said to come within the zone of parental responsibility for a 15 year-old who did not suffer from the conditions with which D has been diagnosed will be of a wholly different order from those decisions which have to be taken by parents whose 15 year-*

402 Para 49.

403 In fact, showing how easy it is to go astray with the language here, Keehan J later corrected himself (when e cam back to consider this case again – see below):"I should have said in the first sentence that 'I am wholly satisfied that D lives in conditions which satisfy the First Limb of the Storck test', [ie objective confinement] rather than how I then expressed myself namely 'which amount to a deprivation of his liberty'."

404 Though he disregarded the authority of *Neilsen*, describing it as "controversial".

old son suffers with D's disabilities. Thus a decision to keep such a 15 year-old boy under constant supervision and control would undoubtedly be considered an inappropriate exercise of parental responsibility and would probably amount to ill treatment. The decision to keep an autistic 15 year-old boy who has erratic, challenging and potentially harmful behaviours under constant supervision and control is a quite different matter; to do otherwise would be neglectful. In such a case I consider the decision to keep this young person under constant supervision and control is the proper exercise of parental responsibility."[405]

He waxed lyrical about the care of the parents:

"On the facts of this case, why on public policy or human rights grounds should these parents be denied the ability to secure the best medical treatment and care for their son? Why should the state interfere in these parents' role to make informed decisions about their son's care and living arrangements?

I can see no reasons or justifications for denying the parents that role or permitting the state to interfere in D's life or that of his family.

I accept the position might well be very different if the parents were acting contrary to medical advice or, having consented to his placement at Hospital B, they simply abandoned him or took no interest or involvement in his life thereafter.

The position could not be more different here…

In my judgment, on the facts of this case, it would be wholly disproportionate, and fly in the face of common sense, to rule that the

[405] Para 55-57. So, taking care with this – D's disability does stop the restrictions being an objective deprivation of his liberty, but does mean that the consenting to the restrictions is a reasonable exercise of parental responsibility and therefore does not meet the subjective element of the definition of deprivation of liberty.

decision of the parents to place D at Hospital B was not well within the zone of parental responsibility."[406]

Remember of course that this finding does not make the care he received any less restrictive. It only, by identifying it as a not a deprivation of liberty, allowed the parents' consent to deny the need (or opportunity) for independent scrutiny and safeguards, in this case by the court.

It was, in some ways, a significant clarification, if not a development of the law. In 2011 the Court of appeal had held that it was well established that

"...that an adult in the exercise of parental responsibility may impose, or may authorise others to impose, restrictions on the liberty of the child. However restrictions so imposed must not in their totality amount to deprivation of liberty. Deprivation of liberty engages the Article 5 rights of the child and a parent may not lawfully detain or authorise the deprivation of liberty of a child"[407]

So Keehan J's judgment was not without controversy itself – branded by some a "baby Bournewood", leaving those under 16 without safeguards, if parental consent were ever given in circumstances which were less benign. And of course, the logic – that those with D's welfare at heart should be allowed to make decisions about his care without excessive intrusion of the state – played out in other cases, not least in *Cheshire West* itself and in the *Rochdale* saga[408]. If that's right, why should it only apply to children?

Keehan J did not restrict himself explicitly to children under 16, as D was at the time, and it was not obvious whether Keehan would take a different approach to children over 16.

---

406 Para 58-64.

407 *RK v BCC* [2011] EWCA 1305

408 See chapter 6.

But as it happens, D himself turned 16 years old just 24 days after that first judgment was handed down, and his case duly came back to Mr Justice Keehan to wrestle with again, in November 2015[409].

In the meantime, D had moved to another placement, with court approval. His new arrangements were that he received 1:1 support throughout the day and night. He was not allowed access to the community unaccompanied. The external doors were locked, and he would need to ask a member of staff to unlock a door to get access to the garden.

Again, the question was not whether this amounts to an objective deprivation of liberty per the *Cheshire West* acid test as modified for children – it plainly did – but whether parental consent could continue to negate what would otherwise have been a deprivation of liberty, now that D was over 16 years old.

The local authority argued strongly that the resource implications for local authorities nationally ought to weigh against a finding that parental consent did not suffice, which would mean that all such cases for 16-17 year-olds had to be brought to court (since DoLS could not be used til 18 years old).

The local authority argued that Keehan J himself had been right to rely on parental consent to negate the existence of a deprivation of liberty, and that he should do so again now D was over 16 in a residential placement. The Official Solicitor, on behalf of D, argued (more courageously) that the judge had been wrong in the previous decision to rely on parental consent at all, and that parents could not consent to a deprivation of liberty of a child of any age.

The judge found a middle way, with (at least) 3 huge implications.

Predictably, Keehan J stood by his decision that parental consent meant it was not a deprivation of liberty when D had been in hospital; but that

[409] *Birmingham City Council v D* [2016] EWCOP 8, judgment given on 21 January 2016.

was when D was 15 years old and – regardless of their lack of capacity – *things change when a young person turns 16*.

The law recognises this in all kinds of ways, he said, not least inclusion of 16 and 17 year-olds in the Mental Capacity Act. *It is not enough to rely on parental consent where a 16 -17 year-old is under continuous supervision and control and not free to leave*.

Pending any reform of DoLS then[410], such a case will therefore always need an application to the Court of Protection for authorisation[411]. This has been enormously significant for providers of residential and other care to young people, including in special schools.

Secondly, in getting to this conclusion, the judge roundly rejected an argument by the local authority that the resource implications made such an outcome unthinkable. That may be so, he said, but (in a passage likely to be quoted loudly and often):-

> *"The issue of the resource implications is a matter for the local authority and, ultimately, the Government; it is not, should not and, in my judgment, cannot be a relevant consideration for this court. The protection of the human rights of those with disabilities or the vulnerable members of our society, most especially in respect of the protection afforded by Article 5 (1), is too important and fundamental to be sacrificed on the altar of resources".*[412]

Finally, he also made a crucial point about imputability to the state, which better falls into the next chapter.

For now, the question of the role of parental consent as negating a deprivation of liberty for 16 and 17 year-olds went on to the Court of Appeal, and then to the Supreme Court.

---

410 As LPS would have done, dropping the age for eligibility from 18 to 16.

411 And, inevitably, annual review by the court, at least until P is 18 and he falls within the scope of DoLS, if it is a registered setting.

412 Para 137-138.

In an echo of the *Cheshire West* case itself, when *Re D* reached the Court of Appeal[413], Lord Justice Munby pushed back on this apparent expansion in the law.

Munby LJ, giving the leading judgment[414], held that where a child of 16-17 cannot make the relevant decisions for themselves, the consent of someone with parental responsibility <u>is</u> sufficient to mean there is no deprivation of liberty that needs authorisation.

Although his exhaustive review of the case law relating to parental responsibility went back to the 1840s, LJ Munby's decision is built on two key cases – the European Court of Human Rights ('ECtHR') judgment in *Nielsen* (from 1988), and the House of Lords judgment of *Gillick* (from 1986). I've already mentioned that *Nielsen* is widely regarded as – to use a technical term – a bit iffy.

Gillick[415] involved a doomed attempt by a mother to establish that a doctor could not provide advice about contraception to her daughters, being under 16, on the basis that they could not consent in law[416]. Instead, the case established that, even under 16, a child may be able to consent to treatment if she has sufficient understanding and maturity. The court rejected a clear bright line at the age of 16 exactly, in favour of a more nuanced approach based on the individual child. The corollary of this, Munby LJ said, is that Keehan J was wrong to say that parents' consent <u>can</u> negate a deprivation of liberty until the age of 16, but <u>cannot</u> after that, simply by virtue of their age. The various bits of legislation referred to by Keehan J which treat 16 year-olds as different were all irrelevant, he said.

> *"In my judgment, in the context with which we are here concerned … parental responsibility is, in principle, exercisable in relation to a 16-*

---

[413] D (a Child) [2017] EWCA Civ 1695, handed down on 1 November 2017.

[414] The other two judges briefly agreed.

[415] [1986] 1 AC 112

[416] See A Practical Guide to the Law of Medical Treatment, chapter 6.

> *or 17-year-old child who, for whatever reason, lacks 'Gillick capacity'.*"[417]

As I understand it, Munby LJ's point is that *Gillick*, essentially, cuts both ways. If we allow that children under 16 may have capacity for certain decisions, depending on their understanding and maturity, then turning 16 should not necessarily preclude use of parental responsibility for decisions where the child does not have *Gillick* competence.

The concept of '*Gillick* competence' is usually only used for under 16s, since the Mental Capacity Act 2005, from the age of 16, prescribes a detailed legislative framework for assessing capacity for particular decisions, and the process of best interests decision making in the event that someone lacks capacity.

In saying that parental responsibility can be exercised to effectively consent to what would otherwise be a deprivation of liberty, how was this supposed to work with the MCA? Even if, presumably, the exercise of parental responsibility is fettered by a requirement that it is in good faith, or even 'reasonable', it is fundamentally deferential to the parents' view of what is best for the child, and far removed from MCA best interests decision making, with its emphasis (ever greater in the recent case law) on P's own wishes, values and beliefs, whether 16 or 61 years old.

Remarkably, over the 160 paragraphs of Munby LJ's judgment there were only 8 mentions of the MCA, every one of which was only in relation to the thinking of Keehan J in the court below.

Predictably, the case was promptly described as '*teen Bournewood*', laden with deference to mum and dad as knowing best and reliably acting in good faith beyond the need for scrutiny. Mum and Dad know best, as much as doctor does?

Inevitably, the case was appealed to the Supreme Court by the lawyers acting for D.

---

[417] Para 128.

***

Though the case was heard in the Supreme Court in early October 2018, the judgment was not handed down until nearly a year later, at the end of September 2019[418].

The 5 judges in the Supreme Court split 3:2, and by a majority overturned the Court of Appeal judgment, reinstating Mr Justice Keehan's view that when a child reaches the age of 16 it is no longer OK to rely on the consent of a parent to negate what would otherwise amount to a deprivation of that child's liberty.

In another echo of *Cheshire West,* Lady Hale again gave the leading judgment, overruling (again) the narrower interpretation of deprivation of liberty adopted by the Court of Appeal judgment led by Lord Justice Munby.

She captured the question like this:

> *"is it within the scope of parental responsibility to consent to living arrangements for a 16 or 17-year-old child which would otherwise amount to a deprivation of liberty within the meaning of article 5?"*[419]

Lady Hale felt that "quite clearly" the restrictions experienced by D were <u>not</u> normal for a 16-17 year-old, absent his disabilities. And his disabilities should not deny him the same protection of his human rights as enjoyed by any other person, in line with the fundamental principle in *Cheshire West.*

---

[418] [2019] UKSC 42

[419] I don't know if it is reading too much into it to note that the two male judges of the Supreme Court hearing the case thought that the answer was "yes", while the three female judges of the Supreme Court, including Lady Hale, thought that the answer was "no". And though it is commonplace of course for the justices of the Supreme Court to hear all kinds of cases, the female majority also included, by the way, the only two of the panel who were family lawyers by background, Lady Hale herself and Lady Black.

And it is not enough simply to rely on parental good faith without safeguards:

> *" [it is]... not within the scope of parental responsibility for D's parents to consent to a placement which deprived him of his liberty. Although there is no doubt that they, and indeed everyone else involved, had D's best interests at heart, we cannot ignore the possibility, nay even the probability, that this will not always be the case. That is why there are safeguards required by article 5. Without such safeguards, there is no way of ensuring that those with parental responsibility exercise it in the best interests of the child... ".*[420]

The point of the safeguards required by Article 5 is precisely that the road paved with good intentions can lead to well-meaning but misguided, over-reaching potential breaches of human rights.

Where the arrangements do amount to the objective element of a deprivation of liberty because they go beyond the "normal parental control" for a child of that age, regardless of disability, and the child cannot consent, then parental consent is not enough to disengage the safeguards of Article 5. Note that because D was 16, on the facts of the case as they were before the Supreme Court, this is interpreted as limited to 16 -17 year-olds, and does not overturn Keehan J's earlier judgment that parental consent can negate a deprivation of liberty under 16 years.

But, Lady Hale said[421]:

> *"Logically, this conclusion would also apply to a younger child whose liberty was restricted to an extent that was not normal for a child of his age, but that question does not arise in this case".*[422]

---

[420] Para 49.

[421] So these comments are what the lawyers who still use Latin would call "obiter" – they are, strictly, just non-binding judicial opinion as they relate to issues which were not directly in question before the court in that case. But they can still be very interesting, and might hint the way the judicial wind is blowing.

[422] Para 50.

And Lady Black noted, similarly, only that:

> *"the position in relation to the confinement of children under the age of 16 might be different for a variety of reasons".*[423]

"*Might be*"…?!

But it was not actually decided in this case.

For the reasons given by Keehan J in his second judgment, there is a principled approach to finding that turning 16 years old does make a difference, and because that was not directly addressed by the Supreme Court, it remains the case that, for a child under 16, a parent's consent can negate what would otherwise be a deprivation of liberty.

This was confirmed in the case of *Lincolnshire County Council v TGA*[424], though Lieven J framed her view in terms that a parent can lawfully deprive a child under 16 of their liberty[425] where there is no dispute that it is in their best interests and where it was clear that the child lacked *Gillick* competence.

Two things:

It is essential, of course, that the parents' decision is in the child's best interests[426]. But it is also important to consider whether this is a decision that the parents can make, not just is it a "good" decision. This is sometimes put in terms of the zone of parental responsibility, but this is not yet well defined. For now, perhaps, remember that this might not only be about the parents doing the right thing, but whether it is within the parents' scope to make this particular decision.

---

423 Para 89.

424 [2022] EWHC 2323 (Fam).

425 As opposed to the parent's consent meaning that is it no deprivation of liberty at all.

426 That is what parental responsibility is for, and it is not to be abused as parental power to make any decision you like.

Second, the caveat that parental consent to negate a deprivation of liberty can only be given for a child under 16 who lacks *Gillick* competence was not explicitly part of Keehan's judgment, but all the reported cases to date have dealt with children who lack competence / capacity. In practice, we would expect to be very wary of reliance on parental consent alone for this with a child who is considered able to make the relevant decisions for themselves.

***

Even if LPS were introduced, this would still be an issue.

LPS would apply from the age of 16, so an application to court wouldn't be needed for every 16-17 year-old who is deprived of their liberty. But at 16-17, the parents' agreement to the restrictions does not stop it being a deprivation of liberty that needs authorisation.

And, reflecting on the logic of the Supreme Court's majority decision in *Re D*, it would be no great surprise if, in a future case involving a child under 16, the Supreme Court were to find that reliance on parental consent alone to negate a deprivation of liberty is insufficient to protect the rights of younger children as well. Then, without further reform, all cases involving deprivation of liberty for children under 16 would need to go to court, as 16-17 year-olds do now.

***

Care Proceedings

As if this were not already a minefield, a further complicating factor is the possibility of care proceedings, in which a local authority also assumes parental responsibility towards a child.

In *A local Authority v AB*[427], in July 2015, Mr Justice Keehan (again) considered the case of a 14 year-old with a moderate / severe learning

[427] [2015] EWHC 3125 (Fam)

disability and attention deficit hyperactivity disorder. He was under an interim care order, and was placed by the local authority at a children's home in circumstances that would meet the objective element of a deprivation of his liberty, with his parents' consent[428]. In this case, can parental consent, or the local authority's consent, mean that there is no deprivation of liberty?

Keehan J held that where there is an interim care order or a care order, it would not be acceptable to rely on the "consent" of the local authority (acting in its role as parent) to negate what would otherwise be a deprivation of liberty. That would just be marking its own homework. And it is not appropriate to rely on the (natural) parent's agreement to the local authority making such a placement either in those circumstances, as the exercise of parental responsibility will have been "seriously called into question".

In one way or another, then, pending significant reforms, cases in which a 16–17 year-old, or any younger child who is in the care of the local authority will need court approval for any objective deprivation of liberty, as there is no way to negate it by "consent".

We will return to the special case of how to go about seeking authorisation for any deprivation of a child's liberty in chapter 14.

Key Points

- Obviously, as a child grows up it is less likely that she would be under continuous supervision and control and not free to leave, and so it becomes more likely that such a situation would be regarded in law as an objective deprivation of her liberty.

- If the arrangements are typical for a child of that age, regardless of disability, then there is no deprivation of liberty per Article 5,

[428] under s20 of the Children Act 1989.

even if the child is under continuous supervision and control and not free to leave (as very young children should be).

- Lady Hale in Re D said that the crux is whether the restrictions "fall within normal parental control for a child of this age"?
- Even if they are not typical of arrangements for a child of that age and would be regarded as confinement, applying the *Cheshire West* acid test as modified for children, this is not a deprivation of liberty if there is consent from someone with parental responsibility if the child is under 16 (ie the objective limb of *Storck* may be met, but the subjective is not)…
- …Unless there is a care order in place, in which case a parent's consent does not suffice, and neither does the local authority's, OR
- If the child is over 16, then parental consent cannot authorise what would otherwise be a deprivation of liberty.
- Where parental consent is relied on to negate what would otherwise be a deprivation of liberty, this must be within the zone of parental responsibility, and exercised in the child's best interests.
- Where there is a deprivation of liberty – objective confinement, lack of valid consent and imputable to the state – it must be authorised to meet the child's Article 5 rights.
- How that is done is covered in chapter 14.

Simples, no?!

Few other areas show the desperate need for reform as clearly as the state of the legal framework around children and young people.

CHAPTER ELEVEN

STATE IMPUTABILITY

As you'll recall, to trigger the protection of Article 5, a person must be[429]:

a) Confined in a particular space for a non-negligible period of time (the objective bit – definitively interpreted (so far) in *Cheshire West* as the "acid test" ie being under continuous supervision and control and not free to leave[430]); <u>and</u>

b) There must be no valid consent (ie in health and social care context, the person typically lacks capacity to consent[431]); <u>and</u>

c) It must be imputable to the state.

We have not said much yet about that third part, state imputability, and we can probably be fairly brief about it now simply because it is rarely in dispute in the case law; and to be honest, I am yet to see a case in which what would otherwise be a deprivation of liberty in a health and social care context is not imputable to the state.

As I mentioned in the last chapter, in finding that after the age of 16 parents can no longer consent to avoid a situation becoming a deprivation of liberty[432], Keehan J also made an important point about imputability.

D's placement had been made under Children Act 1989 s20, with the consent of the parents, and at any stage they could object and remove him, and so, the local authority argued, *it was really the parents, rather than the state*, that was responsible for this. If the parents' consent was

[429] *Storck* [2005] ECHR 406, see chapter 4.

[430] See chapters 4-8

[431] See chapter 9-10

[432] *Birmingham City Council v D* [2016] EWCOP 8.

not enough to stop it triggering article 5 directly, could it do so indirectly by stopping it being imputable to the state?

The judge rejected this, not only on the facts (the placement was identified, arranged, commissioned and supervised by the local authority, and so "*In no sense at all could this set of circumstances be considered a purely private arrangement with no state involvement*"[433]), but also on principle. And when *Re D* reached the Supreme Court, Lady Hale agreed:

> *"Not only was the State actively involved in making and funding the arrangements, it had assumed statutory responsibilities – albeit not parental responsibility – towards D by accommodating him under section 20 of the Children Act 1989, thereby making him a "looked after child". Even without all this, it is clear that the first sentence of article 5 imposes a positive obligation on the State to protect a person from interferences with liberty carried out by private persons, at least if it knew or ought to have known of this."*[434]

There is, however, a strand of case law to the contrary, especially in cases in the context of a family home where judges were inclined to say that there was no deprivation of liberty. In *A and C* in 2010[435], dealing with two individuals locked in their bedrooms for their own safety by their families, as well as holding that they were not objectively deprived of their liberty, Munby J also held that the local authority's mere knowledge of what was going on in the family home was not enough to make the state responsible for this regime.

However, he also said that where the local authority thinks that a deprivation of liberty might be occurring in a private household, it had obligations to:

---

433 Para 132.

434 [2019] UKSC 42, at para 43.

435 See chapter 6.

- Investigate (and continue to monitor) whether there is a deprivation of liberty;
- Take steps to intervene to bring any deprivation to an end – perhaps by providing additional support and resources; and
- If not resolved, to bring the case to court.

Similarly, in Mrs L's case[436], Mr Justice Bodey held that care arrangements that locked Mrs L in her home was not an objective deprivation of liberty and in any case were not imputable to the state due to the "strong role" played by the family in making the arrangements, which "diluted" the responsibility of the state.

On the other hand, while Parker J in *MiG and MeG* had held that neither were objectively deprived of their liberty, she did find that the foster mother looking after MiG was "undoubtedly the local authority's agent".[437]

The law has been settled though by a Court of Appeal judgment squarely on the point in 2016, *Staffordshire County Council v SRK*[438].

In his late 30s at the time of the judgment, SRK had suffered multiple injuries, including brain injury, after a road traffic accident in 2005, and lost the capacity to make decisions about his care and residence.

SRK received a substantial award compensation to settle the claim arising from his accident, which funded adaptation of a property to meet his needs and for a 24-hour care package for the rest of his life.

SRK's accommodation and care package was arranged and provided without any input from the local authority, Staffordshire County Council, or any other public body. The care was supervised by a private

---

436 See chapter 6.

437 [2010] EWHC 785 (Fam), at para 196. See chapter 4.

438 [2016] EWCOP 27

specialist brain injury case manager and was provided by private carers, all funded from his compensation.

The council knew nothing of SRK, and was unaware of his private care arrangements, until it received a letter from the deputy, who had been appointed by the court to manage SRK's finances, which informed the council that the arrangements for SRK's accommodation and care at the property may amount to a deprivation of his liberty[439]. The council agreed that the situation could meet the *Cheshire West* test, and that he lacked the capacity to consent to it himself due to his brain injury. While it was clearly put in place in SRK's best interests, the local authority argued that it was not imputable to the state, in these circumstances, to trigger the protection of Article 5 and need court authorisation.

Mr Justice Charles held that while the arrangements for SRK's care and accommodation were made entirely privately, nonetheless it was attributable to the state because it knew or ought to have known about it. There had been court approval of the damages award (as there must be where a claimant lacks capacity to make a decision about settlement for himself); a court had appointed the deputy, who is overseen by the Office of the Public Guardian.

The state not only has a "negative" obligation not to unlawfully deprive individuals of their liberty itself; it also has a positive obligation to take reasonable steps to protect people from others doing so.

On an appeal by the Secretary of State, the Court of Appeal[440] agreed with Charles J. It was not enough to rely, as the Secretary of State argued, on the role of the Care Quality Commission, as the regulator of the registered care professionals. The CQC does not go into private family homes to inspect the care given to individual patients and service users,

[439] In the largest compensation claims, the lawyers acting for the claimant will often argue that the care package needed, such as round the clock care in adapted accommodation, will amount to a deprivation of liberty and will therefore need court approval, which means that the costs of making such an application to court (and its annual renewals for the rest of P's life) are added to the value of the damages claimed.

[440] [2016] EWCA Civ 1317

and in any case its role is not focused on the prevention of arbitrary detention, which is the purpose of Article 5. The court also referred to the safeguarding role that rests on the local authority.

And it was not enough to rely on the possibility that criminal law provisions that might apply, after the event, if SRK's welfare was not being protected appropriately[441].

In the absence of Court of Protection proceedings to oversee the deprivation of SRK's liberty, there is no provision for a regular assessment and review to meet his Article 5 rights.

Obviously, the question of imputability to the state comes up most in the family home, and where care arrangements are made or implemented without the involvement of public bodies. So, as we saw in Chapter 6, in the case of *A and C* in 2010, so before the *Cheshire West* judgment, Mr Justice Munby, before his elevation to the court of appeal, considered the role of the state in relation to care arrangements made in the family home by the families themselves, but *SRK* has made the law clear.

In *AEL*[442] in 2021, a case of care being provided in the family home, led by the patient's father, there was no question that it failed to trigger Article 5 for lack of being imputable to the state.

In the health and social care context, the NHS or local authority (obviously organs of the state) are often involved in either commissioning or provision of the care involved. And as we have seen, even in cases that are wholly privately funded, professional provision of care will be delivered by an organisation registered with the CQC as the regulator (another organ of the state). Often "private" care packages, where they amount to continuous supervision and control, may well be the result of large awards of compensation ordered or approved by the court (an organ of the state).

---

441 See chapter 15.

442 [2021] EWCOP 9 – see chapter 6.

Compensation aside, often people who are paying for their own care, rather than being commissioned by the NHS or local authority, may feel that they are neglected by our system. In fact, the DoLS Code of Practice only makes a single passing mention of self-funders[443] and it is clear that DoLS applies whether the care is provided / commissioned by the state or not.[444]

Even if care were paid for and provided wholly privately, in a family home, the local authority would still have a safeguarding duty towards any individual. And any application to the court would, by definition, bring the case to the attention of an organ of the state.

It *might* be possible to come up with a scenario of a health and social care case in which court might find the *Cheshire West* acid test is met but the situation is not imputable to the state, but I haven't seen an example yet.

Key Points

- A situation is imputable to the state not only if the care is provided or commissioned by a public body, but also if the state knew or ought to have known about the potential deprivation of liberty.

- It is overwhelmingly likely that a situation in health and social care will be attributable to the state, whether by provision / commissioning through the NHS or local authority, a private care provider being regulated by the state, the involvement of the court, or the local authority's safeguarding duties.

So, this is the final bit of the definition of deprivation of liberty, along with the objective element (the *Cheshire West* "acid test") and the lack of

443 Para 5.23, saying that this presents a particular problem when a DoLS authorisation is rejected, because other arrangements for the person's care might not be made without discussion with those controlling P's funds.

444 MCA s64(6).

valid consent. Now we know what a deprivation of liberty is, what do we do about it if we think there might be one?

PART THREE

WHAT DO WE DO ABOUT IT?

CHAPTER TWELVE

THE SAFEGUARDS: DOLS

Now we have got as far as we can, perhaps, with what a deprivation of liberty is, and how we could identify that someone might be deprived of their liberty, *now what*, and *so what*? What safeguards does this actually bring?

Let's start with the Deprivation of Liberty Safeguards (DoLS) system in care homes and hospitals here, and then turn to the situation outside those settings in chapter 14. (Chapter 13 tackles the interface between DoLS and the Mental Health Act).

For someone over 18 years, when a care home or hospital[445] (a "managing authority") thinks that there might be a deprivation of liberty, it must make a referral to the relevant local authority[446] (the "supervisory body") for a DoLS authorisation.

The Managing Authorities

DoLS can be used where the individual is a *detained resident*[447] in a care home or a hospital.

[445] Remember we are only talking about hospital inpatients, not those in the Emergency Department – see chapters 7, 8 and 14.

[446] In Wales, DoLS cases in hospitals are referred to the Local Health Board as the supervisory body, but otherwise the supervisory body is the relevant local authority, see below.

[447] Schedule A1 para 6: "Detained resident" means a person detained in a hospital or care home — for the purpose of being given care or treatment — in circumstances which amount to deprivation of the person's liberty.

Care home is defined by s3 of the Care Standards Act 2000:

> *(1) For the purposes of this Act, an establishment is a care home if it provides accommodation, together with nursing or personal care, for any of the following persons.*
>
> *(2) They are—*
>
> > *(a) persons who are or have been ill;*
> >
> > *(b) persons who have or have had a mental disorder;*
> >
> > *(c) persons who are disabled or infirm;*
> >
> > *(d) persons who are or have been dependent on alcohol or drugs.*

"Hospital" is helpfully defined in MCA Schedule A1 para 175 as

> *(a) an NHS hospital, or*
>
> *(b) an independent hospital.*

And in turn,

> *(2) "NHS hospital " means—*
>
> > *(a) a health service hospital as defined by section 275 of the National Health Service Act 2006 or section 206 of the National Health Service (Wales) Act 2006, or*
> >
> > *(b) a hospital as defined by section 206 of the National Health Service (Wales) Act 2006 vested in a Local Health Board.*
>
> *(3) Independent hospital"—*
>
> > *(a) in relation to England, means a hospital as defined by section 275 of the National Health Service Act 2006 that is not an NHS hospital; and*

> (b) *in relation to Wales, means a hospital as defined by section 2 of the Care Standards Act 2000 that is not an NHS hospital.*

And note that the need to be a *detained resident* means that they have to have been admitted to hospital – DoLS cannot be used for patients just attending the Emergency Department, for instance, which can cause problems.

Urgent Authorisations

If the deprivation of liberty is already happening, or the urgency of the person's needs are such that the interventions that may amount to a deprivation of liberty cannot wait for a "standard authorisation" to be done, then the managing authority can grant itself an "urgent authorisation", which is valid for up to 7 days. In "exceptional circumstances", says the Code of Practice[448], the urgent authorisation can be extended by the supervisory body for up to 14 days.

The thinking is clearly that the period of the urgent authorisation should allow time for the process of granting a standard authorisation to be completed, so there should be no gap in the legal framework used to authorise a deprivation of liberty.

Where an urgent authorisation is in place, the standard authorisation process must be completed before the urgent authorisation lapses[449]. Otherwise, if there is no urgent authorisation in place, the supervisory body has 21 days from receipt of the application. How far that is from the reality at the moment, we will see in chapter 16.

---

448 The DoLS Code of Practice from 2008, like the MCA Code of Practice from 2007, is painfully out of date, but sadly, unlike the MCA code, is unlikely to be updated anytime soon, given the debacle over the LPS.

449 Mental Capacity Act (deprivation of liberty, standard authorisation assessments and ordinary residence) Regulations 2008, regulation 13.

For now, note that the urgent authorisation process is largely within the gift of the care home or hospital itself. All it needs is that the managing authority has a reasonable belief that the criteria for a standard DoLS authorisation are met.

Remember that even if an urgent (or standard) DoLS authorisation is in place, this only addresses the deprivation of liberty itself; the underlying issues of the care and treatment that are in the person's best interests must still be determined through the Mental Capacity Act. A DoLS authorisation is not a blank cheque to impose care or treatment.

An urgent authorisation is made by completion of a DoLS form 1[450], and the managing authority must make an application for a standard authorisation at the same time: an urgent authorisation cannot stand alone. And subject to the single extension permitted to a total of 14 days, it cannot be used again. If the standard authorisation is not completed and granted before the urgent authorisation ends, another urgent authorisation cannot be given.

It is up to the care home or hospital who may issue an urgent authorisation, though the code of practice says only that it should be done "at a senior level"[451].

The urgent authorisation can end:

- When the standard authorisation application is determined, whether granted or refused;
- When the urgent authorisation lapses after 7 (or 14) days;
- By an order of the Court of Protection;

[450] Note that the DoLS forms are not statutory, and so they have been adapted by some local authorities, though there is a standard resource of forms here, developed by ADASS. https://www.gov.uk/government/publications/deprivation-of-liberty-safeguards-forms-and-guidance

[451] Para 6.13.

- Or if one of the essential criteria changes, for example if P has regained capacity to make the relevant decisions.

As the safeguards for P under an urgent authorisation are all replicated (and extended) in the standard authorisation process, I will deal with them together below.

Safeguards under DoLS

The key safeguards of DoLS standard authorisations are:

- A due process of scrutiny, by qualified professionals, to assess and determine whether:

    1. Someone lacks capacity to make the relevant decisions (whether to be accommodated for care and treatment);
    2. They have a mental disorder;
    3. They are / will be deprived of their liberty, and that the deprivation of their liberty is in their best interests, taking into account their wishes and feelings;
    4. They are over 18;
    5. They are not ineligible by operation of the MHA; and
    6. There are no valid objections.

These comprise the six assessments for DoLS, reflecting the six qualifying requirements.

In addition:

- The referral should be made before the deprivation of liberty starts, where possible;
- An independent representative;

- A right to review;
- Any authorisation is time limited, and must be subject to renewal if the deprivation of liberty continues; and
- Conditions can be attached to the authorisation.

And, for both urgent and standard authorisations:

- A right to advocacy and representation throughout;
- Notifications to the CQC (or the Care Inspectorate Wales) for independent monitoring; and
- A right to challenge their DoLS authorisation in court under MCA s21A, which attracts non-means tested legal aid.

Let's have a look at each of these in turn.

DoLS assessments and assessors

There must be at least two professionals involved in carrying out the 6 assessments required for a DoLS authorisation.

- The "mental health assessor" must be a doctor, either approved under s12 MHA[452] or with three years' experience of diagnosis and treatment of mental disorder.
- The "best interests assessor" (BIA) must be a health and social care professional – often a social worker, but they can be a nurse, an occupational therapist, or psychologist. They must also have

[452] MHA provides for detention for assessment or treatment of mental disorder on the basis of two medical recommendations, and s12 requires that "one shall be given by a practitioner approved for the purposes of this section by the Secretary of State as having special experience in the diagnosis or treatment of mental disorder".

undertaken an approved BIA qualification and further relevant training within the previous 12 months.

It is, broadly, the responsibility of the local authority to source the relevant assessors. Detailed requirements for the assessors are set out in Regulations[453]. The local authority must be satisfied that they are insured for any liabilities incurred through carrying out their functions; that they have appropriate skills, experience and up to date training; and have a DBS[454] check.

While the legislation is not prescriptive, there is recent guidance from the Chief Social Worker[455] that "*most deprivation of liberty assessments should be face to face*", suggesting that there may be some circumstances where it is acceptable for them to be done remotely.

The CQC State of Care Report 2022/23, published 20 October 2023[456] was also quite sniffy about the use of remote assessments:

> *"Frequently used during the pandemic, we found that a remote assessment may not always provide enough detail to assess the care environment. A member of our Expert Advisory Group questioned the suitability of this type of assessment, especially for people who have conditions such as advanced dementia, which may affect communication".*

[453] The Mental Capacity (Deprivation of Liberty: Standard Authorisations, Assessments and Ordinary Residence) Regulations 2008.

[454] Disclosure and Barring Service.

[455] https://www.gov.uk/government/publications/proportional-assessment-approaches-a-guide-from-the-chief-social-worker-and-principal-social-workers/proportional-assessment-approaches-a-guide-from-the-chief-social-worker-and-principal-social-workers#mental-capacity-and-deprivation-of-liberty
7 September 2023.

[456] https://www.cqc.org.uk/publications/major-report/state-care/2022-2023/dols

The Six Assessments

Capacity:

This can be carried out either by the BIA or the mental health assessor.

It goes without saying, I hope, that capacity is decision specific – in this case the decision is "*whether or not to be accommodated in the relevant care home or hospital for the purpose of being given the relevant care or treatment*"[457].

Capacity means the ability to understand / retain / weigh up the information relevant to the decision; in chapter 9 we looked at what that relevant information is (with emphasis on the need to consider the *confinement* as well as the care and accommodation more generally[458]), and chapter 1 sets out some of the key points and pitfalls of assessing capacity.

Unless P lacks capacity for this decision, there is no scope for the MCA to allow best interests decision-making, whether in the Court of Protection or using DoLS.

Mental health:

The mental health assessment can only be done by the mental health assessor. The purpose is to establish that there is a "*mental disorder*", the definition of which is tied to the Mental Health Act: "*any disorder or disability of the mind*". This, of course, allows any deprivation of the person's liberty to come within Article 5(1)(e) covering persons of "*unsound mind*", as we have seen.

The MHA code of practice (para 2.5) sets out a non-exhaustive list of conditions as examples:

---

457 Schedule A1 paragraph 15.

458 See LDV, in chapter 9.

- Affective disorders, such as depression and bipolar disorder;
- Schizophrenia and delusional disorders;
- Neurotic, stress-related and somatoform disorders, such as anxiety, phobic disorders, obsessive compulsive disorders, post-traumatic stress disorder and hypochondriacal disorders;
- Organic mental health disorders, such as dementia and delirium;
- Personality and behavioural changes caused by brain injury or damage;
- Personality disorders;
- Mental and behavioural disorders caused by psychoactive substance use;
- Eating disorders, non-organic sleep disorders and non-organic sexual disorders;
- Learning disabilities (the extra criteria that a learning disability must be associated with abnormally aggressive or seriously irresponsible conduct before it can be the basis for detention under some parts of the MHA does not apply here);
- Autistic spectrum disorder (including Asperger's syndrome); and
- Behavioural and emotional disorders of children and young people[459].

Wide as this is, it is narrower than the MCA definition that there must be "*an impairment, or disturbance in the functioning of, the mind or brain*"[460], which can also include, for example, intoxication, or someone

[459] Though of course DoLS only applies over the age of 18.

[460] MCA s2(1).

sedated into unconsciousness[461]. There are, therefore, some people who could be subject to best interests decisions under the MCA, but outside the scope of DoLS for failing to meet the mental health requirement.

In reality, though, the great majority of people subject to a DoLS authorisation are elderly people with dementia, followed by younger people with a learning disability[462].

The mental health assessor must confirm that they reasonably believe that the person has a mental disorder. A rationale must be given, but there is no need for a specific diagnosis.

Ineligibility:

The mental health assessor must also carry out the eligibility assessment, to confirm that DoLS can be used, rather than P being ineligible because of the Mental Health Act is being, or should be, used instead, picking their way through the legal minefield described in chapter 13.

Age:

DoLS can only be used for people over 18 years, and so there is an assessment to be done, by the BIA, to confirm P's age. This is rarely controversial.

No refusals:

The no refusals assessment, as the name suggests, is to check that there is no formal barrier to the use of DoLS, which could be:

- An advance decision to refuse treatment (ADRT);
- A Lasting Power of Attorney (LPA) for personal welfare; or
- A deputy for personal welfare.

---

[461] See chapter 7.

[462] See chapter 16.

The no refusals assessment can only be carried out by the BIA.

Though the Schedule uses the term "*advance decision*", it refers directly to MCA s24 which specifies that this means an advance decision to refuse treatment (ADRT), not just any generic expression of wishes. If there is a valid ADRT that refuses the treatment proposed[463], and the purpose of the DoLS authorisation was at least partly to enable that treatment, then the DoLS cannot be given for the purpose of that treatment[464].

Likewise, if there is an LPA or a deputy for personal welfare who has made a valid decision that would conflict with the proposed DoLS authorisation, then DoLS cannot be used in a way that would effectively overrule them.

Note, though, that no attorney or deputy has the power to authorise a deprivation of liberty. They may be able to make decisions about where and how P lives, but if it amounts to a deprivation of liberty then the attorney or deputy's say so does not make that lawful; P's Article 5 rights still demand that it be authorised, whether by DoLS or by the court.

If an attorney or deputy refuse the proposed care or treatment in a way that prevents a DoLS authorisation, the supervisory body can and should challenge this in the Court of Protection if it felt that this was not in P's best interests.

Best interests assessment:

Lastly, this is the heart and soul of the DoLS process, and the most detailed of the assessments[465].

---

463 See MCA s24-26, and "*A Practical Guide to the Law of Medical Treatment*" for more detail.

464 It may still be possible to authorise a deprivation of liberty using DoLS where it is justified for other reasons than for the particular treatment that has been validly refused.

465 See chapter 3 for an example of it not going well.

It can only, naturally, be done by the best interests assessor (BIA)[466].

The BIA must establish that:

- P is (or will soon be) deprived of their liberty in the care home or hospital;
- It is in their best interests to be deprived of their liberty there; and
- It is necessary and proportionate to be deprived of their liberty in order to prevent harm.

Self evidently, then, and without repeating all the previous content, the BIA must have a good understanding of the law on what constitutes a deprivation of liberty, especially in the context of a care home or hospital. Documenting their thinking with explicit reference to the case law will make the assessment more robust.

And they must apply the fundamentals of the MCA as regards best interests decision making, and in particular:

- Consult as far a practical and appropriate with others who can inform the best interests decision, for example carers, family and friends, as well as anyone holding an LPA, a deputy or anyone specified by P[467].
- Consult P and encourage them to participate in the process.
- Give appropriate weight to their wishes and feelings, values and beliefs. Though capacity is artificially binary for legal purposes – you either have capacity for a particular decision or you don't –

466 There is lots of useful practical guidance in the excellent "*Best Interests Assessor Practice Handbook*", by Rachel Hubbard and Kevin Stone, Policy Press, 2018.

467 MCA Schedule 1A para 185 provides a list of "interested" people to consult, if possible. The BIA must include on the form the name and address of each person consulted.

in reality it is a spectrum, and the closer P is to having capacity, the greater weight should be given to their views.[468] The consistency and strength of their views may also be relevant.

- Take a holistic view of best interests – there is more to this than the safest choice, or the best outcome in terms of medical or care needs. It should fully consider social and emotional benefits, for example, and the burden on P if their wishes are to be overridden.

- To justify not only a best interests decision that P should reside in that care home or hospital, but to justify their deprivation of liberty there, the BIA should carefully identify the harm[469] that this is intended to avoid, and whether the restrictions imposed are necessary to prevent that harm and proportionate to its likelihood and seriousness.

- Consider whether there is a way to meet P's best interests that is less restrictive of their rights and freedoms.

NB on the law as it stands, all this is relevant to the question of best interests but <u>not</u> to whether or not P is deprived of their liberty.

---

[468] *ITW v Z* [2009] EWHC 2525.

[469] Note that this is harm to P themselves – DoLS does not permit P's deprivation of liberty in order protect others from harm (though this is sometimes stretched a little, eg in cases of P offending where the public is effectively protected by restrictions imposed on P which are then framed in terms of protecting P from the harm of offending, or the risks of facing retaliation. For example, *Y County Council v ZZ* [2012] EWHC B34, and also *DY v A City Council* [2022] EWCOP 51. The Law Commission proposed dealing with this a little more honestly and allowing harm to others as a factor, but this is controversial as it moves away from the roots of the MCA being all about P, and it was not adopted in the proposed LPS system. There are also some cases where the impact on others is considered within the scope of the MCA, for example in making decisions about sex – see JB [2021] UKSC 52 https://www.supremecourt.uk/cases/uksc-2020-0133.html

Conditions

One of the BIA's powers is to recommend conditions to attach to the DoLS standard authorisation, if it is granted, with a view to reducing the restrictions in a care plan[470].

Some examples are given in the DoLS code of practice[471]:

> *"For example, [the BIA] may make recommendations around contact issues, issues relevant to the person's culture or other major issues related to the deprivation of liberty, which – if not dealt with – would mean that the deprivation of liberty would cease to be in the person's best interests. The BIA may also recommend conditions in order to work towards avoiding deprivation of liberty in future. But it is not the BIA's role to specify conditions that do not relate to the deprivation of liberty".*

And:

> *"In recommending conditions, BIAs should aim to impose the minimum necessary constraints so that they do not unnecessarily prevent or inhibit the staff of the hospital or care home from responding appropriately to the person's needs, whether they remain the same or vary over time."*

This is a powerful tool, as any conditions which are applied by the supervisory body are not optional for the provider: "*the relevant hospital or care home must ensure that any conditions are complied with*"[472]. And while the local authority has no power to directly enforce conditions, if they are not met then the DoLS authorisation may not protect the provider from any liabilities.

---

[470] Schedule A1 para 53.

[471] Para 4.74.

[472] Schedule A1 paragraph 53(3).

In a number of cases, failure to comply with conditions had been criticised by the Ombudsman, or explicitly featured prominently in a poor rating by the CQC, and as a breach of their regulations[473].

In practice, we often see conditions used to leverage improvements in a person's care package, such as adding more access to the community or activities, and making a significant difference to the person's quality of life. There may be a question, though, whether someone should be put at an advantage against other residents, perhaps, who might not have the same leverage, where we are dealing with limited resources. In any case, there is no point in proposing "ideal world" conditions if there is little prospect of them being possible, however desirable, and it is prudent to have a sensible discussion with the provider about what is practical.

Duration

Alongside recommendation of conditions, another key influence for the BIA is to recommend the duration of any standard authorisation to be granted. The maximum period is for a year, but this should not be regarded as a default.

The BIA "should set out the reasons for selecting the period stated"[474].

In some cases, this may only be a much shorter period, in which is it expected that things might change, for example alongside a condition that within X weeks or months the case should be referred to the Court of Protection.

Some features, for example the use of covert medication, might demand a more frequent review:

> *"While each case will be fact specific, I would suggest that where the use of covert medication is known at the time of the best interests*

---

[473] Health and Social Care Act 2008 (Regulated Activities) Regulations 2014, regulation 13(5).

[474] DoLS code of practice para 4.71.

> *assessment, it would be inappropriate for the standard authorisation to be for the maximum period without either conditions being attached for review or preferably for there to be a shorter period of authorisation. On the facts of this particular case a six month period would have been more appropriate."*[475]

Prospective authorisation

Crucially, a DoLS authorisation can be granted up to 28 days in advance of an anticipated deprivation of liberty starting, and in *AJ*[476], a case we will come back to throughout this chapter, Mr Justice Baker said:

> *"... in the vast majority of cases, it should be possible to plan in advance so that a standard authorisation can be obtained before the deprivation of liberty begins. It is only in exceptional cases, where the need for the deprivation of liberty is so urgent that it is in the person's best interests for it to begin while the application is being considered, that a standard authorisation need not be sought before the deprivation begins"*[477].

AJ was an 88 year-old lady who was increasingly dependent due to vascular dementia. She moved into an annexe to the home of her niece and her husband, Mr and Mrs C, who had been appointed as her attorneys, both for personal welfare and finances. When the couple went on holiday for two weeks, AJ was placed into a case home against her wishes "for respite", though it was apparent that their intention was for her to stay there longer. A DoLS authorisation was only put in place afterwards.

It is, sadly, fair to say that it is far from exceptional in practice at the moment for the process of referral to DoLS to begin only after someone has been placed into a situation that may amount to a deprivation of their

---

475 *Re AG* [2016] EWCOP 37, per District Judge Bellamy. See chapter 8.

476 [2015] EWCOP 5.

477 This is also, almost word for word, in the introduction to chapter 3 of the DoLS code of practice.

liberty. Asking for forgiveness, not permission. That is especially damaging given the backlogs and delayed timescales for these to be dealt with just now – see chapter 16.

Not only should someone's rights be considered and protected appropriately and promptly, there are real practical consequences from getting this backwards. In many cases, the move into residential care will take a toll on the person involved, especially if they are very frail or upset by the change, and this can itself affect the balance of risk and benefit when it comes to considering their best interests in making another move, for example back to their own home that they never wanted to leave in the first place[478].

If a DoLS authorisation is in place in anticipation of a move, it can be challenged in court ***before*** the move takes place, rather than only once it has already happened.

For AJ, by the time her case eventually got to court the substantive issue of where she should be living was not pursued, given the evidence of the deterioration in her condition and her behaviour since the move to the care home, and the lack of a viable option for domiciliary care. This meant that there was no proper consideration of the alternative options for AJ's care, and nor was she given a chance to have her own views taken into account, before the move to the care home. The judgment focussed instead on the (mis)use of the safeguards that left her in that position.

Advocacy

The Mental Capacity Act created a specialist advocacy role called, unimaginatively, Independent Mental Capacity Advocate, or IMCA. For the purposes of DoLS, this was expanded, with provision that an IMCA must be appointed if:

[478] As happened in *AJ*, cited above.

- There is no friend / family etc appropriate for the BIA to consult for the best interests assessment, as set out above (MCA s39A).

- There are gaps in appointment of a relevant person's representative (RPR – see below) (MCA s39C).

- P, or their RPR (if they are unpaid), requests an IMCA (MCA s39D);

- Broadly, that the local authority has reason to believe that P's rights have not been properly exercised, or are unlikely to be properly exercised, without the support of an IMCA (MCA s39D).

Note that there is still an obligation to appoint an IMCA in these situations, even if there is an LPA for personal welfare.[479]

The role of the IMCA, then, is crucial – not only in ensuring a meaningful consultation as part of the best interests assessment where there are no non-professionals to involve, but also in then making sure that P's rights and procedural safeguards are used effectively.

I am yet to see a case that has not been improved by the involvement of an IMCA; the main concern about them is whether they are appointed as often as they should be, and whether there are enough of them.

It was only when an IMCA became involved that professional support was given to Mark Neary to get Steven home.

Especially if appointed for the broader role under s39D, the role of an IMCA is extensive, explicitly including taking such steps as are practicable to help P understand the relevant legal framework, their rights and how to exercise them, as well as to take reasonable steps to exercise the right to apply to court or for a review.

---

[479] *AJ*, again.

I'll come back to the onus on the IMCA / RPR to do this later, when we get to those processes.

Representative

Everyone under a standard DoLS authorisation must have a relevant person's representative (RPR) appointed. Again, the recommendation of an appropriate RPR falls to the BIA, subject to approval by the supervisory body. It can be a family member or friend, or can be a (paid) professional if there is no one else suitable and available.

The RPR must be over 18 years old, and must be willing to take on the role. A different RPR can be appointed in a successive DoLS authorisation; whether the RPR is appropriate should be considered afresh at each renewal.

The starting point for selection of an RPR should be for the BIA to assess whether P has capacity to make that decision for themselves, and to allow them to do so if they do, though the BIA still has to check that the RPR would meet the criteria.

If P lacks capacity for that decision, then any attorney or deputy in place can select the proposed RPR, including themselves, again subject to meeting the criteria[480].

If there is no attorney or deputy, then the BIA can select a proposed RPR, but should not propose someone who P (or a deputy or attorney) objects to.

---

480 See *London Borough of Hillingdon v JV*, [2019] EWCOP 61, in which it was appropriate for the BIA to exclude JV's son from consideration as a potential RPR due to concerns about his suitability, but because he was also JV's attorney the BIA should have given him the opportunity to nominate someone else before moving on to propose appointment of a paid RPR.

A conflict of interest would prevent someone acting as an RPR, for example having a financial interest in P's care home or hospital, or being employed there, or employed by the supervisory body[481].

The RPR's role is to represent P and to support them in relation to the DoLS authorisation, for example by asking for a review (see below), requesting an advocate, or bringing a challenge to court. As such, it may be risky to appoint someone as an RPR who is so strongly supportive of the placement and care plan that amounts to a deprivation of liberty that it might compromise their ability or appetite to do that role, reflecting P's own wishes.

Appointment as an RPR must not be made unless it appears to the person making the selection that the prospective RPR would, if appointed "*maintain contact with P*", and would "*represent*" and "*support*" them in matters related to the DoLS authorisation[482].

How much contact the RPR must have is not prescribed, and has not yet been tested in court. The Code of Practice says that face to face contact is required,[483] though of course that was stretched during the pandemic. There is an onus on the care home or hospital to allow visits by the RPR and, when reviewing the care plan, to consider whether there is sufficient contact for the RPR to offer effective support.

For the DoLS authorisation under which my mum was placed in a dementia specialist care home, my dad was appointed the RPR. For *AJ* [484], sadly, the RPR appointed to protect her rights was Mr C, her niece's husband, who was clearly disinclined to bring a challenge against his own decision to move AJ out of his own house.

The supervisory body was criticised by the court:

---

481 Mental Capacity Act (Deprivation of Liberty: Appointment of Relevant Person's Representatives) Regulations 2008.

482 Schedule A1 para 140.

483 Para 7.25.

484 [2015] EWCOP 15.

> *"... the local authority ought not to have appointed Mr C as RPR notwithstanding the fact that he was selected by the BIA... [and] ought quickly to have realised (1) that AJ was extremely unhappy in residential care and wished to challenge the authorisations and (2) that Mr C was not taking any or any sufficient steps to represent or support her in pursing that challenge. The local authority should therefore have taken steps to replace Mr C as RPR when it became apparent that he was not intending to issue proceedings promptly and that there was not going to be a speedy review of AJ's detention by the court."*

The RPR's appointment will end when the DoLS authorisation ends, the RPR dies or they tell the supervisory body that they want to end the role, if P or their attorney or deputy now objects to that RPR, or it can be brought to an end by the supervisory body if it feels that the RPR is not fulfilling their responsibilities, for example sufficient contact, or they no longer meet the eligibility criteria.

If there is a gap in the appointment of an RPR, then an IMCA must be appointed in the interim.

Part 8 review

There is no mechanism to review an urgent authorisation, but a standard authorisation can be reviewed by the supervisory body at any time, and it must carry out a review on the request of P, their RPR or the care home or hospital.

The process is set out in part 8 of Schedule A1, so this is referred to as a part 8 review.

When a supervisory body receives a request for a review it "*must first decide which if any of the qualifying requirements need to be reviewed... If the supervisory body concludes that none of the qualifying requirements need to be reviewed no further action is necessary.*"[485]

[485] Code of Practice para 8.9-8.10.

If a review is done, only the original assessment/s that are in question need to be reassessed, not all six.

Of course, if reviewing one or more of the original assessments finds that one or more of the qualifying criteria for a DoLS authorisation are no longer met, then the standard authorisation will end.

There is a useful role for a part 8 review where, for example, circumstances have changed and the restrictions are now more significant that those considered by the BIA, so that it is appropriate to review the best interests assessment[486], but the remainder of the assessments do not need to be repeated.

There is a huge variation in the frequency of reviews around the country, but overall they are relatively rare and, as it is effectively a second opinion from the supervisory body that authorised the deprivation of liberty in the first place, it is not to be seen as a substitute for a challenge against the DoLS authorisation in court.

The function of the signatory / supervisory body

When DoLS was introduced, the relevant local authority was the supervisory body for care home cases, but cases in England's hospitals were dealt with by the relevant NHS Primary Care Trust (PCT). Since then, NHS reforms have not only abolished PCTs, in April 2013, replacing them with Clinical Commissioning Groups, but CCGs themselves ceased to be in July 2022, replaced by Integrated Care Boards. Who knows whether ICBs will still be around by the time you read this!

So, since April 2013 all English DoLS cases, whether care home or hospital set, have been overseen by local authorities, and the NHS part

[486] For example, where additional medication with a restrictive effect or given covertly is introduced after the best interests assessment was done and the DoLS authorisation is granted, as in *Re AG* [2016] EWCOP 37.

of the supervisory body role has ended[487]. In Wales, the supervisory body role is still split between the Local Health Board for hospital cases, and the local authority for care homes.

Which local authority? The one where P is ordinarily resident, ie the one that holds all the other usual duties towards P under the Care Act 2014, which deals with social care provision.

"*Ordinary residence*" is a legal term of art, and can cause confusion enough to warrant another book, but this is not the place to get into it, and it is reasonable to approach it on a common sense basis. It is rare in deprivation of liberty for there to be a genuine dispute over which local authority is the supervisory body.

On receipt of a referral for a DoLS authorisation, the supervisory body must arrange for the six assessments to be carried out appropriately, as above.

If all the assessments are positive, then Schedule A1 paragraph 50 says that the supervisory body "must" give a standard authorisation, though as we saw in the *Neary* case (in chapter 3) this does not excuse the supervisory body from proper consideration of the evidence put before it by the assessors.

> *"The responsibilities of the supervisory body, correctly understood, require it to scrutinise the assessment it receives with independence and a degree of care that is appropriate to the seriousness of the decision and to the circumstances of the individual case … Where, as here, the supervisory body grants authorisations on the basis of perfunctory scrutiny of superficial best interests assessments, it cannot expect the authorisations to be legally valid"*[488].

[487] Though the Liberty Protection Safeguards, if implemented, would have restored it to some extent, with a role for England's NHS hospitals and for ICBs. See chapter 18.

[488] [2011] EWCOP 1377, per Jackson J. See chapter 3.

As such, though the individual "signatory" at the supervisory body is not specified by the legislation, it will typically be a senior and experienced professional. It is a role with considerable responsibility.

Much of what the BIA recommends (the maximum duration, the identity of the RPR and any conditions to be attached for example) is ultimately up to the signatory at the supervisory body to decide. Though the signatory is obliged to scrutinise all the evidence and take an independent view, they would need a fairly high bar to depart significantly from the recommendations of a BIA who will have spent much longer with the case, and actually met the people involved.

The court has made clear that the supervisory body's job is not done once the authorisation is granted. If the RPR / IMCA are not acting appropriately to bring a challenge to the DoLS authorisation to court, then the supervisory body should do so itself[489] – see below.

On the other hand, the onus to request a renewal of a DoLS authorisation as it approaches its expiry falls on the managing authority rather than the supervisory body[490].

Access to information

The managing authority is obliged to inform P of their rights under an urgent or a standard authorisation, both verbally and in writing. It must also take all practicable steps to ensure that P understands their rights.

The information given must include the effect of the authorisation, the right to appeal to the Court of Protection, and (for standard authorisations only) the right to request a part 8 review and the right to an advocate and how to get one appointed.

---

[489] Again, *AJ* cited above.

[490] Schedule A1 para 29.

The RPR must also be told about all these rights in writing[491].

The supervisory body also is obliged[492] to provide a copy of all completed standard authorisations, whether or not the authorisation is granted, as soon as practicable to:

- P
- The RPR,
- The care home or hospital,
- Every interested person who was consulted by the BIA for the best interests assessment, and
- Any s39C IMCA (ie one appointed due to a gap in RPR appointment).

There is also a duty on supervisory bodies to record in writing all standard authorisations granted / not granted, and all requests and decisions about extensions to urgent authorisations.

Monitoring by the regulator

All care homes / hospitals must notify the CQC (in England) or the CIW (in Wales) of all applications made to deprive someone of their liberty, whether under DoLS or by the court[493].

---

[491] Given that deprivation of liberty is – evidently – a complex topic, it is no small challenge to create a written resource that is both accurate but accessible, and it is regrettable that there is no central or standardised resource for this, with each care home / hospital left to create their own. A useful unofficial example is given in the Deprivation of Liberty Safeguards Handbook (second edition), https://www.bookswise.org.uk/deprivation-of-liberty-safeguards-d

[492] Schedule 1A para 57 – 58.

[493] Care Quality Commission (Registration) Regulations 2009: Regulation 18(4).

As the CQC emphasise in their guidance, the duty is as regards the outcome of any application, so only arises once the outcome is known. The current very long delays in processing DoLS referrals may dilute this safeguard in any individual case, though data is monitored overall.

As we will see in chapter 15, the CQC can take a keen interest in deprivation of liberty, and especially unauthorised deprivations, when it comes to inspections and ratings. Remember that the Health and Social Care Act 2008 (Regulated Activities) Regulations 2014, Regulation 13(5) imposes a strict duty that:

> *"A service user must not be deprived of their liberty for the purpose of receiving care or treatment without lawful authority".*

Court of Protection

As distinct from the role of the Court of Protection in making decisions about deprivation of liberty for someone who is outside the scope of DoLS[494], the Court of Protection also has a function as the route of appeal against a DoLS authorisation.

This is set out in s21A of the Mental Capacity Act and so, of course, these are called "section 21A cases". Crucially, for a s21A case you are entitled to legal aid as of right, without having to pass the means testing which would otherwise exclude almost everyone.

From outside the DoLS process, s21A cases might well be the most visible part of the safeguards; certainly so for the lawyers involved, or those paying their bills. Judgments in the Court of Protection can be published, and though there will usually be an order that prevents anyone from breaching the confidentiality of the individual involved, the cases are usually heard in public, meaning that anyone can attend, whether in person or remotely. The terrific work of the Open Justice Project[495] has

---

494 If the person is over 16 and lacks capacity for the relevant decisions, otherwise the High Court.

495 https://openjusticecourtofprotection.org/

been hugely effective in bringing the Court of Protection process into the light, starting in the pandemic, when all hearings were moved online, and continuing now that we have reverted to a mix of remote and in person hearings.

However, not every case generates a written judgment, especially when they are dealt with at the lower levels of the judiciary, as almost all s21A cases are.

And in reality, very few cases go to the Court of Protection[496], and in turn the outcome of most of those that do will simply affirm a situation, though meeting P's rights to challenge it.

The stories of Steven Neary and others who are "released" from detention after a successful challenge using s21A are powerful, but rare. I do not know if that is a reassuring sign or not. Does a low success rate in s21A challenges show that the DoLS system is getting it right at the start? Or that the challenge process is too weak, especially once the detention is essentially a done deal?

In my own experience of s21A cases, it is relatively common for the capacity assessment to be in dispute, or the best interests assessment, especially when P does not want to stay there. It is rare to have a litigated case on whether or not there is a deprivation of liberty at all, hence the relative lack of helpful case law on this directly.

Conversely, though s21A cases are relatively rare compared to the number of DoLS authorisations, the work they create can be a very substantial part of the legal spend / focus of a local authority or ICB. Given the even greater rarity of a DoLS authorisation being discharged by the court, is this really worth it in terms of the protection effectively offered to P?

Perhaps "success" needs to be drawn a little wider – even if the DoLS authorisation is upheld, the court can impose conditions that may be to P's benefit, or bring scrutiny to the care package that may lead to positive

[496] See chapter 16.

changes. Even the threat of a challenge can focus the mind of the care provider or commissioner.

But there is no getting away from the fact that a lot of the hard yards in protecting P are not achieved in court, but are hidden inside the system: the BIAs and IMCAs challenging care providers to find less restrictive ways to meet P's care needs, to amplify and heed P's voice, and sense checking the views taken of best interests and risk.

Even so, it is clearly essential, to meet the requirements of article 5(4) that there must be a way in which any deprivation of liberty must be challenged in a judicial process. So it is important to be clear when that process should be triggered.

Going back to *AJ* again, in addition to the points already highlighted, Mr Justice Baker said:

- Professionals need to be "on their guard" against cases where there is ostensibly a respite placement but, as for AJ, the intention is clearly for it to be a permanent placement, sidestepping the proper protection of her Article 5 rights.

- The care plan and other documentation must fully and faithfully record the real situation, and in particular the constraints actually imposed on P. In this case, he felt that the care plan had initially underplayed the extent of the use of restraint.

- Failure to act with "*diligence and urgency*" to bring a case to court in good time will lead to "*the evaporation of P's Article 5 rights*".

- The right to challenge the deprivation of liberty should not be contingent on another person's exercise of discretion, for example whether or not the RPR happens to want to bring the challenge.

- Nor should that right be dependent on anyone's assessment of the prospects of any challenge being successful, ie there is no role for *gatekeeping* before a challenge is brought, if that is what P wants or would want. It would be wrong to dismiss the idea of a challenge simply because what P is saying they want something that is impossible, for example to return to a childhood home that no longer exists.

- The local authority remains under "*a continuing and positive obligation to ensure that AJ's Article 5(4) rights were respected*", and so if it was not satisfied that either the RPR or the IMCA were taking the necessary steps to bring the case to court in good time, it should have brought the proceedings itself.

In some ways, if *Cheshire West* showed us the breadth of the obligations under Article 5 in terms of how many people and situations are caught, *AJ* showed us how deep are the obligations on the local authority in any individual case.

We must recognise where interventions may create a deprivation of liberty, however well intended, and be honest about what the proposals / existing care plan really involves. We must really consider if there is a less restrictive way of meeting P's best interests, and – if an authorisation of a deprivation of liberty is needed – do everything possible to see this is done before the steps are taken. And even once a DoLS authorisation is in place, "*there is an obligation on the state to ensure that a person deprived of liberty is <u>not only entitled but enabled</u> to have the lawfulness of his detention reviewed speedily by a court*".[497]

The year after *AJ*, Mr Justice Baker heard five test cases[498] which were brought together to test the circumstances in which s21A cases should be brought.

He reiterated that the RPR's role includes taking all reasonable steps to identify whether P wishes to exercise the right to apply to the Court of Protection (or the right to Part 8 review); that if the RPR concludes that P wishes to apply to the Court it is the RPR's duty to ensure that application is brought; and that it is not the function of the RPR to

---

497 *AJ*, cited above.

498 *RD* [2016] EWCOP 49.

consider whether such an application is in P's best interests, and he gave this guidance:

> *"In seeking to identify P's wishes the RPR must consider not only the direct evidence of expression of wish, but also indirect evidence of P's wishes as inferred form behaviour taking into account all the circumstances …"*
>
> *"Where P is unable to communicate his / her wishes, the RPR should consider what those wishes would be, were he or she able to communicate them"*
>
> *"In considering whether P's behaviour constitutes an objection, regard should be had to:*
>
> > *(a) the possible reasons for P's behaviour,*
> >
> > *(b) whether P is being medicated for depression or being sedated,*
> >
> > *(c) whether P actively tries to leave the care home,*
> >
> > *(d) whether P takes preparatory steps to leave, e.g. packing bags,*
> >
> > *(e) P's demeanour and relationship with staff,*
> >
> > *(f) any records of challenging behaviour and the triggers for such behaviour.*
> >
> > *(g) whether P's behaviour is a response to particular aspects of the care arrangements or to the entirety of those arrangements.*
>
> *Consideration should be holistic and usually based on more than one meeting."*

The idea of "*objection*" is important, as we will see in more detail in the next chapter, when we come to the interface with the MHA.

Conclusion

Extensive as these safeguards are, they have their limits.

Like any other issue under the Mental Capacity Act, best interests decisions can only be made among the options that are actually available. In AJ's case, once her niece and her husband decided that she was no longer welcome at their home, and assuming the AJ had no property right to stay there, then a move was inevitable, however much she may have wanted to stay there. Of course, it may be that there were other places she would have preferred to move to than the care home she was placed in against her wishes, and she was entitled to that being considered properly and, if need be, tested in court.

Similarly, P's chance to stay in their own home might really depend on the willingness of a local authority to fund a particular domiciliary care package; and if it will not fund this then, short of that decision itself being unlawful, there may be little that the court can do about it, and the s21A process may well feel hollow from P's point of view.

In reality, as with so much else in this context and more widely, the outcome from P's perspective is likely to be closely tied to the resources that can be made available for them, at a time when far too many people are being left far too short of what they want or need.

Easier said than done when faced with the scale of the workload now[499], but remember the gravity of each individual case for that individual, and try to treat them individually. Be wary of the temptation to cut and paste from one form to another: In *YC*[500] the DoLS authorisation was criticised by the court for repeatedly using the wrong patient's name in the paperwork, though it was upheld as valid nonetheless.

---

[499] See chapter 16.

[500] YC [2015] EWCOP 54 –

If you only read one case, read *AJ*.[501] And, again, reflect that when things go wrong with DoLS it is almost always the fundamentals of the MCA that have gone awry than any of the complexities around the DoLS regime itself.

That said, the interface with the MHA is where this is most complex, so we will look at that in a separate chapter next.

501 [2015] EWCOP 5 – https://www.bailii.org/ew/cases/EWCOP/2015/5.html

CHAPTER THIRTEEN

MENTAL HEALTH ACT / DEPRIVATION OF LIBERTY INTERFACE

It is worth taking some care over the interface between the Mental Health Act and the law on deprivation of liberty for a few reasons:

- It is important, certainly for the individuals involved, to make sure that the proper legal framework is in place and their rights are met, and there are significant differences between the MHA and DoLS;

- the interface is complex and confusing, even for the most experienced practitioners (it was this bit of the law that Mr Justice Charles was referring to when he talked about feeling like he was in a tumble dryer[502]); and

- It is unlikely to change anytime soon – the Liberty Protection Safeguards proposals left the current dog's dinner substantially unchanged, and even though there may (or may not) be a new Mental Health Act on the way, it is also unlikely to tackle this.

There is a simple version to this, and a complicated one.

The simple version is: DoLS were developed to plug the *Bournewood* gap, ie where a patient is deprived of their liberty and the Mental Health Act is not being used for whatever reason, leaving the person without any procedural safeguards.

---

[502] Quoted in the Introduction.

So, where the Mental Health Act is being used (or *should be* used) in a way that authorises the deprivation of liberty in question, then there is no gap, and no need for the deprivation of liberty safeguards.

The complicated version is everything else in this chapter. I am sorry it's a mess, but I'll do my best.

The Mental Health Act

For centuries there have been laws dealing with people regarded as mentally unwell, often in terms we would not be comfortable with today. Much of the concern in legal terms was about managing the finances where a wealthy family member went a little beyond what was regarded at the time as "eccentric". An earlier version of the "Court of Protection" dealt with those issues, dealing with those who were considered at the time to be "*lunatics*" and "*idiots*".

The current version of mental health legislation is the Mental Health Act 1983 (MHA), as was substantially amended by the Mental Health Act 2007.

The focus of the MHA is on *detention and treatment for a mental disorder*. As I said earlier, one of the things I dislike about the title of the Mental Capacity Act is the potential confusion from the word "mental", when in practice the treatment of mental disorder without a patient's consent is the preserve of the Mental Health Act.

Just as the Mental Capacity Act has no jurisdiction unless the patient has an impairment or disturbance in the functioning of their mind or brain which means they lack capacity for a particular decision, so the Mental Health Act only kicks in when a patient has a mental disorder. But the MHA does not require that a patient lacks capacity for a particular decision – treatment can be given for their mental disorder under the MHA when detained in hospital even for a patient who is refusing the treatment and has capacity to make that decision.

Under the MHA there is scope to be a voluntary patient – ie the person has capacity to make the decision and is consenting to their admission to hospital for the purpose of care and treatment of their mental disorder. But care must be taken not to mistake passive compliance for voluntary consent, depriving the patient of the stronger safeguards that accompany formal admission through detention under the MHA.

The Mental Health Act defines mental disorder as any disorder or disability of the mind. For the purposes of the MHA, a learning disability is not a mental disorder. However, the MHA provides an exception known as the "qualifier" where the person has a learning disability that is associated with abnormally aggressive or seriously irresponsible conduct. In that case, the person "qualifies" for the use of the MHA and this should be used to authorise their detention to hospital.

There is no such qualifier for people whose only presentation is that of alcohol or other substance misuse. Such addictions fall outside the definition of mental disorder under the HA.

A new Mental Health Act may (or may not) be in the pipeline, and one of the significant reforms proposed is to exclude patients with learning disability or autism spectrum disorder from the criteria for detention under Section 3 entirely.

Detention under the Mental Health Act most commonly refers to use of the civil sections, which are section 2 and section 3[503]. Section 2 allows a patient to be detained for assessment (which can include treatment) for up to 28 days, which cannot be renewed. Section 3 allows for detention for treatment in the longer term, initially up to 6 months, which can then be renewed for up to 6 months, and then can be renewed annually.

Both sections include procedural safeguards which meet the ECHR Article 5 rights of the patient detained. These include the prescriptive criteria by which detention can be recommended and authorised, rights

[503] A full review of the MHA is obviously not "within the scope" of this book. The leading text if you want more is the Mental Health Act Manual by Richard Jones, currently in its 25th edition.

of advocacy, the set time scales for detention, and rights to challenge the detention by several options including appeal to the Independent Associate Hospital Managers, review at renewal by the Independent Associate Hospital Managers, the exercise of rights by the patient's "nearest relative"[504] to discharge the patient, and a right of appeal to the first tier Mental Health Review Tribunal.

The Deprivation of Liberty Safeguards do us few favours in explaining they fit alongside the Mental Health Act (usually called the "interface"). It is mostly dealt with in Schedule 1A of the Mental Capacity Act, which sets out which patients are "ineligible" for DoLS (or for a Court of Protection to authorise any deprivation of liberty[505]) as a result of the Mental Health Act.

The general idea is that patients who ought to be detained under the Mental Health Act should be in that regime, with DoLS (or the Court of Protection's jurisdiction to authorise a deprivation of liberty) only intended to plug the gap where procedural safeguards are needed but the Mental Health Act is not or cannot be used.

This is the idea of "ineligibility", which is assessed by the DoLS mental health assessors, as set out in the last chapter.

Ineligibility

Good law should be accessible and clear.

No-one is, or should be, proud of this bit of the law. I can only ever get my own head round it for a short period of time when I have to, and only then after a little lie down in a dark room with a damp towel.

[504] Note, not the same as "next of kin".

[505] MCA s16A provides that anyone ineligible for DoLS, per Schedule 1A cannot be deprived of their liberty by an order of the Court of Protection either, though for brevity in this chapter I may just refer to being ineligible for DoLS, in reality it also makes P ineligible for the jurisdiction of the Court of Protection as well, as far as authorisation of a deprivation of liberty is concerned.

Essentially, to avoid overlap with the Mental Health Act, Schedule 1A sets out situations in which P will be "ineligible" for DoLS or the Court of Protection to authorise a deprivation of liberty in 5 situations[506], where the MHA is being (or *could be*) used:

- Where P is already detained under the MHA (case A);

- Where P is on leave of absence or a conditional discharge (case B), a Community Treatment Order (case C) or guardianship (case D) under the MHA, and they are subject to a requirement that would be inconsistent with the DoLS authorisation; or a proposed DoLS authorisation would be for the purpose of medical treatment for a mental disorder in hospital;

- Where P is "within the scope" of the MHA and objecting to proposed treatment for a mental disorder in hospital (case E).

Case A is straightforward – P is already being detained in hospital under the MHA[507] and so is ineligible for DoLS.

So, it is not quite right to say that DoLS or an order from the Court of Protection depriving P of their liberty cannot coexist with use of the MHA at all. They <u>can</u> be used together as long as the provisions of any leave / conditional discharge / CTO / guardianship are consistent with any DoLS authorisation / court order sought. For example, if the guardianship requires that P lives at a particular address, then he would not be eligible for a DoLS authorisation for a care home, or a court order for a deprivation of liberty in the community, that was not at that address.

It is possible for these powers under the MHA and a DoLS authorisation to work alongside each other, not least as those particular MHA powers

---

506 Schedule 1A paragraph 2.

507 Though using it in practice can be complex – see Chapter 14 on the inherent jurisdiction – the Dr A case.

may not in themselves make a deprivation of liberty lawful, and so a DoLS authorisation / court order may be needed for that.

In particular, since a pair of Supreme Court cases in 2018, we know that a Community Treatment Order cannot be used to impose conditions which amount to a deprivation of liberty[508]; and that a conditional discharge cannot be used by a tribunal or the secretary of state to impose conditions that amount to a deprivation of liberty, even when a patient purports to consent to this[509]. How could such "consent" be real, if agreeing to those conditions is seen as the only way out of detention?

This has a real impact for a patient who has capacity to make the relevant decisions: If a necessary care plan on discharge amounts to a deprivation of liberty, and their "consent" to such conditions in a conditional discharge cannot be taken at face value, it may be very much harder to secure and authorise this for a patient with capacity than for one without capacity, for whom the Court of Protection / DoLS can be used instead.

Until this bit of law is reformed, it can often lead to artificiality, or judicial creativity, for example with long term s17 leave under MHA being used to find a way around this for patients in that situation[510].

Case E – "could be"?

But back to the five cases of ineligibility: The real confusion comes from the last of these – case E – in which we are speculating about the *possibility* of using MHA powers to detain, which are not actually already being used, as a reason to exclude the use of DoLS.

So, let's look closer at the wording of case E. It provides that P is ineligible if they are "*within the scope of the Mental Health Act*" but are not subject to any of the MHA, if they meet the criteria in paragraph 5.

---

508 *Welsh Ministers v PJ* [2018] UKSC 66.

509 *Secretary of State for Justice v MM* [2018] UKSC 60.

510 See for example *CNTW NHS FT v EG*, [2021] EWHC 2990 (Fam).

The criteria in paragraph 5 are that:

- The (proposed) Court of Protection order or DoLS authorisation authorises P to *be a mental health patient* (ie a person accommodated in a hospital for the purpose of being given medical treatment for mental disorder)[511];

- That, taking into account P's behaviour, wishes and feelings, views, values and beliefs, *P objects* to being a mental health patient or to being given some or all of the medical treatment for his mental disorder; and

- There is no valid decision by a Deputy or someone holding a Lasting Power of Attorney to consent to the things the P objects to.

But the confusion is more often about being "*within the scope of the MHA*" itself, which means that "an application *could* be made" under MHA s2 or s3, and that, if made, P "*could* be detained in hospital".[512]

What does "could" mean?

This has most recently been considered in *JS v Manchester University Hospitals NHS FT*[513].

JS was a 17 year-old girl with a diagnosis of autism, ADHD, learning disability and an attachment disorder. She was admitted on an informal basis (having initially been assessed to have capacity to agree to this), but was then detained under MHA s2 for assessment. Her challenging

[511] Schedule 1A paragraph 16(1).

[512] Emphasis added, defined in Schedule 1A para 12. There are also some assumptions that the necessary medical recommendations for detention are made, and that the treatment referred to in MHA s3(2)(c) (it is necessary for the health or safety of the patient or for the protection of other persons that he should receive such treatment and it cannot be provided unless he is detained under this section) cannot be provided under the MCA.

[513] [2023] EWCOP 33.

behaviour included acts of serious deliberate self-harm and suicide attempts. She was managed on a mixed acute hospital ward by "*physical containment and the use of restraint both by physical intervention and medication*".

She remained under the same restrictions after the s2 detention had lapsed, and – the assessment of her capacity having changed – an application was made to the Court of Protection to authorise her continued detention. HHJ Burrows authorised her deprivation of liberty, but queried whether she may be ineligible for this under Schedule 1A, and at a later hearing he determined that she was ineligible. The hospital appealed, arguing that she was not getting any treatment for her mental health, but was simply being kept in hospital, in the best way they could to keep her safe, for lack of anywhere better for her to be, and so she should not be ineligible under the MCA Schedule 1A, so that the Trust could seek a Court of Protection order to authorise the restrictions.

On appeal, Ms Justice Theis upheld HHJ Burrows' decision, and reaffirmed the approach to ineligibility in case E set out in the earlier case of *GJ*.

Acknowledging the Trust's concerns, Theis J made clear that mental health treatment under MHA s145(1) has a wide interpretation, including nursing, psychological intervention and specialist mental health rehabilitation and care; there was no doubt that the clinicians saw her behaviour as a manifestation of her mental disorders, and that the restrictions imposed were in response to this; the care plan remained the same as it had when she was detained under MHA s2.

HHJ Burrows had been perfectly entitled to find that:

- JS was a mental health patient;
- She was clearly objecting; and
- That she "could" be detained under MHA s3

… making her ineligible under MCA Schedule 1A for DoLS or for the Court of Protection to make an order authorising a deprivation of liberty.

The case of *GJ*[514] was previously the leading authority on what "*could*" means (makes you proud to be a lawyer, no?) and still needs inclusion, though the *JS* case is useful as it is a little more accessible.

GJ was a 65 year-old man with a diagnosis of vascular dementia, as well as Korsakoff's Syndrome and amnesia, due to alcohol. But he also had insulin dependent diabetes, which he had managed reasonably well in the community until his partner died in 2008. After that, his glycaemic control was "appalling", and he was at high risk of brain injury and death without support for management of his diabetes. He was initially detained under the MHA, but was in hospital under a DoLS authorisation by the time of the application to court in 2009.

Whether an application "could" be made, and he "could" be detained under the MHA, depended on how "could" is interpreted.

It was argued on GJ's behalf that he was caught by case E – ineligible for DoLS if an application under MHA s2 or 3 *could* be made – if this was a mere "*possibility*". The NHS bodies involved argued that there was a much higher bar: that "could" meant a "*high probability*" – effectively that no reasonable psychiatrist or doctor involved in the decision making whether to detain P under the MHA would refuse to do so.

The judge, Charles J, rejected both, and went for a different approach, advocated by the Secretary of State – the "*what the decision-maker thinks*" test.

As it says on the tin, this simply defers to the person considering whether or not P is ineligible for DoLS – ie the Court of Protection judge or the DoLS assessor – to take their *own view* on whether or not the MHA s2 or 3 criteria are met.

---

514 *GJ v The Foundation Trust* [2009] 2974 (Fam) Charles J.

This has the obvious problem that this person speculating on whether the MHA criteria are met (the DoLS assessor, say) is not the same person who actually decides whether they are (ie the assessors for the MHA). It is quite possible that a DoLS assessor / judge may feel that the MHA could be used to detain someone (making them ineligible for DoLS if they object to that) but that the assessment for detention under the MHA is actually refused. Then what?!

Before we get to that stalemate, there's another useful bit of the *GJ* judgment, in which Charles J considers how to tease out the reality of the situation in complex cases in which there is both physical and mental health care involved: a "*but for*" test. This means asking yourself whether P would still be detained under the MHA if not for the physical health treatment (unrelated to the mental health needs).

In this case, though the judge considered it to be "borderline", he concluded that if GJ had not needed the physical treatment for his diabetes he would not have been detained in hospital. He was, therefore, *not within scope of the MHA*, and *was eligible* for DoLS to be used to authorise the deprivation of his liberty.

Of course, since detention under MHA s2 or 3 can only take place in a hospital, case E has no relevance to someone in a care home or elsewhere in the community.

Subject to that, Charles J also asserted the "*primacy of the MHA*", by which he means that the question of whether or not P is within scope of the MHA must be approached with an assumption that the powers of the MCA / DoLS are not available: the MHA route falls to be considered first, and only if P is not within scope of the MHA should the mind turn to the MCA/DoLS:

> *"(a) the MHA 1983 is to have primacy when it applies, and*
>
> *(b) the medical practitioners referred to in ss. 2 and 3 of the MHA 1983 cannot pick and choose between the two statutory regimes as they think fit..."*

Primacy of the MHA and picking and choosing

That changed when Charles J came back to the issue of "primacy" of the MHA in 2013 in *AM v SLAM*[515].

AM was a 78 year-old woman who had been removed from her home[516] to be assessed in hospital under MHA s2. A mental health tribunal refused an application for discharge, concerned that she would not be compliant with her medication if she went home. A second tribunal proposed that she could be discharged from MHA detention as she would agree to remain in hospital voluntarily, as it was not in dispute that she lacked capacity to make decisions about her care and treatment, and so it was said that she could be treated under the MCA, with any deprivation of her liberty authorised by DoLS.

On reflection, Charles J considered that in some circumstances there may in fact be a choice to be made where it is possible for either the MHA or MCA/DoLS to be used.

There should be three questions:

1. Does P have capacity to consent to admission as an informal patient?

If they do have capacity then the MCA / DoLS of course cannot be used, as their jurisdiction depends on incapacity for the relevant decisions. Only the MHA can be used.

2. If they lack capacity for the relevant decisions, might the hospital be able to rely on the MCA to lawfully assess or treat P?

[515] *AM v South London and Maudsley NHS Foundation Trust* [2013] UKUT 0365.

[516] Under MHA s135(1).

This depends on likely compliance – the MCA cannot be used to lawfully assess or treat an objecting mental health patient, as they would normally be ineligible for DoLS[517].

3. If there is a choice between the MHA and MCA/DoLS (ie P lacks capacity for the relevant decisions, but is not objecting to the proposed treatment), which is the least restrictive way of best achieving the proposed assessment or treatment?

It is not to be taken for granted that use of DoLS is necessarily less restrictive than detention under the MHA, notwithstanding the stigma that remains attached to being "sectioned". There is, conversely, benefit to P in access to the non-means tested package of health and social care that follows discharge from detention under the MHA designed to prevent re-detention[518], as well as the significant procedural safeguards of the MHA, including those set out earlier.

The Mental Health Act Code of Practice[519] has a useful table of the options available depending on capacity and objection:

[517] MCA s28, and Schedule 1A paragraph 2 case E, as above.

[518] MHA s117.

[519] Para 13.52.

	Individual **objects** to the proposed accommodation in a hospital for care and/or treatment; or to any of the treatment they will receive there for mental disorder	Individual **does not object** to the proposed accommodation in a hospital for care and / or treatment; or to any of the treatment they will receive there for mental disorder
Individual has the capacity to consent to being accommodated in hospital for care and / or treatment	Only the MHA is available	The MHA is available. Informal admission and treatment might be appropriate. Neither DoLS nor Court of Protection order to authorise a deprivation of liberty are available.
Individual lacks the capacity to consent to being accommodated in hospital for care and / or treatment	Only the MHA is available	The MHA is available AND DoLS authorisation / Court of Protection Order to authorise a deprivation of liberty is available

In short:

- If P is objecting to an admission for treatment of a mental disorder then only the MHA can be used. That is what it is for.

- If P is not objecting then MHA can still be used, regardless of P's capacity.

- Only if P is not objecting AND lacks capacity for the relevant decisions (the bottom right box) can there be a choice between using the MHA or MCA/DoLS.

Stalemate

If JS *had been* detained under the MHA, there would have been no problem.

The problem with case E is one of "stalemate": If P becomes ineligible for the MCA / DoLS to be used for any deprivation of liberty because the MHA *could* be used in the opinion of the decision-maker under the MCA (ie the court or a DoLS assessor), *what happens if the MHA actually isn't used because the MHA assessors take a different view?*

Note that where there is uncertainty about ineligibility, MCA s4B can still work to authorise a deprivation of liberty while the court resolves this[520].

In *JS*, the court also suggested:

- In any application for deprivation of liberty of a 16-17 year-old, the applicant should consider carefully whether an application should be made to the Court of Protection (rather than to the High Court as you would have to for a younger child).

- If an issue of ineligibility (case E) is anticipated, evidence should be obtained and filed with the application to cover the questions asked in GJ so this is available to the court.

---

520 See chapter 8.

- If P is found to be ineligible for MCA / DoLS to be used for any deprivation of liberty, and the MHA is not used, the professionals involved "*should liaise urgently*".

- The hospital can:

    - press for detention under the MHA (and may be well advised to seek a referral to an AMHP[521] to start the process for assessment for detention under the MHA before making an application, so the outcome of this is clear[522]);

    - Seek detention in a setting outside hospital, such as a care home, where case E does not apply; or

    - Remove the restrictions that amount to a deprivation of liberty.

- And where P is truly left in a gap, with neither the MCA / DoLS or MHA available to authorise any deprivation of their liberty, then the inherent jurisdiction of the High Court can be used[523].

Of course, much the better approach is for there to be a constructive and collaborative approach between the MCA and MHA decision-makers from the outset to avoid the gap if possible[524].

---

[521] Approved Mental Health Professional, who has a role under the MHA in starting the process of assessment for detention.

[522] In practice, this usually begins with the AMHP service receiving a first medical recommendation, so the issue becomes finding a s12 doctor who will make the recommendation.

[523] See Chapter 14 on the inherent jurisdiction.

[524] Even without the stalemate over case E ineligibility, the use of the MHA alongside MCA / DoLS can bring real dilemmas beyond the scope of this book. For instance in *Nottinghamshire Healthcare v RC* [2014] EWCOP 1317 (deciding not to use MHA s63 to give blood products to someone detained under the MHA for self-harming due to a personality disorder where he had a valid ADRT rejecting this); and *A NHS Trust v Ms X* [2014] EWCOP 35 (deciding not to admit a patient to treatment under the

Residual liberty

One final point – where P is already detained under the MHA for treatment of a mental disorder, this can extend to treatment of physical health needs which are caused by or related to that mental disorder[525]. But what about treating a patient detained under the MHA for unrelated physical health needs where that treatment would itself involve a deprivation of her liberty?

HJ[526] was a 64 year-old woman detained under MHA s3, with bipolar affective disorder and psychotic symptoms. The pressing issue, though, was physical health unrelated to her mental disorder (so which could not be treated under MHA s63). She had chronic constipation which needed occasional enemas, for which restraint with 4-5 staff was required, lasting 3-5 minutes each time.

Initially the treating hospital and the Official Solicitor agreed that this would amount to a deprivation of liberty, and so would need approval by the High Court (since her MHA detention took her outside the scope of DoLS and the Court of Protection for these purposes).

The judge referred to the idea of "residual" liberty[527], but in summary held that:

- HJ lacked capacity for decisions about her medical treatment, and these decisions were made in her best interests by clinicians in good faith, holding a duty of care towards her;

- That duty of care, plus following the MCA properly, is enough protection of her rights, under MCA s4 to make a best interests

---

MHA was in her best interests for a young woman with enduring and severe anorexia and alcohol dependence).

525 MHA s63.

526 *Norfolk & Suffolk NHS Foundation Trust v HJ* [2023] EWFC 92.

527 See also NHS Trust v Dr A [2013] EWHC 2442 (COP), addressed in chapter 14 on the inherent jurisdiction.

decision involving HJ herself, and s6 to ensure that any restraint is proportionate and necessary to prevent harm;

- She also has the protection of safeguards on use of restraint from Seni's Law (the Mental Health Units (use of force) Act 2018)[528];

- Though a deprivation of residual liberty is possible for someone already detained, it should be exceptional – Article 5 (right to liberty) is not interested in the nuts and bolts of care planning[529], and her article 8 rights were met by the MCA / MHA / Seni's law.

- The judge did not approach it by saying that the duration (3-5 minutes of restraint) was a relevant factor in it not being regarded as a deprivation of liberty, instead making a more general point, it seems, that only in exceptional circumstances will treatment of a physical medical condition constitute a deprivation of liberty for someone already detained under the MHA.

Though there has been no appeal in this case, it might best be treated with some caution for now. There is more than a whiff in this of the *Cheshire West* Court of Appeal approach of deference to treating professionals and that providing appropriate care is no deprivation of liberty, at least for those who are already detained under the MHA.

In anything like this situation, it would be prudent to seek urgent legal advice.

---

[528] This is legislation introduced after the death of Olaseni Lewis in 2010 soon after being restrained in a mental health hospital. The legislation, which came into force on 31 March 2022, is focussed on identifying and documenting incidents of physical restraint in hospitals, to increase transparency and accountability.

[529] See chapter 7 on acute medical treatment.

Final thoughts

Few parts of the law are in such urgent need of reform. In the State of Care Report for 2022/23, the CQC wrote:

> "*In mental health settings we continue to see a variable understanding of the interface between the MCA, which DoLS are part of, and the MHA. Where both frameworks could be used, it is not always clear how staff decided that using the DoLS framework would be most appropriate for a particular patient.*
>
> *These issues are compounded by the lack of certainty around the future of DoLS, leaving providers feeling confused and frustrated. We have observed some providers not delivering adequate training on DoLS, resulting in a lack of understanding among staff.*"

But the prospect of reform seems distant at the moment[530].

And the law might be easier to manage in this area if there were not such a gulf, and an often-artificial distinction, in the way we treat physical and mental health issues, which so often co-exist in a system in which we seem driven to compartmentalise.

530 Both the Liberty Protection Safeguards (though dropped at least for now) and the proposals for reform of the Mental Health Act (long promised but also missing from the King's Speech on 7 November 2023, so evidently not being pursued until the next general election) would have left the interface between the MHA and MCA/DoLS untouched.

CHAPTER FOURTEEN

THE SAFEGUARDS BEYOND DOLS

We have looked at those who may be deprived of their liberty who are within the scope of the DoLS, but what about everyone else? Everyone under 18 years old, or who may be deprived of their liberty somewhere other than a care home or hospital[531], or who may be *ineligible* for DoLS for another reason?

The short answer is that any deprivation of liberty for anyone outside the scope of DoLS can only be authorised by the court, unless some other legal framework such as the Mental Health Act is used.

Typically, this will be in the Court of Protection where P is over 16 and lacks capacity for the relevant decisions, giving the court jurisdiction under the Mental Capacity Act. Otherwise, you are likely to be in the High Court, using the powers of the Children Act 1989 (for under 18s) or the inherent jurisdiction.

I will split this chapter into three:

1. Adults
2. Children and young people
3. The hospital Emergency Department (as this raises some distinct issues).

[531] NB "in hospital" means a patient who has been admitted, and does not include someone who might be in ED, for example, where any deprivation of liberty might raise difficult questions how it might be authorised. I will come back to this at the end of the chapter.

Let's start with adults, and with the role of the Court of Protection.

Part 1 – Adults

The Court of Protection

The Court of Protection has the power to declare whether P lacks capacity for particular decisions, to determine what is in their best interests if they do. That can include approving care packages that amount to a deprivation of the person's liberty[532]. The court process itself protects P's Article 5 rights, and includes the possibility of an appeal to a more senior judge if need be.

In practical terms, an application to the Court of Protection to authorise a deprivation of liberty will almost always be brought by a public body, usually an NHS body or local authority, whether as the provider or commissioner of the care.

Often an application will be necessary to consider the care / treatment proposed itself. The question of whether it also amounts to a deprivation of liberty, and authorising it, may be ancillary, for example in asking a court to approve a plan for P to be brought into hospital against their wishes for medical treatment.

Given the cost of bringing proceedings, there can sometimes be tension between the public bodies involved as to which should take responsibility. But generally, the court takes a very dim view where this causes any delay in a case, especially where delay adversely affects P, for example reducing the prospect of successful treatment. There are several cases in which both local authorities and the NHS have been strongly criticised in these circumstances. Where there is a real dispute about taking this responsibility, it is always possible to start the proceedings and argue at the first hearing that it should be taken over and driven by another body. These cases rarely improve with keeping.

---

532 As long as they are not ineligible – MCA s16A, Schedule 1A – see chapter 13.

There is not space for a full account of proceedings in the Court of Protection, but it is worth noting that:

- P would normally be a party to the proceedings, so they can be represented and involved[533].
- The question whether P has *capacity to litigate* – ie make decisions within the proceedings and instruct their own lawyers – is, logically, distinct from the question whether they have capacity for the decisions about their care and residence which are in issue. It is possible for someone to lack capacity about the substance of the case, but to have capacity to litigate about it, but they are so closely related that in practice that is rare.
- If P lacks capacity to litigate, then a litigation friend must be appointed to act on their behalf, who may in turn instruct solicitors. This could be a family member, if there is no conflict of interest that would make this inappropriate.
- If there is no other suitable litigation friend, the Official Solicitor[534] can take on this role, and in disputes about serious medical treatment this is usually the case.
- In contrast to the s21A proceedings described in chapter 12, other Court of Protection proceedings do not attract non-means tested legal aid, even though the issues and implications to P can be just as grave where they may be deprived of their liberty by the court's own order rather than the DoLS process. So if P has more than the (very paltry) financial limits, they can end up having to pay or contribute to the legal costs of their representation in proceedings that they did not start, and which are designed to

533 Contrast the *Re X* process, below.

534 A public official, currently Sarah Castle, who often acts as a litigation friend of last resort, subject to suitable funding being available.

protect their fundamental rights, as a result of which they can be deprived of their liberty[535].

- Really urgent issues – such as vital medical treatment – can be dealt with very quickly, out of hours and 365 days a year, if need be. Sadly, other proceedings in the Court of Protection may not be a quick as we would like, and can take months or even years, reflecting the overwhelmed resources of every part of the system.

- Typically, proceedings will involve case management hearings along the way which would deal with the housekeeping of the case – what evidence is needed and the timetable for this, working towards a final hearing.

- It is possible for proceedings to be concluded without a final hearing to determine any substantial issues where these are compromised by agreement, or perhaps overtaken by events, such as P's death, or P moving out of the placement to which they objected.

But if the public body involved does not initiate proceedings in good time, or at all, to draw this to the attention of the court, what safeguards remain then?

Such individual situations, beyond the scope of DoLS, are often also outside the gaze of the CQC, which regulates organisations that provide care, but does not reach into a someone's home or supported living. The prospect of a claim being brought by an individual unlawfully deprived of their liberty outside the scope of DoLS might seem as fanciful as the idea that they would start proceedings to authorise it themselves, where the public body does not. We will get to accountability in this next chapter.

---

535 Adding insult to injury, indeed, and I suspect that this might be challenged as discriminatory sooner rather than later.

The most commonplace application to the Court of Protection in relation to deprivation of liberty is where there may be a deprivation in the community, such as in P's own home.

These are sometimes referred to as deprivation of liberty in the community (or "DOLIC") cases. Sometimes, "community DoLs" (as in the plural: deprivations of liberty), though I think that tends to promote confusion with DoLS (ie the Deprivation of Liberty *Safeguards*), which by definition cannot be used in the community, since they only apply to care homes and hospitals. Likewise, it is confusing that orders made by the court authorising a deprivation of liberty can be referred to as "DoLS orders" when they are being made precisely because DoLS does not apply. I have also recently seen, for the first time, "DOLO" used by a judge, as shorthand for Deprivation of Liberty Order for a child in the High Court.[536]

Whatever the terminology, though, the scale of these cases, post *Cheshire West*[537], was such as to require a dedicated, streamlined process.

Deprivation of Liberty in the Community – Re X

Ironically, perhaps, given his attempts in the Court of Appeal to keep a lid on this, it was Sir James Munby who stepped up, as President of the Court of Protection at the time, to try to tackle *Cheshire West's* impact on the court.

In the weeks after *Cheshire West*, Sir James arranged for a number of deprivation of liberty cases already going through the Court of Protection to be heard before him all together to consider "*the practical and procedural implications for the Court of Protection of what all informed opinion agrees is the large increase in its case-load which will follow in consequence of the Supreme Court's decision.*"

---

536 By Paul Bowen KC sitting as a deputy High Court judge in *Re EBY* [2023] EWHC 2494 (Fam) – see below in part 2 of this chapter.

537 See chapter 16.

As such, at a hearing before him on 5-6 June 2014, in a case called "*Re X*", there appeared:

> *"...a large number of advocates, representing between them, in addition to the Official Solicitor as advocate to the court, the Secretary of State for Health and the Lord Chancellor and Secretary of State for Justice, the Law Society of England and Wales, the Association of Directors of Adult Social Services, Mind, eight local authorities, two NHS clinical commissioning groups, an NHS trust and four individuals".*

He explained that:

> *"The immediate objective, in my judgment, is to devise, if this is feasible, a standardised, and so far as possible 'streamlined', process, compatible with all the requirements of Article 5, which will enable the Court of Protection to deal with all deprivation of liberty cases in a timely but just and fair way. The process needs, if this is feasible, to distinguish between those deprivation of liberty cases that can properly be dealt with on the papers, and without an oral hearing, and those that require an oral hearing".*

The challenge, essentially, was to find a process that is streamlined enough for the court not to be swamped, but still meets the Article 5 rights of the person being deprived of their liberty. How many corners can safely be cut?[538]

Dealing with the fundamentals of the process, Sir James held that:

---

[538] This reflection on optimising the ruthless efficiency of the system involved 19 barristers bobbing up and down, as well as countless solicitors and others – including myself – sitting packed into court behind them, an irony that seemed to be lost. I was there, acting for one of the CCG parties. I remember the words "irreducible minimum" being used a lot to discuss the extent of the evidence that might be required of the applicant in such a case, and thinking that just "minimum" would have done it.

- It was not enough to comply with Article 5 for a deprivation of liberty to be authorised by a court official; it must be done by a judge;
- And a separate application must be done for each individual (it would not be good enough for a local authority to apply in respect of a list of people all in one go);
- But, it was not necessary for there to be a hearing – a suitable case (where there is no dispute over P's capacity, that they are deprived of their liberty, and that it is in their best interests) could be dealt with "on the papers".
- And, crucially, it was not necessary, he said, that the person deprived of liberty had to be a party to the proceedings in every case.

Munby LJ set out in quite some detail the streamlined process he proposed, which came to be known as the "*Re X*" process, in a pair of judgments handed down on 7 August 2014[539], and on 16 October 2014[540].

The second judgment picked up in more detail that last point, about P not needing to be a party, which makes a huge difference. If P must be a party to any proceedings, with a litigation friend, and all the issues of access to representation and funding which that involves, this will inevitably be a lot less streamlined than Sir James Munby may have hoped, with consequences for delay, costs and the resources and time needed generally to get the huge number of cases through the process.

539 https://www.bailii.org/ew/cases/EWCOP/2014/25.html

540 *Re X (No 2)* [2014] EWCOP 37
https://www.bailii.org/ew/cases/EWCOP/2014/37.html Why it was done in this way, I cannot explain.

Reflecting these judgments, a new practice direction and Court of Protection form (COPDOL10[541]) were published in November 2014, establishing the '*Re X*' process along these lines, and a raft of judges around the country were trained up, ready to deal with the expected flood of cases. There's also been an amendment to the Court of Protection Rules, with effect from 1 July 2015, which requires the court to consider whether P's participation can be secured and interests protected in another way, without being a party to proceedings, for instance by the appointment of a "Rule 1.2 representative" (usually a family member relied on to inform the court about P's wishes and feelings, values and beliefs, so these can be taken into account).

It was, predictably, on this issue that there was immediately an appeal brought by lawyers acting on behalf of two of the individuals deprived of their liberty in these cases. They argued, among other things, that natural justice simply required that the individual ought to be a party to any proceedings that would determine whether they were deprived of their liberty and its lawfulness.

Re X – The Court of Appeal

The Court of Appeal heard the case[542] on 17 and 18 February 2015, and the judgment, handed down on 16 June 2015, is something of a legal oddity[543]. The leading judgment, by Lady Justice Black, tackled first the question of whether the Court of Appeal had any jurisdiction at all, and came to the view that it did not.

The Court of Appeal needs a decision about a case made by a lower judge for it to review. What was the *decision* about a case made by LJ Munby? He had, instead, essentially been thinking out loud about the design of a

[541] Later replaced by COPDOL11, which remains in use, though an update may be coming.

[542] Involving a positively thrifty 8 barristers.

[543] [2015] EWCA Civ 599 https://www.bailii.org/ew/cases/EWCA/Civ/2015/599.html

new court process in general terms. When he announced a view that the person deprived of their liberty need not be a party to proceedings about that, it did not actually affect the individuals in front of him at the time – the two patients who brought this appeal, for instance, in fact *were* parties to their proceedings already. There was no *decision that affected them* to give them standing to appeal, or to give the Court of Appeal traction.

Black LJ said that while this might be a "*finicky*" analysis, "*this case demonstrates the problems that can arise where formalities take second place to expediency, even when that happens for the very best of reasons*".

She said that she was sympathetic with Munby LJ's understandable desire to address a very real problem, but that this should properly have been done by a formal Practice Direction, which could then be challenged by judicial review.

Agreeing that the Court of Appeal had no actual decision in a case to review, Gloster LJ was more critical:

> "*...the President engaged in an illegitimate approach to the determination of what he and all legal representatives regarded as generic academic issues without any, or any proper, identification of the particular issues which arose in the specific cases before him, he had no jurisdiction to make the determinations which he did.*"

But then – "*look at what you could have won!*" – the Court of Appeal went on to say:

> "*As we have heard such full argument on the substantive issues in the appeal, I am prepared to set out what I would have decided, had this court had jurisdiction ....*"

All three Court of Appeal judges would have said that P *should* be a party to any deprivation of liberty proceedings.

Lady Justice Gloster, for example, said that Sir James Munby's conclusion that P need not be a party "*is not consistent with fundamental principles of domestic law and does not provide the degree of protection required by the Convention or the Strasbourg jurisprudence*".

Ironically, the Court of Appeal's comment on this is arguably just the sort of non-binding thinking out loud[544] that it criticised LJ Munby for, as the court had already decided that it didn't have jurisdiction to decide these issues in this appeal. But on any view, it casts a shadow over the legitimacy of an approach that denies P party status in court proceedings that may decide on depriving someone of their liberty.

Re NRA

The *Re X* process was put on hold after the Court of Appeal judgment, and was only restored, with some amendments, after Mr Justice Charles grappled with the same issues again in a case called *NRA*[545].

Charles J explicitly weighed the benefits of a streamlined process against the comments in the Court of Appeal and came down on the side of pragmatism. He said that the *Re X* process was necessary and should be reintroduced, albeit with some amendments aimed at getting more information from the pubic bodies at the outset.

The essential things to include to protect P were to:

- Elicit P's own views and present them to the court;
- Critically examine the pros and cons of the proposed care package and whether it was in P's best interests; and
- Keep the implementation of that care package under review, and raise concerns as need be.

---

544 *Obiter*, if you like your legal latin.

545 [2015] EWCOP 59 https://www.bailii.org/ew/cases/EWCOP/2015/59.html

He held that in the great majority of cases it is reasonable to trust the judgement of family members to do this, without P needing to be a party to the proceedings. The risks to P of such a streamlined approach are outweighed by the practical advantages of proportionality.

So here we are, 8 years after the critical Court of Appeal judgment, with LJ Munby's *Re X* process, in essence, still in use.

COPDOL11

While the initial COPDOL10 court forms used for the process was updated to "COPDOL11"[546] from December 2017, following the *NRA* case, the approach remains explicitly rooted in the *Re X* judgments.

The process is intended for only the least controversial cases, where there is no real dispute that P lacks capacity for the relevant decisions about their care and residence, that they are deprived of their liberty, and that it is in their best interests and cannot be done in any less restrictive way. Anything more complex or controversial should be brought to court in full proceedings, in the expectation that P would be a party to the proceedings and that there may need to be a hearing.

The application is usually brought by the local authority with responsibility for the care package involved, or by the ICB (the NHS commissioner that has replaced Clinical Commissioning Groups).

The obligation on the ICB is explicit in the National Framework for Continuing Healthcare, most recently updated in July 2022[547], which says (at paragraph 346):

---

[546] https://www.gov.uk/government/publications/form-copdol11-application-to-authorise-a-deprivation-of-liberty-sections-4a3-and-162a-of-the-mental-capacity-act-2005

[547] https://assets.publishing.service.gov.uk/government/uploads/system/uploads/attachment_data/file/1170290/National-Framework-for-NHS-Continuing-Healthcare-and-NHS-funded-Nursing-Care_July-2022-revised_corrected-July-2023.pdf

"Where the individual who lacks the relevant capacity is in receipt of NHS Continuing Healthcare in their own home, including tenancy based accommodation (e.g. supported living), and is subject to restrictions that may constitute a deprivation of liberty, the deprivation of liberty cannot be authorised using the Deprivation of Liberty Safeguards (DoLS) process, instead authorisation must be obtained from the Court of Protection. In these circumstances, because the ICB is the primary funding authority, it is responsible for applying to the Court of Protection for this authorisation and should seek their own legal advice for this reason. The ICB is responsible for its own associated legal costs, but is not responsible for the legal costs of the individual concerned. However, the ICB should ensure that the individual has access to legal advice in their own right".

The application usually consists of:

- The COPDOL11 application form, which sets out information about the applicant and P;

- Annex A – supporting evidence, describing the care being provided and reasons why this is considered to be a deprivation of liberty, why this is considered to be in their best interests, the harm that it is avoiding (*necessarily* and *proportionately*), and why this is the least restrictive option to meet their best interests;

- Annex B – evidence of consultation with the relevant people in making the best interests decision that may amount to a deprivation of liberty[548].

- Annex C – evidence of consultation with P themselves.

- COP3 – the form that provides evidence of P's lack of capacity to make the relevant decisions. Or (if the COP3 is not completed

548 Essentially, the same categories of people who ought to be consulted under MCA s4(7) for best interests decisions generally.

by a doctor) Mental Health Assessment – usually a letter from the GP to confirm that P has a mental disorder.[549]

- Other relevant documents – such as any advance decision to refuse treatment, any LPA or previous court orders.
- The care plan.
- There may also be a witness statement on behalf of the public body to explain the basis of the application, and from the rule 1.2 representative if there is one.

There is guidance at the back of the COPDOL11 form on how to complete it and the information to give.

The care plan is absolutely key. It should be clearly dated to ensure that it is up to date, or the court may return it (though it can be galling to get the application back from the court because the care plan is out of date when this is a result of a delay in the court itself dealing with it).

The intention is that the application is reviewed and an order given "*on the papers*", ie without a hearing. *Re X* cases are supposed to be vanilla – the uncontentious cases in which we just need a due process to comply with P's Article 5 rights, but there is no real issue in dispute. Equally, it should not routinely be used for 16 and 17 year-olds, where the factual situation is typically more complex and restraint more common, the court said in *Bolton Council v KL*[550], in which Senior Judge Hilder noted that:

---

549 For the reasons described earlier, this is necessary, as well as evidence of P's lack of capacity for the relevant decisions, to bring P within the "unsound mind" category to allow them to be deprived of their liberty at all, subject to the other safeguards of Article 5. In practice getting this evidence from GPs can be a real bottleneck, given the other demands on their time, and there has been controversy over whether GPs are entitled to be paid for doing this.

550 [2022] EWCOP 24.

> *"... the process is very definitely not a "rubber stamping" procedure, but it relies on judicial antennae alone to identify from paperwork if/where further enquiry is required".*

Without P being a party and represented in a *Re X* application, those "*judicial antennae*" are wholly dependent on the information provided by the applicant public body, and the court only gets their side of the picture, emphasising the need for the information to be complete and accurate.

If it appears to the court that the *Re X* process is not appropriate in any particular case then it can order that proceedings be transferred into the main court process, out of the streamlined scheme.

Increasingly, we are seeing "maybe orders", where the court's response is to ask for more information before making a decision, such as an update on the care plan.

Like any other court order to authorise a deprivation of liberty, and in line with DoLS, an order made by the court under the *Re X* scheme would be for a maximum of 12 months, and so would then need to be renewed regularly[551]. The majority of cases suitable for *Re X* are likely to be long term arrangements.

Clearly, even for a "streamlined" process, this is still onerous and costly for the public bodies involved[552]. And as we will see[553], there are a great many more people deprived of their liberty in the community than the number of applications being brought, leaving unlawful deprivation of liberty widespread and unavoidable.

It is crying out for reform. If the Liberty Protection Safeguards are not coming soon, which would have brought community deprivation of

---

[551] See chapter 16 for the impact and implications of this.

[552] Many specialist firms of solicitors offer a fixed fee process to try to make this cost effective and predictable.

[553] Chapter 16.

liberty cases into the same scheme as care homes and hospitals, this may now come under renewed scrutiny.

At the time of writing, there is an updated form under consideration at the Court of Protection Rules Committee (a "COPDOL12"?), which I hear may take a wider view of a person's care, to include issues that are important but may be more about Article 8 than Article 5, such as restrictions on contact or use of social media[554]. The form may allow for a *Re X* process to include non-contentious applications for authorisation of restrictions on such Article 8 issues, alongside authorisation of any non-contentious deprivation of liberty. We will see. Such a broader view would certainly be welcome, though it does not by itself address all the challenges we face here, and in fact may increase the *Re X* workload.

Inherent Jurisdiction

This is the "great safety net"; the power of the court to do the right thing, especially to intervene to keep someone safe where they are vulnerable, and there is a gap in the powers set out by legislation.

The slight mystical feel to it, referred to sometimes as acting in *parens patriae* – on behalf of the monarch as the parent to the nation – is emphasised by the fact that when it is called upon by parties in court or by judges, it is usually described as being "*invoked*", like some kind of magic.

Often the inherent jurisdiction is used where someone has capacity but their decision making is overborne by undue influence, or coercion, for example. Typically, then, the extent of the court's intervention is only to remove that undue influence in order to allow the person to make their own decision. For example, in *DL v a Local Authority*[555], the court was dealing with an elderly couple whose son was living with them and essentially bullied them, verbally and physically, including pressing them

---

[554] See Chapter 8.

[555] [2012] EWCA Civ 253.

to decide that the mother would be placed into a care home against her wishes, and that the house would be transferred to himself. There was no reason to think that the parents lacked capacity for the relevant decisions, so there was no way to use the MCA in their best interests, and the son argued that the court was powerless to intervene. An abuser telling a judge that there is nothing the court can do to protect someone from his abuse rarely goes down well, and the court found that the inherent jurisdiction of the High Court had survived the advent of the MCA, and gave an injunction preventing the son from continuing that behaviour. This was upheld by the Court of Appeal.

Part Two of this chapter will deal with the court using its own powers under the inherent jurisdiction to authorise a deprivation of liberty for children, when it is working around the edges of the legislative framework of the Children Act, for example.

The inherent jurisdiction may also be available for adults, and especially where they fall outside the protection of the MCA because they have capacity for the relevant decisions, or they fall into the gap between the MHA and MCA / DoLS, as set out in the last chapter.

An example of that is the case of *Dr A*[556]. Dr A was a 50 year-old Iranian immigrant who was on hunger strike in protest against the decision of the UK Border Agency. He was also suffering from a delusional disorder, for which he was detained under the MHA. Wrestling with this, Mr Justice Baker held that the MHA could not be used to authorise force feeding as his hunger strike was related to political protest and not a manifestation of his mental disorder[557]; and that his detention under MHA s 3 meant that Dr A was ineligible under Schedule 1A and therefore the court had no power under s16 to make an order to authorise force feeding, which would amount to a (further) deprivation of his liberty[558].

---

556 *An NHS Trust v A* [2013] EWHC 2442 (COP).

557 So could not be treated under MHA s63.

558 MCA s16A.

Baker J found an answer by using the inherent jurisdiction of the court to authorise the force feeding[559]. Despite the treatment amounting to a deprivation of his liberty, he lacked capacity for the relevant decisions, and so the use of the inherent jurisdiction to authorise this could be compliant with Article 5(1)(e) as Dr A fell in the category of someone of "unsound mind".

In *Southend-on-Sea Borough Council*[560], the court had to consider what could be done to help a 97 year-old blind man who was living, together with his son, in deeply squalid conditions. Hayden J accepted that Mr Meyers had capacity for his own decisions, he was not of unsound mind, and that he was not "*vulnerable*" for the purposes of the inherent jurisdiction simply because he was blind. This would seem to have left the court without power to intervene, but Hayden J also found that the "*needy, irrational, frequently out of control as well as manifestly emotionally dependent*" son had an influence on his father that was "*insidious and pervasive [and] … is malign in effect if not in its intention. The consequence is to disable Mr Meyers from making a truly informed decision which impacts directly on his health and survival*".

Though the judge "*instinctively recoils from intervening in the decision making of a capacitous adult…. Here Mr Meyers' life requires to be protected and I consider that, ultimately, the State has an obligation to do so*".

He made an order that Mr Meyers may be prevented from living with his son, either at their current home or anywhere else, and though counsel for the parties did consider that this raised an issue over Article 5, the judge held that it did not amount to a deprivation of liberty. As he saw it, he was restricting Mr Meyers' options to be sure, but this was properly seen as a proportionate interference with his Article 8 rights to private and family life, rather than a deprivation of liberty.

---

[559] A postscript to the judgment notes that after a period of force feeding requiring the use of restraint, and his mental health improving with the use of medication, he was discharged from the MHA and Dr A then made a capacitous decision to return to Iran.

[560] [2019] EWHC 399 (Fam).

That may or may not be right[561], but it is clearly an example of a very serious interference in someone's life, and if it were a deprivation of liberty it is doubtful whether it could be squared with Article 5(1)(e) where the person involved is not of unsound mind.

In *Mazhar v Birmingham Community NHS Trust*[562], an NHS Trust obtained an order on an urgent basis out of hours that Mr Mazhar could be removed from his home and taken to hospital against his and his family's wishes, which was effected at around 3am by uniformed police and paramedics. There was no evidence that he lacked capacity to make his own decisions about care and treatment, but he was dependent on a ventilator which needed skilled carers 24 hours a day on a 2:1 basis, and (as a result of concerns raised by his family about some of the carers involved with his package) a point had been reached where no carers could be found to staff the package overnight. Mr Mazhar refused to go to hospital as a place of safety while that was addressed. The clinicians were concerned that the risks he faced without professional care overnight were unacceptable, and that there may have been some improper influence over him by his family.

The Court of Appeal were critical of the Trust's application, and said that the order should not have been made in this way[563], even allowing for some sympathy for the difficulties of dealing with urgent situations out of hours. But the court declined the opportunity to consider whether, in principle, the inherent jurisdiction could ever be used to authorise a deprivation of liberty for someone with capacity.

---

561 In *JE v DE* [2006] see chapter 4, Munby J rejected the local authority's submission that there was no deprivation of liberty where it simply sought to prevent DE living with JE at home.

562 [2020] EWCA Civ 1377.

563 The application was made without notice, meaning that Mr Mazhar and his family were not represented, and in fact the judge made the order based on the written evidence of the Trust alone, without even a hearing to test the evidence and urgency with the Trust's barrister; no reference was made in the order to reflect consideration of the court's jurisdiction to make such an order, and there was not nearly enough evidence of undue influence to justify invoking the inherent jurisdiction.

We are still exploring the edges of this map and, as with the MHA/DoLS overlap, the use of the inherent jurisdiction for vulnerable adults is not straightforward; it's a good idea to get detailed legal advice asap if you think this may be an issue.

Part 2 – Authorising a deprivation of liberty for Children and Young People

Just as children raise different issues for identifying a deprivation of their liberty, so there are differences in the way that they can be authorised. DoLS cannot be used under 18, and the *Re X* streamlined process is discouraged for 16-17 year-olds, and under 16, of course, the Court of Protection and the MCA itself do not apply.

Article 5(1)(d)

There is also a difference in the ECHR Article 5 for children. Up to now, we have been dealing with Article 5(1)(e) – deprivation of liberty being lawful for someone of "unsound mind", which can apply at any age.

But for children there is also Article 5(1)(d) – "*the detention of a minor by lawful order for the purpose of educational supervision*", which does not require a mental disorder or disability, and can be interpreted very widely to include all the child's welfare needs[564], though "*it is not the same thing as child protection*"[565].

There is also a distinctive statutory power set out in the Children Act 1989 s25.

Before that, let's just deal with detention of children under the Mental Health Act.

---

564 Article 5(1)(d) – see *Re T (A Child)* [2021] UKSC 35, see below.

565 See *Derbyshire County Council v EF* [2023] EWHC 1574 (Fam).

CAMHS Tier 4

Child and Adolescent Mental Health Services (CAMHS) can get involved when there is a question of detaining a child under the Mental Health Act as an inpatient. An inpatient bed is described as "Tier 4" of CAMHS, and they are commissioned nationally by NHS England rather than locally by each individual ICB.

As such, as well as needing the usual recommendations for detention under the MHA, there is an established *gatekeeping* process by which NHS England assesses whether an admission to a Tier 4 bed is appropriate. Sadly, often there is simply no Tier 4 bed available, as they are also vastly outstripped by demand.

There can be tension between the various public bodies involved, when the local authority feels that a child should be but is not detained under the MHA, though the courts have emphasised the need for collaboration[566].

Children Act 1989 s25 – Secure Accommodation

Section 25 of the Children Act 1989 provides a statutory framework for a child who is looked after by a local authority to be placed in "secure accommodation", meaning that it is intended to restrict liberty, ***only*** if he has a history of absconding and is likely to abscond from any other accommodation, and is likely to suffer significant harm if he did.

The specific accommodation must be specially approved for this purpose[567], and still needs consideration by the court in proceedings in which the child must be represented. This is the process by which the child's Article 5 rights are protected.

---

[566] *Blackpool Borough Council v HT* [2022] EWHC 1480 (Fam) https://www.bailii.org/ew/cases/EWHC/Fam/2022/1480.html

[567] The Children (Secure Accommodation) Regulations 1991.

In Wales, the equivalent is found in section 119 of the Social Services and Well-being (Wales) Act 2014.

The Supreme Court has accepted that the inherent jurisdiction can also be used to authorise a child's deprivation of liberty, if need be, where s25 cannot be used, for example where – all too often – there is no s25 compliant accommodation available[568].

Inherent Jurisdiction

As you might expect, the judiciary often find a way in which they can exercise the inherent jurisdiction.

EBY[569] is a "*bright and ambitious*" 17 year-old girl who wants to be a police officer. Her family circumstances have been hard; with her parents split, her mum's disabilities meant that she had to live with her dad, whose work kept him out of the house for long and antisocial hours. She has regularly been left unsupervised, and had fallen into involvement with a criminal gang, where she had been exploited, repeatedly beaten up and raped.

She was placed by the local authority into an unregistered children's home (see below) an hour away from her home, to which her mother and, later, her father consented[570], but EBY opposed this herself, and was being kept under 2:1 supervision in the placement, and 3:1 in the community, to prevent her absconding and to keep her safe. This was clearly a deprivation of her liberty that needed court approval.

568 *Re T (A Child)* – as above. And see *Re X (secure accommodation)* [2022] below.

569 [2023] EWHC 2494 (Fam). https://www.bailii.org/ew/cases/EWHC/Fam/2023/2494.html

570 Section 20 Children Act 1989 allows for the local authority to arrange accommodation for a child with the parents' consent.

Children Act 1989 s100 contains barriers intended to trim the scope for discretionary intervention where there is already a statutory scheme, essentially that the court cannot use the inherent jurisdiction:

- if it would require the child to be accommodated or placed into care by the local authority;
- if the court does not give permission for an application under the inherent jurisdiction;
- and that such permission should only be given if what the local authority wants to do cannot be achieved by any other statutory power, and (if the inherent jurisdiction were not used) the child is likely to suffer serious harm.

In *EBY*, the court carefully picked its way round these limits and held that it could still use the inherent jurisdiction in this case. The judge authorised her deprivation of liberty for short period, as necessary and proportionate to the risks she faced, pending review with updated evidence.

In *Re A-F*[571], Lord Justice Munby gave a steer as to how applications under the inherent jurisdiction should be brought:

- No substantive or final order should be made without an oral hearing in the family division of the High Court;
- The child must be a party to the proceedings and have a guardian, ideally the children's guardian acting in the care proceedings;
- The child should be permitted to speak to the judge in person if of an age to express their wishes and feelings;

571 [2018] EWHC 138 (Fam), at paragraphs 49-53. https://www.bailii.org/ew/cases/EWHC/Fam/2018/138.html

- It would not be lawful to make a "bulk" application in respect of several children at once.

As you can see, the proceedings to authorise a deprivation of liberty for a child using the inherent jurisdiction are likely to be significantly more involved than LJ Munby thought appropriate for the *Re X* scheme for deprivation of liberty in the community generally.

<u>"National DoLS Court" / List</u>

Nonetheless, to keep up with the increase in cases of deprivation of liberty for children, the High Court introduced a "*National Deprivation of Liberty Court*" in July 2022, for a 12-month trial.

This was always something of a misnomer[572] as it was not a new court but simply a request that all such applications were issued at the Royal Courts of Justice in London, and then allocated to judges there, just as a way of better organising the cases of deprivation of liberty authorisations that were going through the High Court.

In July 2023, Sir Andrew McFarlane confirmed that the pilot would be continued, though it would be renamed with a "more accurate title" of "National DoLs List"[573].

One positive result though was more transparency in the number of cases being processed in this way, especially with regular reports from the Nuffield Family Justice Observatory[574].

---

[572] Calling it a "*national DoLS court*" was even worse – it had nothing to do with the Deprivation of Liberty Safeguards, of course, as it dealt exclusively with children to whom DoLS does not apply.

[573] https://www.judiciary.uk/guidance-and-resources/a-view-from-the-presidents-chambers-july-2023/ though of course the reference to "DoLs" is still confusing.

[574] See chapter 16.

Un/Regulated placements

The scarcity of appropriate options has also raised the question of the use of unregulated and unregistered placements.

An unregulated placement is a setting which does not, for whatever reason, meet the criteria for registration with a regulatory body – such as the Care Quality Commission or Ofsted. It does not need to be registered.

An unregistered setting is one that is regulated – ie it should be registered, but it is not, for whatever reason.

On 30 July 2021, the Supreme Court ruled in re *T (A Child)*[575] that the inherent jurisdiction of the High Court could be used to declare that it was lawful for a local authority to place a child in an *unregulated* placement where the child was deprived of his or her liberty, however undesirable, if it was the only practical option available to the local authority.

On 9 September 2021, regulations[576] came into force in England which provided that placement of looked after children under 16 in an unregulated setting by a public body would be unlawful.

Just a day earlier, though, Mr Justice McDonald[577] had ruled that this did not stop the High Court declaring that such a placement of a child under 16 by a local authority was lawful, if there was no alternative. This apparent contradiction is not helpful.

---

575 [2021] UKSC 35.

576 The Care Planning, Placement and Case Review (England) (amendment) Regulations 2021.

577 MBC v AM (DOL Orders for Children Under 16) [2021] EWHC 2472 (Fam).

Sitting in the Court of Appeal, the current President of the Family court, Sir Andrew McFarlane confirmed that deprivation of a child's liberty at an *unregistered* placement can be authorised:

> "... *where conditions of imperative necessity require, the common law steps in and allows the High Court to exercise its inherent jurisdiction*"[578] *(emphasis added).*

On 14 August 2023, Ofsted issued some guidance to remind providers that the existence of a court order authorising a deprivation of a child's liberty does not negate the need for a children's home to be registered with them (or with Care Inspectorate Wales)[579].

Until very recently, the courts used to monitor this. Guidance issued by Sir Andrew McFarlane in 2019[580], updated in 2020[581], set out that if the court were authorising a deprivation of liberty at an *unregistered* setting it must:

- Require in the Order that the placement applies for registration with Ofsted or the Care Inspectorate Wales within seven working days;
- Ask the local authority to confirm within 10 days that the application has been made;
- List another hearing immediately if it hasn't; and

---

[578] *A Mother v Derby City Council* [2021] EWCA Civ 1867. https://www.bailii.org/ew/cases/EWCA/Civ/2021/1867.html

[579] https://www.gov.uk/government/publications/placing-children-deprivation-of-liberty-orders/placing-children-deprivation-of-liberty-orders.

[580] https://www.judiciary.uk/guidance-and-resources/practice-guidance-placements-in-unregistered-childrens-homes-in-england-or-unregistered-care-home-services-in-wales-2/

[581] https://www.judiciary.uk/guidance-and-resources/addendum-to-practice-guidance-placements-in-unregistered-childrens-homes-in-england-or-unregistered-care-home-services-in-wales/

- Review the registration status after 12 weeks.

However, on 11 October 2023, Sir Andrew published revised guidance[582], watering down the courts' role, Though the new guidance still says that the court "may" (no longer "must") order that the provider applies for registration within 7 days, the court oversight to check this is actually done is scrapped. "*It is not for the Court to become a regulatory body or the overseer of the regulatory process*", he writes, but acknowledges that this is driven by the "*very considerable burdens*" this had put on the court system given the growth in the number of deprivation of liberty orders sought in unregistered placements.

It would be helpful, of course, if all this confusion could be cleared up, but it is, at bottom, a symptom of the shameful lack of suitable placements and resources.

Un/Suitable placements

We cannot leave the topic of authorisation of deprivation of liberty for under 18s without the grim reality of the struggle – all too often – to find any suitable placement option at all. Sometimes the problem is not the complexities of the legal test, or the niceties of the legal framework, but simply the raw reality of having nothing to offer to actually meet a child's needs.

There is no doubt that the problems have got worse recently, but they are not new.

In 2017 Lord Justice Munby, none other, attracted headlines with a stark warning to the public bodies involved in a tragic case[583]. He was dealing with an application[584] about a 17 year-old girl, "X", who had made a

[582] https://www.judiciary.uk/wp-content/uploads/2023/10/PFD-Revised-DoLs-Guidance-September-2023.pdf

[583] https://www.theguardian.com/society/2017/aug/03/judge-warns-of-blood-on-our-hands-if-suicidal-girl-is-forced-out-of-secure-care

[584] Re X (A Child) (No 3) [2017] EWHC 2036 (Fam), 3 August 2017

number of "determined attempts" to take her own life. She was in desperate need of a secure setting to keep her safe, but nowhere suitable could be found.

LJ Munby said:

> *"If ... we, the system, society, the state, are unable to provide X with the supportive and safe placement she so desperately needs, and if, in consequence, she is enabled to make another attempt on her life, then I can only say, with bleak emphasis: we will have blood on our hands".*

And:

> *"We are, even in these times of austerity, one of the richest countries in the world. Our children and young people are our future. X is part of our future. It is a disgrace to any country with pretensions to civilisation, compassion and, dare one say it, basic human decency, that a judge in 2017 should be faced with the problems thrown up by this case and should have to express himself in such terms."*

He went on to say that he felt "ashamed and embarrassed" that no suitable hospital place could be found that could take proper care of a vulnerable 17 year-old girl.

The judge directed that copies of the judgment be sent immediately to the Chief Executive of NHS England, and to the Secretaries of State for the Home Office, Health, Education and Justice.

Sadly, that in itself does not conjure up the further resources so obviously required, and if anything things have got worse since 2017, while this has become a familiar theme in the cases. It was also highlighted in a powerful report in 2020 by the Children's Commissioner – "*The Children who no-one knows what to do with*".[585]

---

585 https://www.childrenscommissioner.gov.uk/report/the-children-who-no-one-knows-what-to-do-with/ 11 November 2020.

Speaking about s25 placements specifically, in *Re X (secure accommodation)*[586] in 2023, Sir Andrew McFarlane lamented the "*wholesale failure to provide adequate resources*", and said that there were 60-70 children waiting for a secure placement on any given day:

> *"All the courts can do is seek to draw attention to the problem in the hope that those with responsibility for these matters in Parliament and Government will take the issue up ..."*

When the judge asked the Secretary of State for Education to address this, the initial response was that this is simply up to the local authorities, which the judge described as:

> *"... shocking to see that the Department for Education seemed to be simply washing its hands of this chronic problem"*[587].

Refusal to authorise a deprivation of liberty

Another side of the same problem is that, at times, a child or young person can be brought into hospital (being seen as a place of relative safety), as a result of a failure of a placement, rather than them having any need for medical treatment. Often there are challenges are around self harm or attempting suicide which would be all but impossible to manage in any kind of placement. But where she does not meet the criteria for detention under the Mental Health Act (ie she does not have a mental disorder, the nature or degree of which warrants detention for assessment or treatment) there may be few legal tools available.

If a 16-17 year-old patient lacks capacity to make decisions about care and residence, then it may be possible to make MCA based best interests decisions about staying in hospital, but any deprivation of their liberty can only be authorised by a court order. If they have capacity, (or are

586 [2023] EWHC 129.

587 The judge refused the request for the Secretary of State to be excused from the next hearing, and the government did, eventually, acknowledge that there needed to be more support given to local authorities.

under 16[588]), then we look to the inherent jurisdiction of the High Court, as the Court of Protection has no powers.

We certainly cannot rely on *Ferreira*[589] to argue that they are not deprived of their liberty, if they have no medical need to be in hospital at all.

Such situations can have a huge impact on the functioning of a hospital. Often many staff are required; the staff in an acute hospital setting may not be trained in skills that they might need, such as physical restraint; this may involve closing part of the rest of a ward to avoid the disruption causing distress to other patients. Often the moral distress and emotional cost to staff is devastating: trying to manage a situation without the proper tools or resources, for a patient with no medical need to be in hospital.

But above all, of course, there is a vulnerable young person who is simply in the wrong place – often a teenager either on an adult ward, or among very young and very sick children and their families – for lack of anywhere better.

Because any deprivation of liberty in those cases cannot be authorised by DoLS (even if they do lack capacity for the relevant decisions, because DoLS only applies at age 18) such cases have to go to court for approval. Often, despite all the issues above, the hospital trust will be seeking the legal authority to keep the patient in the hospital, though they don't need to be there, simply because allowing them to leave with nowhere suitable to go would be worse. The court application can be little more than an exercise in trying to apply some pressure to the body responsible for finding a more suitable placement (usually the local authority), but of course they can no more conjure a suitable placement than anyone else, when they simply don't exist.

---

[588] It may be thin legal ice to try to rely on parental consent alone to keep a child even under 16 in hospital where this amounts to a deprivation of liberty without any medical need to justify this, especially perhaps if the child is *Gillick* competent. See also chapter 10.

[589] See chapter 7.

Often, the courts have felt that there is little option but to authorise a deprivation of liberty in this situation, where there is simply no alternative, often repeating Lord Justice Munby's concerns. But recently this has started to change.

In *Wigan MBC v Y and others*[590], Mr Justice MacDonald was concerned with a 12 year-old boy ("Y"). After explaining that Y had complex medical and behavioural issues, and demonstrates "challenging, violent and increasingly self-harming behaviour", the judge summarised, grimly, that Y did not have a mental disorder to justify detention under the MHA, but:

> *"At the same time, the therapeutic treatment within a restrictive clinical environment for acute behavioural and emotional issues arising from past trauma that he does urgently require is simply unavailable".*

As a result,

> *"… Y is currently and inappropriately placed on a clinical ward at the [named hospital], where he has had to be subject to chemical restraint, physical restraint and 5:1 staffing in order to attempt to control his behaviour. At times there have been up to thirteen police officers present on the ward in an effort to control Y's behaviour. That paediatric ward has now had to be shut to new admissions due to the risk presented by Y and parts of the ward have been closed entirely. Other gravely ill children have had to be moved to alternative hospitals across the North West of England and lists of elective surgeries for children in urgent need of such treatment have been cancelled. Nurses and other hospital staff have been injured. Other sick children and their parents have been alarmed and frightened. At present, Y has nowhere else to go."*

Y was in the care of the local authority, and so parental consent to negate any deprivation of liberty was not possible. In the circumstances, the local

590 [2021] EWHC 1982 (Fam) https://www.bailii.org/ew/cases/EWHC/Fam/2021/1982.html

authority sought a court order to make it lawful that Y be deprived of his liberty by keeping him there in hospital.

In contrast to earlier cases in which the same judge had authorised placements that were "sub-optimal", especially where there was no real alternative[591], in this case there was nothing positive to say about the situation at all. The judge decided that:

> "... *the only possible conclusion regarding Y's current situation on the hospital ward is that it is an inappropriate, demeaning and, quite frankly, brutal one for a 12 year-old child.*
>
> *The primary purpose of a paediatric hospital ward is to treat children, not to deprive them of their liberty by means of locked doors, sparse belongings and chemical restraint. There is now no clinical basis for Y to be on the hospital ward and he is medically ready for discharge. .... Within this context, Y currently remains contained on the ward in a sectioned off area that is not designed to restrict the liberty of a child but rather to provide medical treatment to children. The doors to the paediatric ward have been securely shut and the area cleared of all movable objects. Accordingly, not only is there no connection at all between purpose of the hospital ward on which Y is held and the deprivation of Y's liberty, but the arrangements that are in place to restrict his liberty in that setting are, accordingly and necessarily, an entirely ad hoc arrangement that is not, and indeed can never be, designed to meet his needs*".

As such,

> "... *I cannot in good conscience conclude that the restrictions in respect of which the local authority seeks authorisation from the court are in Y's best interests, having regard to Y's welfare as my paramount consideration. Indeed, I consider that it would border on the obscene to use the protective ... jurisdiction of the High Court to authorise Y's current situation. I am further satisfied that this conclusion is not*

[591] See for example *Tameside MBC* [2021] EWHC 1814 (Fam).

> *altered by the fact that, as at 12 noon yesterday, there was no alternative placement available capable of meeting Y's needs. In this case, I consider that the current arrangements for Y are so inappropriate that they constitute a clear and continuing breach of his Article 5 rights".*

He concluded that:

> *"Judgments given by a court should be sober and measured. Superlatives should be avoided. It is likewise prudent that a judge carefully police a judgment for the presence of adjectives. However, and as the hearing proved, in this case it is simply not possible to convey the appropriate sense of alarm without recourse to such language. In this case, having observed that in his thirty years at the Bar he had never been in a position of having to ask a court to authorise a regime for a child "as shameful as this one is", [the local authority's barrister] conceded on behalf of the local authority that, boiled down to its essence, his submission was simply that the court must today prefer the lesser of two acknowledged evils, the hospital ward or the street, in circumstances where there is currently no alternative placement. But that is not a solution that can be countenanced in a civilised society. The test laid down by the law is not which is the lesser of two evils but what is in the child's best interests having regard to the child's welfare as the paramount consideration. The parens patriae[592] inherent jurisdiction of the court is protective in nature. As I have observed above, it would border on the obscene to use a protective jurisdiction to continue Y's current bleak and dangerous situation simply because those with responsibility for making proper provision for vulnerable children in this jurisdiction have failed to discharge that responsibility".*

592 See part one of this chapter: A bit of legal Latin referring to the power of the courts on behalf of the monarch to protect those unable to protect themselves – like a parent to the nation.

There is now a depressing, growing body of similar cases in which a judge has refused to authorise a deprivation of liberty in circumstances where there was no viable alternative available[593].

In a case[594] involving a 13 year-old girl being detained in a hospital for several months with no medical need to be there, for lack of a suitable placement, Mr Justice Poole said:

> *"This case, as do many others involving the care of children with complex needs, calls into question the court's role. Very often the court is told that there is only one place where the child can be accommodated. The court's role is therefore very limited. There are no real choices for the court to make. The court cannot direct that placements shall be made available. The court is not a regulator and cannot inspect potential placements or oversee care regimes. On the other hand, even when there are no other placement options, the court does not merely provide a rubber stamp for the restrictions sought, and there are decisions to be made about the extent of the restrictions that are necessary and proportionate and in a child's best interests. However, the courts, like the parties, continue to be confined by the consequences of what Lord Stephens called a "scandalous lack of provision" for which it appears that there is no end in sight". (emphasis added).*

Note that even where the application is refused, bringing the case to court was the right thing to do.

"Holding the baby"

We will come back to the question of the value of safeguards in the absence of a viable alternative[595], but whatever the merit of this as a moral

[593] For example, *Nottinghamshire County Council v LH* [2021] EWHC 2584, *A County Council v A Mother (refusal to make a DoLS Order)* [2021] EWHC 3303, *An NHS Trust v ST (refusal of deprivation of liberty order)* [2022] EWHC 719 (Fam).

[594] *Manchester City Council v J* [2022] EWHC 2687 (Fam) at para 36.

[595] See chapter 19.

stand, refusing to "*approve*" a situation so awful for the child, it does little to help a hospital.

Staff still face the dilemma of imposing restrictions on children like Y, intended to keep him safe, for fear of something worse if he was allowed to leave without a suitable alternative placement, only to be told that a court had refused to authorise it!

In these circumstances, though not ideal to say the least, the hospital trust is not entirely without legal cover, and might rely on some of these other powers:

- The Children Act 1989 s3(5) gives a power to anyone who has a child in their care, but does not have parental responsibility for them, to "*do what is reasonable in all the circumstances of the case for the purpose of safeguarding or promoting the child's welfare*".

- There are common law powers, such as intervention to prevent a breach of the peace[596], or to prevent harm, or to intervene for "necessity"[597]. Though it can be uncomfortable to rely on only these fairly woolly ideas, as we saw in *Bournewood* itself, they have been recognised by the courts, for example in the Court of Appeal in *Munjaz v Mersey Care NHS Trust*[598], where it was noted that there is a "*... general [common law] power to take such steps as are reasonably necessary and proportionate to protect others from the*

596 This can be exercised by anyone, not only the police – see *R v CC of Gloucestershire Constabulary* [2006] UKHL 55 "*every constable and citizen enjoys the power and is subject to the duty to seek to prevent, by arrest or other action short of arrest, any breach of the peace occurring in his presence, or any breach of the peace which (having occurred) is likely to be renewed, or any breach of the peace which is about to occur*".

597 For example, in *Black v Forsey* [1988] SLT 57, Lord Griffiths said that there is a power which is "*confined to imposing temporary restraint to a lunatic who has run amok and is a manifest danger either to himself or to others – state of affairs that is as obvious to a layman as to a doctor*".

598 [2003] EWCA Civ 1036.

immediate risk of significant harm. This applies whether or not the patient lacks capacity to make decisions for himself'.

- If the child is 16-17 and lacks capacity for the relevant decisions, the MCA s6 gives an authority to restrain them if in their best interests and necessary to prevent harm and proportionate to the likelihood and seriousness of the harm (though it should not extend to authorisation of a deprivation of liberty).

- Section 3(1) of the Criminal Law Act 1967 allows reasonable force to be used to prevent crime, including in self-defence, defence of others, or protection of property.

- Finally, though it depends on the discretion of the police rather than the hospital, section 46 of the Children Act 1989 gives a power to impose a Police Protection Order, under which a constable acting on a reasonable belief that a child would otherwise be likely to suffer significant harm, can "*take such steps as are reasonable to ensure that the child's removal from any hospital, or other place, in which he is then being accommodated is prevented*". This comes with some procedural requirements, and is only valid for up to 72 hours.

Holding powers under the Mental Health Act s5 are mainly for use to keep someone in hospital where they need to be assessed for detention under the MHA, and may not be useful for someone who has already been assessed as not detainable under that Act.

Invidious as it is, the trust may face a potential liability for an unlawful deprivation of the child's liberty, but must balance that against the competing potential liabilities should the child come to harm from the trust allowing them to leave.

In all such cases, of course, anybody left in this position should seek prompt legal advice; proceed with great care; document decision-making scrupulously; consider seeking an indemnity for any potential liabilities from the body responsible for placing the child appropriately, who have left them "*holding the baby*" in this way; and be very conscious of the strain on the staff involved and their need for support.

Part 3 – Hospital Emergency Departments

At the risk of going over some ground again, the situation in a hospital Emergency Department is worth thinking about separately, even if many of the same tools already discussed apply.

The Emergency Department is a distinctive scenario because:

- DoLS cannot be used to authorise any deprivation of liberty, as P needs to be a detained resident of the hospital or care home for DoLS to be used, which excludes those not yet admitted.
- The holding powers of MHA s5 also only apply to patients who have been admitted[599];
- Things can naturally be fraught and urgent, with life or death consequences;
- Even with 24/7 access to a judge out of hours, if need be, the timescale for necessary decisions in ED may not allow for applications to court before taking action;
- At the moment, we are seeing greater demand and ever longer waiting times in ED, as elsewhere in the system, applying more pressure to the timescale in which we might regard a deprivation of liberty as possible, and to the resource and headspace for staff to deal with such issues alongside the substantive care.

599 Though it has been suggested that this could be extended to ED if the Mental Health Act is reformed, but the government has not yet committed to pursue the Mental Health Bill in this Parliament.

So, some advice for ED specifically[600].

The starting point is the assessment of the patient's capacity to make their own decisions about any proposed investigations or treatment, and about staying in hospital for that to be done. As with any decisions, it should be assumed that they have capacity. But that does not mean that capacity shouldn't be assessed specifically where there are reasonable indications to do so. It is not good enough to rely on the presumption of capacity as an abdication of responsibility to take a view on whether the patient in front of you has capacity or not to make their own decisions.

Without capacity there can be no consent, and treatment without consent is not ok, bringing potential criminal, civil and regulatory consequences, as well as breaching the patient's rights, unless the MCA is followed appropriately.

It is perfectly OK for the assessment of capacity to be proportionate to the situation and the urgency. No one is suggesting a long-winded process of box ticking while the patient dies untreated.

Of course, someone with capacity to make the relevant decision can lawfully refuse treatment, even if they will die without it. This does not mean that someone assessed to have that capacity cannot be helped, just that it is outside the scope of the MCA to force help on them.

For instance, someone may be assessed for detention under the MHA if they are at risk of dying by suicide. There is a positive duty on the state to act to protect individual lives under Article 2, balanced with individual rights to autonomy, liberty and private life. Suicide is no longer a crime, since the Suicide Act 1967, but it can be dangerously misleading to see it in terms that a patient who "has capacity" must simply be left to their own devices.

---

[600] This is focussed on deprivation of liberty issues, and not intended to be a full account of medical treatment decision making, for which I, obviously, recommend: A Practical Guide to the Law of Medical Treatment Decisions.

Even where someone cannot lawfully be stopped from leaving ED, it is appropriate to think what support can be offered, for example by alerting other health or social care services (safeguarding referrals for self-neglect do not need the patient's consent) or the police, requesting a safe and well check.

If the patient does not have capacity then we are into best interests decision making. Ideally this involves a collaborative discussion with the patient themselves and with those that know them best to make sure that their wishes and feelings, values and beliefs are fully taken into account. But again, this can reasonably be tempered by the reality and urgency of the scenario you are in.

There may be cases where it is clear that it is not in that person's best interests to provide emergency treatment, where they cannot decide for themselves.

Otherwise, provision of life saving treatment is the priority; as I have said, I much prefer to explain myself to a judge than to a coroner.

Any doubt about capacity or best interests can be referred to court to resolve, but it is appropriate to provide life sustaining treatment in the interim.

As long as your view is reasonable that the patient lacks capacity for the relevant decisions, and that what you are doing is in their best interests, you should have the protection from liability of MCA s5.

That will extend to any restraint that is used, as long as it is necessary to prevent harm and proportionate to the likelihood and seriousness of the harm, under MCA s6.

MCA 5-6 do not authorise any deprivation of liberty, but *Ferreira* says that life saving medical treatment[601] is no deprivation of liberty, as long as it is the same as for anyone else with that physical health need.

---

[601] At least – see chapter 7.

Where we cannot rely on *Ferreira* because the treatment is different due to the patient's mental health condition, we need to consider whether the restrictions imposed meet the acid test (continuous supervision and control, and not free to leave[602]) for long enough (a non-negligible period of time[603]) to amount to an objective deprivation of liberty. Any confinement in ED will obviously be imputable to the state, and lack of valid consent (where the patient lacks capacity to make the decision) will leave this as a deprivation of liberty that requires authorisation to comply with Article 5.

We know we cannot use the Deprivation of Liberty Safeguards. What other tools might be available?

Of course, a court order could authorise any deprivation of liberty, but that would be likely to take some time.

We saw in chapter 8 that MCA s4B allows for a deprivation of liberty to provide life sustaining treatment or carry out a vital act in an emergency *while seeking a decision from the court.* Note that the emergency itself, and the vital nature of the treatment itself, are not enough to make any deprivation of liberty lawful, *unless the decision from the court is being sought.*[604] This seems likely to mean at least that the hospital legal team are involved and are taking steps to start proceedings, before s4B can be relied on.

Otherwise, we are looking at largely the same tools as for the scenario where a court refuses to authorise a deprivation of liberty for a child considered in more detail at the end of Part Two:

---

602 See chapter 7.

603 See chapter 8.

604 See chapter 8 – The version of s4B amended by the LPS legislation would change that, but that has not been brought into force, and we do not know if or when it will be.

- Common law powers, such as intervention to prevent a breach of the peace, or to prevent harm, or to intervene for "necessity".
- Section 3(1) of the Criminal Law Act 1967 allows reasonable force to be used to prevent crime, including in self defence, defence of others, or protection of property.

And for children,

- Use of the Children Act 1989 s3(5)[605]; or
- A Police Protection Order under the Children Act 1989 s46.

Finally, in addition, an Emergency Department is considered to be a public place for the purposes of using MHA s136, the power to remove someone from a public place to a place of safety.

Reform of the law to provide more certainty in Emergency Departments, both over the scope of the *Ferreira* exception and the legal basis for authorisation of any deprivation of liberty, would be very welcome.

Key Points

- Where there is a deprivation of liberty, it must be authorised to meet Article 5 rights, and where DoLS cannot be used, we must turn to the court[606].

[605] Though note that the Mental Health Act Code of Practice (Para 26.61) says: "Staff should be aware that under section 3(5) of the Children Act 1989 they may do "what is reasonable in all the circumstances of the case for the purposes of safeguarding or promoting the child's welfare". Whether an intervention is reasonable or not will depend, among other things, upon the urgency and gravity of what is required. This might allow action to be taken to prevent the child from harming himself, however it would not allow restrictive interventions that are not proportionate and would not authorise actions that amounted to a deprivation of liberty".

[606] Unless the Mental Health Act 1983 is used, which has no lower age limit.

- That can mean the Court of Protection for those over 16 who lack capacity for the relevant decisions, or the High Court using powers of the Children Act or the inherent jurisdiction for children under 18 or (rarely) for vulnerable adults, or those ineligible for DoLS.

- The number of potential applications is such that the Court of Protection has developed a streamlined process (*Re X*, or COPDOL11) for uncontroversial cases which can be authorised without a hearing, though concern has been raised that it is not enough to meet heir Article 5 rights if P is not a party to those proceedings.

- It seems unfair that applications to court to deprive someone of their liberty do not bring access to non-means tested legal aid, which is available to challenges to DoLS authorisations under MCA s21A.

- For children in particular, there are further issues about the lack of appropriate placements, which has led to use of unregistered placements for which the court has wanted further oversight, though this has been diluted recently.

- There have also been cases in which the court has said that a placement for a child is so unsuitable that it has refused to authorise it, even in the absence of any meaningful alternative, leaving the provider "holding the baby" and concerns about the legal basis for this.

- There are similar concerns about the legal basis for deprivation of liberty if it occurs in a hospital Emergency Department, where DoLS cannot be used, and a court application may not be practicable in the timescale required, though there are some legal tools available; and it is important to remember that critical clinical care comes first.

- As with so many bits of the system, the failings and complexities of the legal framework are magnified by the appalling mismatch between the scale of the task and the resources available.

CHAPTER FIFTEEN

ACCOUNTABILITY

When we fail to bring proper scrutiny and safeguards where someone may be deprived of their liberty, the cost will inevitably fall most heavily on that individual herself. Care may be given and constraints imposed in a way that is not the least restrictive way to meet her best interests, or not necessary to prevent harm or proportionate to that harm. She may be forced to live somewhere she should not be, and under conditions that she should not bear, and without the right to challenge it there should be.

Criminal Law

This can be a matter for the criminal law. The Mental Capacity Act 2005 created a criminal offence of ill treatment or wilful neglect of someone who "*lacks capacity*"[607], carrying a potential prison sentence of up to 5 years.

[607] For all the appropriate emphasis on "capacity" being meaningless without reference to the decision being considered, it is a quirk of the MCA that this section just establishes a criminal offence in relation to someone who "lacks capacity" full stop. This was actually used as a basis to challenge a conviction in *R v Dunn* [2010] EWCA Crim 2935. The Court of Appeal was having none of it. Though it recognised the inconsistency, as a matter of policy to avoid making prosecutions even harder, they held: "*...the stark reality is that it was open to the jury to conclude that the decisions about the care of each of these residents at the time when they were subjected to ill-treatment were being made for them by others, including the appellant, just because they lacked the capacity to make these decisions for themselves. For the purposes of section 2, this was "the matter" envisaged in the legislation*".

There was already an offence of ill treatment or wilful neglect of patients receiving treatment under the Mental Health Act 1983[608], and there is also an offence of wilful ill treatment or neglect of children[609].

Following the Francis report into the scandal at Mid-Staffordshire hospitals, in 2015 the Criminal Justice and Courts Act s20-21 introduced a similar offence for those who have full capacity, which can apply both to individuals and organisations providing care.

Most convictions are of professional carers in working in institutional settings. A recent case, though, saw the wife of a disabled man, as well as his carer, jailed for eleven years.

Tom Somerset-How, aged 40, weighed just 6 stone when he was rescued from his home. He has cerebral palsy, is almost blind and uses an electric wheelchair. He was left in bed almost constantly over four years, often without enough food and drink, unwashed and lying in his own excrement, by his wife and a live-in carer who became her lover. He went a year without brushing his teeth. They stole the money from his benefits, treating him, the judge said, like "*a cow to be milked*". They were convicted of "wilful neglect"[610] and offences under modern slavery legislation.

This appalling abuse was eventually uncovered by a friend and family member. If Mr Somerset-How had lacked capacity for decisions about care and residence, would his abuse have been more effectively prevented, or caught sooner, if his care arrangements were treated as a deprivation of liberty that required scrutiny and authorisation, despite it being in his own home?

---

608 MHA s127.

609 Children Act 1933 s1.

610 Often, as here, it is not clear in the media coverage of ill treatment or wilful neglect cases exactly what offence is being alleged; there is no suggestion in the media coverage that Mr Somerset-How "lacked capacity" for the MCA s44, but the CJAC s20-21 does not catch unpaid, family carers, so it is not clear on what basis his wife could be prosecute under that.

The Regulator

For the organisations where such abuse happens in an institutional setting, it can be terminal. Winterborne View's owner (Castlebeck) went out of business after the scandal there and, likewise, Whorlton Hall was quickly closed.

The CQC[611] has a significant role to play. Regulation 11 of the fundamental standards[612] makes it an offence to provide care or treatment without the patient's consent or – if they cannot give it – without properly applying the MCA. Regulation 13(5), dealing with safeguarding, is explicit:

> *"A service user must not be deprived of their liberty for the purpose of receiving care or treatment without lawful authority".*

CQC inspections of NHS hospital trusts in the last few years often make critical findings about the number of people apparently unlawfully deprived of their liberty, and insist that this be addressed within a particular timescale. This can leave the trust in some trouble, when their referrals to the local authority are being made appropriately and the backlog is the result of the local authority's approach / resources / (de)prioritisation of hospital cases[613]. Hospitals can face regulatory action, and need pragmatic legal advice.

It is certainly the case that for any care provider, a failure to get the MCA right, including DoLS processes, is very strongly correlated with very poor inspection and rating outcomes and regulatory action.

In November 2022, the CQC fined an NHS trust £8,000 in total for failures to provide for appropriate support to secure consent or to comply

---

611 Care Quality Commission, the regulator of health and social care in England. In Wales it is the Care Inspectorate Wales or Health Inspectorate Wales, though this section focusses on the CQC as there are more prominent recent examples of their action on these issues.

612 Health and Social Care Act 2008 (Regulated Activities) Regulations 2014.

613 See chapter 16.

with the MCA if the patient cannot consent, where it did not provide a British Sign Language interpreter for a patient who was deaf, and did not contact someone holding a Lasting Power of Attorney for the patient.

In February 2023, another NHS trust was issued with a warning notice by the CQC, citing failures to have effective systems and processes to ensure consent / compliance with the MCA, including those who presented at A&E and may have been prevented from leaving as a best interests decision.

But that does not mean that patients should be left to their own devices. In March 2023, another NHS trust was fined more than £200,000 after the death of a man with advanced dementia, who had managed to abscond from A&E and fell down a grassy bank and died after hitting his head on the concrete at the bottom.

In the State of Care Report for 2022/23, published on 20 October 2023[614], the CQC said:

> *"We are concerned that poor understanding of the MCA and issues with the management of DoLS are contributing to the overuse of restrictive practice."*

Compensation and barriers to claims

There are also a number of cases in which unlawful deprivation of liberty has led to a hefty award of damages and some very public criticism by the court.

Though the focus of the Court of Protection is squarely on the future – looking *forwards* to determine the right thing to do now, rather than *backwards* to criticise conduct in the past – it is well established that the court does have the power to order compensation where appropriate[615].

---

614 https://www.cqc.org.uk/publications/major-report/state-care/2022-2023/dols

615 *YA(F)* [2010] EWCOP 2770.

It is worth taking stock on the relatively few cases in which we have seen compensation awarded so far, because there is no reason to think that these would have been buried with DoLS even if they are eventually dumped in favour of the LPS[616], or any other reforms. And, if anything, delay in such reform is only likely to increase the focus on the potential liabilities we may face while the tools we have are outstripped by the task.

The starting point is ECHR Article 5(5):

> *"Everyone who has been the victim of arrest or detention in contravention of the provisions of this article shall have an enforceable right to compensation."*

At face value, that is quite startling.

There is no equivalent provision in any other Article of the ECHR. Even Article 2 (right to life) and Article 3 (right to not suffer torture of inhuman or degrading treatment) are not protected by the same explicit right to "compensation".

And this is no trivial issue; there may be hundreds of thousands of people unlawfully deprived of their liberty as a result of a combination of the *Cheshire West* widening of the group of people regarded as deprived of liberty, and the consequent backlog of DoLS assessments to be undertaken, and with very few of the cases outside DoLS having yet been brought to court[617].

---

[616] The government declined the opportunity to legislate more clearly on the issue – the Law Commission had recommended a clearer remedy should be set out, but this was not adopted. See para 15.39 onwards of the Law Commission report on proposed reform on deprivation of liberty (2017) https://www.lawcom.gov.uk/project/mental-capacity-and-deprivation-of-liberty/ and see chapter 17.

[617] There was a backlog of 126,000 unprocessed DoLS applications in England as at 31 March 2023, and the Impact assessments for LPS consider there are 53,000 people deprived of their liberty in the community in England needing authorisation by the court, as well as 6,600 16-17 year-olds according to the Department of Education, of which only a few thousand cases per year seem to be brought. In Wales the backlog was "only" around 4,300 cases unprocessed as at 31 March 2022, albeit from a total of

The Joint Committee on Human Rights said:

> *"Every person who is deprived of their liberty without the completion of an application within statutory timeframes is unlawfully deprived of their liberty. Where this happens, it is clearly unacceptable and constitutes a breach of the right to liberty and security".*[618]

It is hard to think of another scenario where the law, policy and public funding have combined to create such an inevitable and widespread unlawfulness. But as we have seen, substantial compensation does not always follow.

The Human Rights Act 1998, which incorporates the fundamental ECHR rights, including Article 5, into domestic law provides[619] that

> "*No award of damages is to be made unless ... the court is satisfied that **the award is necessary to afford just satisfaction** ...".*

In many cases, a court has held that the declaration of the breach of rights is in itself "*just satisfaction*".

In the Court of Appeal in *Bournewood*, in which HL and his family had won and a declaration was made that he had been deprived of his liberty unlawfully, you may recall that the handsome sum of £1 was awarded in compensation[620].

This reflects another aspect of the law which stands in the way of substantial awards of damages – what you might (glibly) call the "*no harm no foul*" principle. By and large, the purpose of *compensation* in our system is, well, to *compensate* rather than to punish or even to hold accountable. And the value of compensation is geared to the extent of the

---

only around 16,000 applications being made pa (the 2022/23 figures for Wales are not available at the time of writing). See Chapter 16.

618 "Protecting human rights in care settings", Fourth Report of Session 2022-23, para 53. https://publications.parliament.uk/pa/jt5803/jtselect/jtrights/216/report.html

619 Section 8(3), emphasis added.

620 Allowing for inflation since 1997, that updates to £1.88 in 2023.

injury and harm caused, rather than the degree of culpability. For claims for breach of human rights specifically, the approach is "*vindicatory*" rather than *restitutionary*, which can make it more unpredictable still.

In *A County Council v MB*[621], Charles J held that a woman had been unlawfully deprived of her liberty in a care home for 2 weeks, but "*in my view correctly*", he said, no award of compensation was sought.

In *Bostridge v Oxleas NHS Foundation Trust*[622] there were failures to follow the Mental Health Act correctly, making the patient's detention unlawful. However, it was apparent that if it had been followed properly he would equally have been detained in exactly the same way. Winning his case meant a declaration that his rights were breached, and an award of £1. And there are further cases of such nominal awards involving breaches of immigration law leading to unlawful detention, for example, on the basis that "*nothing more than nominal damages can be awarded where the claimant would have been detained anyway*" [623].

This is the "technical breach" argument – that there may be an unlawful deprivation of liberty, but it made no substantive difference to the patient's care, treatment or residence. Had it been properly scrutinised and authorised, the argument goes, the outcome would have been just the same. So compensation, if any, should be limited to a nominal award to recognise that the person's rights have technically been breached, but it made little or no difference in practice.

It is, of course, for the detaining authority to prove that there has be no harm from their breach, but even so this can operate as a powerful disincentive to bring claims for unlawful deprivation of liberty in such circumstances, both for the individual claimants / families, and for the lawyers who might want to bring them, since there might well be an argument whether the legal costs of even a "successful" claimant ought

---

[621] [2010] EWCOP 2508 (CoP)

[622] [2015] EWCA Civ 79.

[623] *Lumba v Secretary of State for the Home Office* [2011] UKSC 12.

to be recoverable from the losing defendant, where they are massively disproportionate to any actual or likely award.

There have, however, been a handful of cases of substantive awards.

Substantial compensation

We saw in chapter 3 the story of Stephen and Mark Neary, in which Hillingdon were held to have unlawfully deprived Stephen of his liberty for a year as well as breaching article 8 rights to family life. The court approved a settlement of £35,000 in compensation for Steven alone, in July 2012; the local authority was also ordered to pay the Nearys' legal costs[624].

In 2013, an anonymous local authority agreed to pay £15,000 to Mrs D and £12,500 to her husband in settlement of claims for alleged breaches of their rights under Article 5 and Article 8 of the ECHR, a settlement which was approved by the court[625]. Mrs D had Huntingdon's and a high level of care needs. She was unable to make her own decisions about her care and residence, and the local authority was responsible for meeting her needs.

In August 2011 the couple had been married for 37 years and were still living together when the local authority, with both Mrs and Mr D's agreement initially, arranged 2 weeks of respite care for Mrs D. On 8 September 2011, Mr D asked the local authority when he might be able to bring his wife home, as they both wanted, and was told that he would not be allowed to do so as the local authority had concerns about his ability to care for her. It was recognised that this amounted to a deprivation of her liberty, but no DoLS authorisation was put in place until 25 October 2011; it was only granted for 2 weeks, and on the

624 [2011] EWCOP 3522. I understand from Mr Neary that although the judge made clear that his own Article 8 rights had been breached as well as Steven's, damages were only sought and were only awarded for Steven's claim.

625 [2013] EWCOP B34.

condition that an application to the Court of Protection was made. It was not.

A further 4 weeks' DoLS authorisation was granted, again on condition of an application being made to court. Again, it was not.

And a third DoLS authorisation was then granted in December 2011 and the local authority confirmed its intention to "*begin to prepare*" court proceedings. A fourth DoLS authorisation was granted, still without an application being made.

In fact, no application to the court was made until 10 April 2012. Even then, the local authority failed to make clear there was an ongoing deprivation of Mrs D's liberty, against her wishes, and it was not dealt with urgently, only reaching a hearing on 27 September 2012. The court declared that Mrs D had been unlawfully deprived of her liberty for a period of around 21 weeks (which was the figure conceded by the defendant local authority, and in fact it was likely to have been considerably longer).

In November 2012, two independent experts reported, both recommending that she go home, though the local authority continued to resist this until it eventually enabled her discharge home with a suitable care package in early January 2013. The 2 week agreed respite placement had lasted around 17 months.

While continuing to deny a number of the allegations of breach of their rights, the local authority offered to settle the compensation claim brought by Mr and Mrs D at a total of £27,500 plus their reasonable legal costs. The court referred to the benchmark from the *Neary* case, and approved the settlement.

Note that in both these cases, compensation claims were settled between the parties and then brought to the court for approval, where the claimant does not have capacity to manage the litigation themselves, and so needs the protection of the court against an unfavourable settlement being agreed on their behalf. In terms of a precedent it does not, therefore, carry quite the same heft as a case in which a judge considers and determines the award, but they have been influential, nonetheless.

Mr CP[626] was 91 years old, a former World War 2 RAF gunner, who had lived alone, other than his cat "Fluffy", for some years since his sister's death. He had dementia, increasing difficulty mobilising and other health problems. It appears that the local authority became concerned about CP's vulnerability to financial exploitation and decided to intervene to safeguard him. To do this, a social worker turned up at CP's home at 8.30 one morning and told him, on his doorstep in just his dressing gown, that he had to accompany her to a hotel. When he refused, she said he had to go, or she would call the police. He was very distressed, but was persuaded to go with her by a friend. The local authority placed him, not in a hotel, but in a locked dementia unit.

No DoLS authorisation was put in place until some weeks later, but was allowed to lapse without renewal. A further standard authorisation was only put in place nearly 9 months after the previous one expired, and only at the suggestion of the Official Solicitor. Even then, the BIA said it was in CP's best interests to go home. CP consistently said he wanted to go home, but in total was detained at the unit against his wishes for 17 months, during which his contact with his friends and his access to his usual activities and church attendance had also been restricted.

Eventually a challenge to this was brought to court on his behalf by a close friend, who argued it was still in his best interests to go home, though by that stage some of CP's family felt it was better for him to stay in residential care.

By the time of a hearing, in October 2014, it was established by independent expert evidence and accepted by all parties that in fact CP <u>had</u> capacity to make his own decisions about care and residence. By the time of a further hearing to deal with compensation in November 2014, the judge was "*gratified to learn that CP had returned home to his cat Fluffy*", with a social care package provided by the local authority, with

[626] *Essex CC v RF* [2015] EWCOP 1

the judge "*heartened by their new found commitment to ensuring that CP is able to remain in his own home...*"

As he went on, the judge was less subtle:

> 65. "*As far as P was concerned ECC [the local authority] failed:*
>
> - *To heed the presumption in favour of his capacity*
> - *To adopt the course of action which was less restrictive of P's rights and freedom of action.*
> - *To have regard the independent evidence of P's capacity by either ignoring it or immediately countermanding it*
> - *To take seriously or act upon his consistently expressed wish to return home*
> - *To appoint an IMCA for him*
> - *To refer the matter to the court*
>
> 66. *There is no doubt that P has been failed by ECC. The protection for the individual enshrined in the MCA and the Codes of Practice was ignored by ECC.*
>
> 67. *The conduct of ECC has been totally inadequate and their failings significant.*
>
> 68. *It is hard to imagine a more depressing and inexcusable state of affairs. A defenceless 91 year-old gentleman in the final years of his life was removed from his home of 50 years and detained in a locked dementia unit against his wishes. Had it not been for the alarm raised by his friend RF he may have been condemned to remain there for the remainder of his days.*
>
> 69. *There can be no doubt that ECC's practice was substandard. They failed to recognise the weakness of their own case and the strength of the case against them. They appeared unprepared to countenance any view contrary to their own. They maintained*

> *their resolute opposition to P returning to his home until the last possible moment. In my judgment the conduct of ECC has been reprehensible. The very sad and disturbing consequences for P cannot be ignored.*
>
> 70. *The significant wrong done to P must be adequately compensated*".

The echoes of *Neary* are obvious, and referring to that case and to *Mrs D* as benchmarks, the judge said:

> "*Taking these cases into account the level of damages for the unlawful deprivation of an incapacitated person's liberty is between £3,000 and £4,000 per month*"[627].

Again, however, rather than the judge determining damages, a settlement was actually agreed between the parties, and put to the court for approval, on the basis of:

- A declaration that the local authority unlawfully deprived P of his liberty for at least 13 months.
- £60,000 damages (which put the award "*at between £3,500 and £4,600 per month*")
- Waiver of any fees payable by CP to the care home in which he was detained for the period of his detention (around £23,000 to £25,000)[628].
- Exclusion of CP's damages award from means testing for any contribution to his community care costs.

---

[627] Para 77.

[628] A person placed against their wishes into a care setting still has to pay for the privilege, subject to the usual means testing provisions for social care – see *DM v Doncaster MBC* [2011] EWHC 3652 (Admin).

- The payment of all CP's costs.

And, public bodies will note, this case was on the front pages of the newspapers (a 91 year-old RAF veteran in his pyjamas removed by social workers from his home, and his cat Fluffy, being pretty much catnip for certain kinds of newspaper).

All these cases involve local authorities; there is (as yet) just one reported case of a substantial award against an NHS body.

In *Esegbona*[629] there was a failure to follow the MCA when it came to planning a patient's discharge from hospital. Mrs Esegbona, a 68 year-old lady, was admitted to hospital with shortness of breath, needed treatment in Intensive Care, and ended up with a tracheostomy[630]. She did not tolerate this well, and kept trying to pull out the tube. When she was medically fit for discharge, it took 4 months to find a suitable nursing home placement to take her. But when she was discharged there she died within 10 days, when she removed the breathing tube and had a cardiac arrest. A claim against the hospital was framed primarily in clinical negligence, as the failure to advise the nursing home of her earlier efforts to remove the tube meant that they were not aware to take the appropriate extra precautions to prevent this.

That claim was successful but, for our purposes, the key issue is that before her discharge Mrs Esegbona had repeatedly said that she wanted to go home. The hospital did not properly and promptly assess her capacity to make that decision for herself, but instead proceeded as if a best interests decision could be made. To compound that error, the hospital specifically planned to arrange the discharge <u>without</u> the family being involved. The notes refer to the arrangement of a specific care home, saying it was "*not to be discussed with patient's family*", and "*family*

629 [2019] EWHC 77 (QB)

630 A tube inserted into her throat through an incision in her neck to help her breathing.

are not to be informed until we receive a decision from the care home", apparently to stop any family objections derailing the plans[631].

The judge held that there should have been a comprehensive assessment of Mrs Esegbona's capacity to make her own decision about discharge at the point when she said she wanted to go home, and upheld the family's claim for *false imprisonment*[632] for the rest of the time that she was in hospital after that.

For the 119 days she was an inpatient, saying she wanted to go home, before her discharge to the nursing home, the judge awarded £15,470, explicitly based on a rate of £130 per day, which was extrapolated from the award in the *Fluffy* case. In addition, an award of £5,000 was made as "*aggravated damages*" for the "*high handed*" and "*oppressive*" approach taken by the hospital in their failure to follow the MCA properly[633].

The most recent key case on compensation for unlawful deprivation of liberty (at the time of writing) is a rather startling judgment from 18 December 2020, again involving a local authority[634]. The local authority was concerned and intervened to place Mrs Emile, a lady with dementia, into a care home for her own safety when she was the victim of abuse at home by her husband, who also had dementia[635]. She remained in the care home, then in a nursing home, until her death 11 years later, but for the first 8 ½ years there was no DoLS authorisation in place.

---

631 Bear in mind that anything written in the notes for a patient can be seen by a judge, and can end up in the newspapers via a published judgment.

632 The claim was framed on this common law basis, perhaps because the one-year time limit had been missed for a claim to be brought under the Human Rights Act for unlawful deprivation of liberty in breach of Article 5.

633 In contrast, only £3,500 was awarded in the clinical negligence compensation for Mrs Esegbona's own pain and suffering as a result of the negligence leading to her death.

634 *Emile* [2020] MHLO 70 (CC).

635 The judgment does not explain why it was not more appropriate to remove him, or to find a way to protect her in her own home.

Proceedings were started by the local authority against Mrs Emile and then, after her death, against her estate, to recover £80,000 or so in unpaid care home fees.

But the family counter-claimed for damages for the period when her deprivation of liberty was unlawful, and were awarded £130,000! That decision was made by a district judge, at the lower end of the judicial hierarchy, but then upheld against the local authority's appeal by a Circuit Judge (HHJ Saggerson), which is the reported judgment.

The court flatly rejected the local authority argument that there should be only nominal damages for the unlawful deprivation of liberty period on the grounds of a technical or procedural fault only. The care home placement was not "*inevitable*", if appropriate care, scrutiny and due process had gone into the arrangements made for Mrs Emile. In particular, little if any thought was given to the prospect that she might return home at any point, including when her abusive husband died, removing the threat which had initially prompted the local authority to remove her.

The district judge calculated the compensation at £1,400 pcm, by reference to the benchmark of the *Neary* case, and though HHJ Saggerson hinted that this might have been "*very generous*", and perhaps at the very top of the permissible range for this sort of "benign" confinement, he would not interfere to reduce it on appeal. Even though "*this was not a case where matters were aggravated by oppressive, vindictive or high-handed conduct by the local authority*"... "*limits on a citizen's freedom of movement in circumstances that are not lawful, warrant appropriately substantial damages*".

And there were to be no excuses:

> "*... the fact that the local authority perceives itself to be beleaguered by what it may see as the shifting sands of guidance and continuing changes in emphasis regarding their legal obligations under DoLS standards with significant impact on its resources, these factors ....are not grounds for reducing any damages awarded*".

He put the impact of the local authority's actions in very stark terms:

> *"... [Mrs Emile's] freedom was unlawfully compromised for the greater part of the last decade of her life where less intrusive options of accommodation and care should have been considered. The good intentions and benign motives of the local authority are scant consolation to the person deprived of their liberty".*

Publicity and legal costs

Getting it wrong can also result in very public criticism.

In the *G v E*[636] case, in which a local authority (initially anonymised) wrongfully removed a person from their home, the family asked the court to name the council in the proceedings, to hold them to account. The judge agreed:

> *"I therefore name Manchester City Council as the local authority because the arguments in favour of publicity — openness and public accountability — are truly compelling. These arguments manifestly amount to a "good reason" for taking this step and, considering the various factors for and against, the balance manifestly comes down in favour of publication in this case. It would, of course, be a different matter if there was any significant risk that E and other members of the family might be identified as a result of the naming of the local authority. Manchester, however, is a large city and I am satisfied that no such risk arises. It is important that the residents and council tax payers of the city of Manchester know what has happened so that the local authority can be held accountable. And it is to be hoped that the publicity given to this case will highlight the very significant reforms of the law implemented by the Mental Capacity Act and in particular the DoLS in schedule A1, and the consequent very considerable*

[636] See chapter 4, [2010] EWHC 621.

> *obligations imposed on local authorities and others by the complex procedures set out in those reforms".*[637]

Significant adverse media coverage followed from the local authority being named in this way. Salt was rubbed into its wounds by a further decision by Baker J[638] ordering that the local authority should pay for the majority of the legal costs to date of the proceedings for all the other parties, departing from the general rule in the Court of Protection that there is no order for costs (ie each party pays their own, the Court of Protection being non-adversarial and focussed on P's best interests and so the usual "loser" pays the "winner's" costs default approach of normal litigation not being appropriate).

> *"In this case, however, I am entirely satisfied that the local authority's blatant disregard of the processes of the MCA and their obligation to respect E's rights under the ECHR amount to misconduct which justifies departing from the general rule. [The local authority's barrister] boldly*[639] *relies on the ignorance of the local authority's staff as an excuse and submits that the complexity of the statutory provisions left large numbers of professionals uncertain as to the meaning of "deprivation of liberty". Given the enormous responsibilities put upon local authorities under the MCA, it was surely incumbent on the management team to ensure that their staff were fully trained and properly informed about the new provisions. If a local authority is uncertain whether its proposed actions amount to a deprivation of liberty, it must apply to the Court."*[640]

In Court of Protection proceedings there is usually a Transparency Order, which provides for the case to be heard in public (in that observers are allowed to attend), but prohibits certain information being used or published, in particular usually the identity of the parties. Primarily, this

---

637 Para 16.

638 [2010] EWCOP 3385 (Fam)

639 As with the civil service advice given in "*Yes Minister*", it should be alarming to hear a judge describe your argument as "bold".

640 Para 41.

is to protect P's right to confidentiality, but it is often the case that the public bodies are also covered, and sometimes this is justified by the risk of identifying P, perhaps by disparate information allowing identity to be pieced together like a jigsaw, if the public bodies are named. Increasingly, though, it is recognised that this is not such a risk and it is being challenged by journalists and other observers, as well as by P or the family, where there is a sense that anonymity would hinder proper accountability for a public body's actions[641].

Inquests

As we saw in chapter 7[642], it used to be the case that any death "in state detention" meant that there had to be an inquest with a jury[643]. Really this contemplated those detained by the state in prisons and police custody, for example, but it was not until the Policing and Crime Act 2017, in force since 3 April 2017, that it was made explicit that this should not include everyone under a DoLS authorisation.

In the recent case of Jackie Maguire[644], she had died in hospital from pneumonia and a perforated gastric ulcer and peritonitis. She was 52 years old. Jackie had Down's Syndrome and a learning disability, and had previously been placed in a care home by the local authority and deprived of her liberty there under a DoLS authorisation. There were concerns about the initial response when she fell ill, and whether she should have been taken to hospital sooner, even if against her wishes.

641 See for example – Varying reporting restrictions to name Kent County Council in "shocking" delay case – Promoting Open Justice in the Court of Protection (openjusticecourtofprotection.org).

642 Dealing with the case law on deprivation of liberty in hospital, and the case of Ferreira, which arose from a dispute about whether or not a coroner should have a jury at an inquest.

643 Coroners and Justice Act 2009 s7.

644 *R (on the application of Maguire) v HM Senior Coroner for Blackpool and Fylde* [2023] UKSC 20 https://www.bailii.org/uk/cases/UKSC/2023/20.html

Her family argued that Jackie's vulnerability and dependence on others meant that the failure to have an appropriate system to get her to hospital when necessary raised issues of her Article 2 right to life, and the state's positive obligations, which meant the usual fairly narrow scope of an inquest should be broadened into a wider "Article 2" inquest.

The Supreme Court rejected this. It confirmed that the threshold for an Article 2 inquest is high, and an Article 2 inquest will not follow just because the deceased was deprived of their liberty.

Of course, a coroner may well still take an interest in the decision making around someone's deprivation of liberty and their care or treatment under the MCA, where this is relevant to how they came by their death.

The Ombudsman

There are other ways to get into trouble.

In March 2019, the Local Government and Social Care Ombudsman published a report into Staffordshire County Council. It found that the local authority had triaged cases of deprivation of liberty following the *Cheshire West* tsunami, and since 2016 had decided as a matter of policy not to carry out assessments on DoLS applications which were regarded as low or medium priority. This decision was made during an informal cabinet meeting, and was explicitly "*because of lack of financial resources*", whilst well aware that it did not comply with its legal obligations. Even the "high priority" assessments were significantly delayed.

The Ombudsman found this "*a fault leading to injustice*", and recommended that the local authority produce an action plan to deal with the backlog.

There will be many who are sympathetic for the local authority's situation, faced with a 14 fold increase in the scale of the work, with no more resources than they had before *Cheshire West*[645]. But the Ombudsman said:

> *"this is causing a potential injustice to around 3,000 people [the backlog of unassessed referrals in the area at the time] who have had no or delayed access to the proper legal process designed to check that any decision to deprive a person of their liberty is:*
>
> - *Properly made*
> - *Lawful; and*
> - *Implemented only for as long as necessary.*
>
> *Applying the process properly would not change the outcome for most of the people affected, other than confirming that it is in their best interests to be deprived of their liberty. However, it is possible that some of the people stuck in the backlog for years should have never been deprived of their liberty".*

And in November 2020, the Local Government and Social Care Ombudsman upheld an individual complaint by "Mr X" on behalf of his father that Cheshire East[646] had failed to provide a DoLS authorisation for the first 11 months that he was in a care home, from March 2018 to February 2019. His case had also been triaged and prioritised according to the ADASS tool[647].

In a case involving Kent CC in July 2021[648], the ombudsman upheld a complaint that "Ms D" had been placed in a care home without proper best interests decision making, the appointment of an advocate, or an appropriate legal process to authorise the deprivation of her liberty. As

---

645 See chapter 16.

646 19 010 786 – Local Government and Social Care Ombudsman

647 See chapter 16.

648 19 015 406 – Local Government and Social Care Ombudsman

well as recommending an apology and £500[649] in compensation, the ombudsman required the local authority to ensure all current and future requests for DoLS authorisations are completed in the prescribed timescales and to provide evidence that this has been done.

More recently still, in March 2023, Wirral MBC were found to be at fault by an Ombudsman's report into a complaint that "Mrs C" had been deprived of her liberty in a care home for 15 months without a DoLS authorisation[650], recommending an apology to the family, and a "*symbolic payment of £500… to reflect the distress and the unnecessary time and trouble caused by its failings*". The Ombudsman concluded:

> "*the law is clear the Council should act on all requests for [DoLS] authorisation within 21 days of receipt. The Council can reasonably choose to prioritise applications. And I can understand why, in this instance, the Council did not give the request for Mrs C's authorisation the highest priority. But this should not have resulted in a significant delay beyond the 21 day target*"[651].

Also in March 2023, the Ombudsman reported on Surrey County Council[652] that it was failing to assess DoLS referrals in accordance with the proper timescales; it was taking an average of 345 days. The Ombudsman's verdict was that the council should create an action plan to address these delays within three months, and should consider provision for a remedy in those cases where a deprivation of liberty is not approved, such that an unlawful deprivation of liberty may have had a

[649] Recommendations by the ombudsman are typically more modest than the court, usually framed as recognition of distress caused or the need for the complaint to be made, and are strictly only recommendations as the ombudsman has no power to award damages.

[650] 22 010 680 – Local Government and Social Care Ombudsman

[651] If this hints that there is, in the Ombudsman's mind at least, *some* leeway beyond the 21 day target, it does not tell us how much. And, of course, there is no legal basis to rely on this to mitigate any potential liabilities for breach of the very clear legal timescale.

[652] 22 014 808 – Local Government and Social Care Ombudsman

harmful impact, or where a deprivation of liberty is approved but with less restrictive measures than would otherwise have been the case.

The Ombudsman has acknowledged the context and the demand on resources but, pending substantial reform, DoLS are:

> *"the main legal protection available to vulnerable people in care home settings. Having such a backlog of DoLS applications awaiting assessment mean the Council is at fault. For each case in the backlog, the Council is failing to comply with the MCA 2005 and the DoLS Code of Practice. Without an authorisation in place, the people that are the subject of these applications are being unlawfully deprived of their liberty.*
>
> *Applying the process properly may not have changed the outcome for many of the people affected … However, it is possible that some of the people stuck in the backlog should never have been deprived of their liberty or there may have been less restrictive options available to meet their needs"*[653].

That last paragraph is the crux of this. In every pile of cases that may only "*a technical breach*", where the MCA has been properly followed, and any deprivation of liberty would be duly authorised if only resources permitted, there just might be a case or two where that scrutiny would show that something had gone awry; where, perhaps, the best of intentions to keep someone safe has overreached, lost track of the fundamentals of the MCA, and lost sight of the individual and their rights. How can we know which is which if we don't have the resources to look properly?

But is this realistic, given the demands on resources to comply fully with the council's obligations[654]?

---

653 From the decision in the Cheshire East case, see note 38.

654 See the judicial review brought by four local authorities, seeking more funding for the DoLS system after *Cheshire West*, in Chapter 16.

Can criticism by the Ombudsman, some adverse media coverage, or even an award of damages in occasional cases really change the behaviour of public bodies if they just do not have the resources to fulfil their duties?

Does this not just make the case for systematic reform?

Key points

1. The burden of unlawful deprivation of liberty of course falls mostly on the individual involved; but there can also be significant consequences for the providers and commissioners of the care.

2. Extreme cases can involve the criminal law, for individuals and organisations providing care.

3. Despite the "*enforceable right to compensation*" for any unlawful deprivation of liberty on the face of Article 5, there is often an argument that the proper scrutiny would simply have affirmed the situation and made no real difference to P; that it was only a "*technical breach*" for which a declaration of breach of P's rights, or only a nominal award, is sufficient.

4. Substantial awards of compensation have been paid in a handful of cases, though it is difficult to reliably extract benchmarks for awards from these.

5. Public bodies can also face sanctions in awards of legal costs against them, adverse publicity, or criticism by the ombudsman.

6. Getting the MCA and DoLS wrong is strongly correlated to poor CQC ratings, as well as potentially leading to offences[655].

[655] Health and Social Care Act 2008 (Regulated Activities) Regulations 2014, regulations 11 and 13(5).

7. As we saw with the *Neary* case study, the common theme to all this chapter's examples of this going horribly wrong is that the MCA has been forgotten, misunderstood or misapplied.

8. The focus should be not on deprivation of liberty in isolation, but on training and implementation to get the MCA right in practice, for the sake of all the individuals, families, professionals and organisations involved.

PART FOUR

REFORM

CHAPTER SIXTEEN

THE IMPACT OF CHESHIRE WEST AND THE PRESSURE FOR REFORM

There is an argument that the DoLS system would have been fine if only it had not been swamped by the impact of *Cheshire West* (we'll get to that shortly). But I think that would be generous, and would overlook a number of fair complaints about some features that were baked into DoLS from the very beginning:

- The unduly limited scope, leaving deprivations of liberty outside of care homes or hospitals, or for anyone under 18, needing to go to court.

- The lack of a clear definition of deprivation of liberty, allowing extraordinary variation and inconsistency.

- The undue bureaucracy and complexity of the system, nowhere more so than in the uncertainty of the interface with the Mental Health Act (see Chapter 13).

By coincidence, in the week before the *Cheshire West* judgment was handed down, the post legislative scrutiny committee of parliament reviewing the Mental Capacity Act and DoLS[656], established in May 2013, reported.

It described the MCA as a "visionary" piece of legislation, though its implementation had not met expectations because

---

[656] https://publications.parliament.uk/pa/ld201314/ldselect/ldmentalcap/139/139.pdf published 13 March 2014.

> *"the prevailing cultures of paternalism (in health) and risk-aversion (in social care) have prevented the Act from becoming widely known or embedded. The empowering ethos has not been delivered. The rights conferred by the Act have not been widely realised. The duties imposed by the Act are not widely followed."*

On the DoLS, though, their conclusion was brutal:

> *"The provisions are poorly drafted, overly complex and bear no relationship to the language and ethos of the Mental Capacity Act. The safeguards are not well understood and are poorly implemented. Evidence suggested that thousands, if not tens of thousands, of individuals are being deprived of their liberty without the protection of the law, and therefore without the safeguards which Parliament intended. Worse still, far from being used to protect individuals and their rights, they are sometimes used to oppress individuals, and to force upon them decisions made by others without reference to the wishes and feelings of the person concerned.*
>
> ***The only appropriate recommendation in the face of such criticism is to start again"***

And …

> *"The level and breadth of criticism of the Deprivation of Liberty Safeguards, including from the judiciary, demonstrates that the legislation is not fit for purpose. Better implementation would not be sufficient to address the fundamental problems identified".*

To be fair, on the other hand, "*Mr Neary said that without the safeguards and the ability to challenge the authorisation in the Court of Protection "Steven would now be in that care home in Wales that Hillingdon intended to send Steven to""*.[657]

[657] Paragraph 272.

As well as underuse (in places), the committee criticised the regional variation in the use of DoLS, noting a range (in 2012/13) from the East Midlands at 48.6 cases per 100,000 adults down to London at 14.1.

This may be (in part at least) explained by demographics. There is no doubt that the use of DoLS has been slanted by age. Looking at the latest figures (2022/23), 85% of DoLS referrals are for people over 65, and around 42% were for people over the age of 85[658]. It is, perhaps, to be expected that areas where there are greater numbers of older people might have an equivalent high level of DoLS referrals. But there is no doubt that the extent of variation is much greater than that, which raises an interesting point, made by Mr Neary in his evidence to the post legislative scrutiny committee:

> *"If you have two neighbouring boroughs and, say, one has authorised two DoLS and the next borough has authorised 52… is two good, or is 52 good?"*[659].

On balance, I would be wary of any complacency in saying that a very low referral rate actually means low numbers of people deprived of their liberty rather than high numbers of people deprived of their liberty *unlawfully*.

Now, to be fair, DoLS did not have the benefit of the care and thought that went into the MCA itself[660].

Though there was a consultation[661], DoLS was rushed through as an urgent solution to plug the *Bournewood* gap. In hindsight, it might have been better, perhaps, to have taken a little more time and care.

---

658 These are the statistics for England alone, but there is a similar picture in Wales.

659 Post legislative scrutiny report on MCA and DoLS, paragraph 265.

660 Which can be traced back to a Law Commission consultation in 1991 https://s3-eu-west-2.amazonaws.com/lawcom-prod-storage-11jsxou24uy7q/uploads/2015/04/cp119.pdf

Mentally Incapacitated Adults and Decision-Making: An Overview, 12 March 1991.

661 https://www.legislation.gov.uk/uksi/2009/827/pdfs/uksiem_20090827_en.pdf

Equally, to be fair, there is a problem of scale. The Impact Assessment published with the original DoLS legislation in May 2008 estimated that there would be around 5,000 DoLS authorisation in 2009/10, falling to 1,700 by 2015/16, "*as people became more familiar with the safeguards*"!

It put the likely worst-case number of applications at 21,000 pa. On any view, the government's assessment was that the number of cases that DoLS would have to manage was "*relatively small*"[662].

It is hard to read this now without eye rolling hindsight, but look at the impact of the *Cheshire West* judgment at the end of the 2013/14 year.

Year[663]	**DoLS applications received**	**DoLS applications processed**[664]
2009/10	7,200	
2010/11	9,000	
2011/12	11,400	
2012/13	11,900	
2013/14	13,000	13,000
2014/15	137,540	62,645
2015/16	195,840	105,055
2016/17	217,235	151,970
2017/18	227,400	181,785
2018/19	240,455	216,055

662 May 2008 Impact Assessment p9.

663 Source – NHS digital.

664 This does not seem to have been reported separately until 2013/14.

2019/20	263,940	243,300
2020/21	256,610	246,025
2021/22	270,650	254,215
2022/23	300,765	289,150

Giving a lecture later in 2014[665], Lady Hale herself said that the *Cheshire West* judgment had had "*alarming practical consequences*".

Almost overnight, the rate of DoLS referrals increased more than tenfold after *Cheshire West*, and (with the exception of a slight decrease at the height of the pandemic) has continued to increase ever since, now exceeding 300,000 per year, or roughly 15 times more than the original impact assessment's worst case anticipated. It is fair to say that the resources allocated to the system have not increased in proportion.

In the circumstances, the increase in cases *being processed* has been nothing short of heroic, and a tribute to the graft, and craft, of those involved in the system. Any criticism of the DoLS process should never be taken as criticism of the individuals who are working in it, going above and beyond while they wait for reform or resources to do properly what now needs done.

But of course, as the rate of referrals outstripped the ability of the system to process them, an accumulating backlog has grown.

At the end of 2022/23 in England[666], around **126,000 referrals were unprocessed.** Of those, **nearly 40,000 had been outstanding for more than a year.**

---

[665] https://www.supremecourt.uk/docs/speech-141031.pdf – The Lord Rodger Memorial Lecture, 31 October 2014.

[666] These statistics are from NHS Digital for 2022-23, but cover England only. Welsh figures are available for 2021-22 here and show similar issues, but the data is not as detailed and they total only about 1/20th of the scale of the English figures https://www.careinspectorate.wales/230207-we-have-published-our-2021-22-

In 2013/14, 81% of referrals were completed within the statutory timescale of 21 days. In 2022/23 that had fallen to only 19%, and ***the average time for a referral to be processed had reached 156 days.***

Put that into perspective: if you are deprived of your liberty and a referral is made to the system designed to bring independent scrutiny and protect your Article 5 rights, *on average* it'll take roughly 5 months for the process to actually swing into action for you. And around one in five of us could expect to still be waiting for that scrutiny a year or more later. In some parts of the country the situation is worse. By definition, in the meantime, without your consent, you are under continuous supervision and control and not free to leave.

The 288,280 applications "completed" in 2022/23 are artificially inflated by the ***nearly 50,000 cases closed because the person had died*** before they were determined.

More than 100,000 were not granted due to "change in circumstances", which is hardly surprising if it's going to take 156 days (on average) for the assessors to turn up, once a referral has been made!

And among the obvious evidence of a system that is swamped, some statistics call into question whether we are getting meaningful safeguards out of all this. Only 5,610 (less than 2% of the applications completed) were refused due to not meeting one or more of the qualifying criteria. Of those, by far the biggest group (3,650) were where P had capacity (or had regained it by the time they were assessed).

Only 115 cases were not granted on the ground that the best interests requirement was not met. That is fewer than 0.04% (4 in 10,000) of the cases completed.

---

national-joint-review-healthcare-inspectorate-wales-hiw-use In Wales there were around 4,300 cases unprocessed as at 31 March 2022, from a total of around 16,000 applications that year.

Response and rationing

I emphasise, again, that this is no criticism of the individuals involved in trying to make it work, but the inevitable consequence has been dilution of the safeguards as they are intended to protect some of the most vulnerable in society.

This raises a difficult question: For those who lauded *Cheshire West* as a landmark in the protection of the rights of persons with disabilities, has the judgment actually done more harm than good? Now that the system is swamped, is it blinded to those who need it most? Have we, effectively, now spread our limited resource so thinly, like too little butter over too much bread, that no one actually gets anything worth having?

The issue of resources is not explicitly broached in *Cheshire West* as it was, for example, obviously influential in the Court of Appeal's approach in *Ferreira*.[667]

It is not just about throwing money at the problem (even if the money had been there to throw). The system also needs enough qualified and experienced staff.

Quick off the mark, if less than helpful, was the Department of Health and Social Care, with a "Dear Colleagues" letter dated 28 March 2014[668]:

---

[667] I cannot vouch for its truth, but I have heard an anecdote that during the Supreme Court hearing, bearing in mind that the Justices are not experts in the health and social care context, the question was asked from the bench, mindful of the potential consequences of adopting a liberal definition of deprivation of liberty, bringing many more cases into its scope: "how long does it take to carry out one of these DoLS assessments?" I heard that learned counsel who was asked did not know, and asked their instructing solicitor, who didn't know and asked the client local authority representative, who didn't know and asked the senior social worker. As the chain of whispers reached back through the court, row by row, and the answer came back, it may have been a little distorted, as the barrister ultimately told the Justices that it was no big deal and they only take about an hour or so to do, paving the way for their decision.

[668] https://www.39essex.com/docs/newsletters/dh_letter_re_supreme_court_dols_judgment_final_28_march_2014.pdf

> "*to draw your attention to last week's judgment in the Supreme Court to help to ensure that health and social care organisations continue to comply with the law following the revised test now supplied by the Supreme Court about the meaning of deprivation of liberty*".

After summarising the case and the judgment, the letter advises that relevant staff should "*familiarise themselves with the provisions of the Mental Capacity Act*" and in particular with the least restrictive principle; be alert to potential restrictions when designing care plans; and try to avoid potential deprivations of liberty where possible.

But

> "*where the care / treatment plan for an individual lacking capacity will unavoidably result in a deprivation of liberty judged to be in that person's best interests, this MUST be authorised*" (emphasis in the original).

As such, local authorities should

> "*review their allocation of resources in light of the revised test given by the Supreme Court to ensure they meet their legal responsibilities*".

"*Keep calm and carry on*", they may as well have said.

Of course, the inevitable response to *Cheshire West* was to prioritise, where suddenly the scale of the job outstripped the tools that were available to do it.

In 2014 ADASS[669] published a triage tool[670] which gave some guidance on prioritising those who most needed scrutiny. It is colour coded into three categories:

- Red (high priority) category included patients in a psychiatric or acute hospital and not free to leave, who are under continuous

[669] The Association of Directors of Adult Social Care

[670] https://www.adass.org.uk/adass-priority-tool-for-deprivation-of-liberty-requests/

1:1 care during the day or night, where sedation or medication is frequently used to control behaviour, where P objects, or there are objections from a family member or friend or some restrictions on contact with them.

- Amber (medium) included those "*asking to leave but not consistently*", or "*not making active attempts to leave*", or who "*appear to meet some but not all aspects of the [Cheshire West] acid test*".

- Green (low) included those cases where there was "*minimal evidence of control and supervision*", or in end of life situations or (anticipating *Ferreira*, perhaps) intensive care, "*which may meet the acid test but there will be no benefit to the person from the safeguards*".

It is also suggested that those with a DoLS authorisation in place and coming up to expiry should be prioritised for renewal above a new case, which may be controversial as that delays review of cases where no-one has looked at the P's circumstances at all in favour of someone who has already had the assessments within the last year.

Otherwise, this does just seem to put most of the cases where you *really* think there may be a deprivation of liberty into the red category, but it is hard not to sympathise with those prioritising overstretched resources when we are all entitled to the same protection of our Article 5 rights.

Less charitably, this has been referred to as guidance on "how best to break the law"[671].

In August 2014, ADASS issued further "Guidance for local authorities in light of the Supreme Court decisions on deprivation of liberty", in which:

[671] Joint Committee on Human Rights, Seventh Report of Session 2017-2019 (The Right to Freedom and Safety: Reform of the Deprivation of Liberty Safeguards).

> *"ADASS reminds all its members that the Supreme Court Judgment is legally binding and must be adhered to. To do nothing in response to this is not an option"*.

In case that wasn't clear, the same document continued:

> *"ADASS reiterate its position that this judgment stands as law and cannot be ignored. Councils must make arrangements to ensure that they meet their statutory duties and must risk assess the likelihood of not doing so. Councils are advised to make their insurers aware of the risks arising from the judgment"*.

It went on to say that the Law Commission might consider wider reform, but

> *"this is likely to take at least three years*[672]*. Councils must therefore expect the current level of demand and application of the safeguards to continue for the foreseeable future"*.

On 22 October 2015 the Department of Health wrote to "MCA-DoLS Leads in Local Authorities and the NHS"[673], enclosing a new guidance note. That note recorded that DoLS applications had risen approximately 10-fold since the Supreme Court judgment and the additional burden that imposed on local authorities, and that they were struggling to meet the 21 day legal timescale.

It continued:

> *"14. It is clear that implementing the Supreme Court judgment is a journey – such a significant change in frontline practice could never be brought about overnight. The Department and our partners….are clear however, that providers and local authorities should have a plan*

[672] Ha! Now 9 years and counting….

[673] https://www.mentalcapacitylawandpolicy.org.uk/wp-content/uploads/2015/10/DH-Letter-to-MCA-DoLS-Leads-Oct-2015-FINAL.pdf

in force for how to respond to the judgment. A 'do nothing' approach is not acceptable.

15. This plan will inevitably involve an element of prioritisation to ensure that those individuals most likely to benefit from a DoLS application and assessment are afforded attention in a timely manner. ADASS has developed a prioritisation tool that will help in this. It is particularly important, given the level of applications made, that robust procedures are in place to ensure that particularly vulnerable individuals can be identified rapidly and appropriate action taken.

16. Health and care providers will understandably be concerned should applications made to local authorities not be assessed with the statutory time limit. Whilst this is not ideal, this is an inevitable consequence of the unexpected large increase in applications that local authorities are now charged with processing. Providers should not delay in sending DoLS applications to local authorities for individuals whose circumstances they believe may meet the Supreme Court's acid test.

17. Fundamentally it is the Department's view that providers that can demonstrate that they are providing good quality care/treatment for individuals in a manner compliant with the principles of the MCA, and who follow DH and other national guidance should not be harshly treated for technical DoLS breaches." (Emphasis added)

Well grand, but as we have seen the "*harsh treatment*" that may come from unlawful deprivation of liberty primarily falls on the individual without appropriate safeguards; and to the extent that there may be liabilities for organisations, the DHSC's sympathy offers no mitigation against the judgment of the court, the ombudsman or the regulator; nor does lack of resources[674].

---

674 See chapter 15.

Resources Judicial Review

In fact, in March 2017, four local authorities[675] brought a judicial review based on the "unacceptable risk of illegality" given the government's failure to allocate increased resources to cover the increased scope of DoLS work[676].

Government funding for DoLS had been maintained at around £34m a year, but the four claimants said that local authorities in England needed between £450m and £600m a year extra[677] to cope with the surge of DoLS cases since March 2014.

The argument centred on what is called the 'new burdens' doctrine: a government agreement with councils that appropriate funding should follow new responsibilities. But the judge held that this did not apply if a court judgment altered the understanding of what was required of councils.

The judge essentially found that the local authorities had the money to meet their DoLS responsibilities in full, if they simply choose to do so:

> *"Certainly, the evidence shows that doing so is, and will continue to be, extremely difficult; certainly the evidence suggests that complying with those obligations would necessitate diverting substantial sums from other parts of the councils' budgets. But it does not establish that the proper funding of the DoLS regime cannot be achieved."*

The government's position was that the councils should just find the money from other things in their budget. Mr Justice Garnham agreed. He noted Liverpool council's decision to use some of the extra funding provided to councils in the March 2017 budget to invest in libraries,

---

675 Liverpool, Nottinghamshire, Richmond and Shropshire.

676 Liverpool City Council & Others v Secretary of State for Health [2017] EWHC 986 (Admin)

677 These figures were based on the work of the Law Commission, see chapter 17.

which was an "*entirely proper decision*", but showed that councils had discretion over how they spent their funding.

This was probably small comfort to the local authorities, for whom DoLS is not their only responsibility, and which have faced very substantial cuts to budgets in the austere years since 2010 in any case; the idea that there may be slack in other areas of the budget that can just be reallocated to DoLS seems a fairytale.

I have heard it said by more than one local authority that the cost of carrying out their DoLS responsibilities in full would cost the entirety of their adult social care budget.

Indeed, the government's Impact Assessment for LPS[678] includes some figures for what it (with some brass neck) calls "*fully operationalising*" the current system of DoLS and court applications – ie funding it enough to do the scale of the work it now has – and comes to *an additional cost of around £1.92 billion every year*, making the LPS proposals look very cost effective!

And, of course, all this is to focus, understandably, on DoLS, but that is only part of the picture. Indeed, neither P & Q (MiG and MeG) placed by Surrey nor P placed by Cheshire West were within the scope of DoLS, both because the sisters were under 18 when the question of their deprivation of liberty came to be authorised, and because none of them were placed in a care home or hospital. They were deprived of liberty in the community, and could only be authorised by the court.

Impact on the Court of Protection

In March 2014, the post legislative scrutiny committee commented that:

678 There have been three versions of this, the most recent from March 2022. https://assets.publishing.service.gov.uk/government/uploads/system/uploads/attachment_data/file/1061618/LPS-impact-assessment.pdf

> *"Vulnerable adults living in supported accommodation are at risk of being unlawfully deprived of their liberty because they fall outside the scope of the Deprivation of Liberty Safeguards. Although recourse to the Court of Protection is available, evidence of the barriers individuals face in accessing the Court, and of the failure by local authorities to bring cases to Court when necessary, suggests that this is unlikely to provide the safeguards intended."*[679]

It was immediately clear that the impact of *Cheshire West* would not only be felt in a huge increase in DoLS referrals from care homes and hospitals, but also in the cases now recognised to be a deprivation of liberty outside the scope of DoLS, such as in supported living or in a person's own home, where this can only be authorised by the court.

In the calendar year 2013, before *Cheshire West,* there had been 109 applications to the Court of Protection relating to a deprivation of liberty (and had in fact been nil a couple of years before that).

Then[680]:

Year	No of COP applications relating to deprivation of liberty
2009	0
2010	0
2011	152
2012	88
2013	109

[679] Paragraph 296.

[680] https://www.gov.uk/government/statistics/family-court-statistics-quarterly-october-to-december-2020

2014	525
2015	1,497
2016	3,143
2017	3,995
2018	4,557
2019	5,219
2020	4,932
2021	6,286
2022	6,265

Note that:

This is for the Court of Protection. Other cases will be in the High Court family division seeking authorisation of a deprivation of liberty for a child, or – rarely, perhaps – for an adult under the inherent jurisdiction, but the High Court statistics are not broken down enough to pick those out.

This includes <u>all kinds</u> of Court of Protection applications. The data for 2023 so far is broken down further which shows 1,423 applications in Q2 of 2023, of which:

- 142 were under s16 MCA – ie asking the court to make an order depriving someone of their liberty in full proceedings
- 470 were challenges to DoLS authorisations under s21A MCA, and
- 820 were applications to authorise a deprivation of liberty using the streamlined *Re X* procedure.

If that is a typical quarter, then we might guess that only around 3,000 – 4,000 cases are being brought each year to authorise a deprivation of liberty in the community, with the rest of the Court of Protection's work taken up with challenges to DoLS authorisations. Some of those may be repeated applications / renewals relating to the same individuals, so the number of individual patients involved will be somewhat less.

We might speculate whether the imminence (so we thought) of the LPS, removing the need to apply to court in many of those cases, pulling all settings under the statutory scheme, might have been a factor suppressing applications recently, which might otherwise have shown steady growth (bar the anomalous pandemic year in 2020).

In case it needs saying, the court system has no more had a commensurate increase in the resources to deal with these cases than the DoLS system. And so, the court now has to manage more than 6,000 applications with a system initially set up to manage a few hundred or so, leading to the implementation of the *Re X* process described in chapter 14.

Inevitably, the court system has been just as overwhelmed as DoLS. Though similarly heroic efforts have been made to catch up, recently especially, it has not been unusual to wait months or years for the court to deal with an application relating to deprivation of liberty. And as with the DoLS backlog, that means an individual may be deprived of their liberty unlawfully in the meantime.

But even that seems to be dealing only with the tip of the iceberg.

Scale of deprivation of liberty in the community

In the *Re X* hearings, Munby LJ asked the counsel for the Secretary of State for Health the scale of the deprivation of liberty in the community issue. She responded with a figure provided by ADASS of around 30,000 – 40,000 cases pa that would require authorisation.

In a break in the hearing she confirmed, on reflection, that ADASS figures only counted those cases for which local authorities were responsible – ie social care commissioned placements. Where the particular care package was commissioned by an NHS body (a Clinical Commissioning Group, at the time, now an Integrated Care Board), as would be the case for patients receiving Continuing Healthcare funding (CHC), for example, these would not be counted in the ADASS figures.

As at the end of June 2023, there were just under 53,000 patients eligible for CHC in England[681]. Given that CHC tends to only be available to those with the highest level of healthcare need, how many of those patients might you reasonably expect might lack the capacity to make their own decision about their care and residence? And how many of those might well be in a package that amounts to a deprivation of their liberty? Some tens of thousands, would be a reasonable guess.

By coincidence, the Law Commission report in 2017 relied on an updated ADASS estimate that there were 53,000 people deprived of their liberty outside the scope of DoLS[682], which ADASS said now allowed for some CHC cases excluded from their earlier estimate. The 53,000 figure still looks conservative to me, but was then adopted by the government in the Impact Assessments for the LPS reforms[683].

That Impact Assessment also tells us that, after *Re D* made clear that parental consent will not do for 16–17 year-olds, the Department for Education estimates there are 6,600 of those cases per annum that also now need court approval.

Only around 3,000 to 4,000 applications per year are currently being made to the Court of Protection to authorise deprivations of liberty for that whole group of 60,000 or so unlawfully deprived at the moment.

Some of those 16-17 year-olds may come through the High Court, ie not in the Court of Protection statistics above, but the Nuffield Family

---

681 https://www.england.nhs.uk/statistics/wp-content/uploads/sites/2/2023/08/CHC_Statistical_Press_Release_Q1_2023_24_LT42f.pdf

682 https://s3-eu-west-2.amazonaws.com/lawcom-prod-storage-11jsxou24uy7q/uploads/2017/03/lc372_mental_capacity_impact.pdf

683 Cited above.

Justice Observatory data[684] of the National DoL court[685] found that there were 1,249 children subject to applications for deprivation of their liberty in the 12 months of the pilot project.

Conclusion

The LPS Impact Assessment says that "*Thousands of people are potentially unlawfully deprived of their liberty*" in the current system. That looks like something of an understatement.

And for each case, whether under DoLS, or authorised by the court in the *Re X* process or otherwise, it is valid only for a year and requires renewal, with the total cases only growing.

There are cases in which the need for a deprivation of liberty comes to an end: for example, someone regains capacity to make their own decisions about care and residence, or their care is changed so that it no longer amounts to a deprivation of liberty that needs authorisation, or children who turn 18 and can no longer be deprived of their liberty unless they are of unsound mind. But these are a minority.

Overall, the impact of *Cheshire West* is not a spike. *It is a snowball.*

The need for reform is obvious, and growing ever more urgent.

[684] https://www.nuffieldfjo.org.uk/news/1249-children-deprived-of-their-liberty-because-of-concerns-about-their-welfare

[685] See chapter 14.

CHAPTER SEVENTEEN

FROM THE LAW COMMISSION TO THE LIBERTY PROTECTION SAFEGUARDS

In 2014, the Law Commission[686] started work on the law around deprivation of liberty, starting as a review of the relationship between DoLS and the Mental Health Act 1983.

In light of the events of March 2014, first the criticism of DoLS by the Parliamentary Committee reviewing the impact of MCA / DoLS, and then the *Cheshire West* Supreme Court judgment, the government asked the Law Commission to undertake a limited review of deprivation of liberty in supported living and other community settings, and consider what lessons could be applied for DoLS. In response to "*engagement with stakeholders*", this remit was then expanded to cover deprivation of liberty in its entirety.

It published a detailed consultation paper in July 2015[687], which confirmed that "*there is a compelling case for replacing the DoLS*".[688]

July 2015 – Consultation and Proposals

The Law Commission's proposals went through something of a journey to their final form and, even then, there was a gulf between their approach and the legislation ultimately brought forward by the government. It is

[686] The Law Commission is an independent statutory body focussed on promoting and informing reform of the law.

[687] https://www.lawcom.gov.uk/project/mental-capacity-and-deprivation-of-liberty/

[688] And yet, here we are, 8 years later and counting....

worth having a look at the way the approach evolved, as there is a chance that we may yet go back to some of these ideas when reform comes back onto the agenda, if we do not end up with the LPS as they stand[689].

The 230-page consultation in July 2015 was wide ranging and ambitious. It went far beyond the narrow issues of Article 5 of the ECHR, and into rights to family life (Article 8), as well as supported decision-making and care planning much more widely.

The Law Commission accepted the *Cheshire West* definition of objective deprivation of liberty as the starting point. The intention, overall, was to create a replacement for DoLS in which the authorisation of any deprivation of liberty was 'mainstreamed' and gradually involved more independent scrutiny and advocacy as care becomes more restrictive. The proposed system saw safeguards as an integral part of the care planning process, rather than a legalistic box ticking exercise after the event. It would also have to work at large scale, and across a whole range of settings, from acute hospitals, care homes and supported living, through to, in some cases, the private family home.

The approach put forward by the Law Commission was a tiered system, provisionally entitled '*protective care*', with proportionate safeguards according to the extent of the restrictions involved in a person's care, and tailored to the particular care setting. They envisaged, broadly:-

- A "*supportive care*" scheme that would look beyond those deprived of liberty under Article 5 of the ECHR and offer some scrutiny to protect those *not deprived of their liberty* but whose rights to private and family life under Article 8 were at risk. This would avoid there being a such a steep gradient between the safeguards enjoyed by those within the protection of Article 5, and those who may fall just outside it.

- A "*restrictive care and treatment*" scheme, to include those deprived of liberty and in restrictive care arrangements, covering

689 Which we will get to in the next chapter, if you do just want to skip ahead.

not only registered settings, like DoLS, but also the family home; with a key role for a beefed-up best interests assessor (BIA) – rebadged as an Approved Mental Capacity Professional (AMCP) – in authorising the deprivation.

- A separate scheme for hospitals/hospices with a different approach for those deprived of liberty as inpatients allowing doctors to authorise a deprivation for up to 28 days.

- Amendments to the Mental Health Act (MHA) to enable the admission to psychiatric hospitals of people who lacked capacity to consent, who needed to be deprived of their liberty but were not objecting to their care and treatment.

- A first-tier tribunal system to hear reviews of the care and treatment of people under the restrictive care or hospital schemes, replacing this aspect of the Court of Protection's jurisdiction.

Overall, the effect would be comprehensive, principled, and with greater emphasis on prevention of a deprivation of liberty arising. But it was also hugely expensive (the impact assessment put the costs of implementation at £1.8bn over 10 years) and, arguably, even more complex than the DoLS scheme it would have replaced.

May 2016 – Interim statement

In May 2016, the Law Commission published an interim statement saying that its proposals would be significantly scaled back, given a frosty reception from the government to the initial scope (and cost).

The Law Commission reaffirmed that "*legislative change is the only satisfactory solution*", and that "*any notion that the existing system can be patched up to cope, even in the short term, in our view is not sustainable*".

However, many respondents (including, plainly, the government) saw the grand scale of the initial proposals as unrealistic, and simply too costly to implement at the time. While the Law Commission pushed back a little on this ("*we do not accept that safeguards should be restricted to the bare minimum or that we should not consider any reforms that may generate additional costs*") they accepted that reform must "*demonstrably reduce the administrative burden*", and provide "*maximum benefit for the minimum cost*".

As a result, the proposals were trimmed to:

- A "*more straightforward, streamlined and flexible scheme*" focused solely on authorising deprivation of liberty, and going no further, abandoning the aspirations of the wider "*supportive care*" scheme, though some amendments would be made to the Mental Capacity Act to protect Article 8 rights in a way that minimises demands on services. These would include adding emphasis on P's wishes in best interests decisions, and testing the necessity for any removal of P from home into institutional care before any such move is made.

- The responsibility of establishing the case for a deprivation of liberty would be shifted from the provider of the care to commissioner (usually local authority, clinical commissioning group or health board) using, where possible, the same assessments already in place for the care planning.

- Rights to reviews, legal proceedings and advocacy.

- Consideration to be given to "*a defined group of people*" receiving <u>additional</u> independent oversight by an AMCP. However, it appeared that not only would the central role of the AMCP as scrutinising and authorising the deprivation in every case be lost (on the basis that the vast numbers affected by the *Cheshire West* judgment means it is "*not proportionate or affordable*" to offer this to everyone caught by Article 5), but even the current universal role of the BIA under DoLS would dropped, so a proportion of those deprived would apparently have no independent oversight.

- A single scheme applied uniformly across every setting, ie dropping plans for the dedicated hospital / hospice scheme and, presumably, leaving it to the relevant CCG or health board to authorise all inpatient deprivations.

- No amendment to be made to the Mental Health Act (MHA), on the basis that the policy aim can be met by provision that the existing powers under MHA should be used for patients who lack capacity to consent to admission and treatment for their mental disorder, even where they are compliant.

- Further consideration to be given to the proposal for a tribunal to replace the Court of Protection jurisdiction in these cases.

One of the most controversial aspects was the terminology used. We are all familiar with the counterproductive effect it can have to try to discuss "*deprivation of liberty*" in some of the sensitive and emotional situations in which health and social care is delivered. The favourite alternatives suggested were "*liberty safeguards*", followed by "*capacity safeguards*", and the Law Commission explicitly requested further suggestions/feedback on this.

It would be nearly another year before we saw the Law Commission's final proposals.

March 2017 – the Law Commission's Final report

The final report and a draft bill were published on 13 March 2017[690], three years to the day after the critical parliamentary committee report. Its first recommendation was that "*the DoLS regime should be replaced as a matter of pressing urgency*".

In its place, the Law Commission proposed the "Liberty Protection Safeguards" (LPS). This was the first time that the phrase was used, but because the later government proposals adopting the same name were

[690] https://www.lawcom.gov.uk/project/mental-capacity-and-deprivation-of-liberty/

significantly different, I will use the acronym LCLPS for now, to denote the Law Commission's LPS, to avoid any confusion.

The LCLPS was intended to be less onerous than DoLS, but to improve the protection of human rights. LCLPS would extend to all settings, including supported and shared living arrangements, and would also cover 16 and 17 year-olds, so such arrangements would no longer have to be authorised by the court.

Where a potential deprivation of liberty is identified, the onus would be upon the commissioning organisations to arrange authorisation. It would be for the 'responsible body' (local authority, hospital managers and CCGs commissioning care) to seek authorisation, intended to make the authorisation process truly central to the care or treatment planning process, rather than a legalistic afterthought.

The new process would consist of:

Stage 1: An advocate or appropriate person is appointed by the responsible body to represent the individual (P) who may be deprived of their liberty.

Stage 2: The responsible body arranges for three assessments (capacity assessment, medical assessment and the 'necessary and proportionate assessment') to be carried out by a minimum of two assessors, working independently. Crucially, to cut down on paperwork, it was intended that practitioners will be able to rely upon previous/other assessments where reasonable to do so. The draft Bill did not set a time limit on the use of capacity and medical assessments, but provided that such "*equivalent assessments*" could be used where they remain a reliable indicator of P's current condition.

Stage 3: Each application would be checked by a reviewer, who must have 'operational independence', i.e. must not be involved in the day-to-day care of the individual, but can be employed by the responsible body. If the independent reviewer feels that conditions for authorisation are met then they can confirm their approval and the responsible body can proceed with authorisation.

If the independent reviewer was not satisfied that the conditions are met, then the application must be referred to an Approved Mental Capacity Professional (AMCP) who is required to scrutinise the assessments and meet with P, before determining whether or not to approve the arrangements. There would be a duty to refer cases to the AMCP either where there is an objection to the proposed arrangements or where the main basis of the deprivation of liberty is the risk of harm posed to others[691]. Thereafter, a referral to court may still be required, but it was clearly intended that the AMCP should be the first step.

The 'record of authorisation' would become part of an individual's care plan, which would follow the patient, with amendments being made as new arrangements arise. This was clearly intended to end the inefficiency of a DoLS authorisation being tied to one particular placement. Authorisations under the LCLPS would cover multiple settings, including arrangements for transport and arrangements to return P to a particular setting in the event of P absconding, plugging some key gaps in the current regime under DoLS.

Authorisations under the LCLPS would be granted for up to 12 months initially, followed by review and the potential to renew for up to a further 12 months. After that, authorisation could be given for up to three years. (Under DoLS, of course, no authorisation can exceed 12 months).

To give greater teeth to efforts to reduce unlawful deprivation of liberty, LCLPS provided that civil proceedings could be brought against a private care provider where identified care or treatment arrangements giving rise to a deprivation of liberty have not been authorised, creating a new tort of unlawful deprivation of liberty.

The Law Commission also recommended amendments to MCA 2005 as a whole, beyond the narrow issues of deprivation of liberty, notably:

---

[691] The idea that a deprivation of P's liberty could be justified on the basis of preventing harm to others was adopted by the Law Commission but has been especially controversial, so it is important to flag that this was dropped from the later LPS proposals that actually went through parliament.

- Statutory codification of *Gillick* competence to provide for consent from children under 16;
- Strings attached to the 'defence' under MCA 2005, s5[692] so it would only apply for specified serious decisions (long-term accommodation, restrictions on contact, covert medication, serious medical treatment or treatment against P's wishes) if there is a written record of the decision-making covering a prescriptive list of issues; and
- greater weight to be put on P's own wishes, in best interests decision-making.

Again, it would be a year before the next formal step: the government's response to the Law Commission final proposals[693].

March 2018 – Government Response

On 14 March 2018, the Government's final response to the Law Commission review was published, which broadly agreed with most of the proposals, and committed to replace the DoLS system.

The only recommendation specifically rejected was the suggestion of statutory codification of the law relating to children (under 16) and decision-making capacity.

The interface between MCA 2005 and the Mental Health Act was effectively parked until the review of MHA ongoing at the time was also complete.

Though recognising the '*pressing urgency*' of reform, it was a bit woolly on the timescale, referring to the need for further careful consideration,

[692] No liability if you reasonably take a step or make a decision in someone's best interests when you reasonably think they lack capacity for that decision.

[693] By now I was quietly confident that I am unlikely to see DoLS actually replaced in my professional lifetime, which is still looking a good bet….

and to legislation '*when parliamentary time allows*', bearing in mind that this was a government up to its eyes in Brexit at the time.

July 2018 – Draft legislation

As such, many of us were surprised when draft legislation appeared as soon as July 2018. (The rumour was that each department had been challenged to come up with a piece of legislation that was unlikely to be controversial so that it could be pushed through Parliament quickly, as a demonstration of a government that was definitely not paralysed by the palaver over with Brexit, and that this was the Bill proposed by the Department of Health and Social Care).

In summary:

- the Bill would abolish the Deprivation of Liberty Safeguards, by deleting Mental Capacity Act 2005 (MCA) Schedule A1 and 1A, and replaced with a new Schedule AA1, to be known as the 'Liberty Protection Safeguards' (though the Bill did not use that title explicitly).

- the Mental Health Act interface was left to one side, pending the ongoing review of the MHA at the time. Those currently ineligible for DoLS would remain ineligible for the LPS, it seemed.

- the issue of overhauling the law relating to consent / capacity under 16 years of age was also left alone. The Bill's scheme (initially) applied only over age 18, contrary to the Law Commission recommendation to bring this into line with the MCA as a whole at age 16.

- the Bill's focus was on deprivation of liberty alone, rather than the wider amendments to the MCA proposed by the Law Commission.

- there was (initially) no statutory definition of deprivation of liberty, so *Cheshire West* prevailed.

- MCA s4B was to be revised, with a new and apparently wider definition of life sustaining treatment / vital act emergency circumstances in which a deprivation of liberty would be lawful, pending any formal authorisation.

- there was to be a new special procedure for care homes (basically giving them great responsibility for arranging the assessments).

- hospitals (both NHS and independent sector) would become responsible for authorising their own deprivations of liberty.

- authorisation of deprivation of liberty in other settings would be the responsibility of the CCG / local health board (if CHC funded) or the relevant local authority in all other cases.

- for a deprivation of liberty to be authorised, it must be *"necessary and proportionate"*, as determined by the hospital or care home manager, after specified appropriate consultation.

- an Approved Mental Capacity Professional (AMCP) would bring independent scrutiny, where *"it is reasonable to believe that the person cared for does not wish to reside in that place …or to receive that care"*.

- authorisations of a deprivation of liberty could last for up to 12 months initially, and could then be renewed for up to 12 months, with subsequent renewals for up to 3 years.

- the Court of Protection would continue to have jurisdiction over any appeal against an authorisation of a deprivation of liberty, so there would be no new tribunal, as the Law Commission had proposed.

Looking back, I wrote at the time that it was anticipated that the Bill would reach Royal Assent by April 2019 and, allowing for implementation and training, we might expect it to come into force perhaps in late 2019 / early 2020[694].

The government statement accompanying the Bill's launch asserted that £200m per year would be saved by local authorities under the new scheme[695].

Amendments in Parliament

Despite the Bill having been picked out as uncontroversial, in fact its journey from introduction on 3 July 2018 to royal assent on 16 May 2019 was something of a rollercoaster, not least when it nearly fell victim to the government's prorogation of Parliament as a device to deliver its promises on Brexit. This would have had the effect that all legislation passing through Parliament, no matter how close to the finish line, would have fallen and had to start the laborious process all over again. I know a number of people very relieved that in fact that particular trigger was not pulled[696] until after the LPS had safely got through.

Even so, it was far from plain sailing. From the outset, there was controversy about the proposed approach, and in particular what was widely seen as the dilution of safeguards, and a system tainted by conflict of interest, especially in granting care home managers a significant role in the authorisation of deprivations of liberty in their care.

The proposal was that for a deprivation of liberty in a care home, the local authority could ask the care home manager to:

---

694 Ha!

695 Though the minister responsible, Lord O'Shaughnessy, commented that this sounded almost "*too good to be true*" (Hansard, HL Series 5, (2nd Reading) Vol 792 col 1106, 16 July 2018) and of course any such saving would have to be offset against the extra costs from shifting some of the burden on to the NHS.

696 Bringing, in due course, Lady Hale back into our story for a swansong, wearing her spider broach and ruling on the (il)legality of that step in the Supreme Court in *R (Miller) v The Prime Minister* [2019] UKSC 41.

- Identify if the patient was "*objecting*", so as to trigger independent scrutiny by an AMCP;
- Commission the assessors with appropriate skills;
- Decide if an IMCA was required;
- Arrange a pre-authorisation review;
- Carry out the consultation with P and others; and
- Draft an authorisation document for the local authority to sign off.

Assuming that care home managers would be willing and able to find the resources and expertise to do, essentially, all the heavy lifting of the whole process[697], there was an obvious concern about a potential conflict of interest. This went further than the inherent problem of DoLS, with local authorities often marking their own homework as the supervisory bodies authorising a deprivation of liberty of their own making in their role as commissioner or provider of the restrictive care. Care homes are mostly private organisations with a profit motive, built on a business model reliant on high occupancy levels, and so a vested interest in keeping their beds full.

None of my care home provider clients were especially keen to take this on, seeing it as a hiding to nothing in terms of actual / perceived conflict of interest, damaging relationships with residents and families, and a whole load more responsibility and more work, for which extra funding was not assured.

More widely, there were concerns raised across the health and social care community about the relative lack of independent scrutiny in many cases; the failure (initially) to include 16-17 year-olds; the terminology

[697] The Impact Assessment's calculation of the costs made an allowance for a half day of training.

(initially) of requiring P to be proven of "unsound mind"; lack of clarity around the tests to be applied and how they would work in practice; lack of a statutory definition of a deprivation of liberty (for some, though this was not universally desired); and absence of guidance about what would happen to the existing DoLS backlog.

The Bill met stiff opposition. A survey in September 2018 (reported in Community Care, 3 September 2018) found that 88% of professionals involved in DoLS opposed the proposals to make care home managers responsible for assessments; 80% wanted a P's representative in all cases; 91% objected to the lack of specific obligation to consult P.

In a (non-scientific) survey I ran of 200 or so professionals in some training I gave in October 2018, only 11 were effusive enough to say that they were "good proposals, on balance" (the most positive category I dared offer). All the others were more or less critical, with 79 saying that they were "*so flawed that we need to go back to the drawing board*", and 34 driven to say that the proposals were "*so bad we'd be better off keeping DoLS and funding it properly*"!

On 8 October 2018, Care England as the representative body for care providers, wrote on behalf of 200 organisations "*calling on the government to go back to first principles and align the Bill with the Law Commission proposals*". They wrote of "*significant areas of concern to social care providers*", "*an unacceptable conflict of interest for providers*", and a view that the reforms would simply pass the DoLS backlog onto care homes to deal with. The presumed half day of training for care home managers was "*clearly unrealistic*".

Perhaps more startling, the Law Society[698] – the representative body for solicitors, and not known for its militancy – wrote that the Bill would "*weaken important safeguards*", and that "*As it stands, the Law Society does not believe that the Bill has sufficient safeguards and it is not fit for purpose*

[698] Full disclosure, I now sit on the Law Society's Mental Health and Disability Committee, but did not do so at the time.

in its current form". They concluded that "*it requires serious reconsideration and extensive revision*".

Hundreds of amendments were proposed on its way through parliament, and some key concessions were made by the government. Most significantly, the Bill was amended to include 16-17 year-olds in the LPS scheme, a specific obligation to consult P as part of the process was added, "unsound mind" was changed to "mental disorder" per the MHA, and the care home managers scheme was eventually dropped[699].

There was also a legislative hokey cokey where the government said that it would (I kid you not) "*give it a go*" to add a statutory definition of deprivation of liberty, as some sought, and then took it back out again (mercifully, looking at it – see Appendix 3).

More than 200,00 people signed a petition demanding better protection for the rights of disabled people[700], and in the House of Lords it was described as "one of the worst pieces of legislation ever brought before this House".[701]

For many of the ambiguous or controversial aspects, though, the government response was to assure people that it would all be made clear in the Code of Practice that would follow the legislation, and the Bill was pushed through to Royal Assent, received in May 2019.

And then it all went quiet, while we all waited for the vaunted Code of Practice.

It had been announced that LPS was due for implementation in October 2020, but in July 2020 – with no sign, still, of the Code of Practice – it

---

699 Though there is a hint in the Consultation on the draft Code of Practice that the government might consider restoring it – see chapter 18.

700 https://you.38degrees.org.uk/petitions/promoted/protect-the-human-rights-of-people-receiving-care-and-support

701 Baroness Barker, Hansard HK Series 5, Vol 794 col 1247, 12 November 2019.

was confirmed that the implementation would, instead, *definitely* be in April 2022.

In fact, the draft Code of Practice and accompanying raft of draft Regulations, adding some flesh to the bare bones of the LPS process, were not published for consultation until 17 March 2022[702]. We will look at the Liberty Protection Safeguards in a bit more detail in the next chapter.

[702] Just the 8 years after the post legislative scrutiny committee called for urgent replacement of DoLS, and 2 days before the 8 year anniversary of the *Cheshire West* judgment.

CHAPTER EIGHTEEN

THE LIBERTY PROTECTION SAFEGUARDS

Never gonna happen?

The most important thing about the LPS is whether they will ever be implemented, at least in the current form. If I had to put my mortgage on it, I'd bet against it.

The announcement in April 2023 was that LPS would not be implemented this side of a general election, apparently to allow focus on other reforms to health and especially social care to bed in. The reality, surely, included political calculation about the need to avoid any distraction from pre-election focus on the NHS waiting list.

That general election may have happened by the time you read this, but writing in Autumn 2023, we know that it has to happen by January 2025. Then what?

It is *possible* that LPS implementation will be a priority for a forthcoming new government, of whatever flavour. It does not seem likely to me. Even if it is accepted that reform is urgent (and has been since 2014), it is not obvious that the LPS, as they stand, will be the way to go. For a variety of reasons, Labour largely voted against the LPS legislation on its way though parliament.

And even with an appetite to do so, and all the resources this would take, LPS implementation would not be quick. We have not yet had the government response to the consultation on the draft Code of Practice, which was very controversial and needs significant work. It seems likely that there would need to be a further consultation on a new version. Once finalised, training needs to be put in place for the relevant professionals, likely to take perhaps 12-24 months, to allow courses to be developed, filled and completed.

I struggle to see a path to LPS implementation, as it stands, that could possibly get us there sooner than 3 years after the next general election, taking us to, perhaps, 2027. And by then, there's a good chance that we are back to the conversation about rolling DoLS reform together with reform of the Mental Health Act, especially as the current MHA Bill has also been dropped in the run up to the election, presumably for the same reasons.

So for all practical purposes, my advice is to work with the tools we already have as best we can; LPS is not going to save us any time soon, and there is a good chance that when reform eventually comes it might well look quite different.

That said – in the style of the "*look at what you could have won!*" reveal of the prize to the losing game show contestant – it may be useful to see broadly what LPS was all about, and where we got to. It may give a sense of what any future reform may look like; and it is a crying shame for all the work that has gone into trying to address some of the many issues with the current system to be overlooked entirely.

LPS in outline

Let's start with the things that, importantly, would not have changed:

- Despite the hokey cokey around this[703], there was no statutory definition of deprivation of liberty in the Mental Capacity (Amendment) Act 2019. This meant that the definition from the case law, and especially the *Cheshire West* Supreme Court judgment, prevails and we are (or should be[704]) looking at LPS

[703] See Appendix 3.

[704] See below about the draft Code of Practice interpretation of this and case studies.

being concerned with the same, huge group of people at risk of being deprived of their liberty in those terms.

- The Court of Protection would continue to hear appeals against authorisations of deprivations of liberty[705], and there would continue to be non-means tested legal aid for this[706].

- There would be no substantial change to the interface with the Mental Health Act.

- The consequences of any unlawful deprivation of liberty would remain – the government declined to include the Law Commission's recommendations for a new remedy.

- Just like DoLS, the LPS may authorise *the deprivation of liberty caused* by the arrangements for care and treatment, but the decisions about care and treatment itself must be made in accordance with the MCA. The LPS authorisation is no licence in itself to provide that care.

There would also be some big changes with LPS:

- DoLS would be replaced entirely (MCA Schedules A1 and 1A replaced with Schedule AA1) by the LPS.

- LPS would apply to all settings – supported living and private family homes, as well as care homes and hospitals.

- It would apply to multiple settings – authorisation would be for the "*arrangements*" for P, ie the overall care plan, which could include time spent in different places, or moving between them.

---

705 Under MCA s21ZA, rather than s21A.

706 Abolishing the iniquity that deprivations of liberty in the community, outside the scope of DoLS, do not get non-means tested legal aid now, as all settings would be in the scope of the LPS.

- LPS could be used for anyone over the age of 16, rather than 18 for DoLS.

- There would be no equivalent of urgent DoLS authorisations, but reform to MCA s4B would expand the legal cover for deprivation of liberty in emergency situations.

- The assessments are streamlined and should be built into care planning.

- Authorisations could be for longer – initially up to 12 months, renewable for up to 12 months and then, in suitable cases, further renewable for up to 3 years at a time.

- Independent scrutiny would be focused (rationed?) with the new Approved Mental Capacity Professional (AMCP) role mostly only for cases in independent hospitals or where P "*objects*".

- The burden of authorisation (in England) would be spread from only local authorities to include some NHS bodies, for NHS inpatient cases and where the care is commissioned by NHS Continuing Healthcare.

Overall, the intent was to bring deprivation of liberty into care planning itself, as everyone's business not a legalistic afterthought. With almost all kinds of deprivation of liberty brought into scope[707], the role of the court would largely be reduced to hearing the appeals against the LPS authorisations (all with non-means tested legal aid).

[707] With obvious exceptions for under 16 (where we may largely be able to rely on parental consent anyway) and for those who may not lack capacity for the relevant decisions / be of unsound mind, for whom the inherent jurisdiction of the High Court may be appropriate.

The "arrangements"

The focus of LPS is[708] on the "*arrangements*" that enable care or treatment that give rise to the potential deprivation of liberty.

This means it is not restricted to any particular setting, or to only one setting. In contrast to DoLS, which would authorise someone being "*accommodated*" at a particular care home or hospital, and which would need to be replaced if they moved to another care home or hospital, LPS would have the flexibility to authorise the whole care plan. That could include predictable periods of respite in different places, or planned / expected admissions to hospital.

It also makes it easier to include provision for any conveyance between settings that may amount to a deprivation of liberty.

Overview of the process

In outline, LPS process would be:

- A potential deprivation of liberty is identified
- An IMCA / "Appropriate Person" is appointed
- 3 assessments are carried out – mental disorder, capacity, and necessity & proportionality
- Consultation with P and with others
- Pre-authorisation review
- Authorisation by the Responsible Body

[708] I am conscious that I am writing about this in the present tense, having just predicted that it will never happen! To be clear, I am saying what the LPS is, since the legislation has been passed, but this has not yet been brought into force, and my guess is that it never will, at least in this form.

- Rights to challenge the authorisation under MCA s21ZA.

The Responsible Body

In place of the Supervisory Body under DoLS, which (in England) is always the relevant local authority, the LPS Responsible Body would run the process and ultimately grant or refuse the application for an LPS authorisation.

The Responsible Body would be:

- An NHS hospital if the deprivation of liberty is mainly as an NHS inpatient;
- Outside hospital, the NHS Integrated Care Board (ICB, or the Local Health Board in Wales)[709] where the care that amounts to a deprivation of liberty is "mainly through the provision of NHS Continuing Healthcare"[710].
- The relevant local authority (where P is ordinarily resident) in any other case.

Note that there are other ways for the NHS to be funding all or most of a patient's care outside hospital, for example under s117 MHA[711], an Individual Funding Request[712], or as the larger share of a joint package

[709] The legislation and supporting documents of course refer to the Clinical Commissioning Group, but those were replaced by ICBs in an NHS re-organisation in July 2022.

[710] CHC – an entitlement to a package of health and social care to be funded entirely by the NHS (ie non-means tested) on the basis that there is a "primary health need", after assessment through a checklist and Decision Support Tool

[711] Aftercare following discharge from detention under the MHA, which is a joint responsibility for the relevant ICB and local authority to provide appropriate health and social care, non-means tested, but depending on the nature of the patient's needs can be split between them in any way, including the ICB paying 100%.

[712] IFR – a bespoke process for an individual to make a case to the ICB that care or treatment should be commissioned on an individual basis, perhaps because they would

of care agreed between the ICB and the local authority[713]. None of those makes the ICB the LPS Responsible Body; logical or not, the legislation says "*continuing healthcare*" funded, and means only that.

The local authority will still be the Responsible Body in the great majority of cases, including for all patients in private hospitals, but the burden would be shared more with the NHS to some extent.

Appropriate Person / IMCA

Instead of the DoLS Relevant Person's Representative (RPR), the Responsible Body should identify and appoint an "*Appropriate Person*", "*as soon as the LPS process is triggered*"[714]. Their role is to provide representation and support for the person and support them throughout the LPS process[715].

This should be done on a best interests basis, where P lacks the capacity to decide for himself who this should be[716]. This is likely to be a family member or friend[717], though – as we saw with RPRs in the *AJ* case[718] – someone who is directly involved in making the arrangements that are in question may not be suitable for the role. There may also be a conflict of interest if they would benefit from the sale of a property, for instance, if

---

benefit exceptionally from something that is not commissioned for the wider population for which the ICB is responsible.

[713] A joint package of care (JPOC) is just that – agreed between the ICB and local authority, and funding can be split in any proportion, including in some cases with the ICB funding by far the larger share.

[714] Para 15.35.

[715] Para 15.47.

[716] See chapter 15 of the draft Code of Practice.

[717] The draft Code of Practice says that it could be anyone over the age of 16, though it is not clear whether

[718] See chapter 12 above.

P were to be moved into residential care[719]. They must "*be able to act truly independently of their own views or interests in the person's care*"[720].

Where there is no suitable Appropriate Person, the Responsible Body should appoint an advocate instead. The Appropriate Person can also access advocacy support.

Conditions of Authorisation

There are three conditions for an LPS authorisation, tied to the three assessments:

1. P has a mental disorder (the medical assessment)[721]
2. P lacks capacity to make the decision about care and residence; and
3. Deprivation of P's liberty is necessary to prevent harm to P[722] and proportionate to the likelihood and seriousness of the harm.

This appearance of streamlining from the six assessments of DoLS should be taken with a little salt. The three DoLS assessments missing here all still effectively need to be done: to confirm that P is old enough to use LPS (here over 16, over 18 for DoLS); that the use or potential use of the MHA does not make them ineligible (since the interface has not changed); and that there are no ADRTs / decisions by attorneys or deputies that impede the use of LPS.

---

719 Draft Code of Practice para 15.21.

720 Draft Code of Practice para 15.22.

721 Changed from "unsound mind" on the way through parliament, though ultimately it is this condition that brings these cases into compliance with Article 5(1)(e) which allows for deprivation of liberty by due process of law where someone is of unsound mind. This is defined in line with the Mental Health Act, but disregarding the additional requirements for learning disability for MHA detention.

722 The idea of justifying a deprivation of liberty to prevent harm to others having been dropped.

Assessments

Draft Regulations provided that Responsible Body should ensure that the assessments are carried out by someone who appears to have "*appropriate experience and knowledge*". Though exactly what that means is a little vague, it must not be someone with a specified "*proscribed connection*" to a care home, to avoid any conflict of interest.

The mental capacity assessment[723] and necessary & proportionate assessments[724] can both be done by:

- a medical practitioner;
- a nurse;
- an occupational therapist;
- a social worker;
- a psychologist; or
- a speech and language therapist.

Medical assessments[725] may only be carried out by a registered medical practitioner (including GPs and psychiatrists) or a registered psychologist who meets the conditions of these regulations.

The Impact Assessments suggest that the government expects GPs to carry out any assessments without a charge. Experience of trying to get medical evidence of unsound mind for the *Re X* process to authorise deprivations of liberty in the community might suggest otherwise, and this would be a likely bottleneck in the LPS process, especially given the timescale (below).

---

[723] See draft LPS Code of Practice para 16.27.

[724] Para 16.62.

[725] Para 16.45.

There is emphasis, where possible, on reliance on "*equivalent assessments*" for the medical and the capacity assessments, ie taking evidence that is already available, perhaps from within P's medical records, rather than completing all assessments afresh unnecessarily, though an equivalent assessment cannot be used for a necessary & proportionate assessment[726].

Consultation

Before arrangements can be authorised by the Responsible Body, appropriate consultation must have taken place with the following people (unless it is not practicable to so so):

- P themselves
- Anyone named by P as to be consulted
- Anyone engaged in caring for P or interested in their welfare
- Anyone holding a power of attorney for P, and any deputy
- Any IMCA; and
- Any appropriate person.

This, essentially, mirrors the list of consultees for the best interests decision making process in MCA s4.[727] The draft Code of Practice says that the consultation should be carried out by the assessor who does the necessary & proportionate assessment.

The purpose of the consultation is "*to ascertain P's wishes or feelings in relation to the proposed arrangements*".[728] In particular, it is important to

[726] Para 16.5.

[727] Chapter 17 of the draft Code of Practice.

[728] Para 17.16.

establish whether P is *objecting* to the arrangements, to determine whether the pre-authorisation review must be done by an AMCP.

Pre-Authorisation Review

This is a new step, not found in DoLS.

The pre-authorisation review[729] must be carried out by an AMCP if the deprivation of liberty is in a private hospital, or P is objecting, or if the Responsible Body decides it is appropriate to refer the case to an AMCP.

The purpose of the pre-authorisation review is to tell the Responsible Body if it is reasonable for them to conclude that the authorisation conditions are met. It can be a desktop exercise, if it is not being done by an AMCP.

For an AMCP review, this must be done in person, ie meeting P, and the AMCP has the same list of people to consult as the necessary & proportionate assessor as above.

If it is not an AMCP case, the pre-authorisation review must be someone who is not involved in P's day to day care, but it need not be a registered health or social care professional, and could be an employee of the care provider, for example.

AMCP[730]

The AMCP must be a registered nurse, social worker, psychologist, speech and language therapist or occupational therapist, and must complete prescribed additional training. They will normally be employed by a Responsible Body, and the local authority must ensure that there are enough AMCPs for its area.

---

729 Draft Code of Practice paras 13.44 to 13.71.

730 Draft Code of Practice chapter 18.

It is tempting to see the AMCP role as analogous to the BIA in DoLS[731], and it is likely that (if LPS proceeds) many AMCPs would probably come from former BIAs, but their roles are very different.

The BIA – in every single DoLS case – assessed P's situation and whether it was in his best interests. The AMCP will only be involved in some LPS cases, usually triggered by P's objection to the arrangements, and in those cases will be reviewing and challenging the work done by other assessors, in particular the necessary & proportionate assessment.

The only independent scrutiny, then, is if an AMCP gets involved in the pre-authorisation review, making it crucial how "*objection*" is defined and identified, as the main gateway to this.

Objection

The "*objection*" trigger for AMCP referral is that "*there is a reasonable belief that P does not wish to reside or receive care or treatment in a place, and the arrangements provide for this*".[732]

In considering this, the draft Code of Practice says to have regard to:

- Verbal and non-verbal behaviour,
- Possible reasons for P's behaviour,
- Medication for depression or sedation,
- Active resistance, eg trying to leave the place,
- Preparatory steps to leaving, eg packing bags,
- P's demeanour and relationship with the care providers,

[731] See chapter 13, above.

[732] Introduction to chapter 18 of the draft Code of Practice.

- Records of challenging behaviour and triggers for this, and

- Whether P seems to object to the whole care package or particular aspects[733].

Authorisation

There is nothing in the Regulations or draft Code of Practice to specify the individual at the Responsible Body who must complete the authorisation, once they have the assessments and the pre-authorisation review. It is left up to each Responsible Body who should do this.

Perhaps surprisingly, the draft Code even says that it is possible for the person giving the Authorisation to be the same person as did the pre-authorisation review if they can show "*a degree of separation between the roles*".[734]

Like DoLS, the authorisation can be completed up to 28 days in advance and can (and ***should***) be given before the situation that might be a deprivation of liberty starts.

Duration and conditions

As trailed above, the maximum duration of an LPS authorisation would be three years, on a second renewal onwards, but is limited to 12 months when initially granted and on the first renewal.

Like DoLS, conditions can be attached to the LPS authorisation, for example relating to contact or cultural issues.

---

733 Para 18.36.

734 Para 13.63.

Review

Like DoLS, there is provision for a review to be carried out by the Responsible Body:

- According to planned programme in authorisation record;[735]
- where conditions are varied;[736]
- on reasonable request by a person with an interest;
- if P becomes subject to the MHA;
- if the Responsible Body becomes aware of significant breach of conditions; or
- aware that P now objects and initial pre-authorisation review was not by an AMCP.

Appeal

As with s21A appeals under DoLS, there would be a right to appeal to the Court of Protection against LPS authorisations[737] and, crucially, the government has confirmed that these would attract non-means tested legal aid.

For my part, I would expect the number of Court of Protection cases challenging a deprivation of liberty to increase substantially under LPS, because:

- LPS would apparently cover everyone currently within the scope of DoLS (ie around 300,000, based on the applications last year)

---

735 Schedule AA1 Para 27.

736 Schedule AA1 para 38.

737 Now in MCA s21ZA.

and those who are deprived of their liberty outside the scope of DoLS at the moment (the government estimate is an extra 60,000 odd, including 16 – 17 year-olds).

- At the moment, those deprived of liberty outside DoLS do not get the non-means tested legal aid that would be extended to them once they are brought within LPS.

- Cases may go to the Court of Protection more readily when there would be less independent scrutiny for P in the LPS process than there is under DoLS.

Timescale

Though it is not in the legislation, the draft Code of Practice[738] says that the assessment process, from the LPS application through to the Responsible Body's decision, should not exceed 21 days, save in "exceptional circumstances". Bear in mind that the urgent DoLS authorisations that at least provide some cover for up to 14 days in some cases are being abolished, (and that at the moment DoLS authorisations take an average of 156 days, and LPS will cover more people).

MCA Section 4B

At least partly because there is no LPS equivalent to the DoLS urgent authorisation, the LPS legislation makes a substantive amendment to section 4B of the MCA.

As we saw in chapter 8, s4B deals with crisis situations, and allows for it to be lawful for a person to be deprived of their liberty in order to provide "life sustaining treatment" or to do a "vital act", "*while a decision … is sought from the court*".

---

738 Draft Code of Practice para 13.26.

The full text of the amended s4B is set out in Appendix 4, but the key change is that if the LPS process or a court application are not already underway, and it is not reasonably practicable to do so before taking the necessary life sustaining / vital act steps, then *the new s4B in itself authorises that deprivation of liberty, so it seems that no application to LPS or the court is required*[739].

Note that – like LPS – this amendment had not yet been brought into force. But the bit that troubles me is how it should be reconciled with *Ferreira*[740].

The amended s4B says that depriving someone of liberty to provide life-saving treatment in an emergency (so there's no time to apply for an LPS authorisation or to the court beforehand) *is a deprivation of liberty that is authorised by this legislation*. But in January 2017, more than 2 years before this legislation was passed, the Court of Appeal said that life-saving medical treatment, in that situation, did not engage Article 5: it was *no deprivation of liberty at all, and so needs no authorisation*.

So which is it: a deprivation of liberty which is authorised by the legislation, or no deprivation of liberty at all? This stuff is murky enough without making it more complicated.

In a hospital context, at least, I find it quite hard to think of a case in which the criteria are met for a deprivation of liberty authorised by the amended s4B, which don't also meet the criteria for *Ferreira* saying that it is *no deprivation of liberty at all.*

---

739 See *Somerset NHS Foundation Trust v Amira* [2023] EWCOP 25, in which, controversially, the judge held that s4B could be used to deliver obstetric care that would amount to a deprivation of liberty if the patient lost capacity to make the relevant decisions during her labour, rather than the Trust making an application in advance where this was foreseeable.

740 See chapter 7 – the idea that some medical treatment, certainly life-saving or emergency care, is no deprivation of liberty to engage Article 5, so long as it is the same as for any other patient (ie there is no discrimination according to any patient's mental disorder).

One possible explanation rests on the string attached to the *Ferreira* exception – ie that the life-saving treatment is the same as it would be for any patient, regardless of their mental disorder. So if Maria Ferreira, for example, in ICU with her breathing difficulties, was being treated as anyone would be with her physical health needs, then she was not deprived of her liberty at all for the purpose of Article 5. But if her treatment was different in any significant way as a result of her learning disability / Down's syndrome, then the trust could not rely on the *Ferreira* exception to take the case outside Article 5 altogether, so it would be regarded as a deprivation of her liberty if it met the acid test *Cheshire West* criteria. In emergency circumstances, this would be authorised by the current s4B *while seeking a court order or DoLS authorisation* and, under the new s4B (if ever brought into force) would just be authorised by the legislation *without an application to court or LPS*.

The amended s4B may also be about getting some leeway in non-health and social care contexts, for example for detaining someone in a situation of self-harm or suicide, if the formalities of the MHA are not or cannot be used, but the language of the legislation of "*life-sustaining treatment*" does rather lend itself to thinking about a medical context.

And how does an exception for "*life-sustaining*" medical treatment apply to a setting such as a hospice where we may equally not want the *Cheshire West* acid test to be mechanistically applied, but that is perhaps not a comfortable characterisation of what's really going on?

If the amended s4B is ever brought into force, it would benefit from a bit more clarity; sadly, the LPS draft Code of Practice does not shed any light on this.

Code of Practice and Consultation

The draft Code of Practice was published in March 2022, open for consultation to early July 2022.

It was a single document dealing with the MCA (updating the MCA Code of Practice from 2007, which is now wildly out of date after more than 15 years of case law), and the LPS (replacing the DoLS Code of Practice from 2008). Though this meant it came in at a whopping 520 odd pages, it is really positive that the LPS scheme was embedded squarely in the MCA in this way.

More challenging though, is what happens now to the whole thing, with the LPS being dropped (for now at least). The update on the MCA is mostly uncontroversial and helpful, and we could do without waiting years more for that. I imagine that the LPS parts will be stripped out, and we will go back to having an updated Code for the MCA alone. The implication of that is that we will continue to rely on the (equally out of date) DoLS Code of Practice for years more, and continue perhaps to have separate documents for the MCA and for deprivation of liberty (whether DoLS or, in due course, LPS) despite this attempt to join up the thinking.

On the deprivation of liberty elements in particular, the draft Code has some gaps, controversies and inconsistencies. But the tone of the 25 consultation questions was mainly "*have we made ourselves clear?*" rather than "*have we got this right?*"[741].

We are told that the government will publish a summary of the consultation responses, but no timescale has been given for this.

Chapter 12 and definition of Deprivation of Liberty

The single most controversial aspect of the draft Code, and the bit of the consultation response summary I am most looking forward to, is the way it tackled the definition of deprivation of liberty.

Remember that the government decided against using legislation to define deprivation of liberty, and said instead that there would be case

[741] And it included a question about bringing back the care home managers' scheme that had been dropped in the face of overwhelming opposition on the way through parliament, as if that might still be up for grabs.

studies in the Code of Practice that would help to explain the *Cheshire West* acid test in practice. This is in chapter 12 of the draft Code.

Over a dozen or so scenarios, the draft Code gives examples which are mostly, it says, *not a deprivation of liberty* for various reasons which I find very hard to reconcile with the case law as I have set out earlier in this book. For example:

- Jake, who has dementia, is locked in the family home by his wife when she goes out. But "*he is still able to wander around the house*" and "*able to choose what to do in the house*".

- Jennifer, in her 80s living in a care home with the early stages of dementia, "*can freely come and go from the communal areas and into her room*", she can use the garden, and there is not a member of staff with her at all times.

- Marsha, a woman in her 40s with schizophrenia, is allowed to go out from her care home unescorted after mid morning, as long as she is back by 9pm, or the police could be called to fetch her back.

Each of these, and many others, *are declared by the draft Code to **not** be a deprivation of their liberty* on the grounds that they do not meet the *Cheshire West* acid test of being under continuous supervision and control and not free to leave.

This does ***not*** reflect the law, as I understand it. This sets the bar far too high, and denies all these people appropriate safeguards.

Continuous supervision and control does not need you to be confined to one room of a house when you are locked in, or to have care home staff in your own bedroom at all times; having to be back at a placement by 9pm under threat of the police being called is not "*freedom to leave*", which in any case is more properly about your ability to pack your bags and go live where you want.

The language of P being "*happy*" or "*content*" is rife throughout chapter 12, when describing a situation asserted not to be a deprivation of liberty, though the Supreme Court made clear that this is not relevant.

And in describing the exception for medical treatment, *Ferreira* is stretched almost beyond recognition: the draft Code[742] says:

> *"a deprivation of liberty will not occur if the person is treated for a physical illness and the treatment is given under arrangements that are the same as would have been in place for a person who did not have a mental disorder. .... This approach should be applied to any form of medical treatment for physical health problems and in whatever setting the treatment is being delivered".*

It goes on to give an example of Ms K, who has dementia and is placed in a care home after a severe stroke, as a result of which she needs "*constant 1:1 support to help her get about*" and has some medication that makes her feel lethargic and tired.

Now, to be sure, once we say some kinds of medical treatment do not generally engage Article 5 right to liberty issues, as the Court of Appeal did in *Ferreira* for "*life saving treatment*" as an inpatient in ICU, we can question where we draw the line around that exception. And as I said in chapter 7, it should not logically be confined only to intensive care. But it does seem a bit much to say that *Ferreira* also takes outside Article 5's protection anyone in a care home who happens to be there because their care needs, like Ms K's immobility, are caused by any medical condition, like her stroke.

Overall, the strong impression is of an attempt to push the definition of deprivation of liberty backwards, limiting the numbers of people within the scope of Article 5's protection, and out of line with the case law.

The government protest that this is not so, and this is a faithful account of how it interprets the law now, not trying to move the goalposts.

---

742 Para 12.77.

On the other hand, during the consultation on the draft Code, the director general for adult social care said "*we are looking at a new definition of what should constitute a deprivation of liberty. We have consulted on that...*"[743]. And the Impact Assessment[744] said "*the proposed definition of deprivation of liberty, as set out in the Code, is also likely to affect the number of applications [to LPS] per year*" making the impact unpredictable.

This could be thought academic, if LPS are not coming, and the LPS parts of the Code are dead in the water, for now at least. But I have included this because it would be very easy to refer to the scenarios in the draft Code and take at face value, wrongly, in my view, that they accurately represent the current state of the law.

It is also worth remembering that:

- A Code of Practice cannot change the case law;
- Even a statutory duty *to have regard to* a Code of Practice allows professionals to depart from it with good reason, as would be the case if it were inconsistent with the law;
- In almost every scenario the draft Code says is not a deprivation of liberty, I think it is, or at least it could be. And that – much easier – question is the right trigger for DoLS / LPS / a referral to court. *Is there a risk* that P is being deprived of their liberty[745]?

---

743 In evidence given to the parliamentary Joint Committee on Human Rights on 18 May 2022.

744 Para 23.5.

745 See chapter 4 above, and this is retained in LPS, eg draft Code para 13.8: LPS should be triggered where a staff member has "a reasonable belief that the arrangements may amount to a deprivation of liberty...".

In the meantime, do no use the draft Code of Practice as a source for material for training on what a deprivation of liberty is.

Conclusion

So what do we think of the LPS?

Certainly, some aspects would be welcome – more flexibility and inclusion of all settings and of 16-17 year-olds.

But is it really all that streamlined? Really much less onerous than DoLS?

Where there are efficiencies, are they at the expense of appropriate safeguards for P – eg the loss of any independent scrutiny of their situation unless they are in a private hospital or are "objecting"?

And does it matter much anyway, if it is not likely to see the light of day anytime soon?

There would need to be quite a bit of work still to get LPS ready to go and implemented, even with political will to move it on after the next election, and there is a good chance that whatever reform we do eventually see will look rather different.

The reality is, despite all the shortcomings of the current system, and the obvious pressures for reform, the tools we have now are all we are going to have for the foreseeable future, and we will just have to get on with it as best we can.

CHAPTER NINETEEN

WHAT NEXT?

So here we are then.

On an issue that goes to the core of our identity and the control that we have over our own lives, we have a complex and bureaucratic system that is expensive and time consuming, but also offers meaningful protection only too little or too late for the vast majority of people who need it.

Illegality is inevitable and widespread.

Reform, the need for which has been painfully obvious for at least a decade, still looks like it is years away.

No-one seems to be happy: Those who want the widest protection of Article 5 will be frustrated at the failures in practice to deliver the safeguards promised. Those who think it has gone too far will rail against the overreach into someone's own home in particular, even though very few of those cases are actually being scrutinised through the courts.

We obviously need reform for the process of dealing with a deprivation of liberty, but do we also need a rethink who is in the scope of this and why?

It did not have to be this way.

In 1994, while the Law Commission was still chewing over the early stages of what would become the Mental Capacity Act 2005, the Law Commissioner in charge of the project wrote an update on their progress, and reflected on the limitations of law reform generally:

> *"Not all problems can be solved by the law or in the courts. Many may be better solved by professional guidance, which is not our province. Law does have advantages of accessibility and public accountability. It can also be cumbersome and expensive. In England and Wales there*

has been a culture of informality, with decisions governed by professional judgement rather than the law and legal procedures. In relation to hospital admission, for example, the law deliberately does not insist that this be genuinely "voluntary", merely that the patient does not actively object. No one wants to establish a system under which formal procedures have to be invoked before any decision can be taken on behalf of any incapacitated person."[746]

That Law Commissioner was Brenda Hodgett, at the time a judge in the Crown Court and a family law academic. 20 years later, having reverted to her maiden name, Brenda Hale, she gave the leading judgment in *Cheshire West,* doing more than anyone else to impose and expand those "formal procedures"[747].

To be fair, in *Cheshire West* Lady Hale did say that, having identified a deprivation of liberty that needed scrutiny and authorisation:

"Such checks need not be as elaborate as those currently provided for in the Court of Protection or in the Deprivation of Liberty safeguards (which could in due course be simplified and extended to placements outside hospitals and care homes)".[748]

However, with no such reform, nor a step change in the resources available to better match the demands put on it, the net of the existing system was simply cast wider.

Ironically, after *Cheshire West,* Steven Neary came to be regarded as deprived of his liberty when he was happily living in his own home with his dad[749]. They now have to go through the regular paperwork and

746 "Mentally incapacitated adults and decision-making: the Law Commission's project", in *Decision Making and Problems of Incompetence*, edited by Andrew Grubb, 1994.

747 Her biography "Spider Woman", 2022, is great, but given her prominence in our story of deprivation of liberty, I was a little disappointed that *Cheshire West* and the issues it has caused do not get a single mention.

748 [2014] UKSC 19 at paragraph 57.

749 Steven is the tenant in his own flat, with his dad as his live in carer.

assessments for a court order to authorise the care plan at home, which Mark Neary says Steven finds really distressing[750].

Is this *really* what we wanted?

And, if not, can we find a way to move the goalposts to where we do want Article 5 to apply?

"There's no place like home"

We cannot get away from the fact that "home" feels different and there is something special about it.

When one of my daughters, 7 and 10, falls off her bike on our street, there's no argument that our neighbour has a bigger, better box of plasters than we do, so it's in her best interests to go there. She just *wants to go home*. After some days at work, I know exactly how she feels.

Home is the place where we have most choice and scope to express our autonomy and individuality. Even in the homes of my best friends, or closest family, I might hesitate before I answer the phone for them, or the door. I would certainly not take it on myself to start redecorating according to my own taste, or behaving quite as I would in my own home.

A leading academic in this field, Lucy Series writes:

"Most of us want 'to live in the place we call home with the people and things that we love, in communities where we look our for one another,

[750] See Mark Neary's blog – https://markneary1dotcom1.wordpress.com/about/ Mark makes a similar point about the palaver of dealing with the substance of the care package through direct payments: "Why have I found myself as a director of a small company just so Steven can go swimming?" quoted in Lucy Series' book, below, at p69.

doing the things that matter to us', and we have no good reason to believe that older or disabled people want anything different".[751]

Institutions are praised when they foster a "homelike" environment, even if institutional reality means there can only ever be an echo of someone's individuality. I remember looking at the glass box of personal memorabilia wall-mounted outside the door of my mum's identikit care home room; I remember wondering what few small items would best capture the whole of my own life.

And, however "homey" they can be, our culture recognises plucky "escape" from institutions, in literature and cinema[752].

Home is different. But instead of saying so, defining and defending this, at times those trying to roll *Cheshire West* back, away from someone's own home, have picked the wrong fights: He is happy! She isn't trying to leave! He can't walk anyway! The restrictions are just what they need for their care anyway, and everyone means well!

But none of these hold up. The "*paradigm prisoner in his cell*" is no less confined if he's heard whistling a jaunty tune, or is beaten / drugged into unconsciousness, or is just asleep. We might well want to say that Steven Neary is not deprived of his liberty at home with dad, but these alone cannot be the reasons why, without too high a price in denial of safeguards to those we would want to have them, especially in more institutional settings. We would not want access to safeguards to be dependent on a care provider's own view of their care being appropriate or well intentioned, or of P's compliance or contentment with it.

We should, perhaps, have been more honest that we have wanted to treat someone's own home as different. We would need to look for a more

---

[751] "Deprivation of Liberty in the Shadows of the Institution", Bristol University Press, 2022, at p227, quoting Crowther N, 2019, "*Talking about a brighter social care future.*"

[752] For instance, Michael Caine's last film, The Great Escaper, released in October 2023, tells the true story of Bernard Jordan, a D-Day veteran absconding from his care home to attend a commemoration.

principled basis to do this, and then to address the two problems that come with it.

Article 5, institutions and our own home

Lucy Series says that "*following Cheshire West, it is likely that England and Wales have the most far-reaching system of recognition and regulation of social care detention globally*".[753]

Distinguishing between institutions and home settings, Series says that *Cheshire West* "*potentially inserts into family life a form of law geared toward regulating institutional spaces*"[754].

In his blog, Mark Neary writes[755]

> "*I have to say there is not one single moment of one single day as I observe Steven going about his business in his own home where it occurs to me that he might be being deprived of his liberty. Having been through the DoLS process when Steven was in the ATU, there isn't any comparison between his life then and his life now. The doors aren't alarmed. He isn't subjected to face down restraint (or any kind of restraint for that matter). He isn't given bucket loads of anti psychotics to make our job easier. He isn't prevented from going out for three months whilst we risk assess all the venues he goes to. He no longer lives an institutionalized life*".

As the minority in the Supreme Court in *Cheshire West* said, the European Court of Human Rights itself had no judgment in which

[753] Cited above, p4.

[754] P182.

[755] https://markneary1dotcom1.wordpress.com/2017/03/18/the-day-cowley-became-a-gilded-cage/ 18 March 2017. With thanks to Mark for his kind permission, I will quote the whole Blog in Appendix 5, as it bears reading in full.

Article 5 had been applied to someone's own home, and all the ECtHR cases referred to took place "*in institutions of some kind*"[756].

And there is no doubt that institutional settings seem to be the focus of Article 5. For instance, from the ECtHR "Guide on Article 5 of the European Convention on Human Rights"[757], last updated on 31 August 2022:

> "*The detention of persons of unsound mind must be effected* ***in a hospital, clinic or other appropriate institution*** *authorised for the detention of such persons*" (emphasis added).

When the DoLS legislation was going through parliament in 2007, the Joint Committee on Human Rights proposed a statutory definition of deprivation of liberty that would have framed it as a person being:

> "***taken from their home*** *to a place where they will be prevented from leaving, and compete and effective control will be exercised over their movements*" (emphasis added).

That certainly sounds like a deprivation of liberty to me.

So, just as we say that Article 5 does not bear on medical treatment in some circumstances, following the Court of Appeal in *Ferreira*, so we *could* say that it does not *usually* apply in someone's own home[758]. That is not to say that there could not possibly be a deprivation of liberty in someone's home, just as it is perfectly possible that there is still a deprivation of liberty in provision of medical treatment in hospital; but it may be that this is a situation that warrants an adapted approach.

That would leave us with the same two problems we have from *Ferreira* – where do we draw the line where the exception applies, and what do

---

756 The joint dissenting judgment of Lords Carnworth and Hodge, [2014] UKSC 19 at para 97.

757 https://www.echr.coe.int/documents/d/echr/guide_art_5_eng

758 To be clear, this is not what the case law says now, but just to suggest that it might be possible for the courts to take a different approach.

we do about protecting people who are denied the cover of Article 5 in that way?

Defining a home?

In chapter 5 I mentioned "*the Burrito test*" – would you be allowed to get up and make yourself a burrito at 3am? It is a pretty good way to crystallise the question whether you are living in your own home or an institution, but I appreciate that it might not lend itself to legislation.

Lucy Series describes a family home as "*a cluster of sometimes related people muddling along with their own lives together under one roof*", and lacking the structure and routines of an institution (as mine surely does!).

Home is more than somewhere we routinely sleep at night. The core qualities might be having a zone of choice, and control of the threshold.

The sense of control and choice is powerful. Series identifies "decision" as "the base unit of liberty", and the "mortification of the self" that comes from all meaningful decisions being taken out of our hands in institutional settings. She describes the clear research showing the improvement in quality of life and outcomes for people who have a sense of control over some of their living arrangements and environment, even down to doing much better when they have a plant to take care of than when it is looked after for them by staff.

But is it still *entirely my own home* if carers come into it – or even live as well as work in it, making some areas their own and inaccessible to me? What if I do not really have the option to deny them access, either at all or without facing consequences such as consideration of a residential placement?

We are likely to see technology used more often to support people to stay in their own homes, driven both by an ageing population and by a health and social care workforce crisis[759]. That may be positive. But whether it is right to see that as *control that warrants some safeguards*, might depend on the formal response that is likely if the data that we get – whether someone has opened the fridge or got out of bed – is not what we want to see.

Perhaps it makes a difference if the care is provided commercially, or just by family?[760]

Supported living and similar arrangements can be a grey area, where boundaries between home and institution have blurred.

Series notes that it may be better not to agonise over whether or not it is a deprivation of liberty in someone's own home, but rather to ask if there is a useful purpose in treating, and regulating, it as if it is. What's the point?

To some extent, I think that goes to the second issue – if we do not see it in terms of Article 5, then what "safeguards" might there be, and what do we want, for someone in their own home?

What safeguards if not Article 5?

Remember, we are only talking about people who are "*under continuous supervision and control and not free to leave*". Even if they are indisputably

[759] For example, this story on BBC news on 7 October 2023, "Reading vulnerable adults home sensor trial wins £1m grant" – https://www.bbc.co.uk/news/uk-england-berkshire-67038575

[760] Series notes that the County Asylums Act 1828 (in force until the Lunacy Act 1890 was repealed in 1960) extended licensing and regulation to places keeping even a single "lunatic", which had previously been excluded from such regulation on the lobbying of the wealthy who would often place a single "mad" relative with a doctor or clergyman in their own home for payment. As such, *Cheshire West* was not entirely novel in seeing deprivation of liberty in need of regulation in someone's own home, albeit when their "guest" was there on a commercial basis.

in their own homes, does this not warrant some degree of oversight and protection, if not the full palaver of Article 5?

This is a much easier question to tackle in the medical treatment context. Wherever the "*Ferreira line*" is drawn, disapplying Article 5, the patient will still benefit from the legal frameworks of a highly regulated environment: a duty of care on the clinicians towards the patient, enforceable through clinical negligence claims, or regulatory action by the GMC or NMC, for example; decisions about treatment being made only with the patient's consent or, if they lack capacity to make the relevant decision, by following the MCA, with the overall service inspected and regulated against fundamental standards by the CQC / HIW. The criminal law can also intervene if need be.

Among all that, is there really a need to add the protection and process of Article 5, unless the treatment and its restrictions are <u>not</u> just a reflection of the patient's physical health needs but also about managing behaviour as a result of their mental disorder / disability?

Someone's own home, in contrast, is less easily regulated. The CQC may regulate a registered care provider, but would have no regulatory traction on the premises themselves, and have no power to second guess assessments of capacity or best interests decisions for individuals. "*Its focus is on institutional-level processes, not reviewing substantive outcomes for particular individuals*"[761].

And perhaps that is the way that we would want it. Our Article 8 rights to private and family life may be just as important to us as the right to liberty.

Series writes:

> "*perhaps decades of informality have normalised this sate of affairs to the point it sems natural, even unquestionable, that health and care professionals have de facto authority to make health and care substitute*

[761] Series p139.

> *decisions whilst family substitute decision making is regarded with suspicion*"[762].

She argues that:

> "*… where we have cause for concern about family-based care, the ordinary tools of the local authority care assessment, care planning and – if necessary – safeguarding and the involvement of the courts are the appropriate response; there is no obvious benefit in regulating this as a question of detention*"[763].

Appalling cases like Tom Somerset-How[764] should not, perhaps, dictate the approach to be taken to safeguards for the great majority of situations[765]. And anyway, there is nothing to suggest that his situation was identified or treated as a deprivation of liberty in a way that did anything to save him.

On the other hand, a reluctance to simply trust in the good intentions of what goes on behind closed doors lay behind the Court of Appeal judgment on imputability to the state in *SRK*:[766] without the periodic review by Court of Protection oversight,

> "*there are insufficient procedural safeguards against arbitrary detention in a purely private care regime*".

Being confined *in your own home* makes you <u>no less</u> under continuous supervision and control, and <u>no more</u> free to leave, and it is still imputable to the state. If we see too much difficulty, or danger, in trying

---

[762] Series p150.

[763] Series p207.

[764] Chapter 15.

[765] Law students are taught that "hard cases make bad law".

[766] And similarly, perhaps, the concern about deference to parents in Lady Hale's comments in Re D in the Supreme Court, as it was with Lord Steyn's concerns about deference to clinicians in Bournewood itself.

to take the whole private home context out of the scope of Article 5, what else can we try to reduce the (over)reach of *Cheshire West*?

"Consent"

The issue of consent – the second limb of the three-part *Storck* test – has been relatively under-explored. It has largely simply been accepted that there can be no consent without the capacity to make the relevant decision[767], but it may be a little less straightforward than that.

To summarise Alex Ruck Keene's argument on this[768],:

- It is appropriate to see Article 5 as expecting a degree of *coercion* or *compulsion*, the ECtHR sometimes referring to this as an essential factor[769].

- It is likely there may be greater restrictions in place if P is resistant.

- The right to liberty is too important to be waived by mere acquiescence, and some of those most vulnerable and most in need of the protection of Article 5 should not lose it by being regarded as passively compliant.

- But, that said, there is ECtHR authority for the possibility that a patient who might lack capacity in law for a decision about his residence may nonetheless be able to give sufficient consent to it

767 See chapter 9.

768 See Alex Ruck Keene's Discussion paper: Deprivation of Liberty, Cheshire West and the CRPD, December 2017 https://www.39essex.com/wp-content/uploads/2017/12/Valid-Consent-Discussion-Paper-December-2017.docx.pdf

769 3 *Firat v Turkey* (Application no. 34010/06, decision of 10 September 2013) at para 35. See also, e.g. Kasparov v Russia [2016] ECHR 849 at para 36. He proposes as an alternative that the objective acid test might be refined by adding a need for an element of coercion before it could amount to a deprivation of liberty.

for it to fall outside Article 5 in practice. In *Mihailovs v Latvia*[770], the ECtHR distinguished between the care home that Mr Mihailovs objected to and another where he seemed to give "*tacit agreement*", and – though he lacked capacity in law to consent for himself – found that the care home where he seemed content was, thereby, not a deprivation of liberty.

- Therefore, if a patient (notwithstanding their lack of capacity per the MCA for the relevant decisions) manifests "*a positive wish*" to be in that particular place or care package, then this can amount to the subjective "consent" to establish that ***there is no deprivation of liberty***, no matter how restrictive the confinement. This may include cases where P had been able to express a clear view in the past, before loss of the relevant capacity, that would support their "consent" to the current placement.[771]

Ruck Keene also makes the point that this approach would better align with the United Nations Convention of the Rights of Persons with Disabilities, the UNCRPD.

So, let's pause to look at that, as it raises some bigger challenges.

UNCRPD

The UNCRPD was adopted by the United Nations General Assembly in 2006, and the UK agreed to follow it in 2009.

Article 12 is the right to equal recognition before the law. States must "*recognise that persons with disabilities enjoy legal capacity on an equal basis*

[770] *Mihailovs v Latvia* [2013] ECHR 65 at paragraph 134.

[771] He also proposes an alternative, as a "weaker" version of this argument: we could say that someone who is not facing coercion in the care plan is likely to be faced with simpler information and therefore an easier hurdle to surmount to establish that they actually do have capacity for the relevant decisions, and so can consent, excluding any possibility that they are deprived of their liberty. I am grateful that Alex has reviewed and "approved" this summary.

with others in all aspects of life". Article 12(4) in particular requires that any measures to safeguard people with disabilities must respect their "*will and preference*".

Article 14 is the right to liberty: "*the existence of a disability shall in no case justify a deprivation of liberty*".

Article 19 requires states to "*recognize the equal right of all persons with disabilities to live in the community, with choices equal to others, … including …Persons with disabilities have the opportunity to choose their place of residence and where and with whom they live on an equal basis with others and are not obliged to live in a particular living arrangement*".

(The French version of Article 19 is the right to "*autonomie de vie*", which has a particular ring to it, no?).

Though their interpretation is still contested, even at face value these are difficult to reconcile with the MCA, DoLS or even the ECHR Article 5(1)(e).

Indeed, the last time that our progress towards UNCRPD compliance was reviewed by the Committee on the Rights of Persons with Disabilities, they said[772]:

> *34. The Committee is concerned that the State party's legislation provides for involuntary, compulsory treatment and detention both inside and outside hospitals on the basis of actual or perceived impairment.*
>
> ***35. The Committee recommends that the State party:***
>
> ***(a) Repeal legislation and practices that authorize non-consensual involuntary, compulsory treatment and***

---

[772] Concluding observations on the initial report of the United Kingdom of Great Britain and Northern Ireland, 3 October 2017 http://tbinternet.ohchr.org/_layouts/15/treatybodyexternal/Download.aspx?symbolno=CRPD%2fC%2fGBR%2fCO%2f1&Lang=en

> ***detention of persons with disabilities on the basis of actual or perceived impairment;***

There is no sign, yet, of the scale of reform of our current approach that would be needed to get into line with the UNCRPD, though the Law Commission's proposals to put extra weight into P's wishes in any best interests decision under MCA s4 (rejected by the government) would have been a step in that direction.

"Assent" as no deprivation of liberty

For now, Alex Ruck Keene's proposed approach would allow us to say that though Steven Neary lacks the capacity to *consent* to the arrangements for his care and residence, he is *not* deprived of liberty when he is at home with his dad, *because he wants to be there*.

And of course this sort of *incapacitous "consent"* actually already plays a crucial role: "*objection*" determines whether someone must go down the route of formal detention under the Mental Health Act, for example; triggers your access to some of the safeguards under DoLS such as a s21A challenge, and (under LPS) makes the difference between the independent review of an AMCP or not.

As such, this obviously has a lot of appeal, but it has not (yet) found favour with the courts[773]. An argument along these lines was run in the Court of Appeal in *Ferreira* but, as we saw in chapter 7, the court simply found that the *Cheshire West* acid test shouldn't apply in life saving medical treatment due to the different *context.*

Even if it were adopted by the courts, taking a cohort of people outside Article 5 who could be said to be "*consenting incapacitously*" to the arrangements it could raise its own concerns.

---

[773] The Joint Committee on Human Rights did like this approach, and it did make it into a proposed amendment to the LPS legislation, though it did not survive.

Though Ruck Keene emphasises the need to avoid taking mere acquiescence / passive compliance as enough "consent" to negate a deprivation of liberty, this must be a risk in practice. There must be a temptation, especially in commercial care home settings, perhaps, to perceive the "positive wish" to be there. Remember that HL in *Bournewood* was described as if passively compliant, when other evidence suggests that, in fact, he had no toenails left after staff restraining him would stand on his feet.

Sufficient and suitable evidence that P positively wishes to be where he is could be quite hard to come by, and in practice finding this may be barely less onerous than simply recognising and authorising the deprivation of liberty.

And research has found that in fact "*every patient living with dementia we observed, resisted care to some extent*".[774]

The Supreme Court in *Cheshire West* very deliberately excluded these *subjective* factors (contentment, purpose, motive) from the *objective* element of the definition of deprivation of liberty for good reason: to ensure that the protection of important human rights is not lost by simple compliance, perhaps masking the extent of coercion that would be used if need be. Sneaking those factors back into the subjective element to say that there is no deprivation of liberty risks defeating that purpose.

And won't it be confusing to say that someone can lack capacity to make a decision about their care or residence, but that nonetheless their behaviour manifesting contentment in that environment, for example, can amount to "*consent*" for the purposes of Article 5 so that it is <u>not</u> a deprivation of liberty, no matter how restrictive?

It can be hard enough to get it clearly understood that there can be *no consent to treatment if the patient lacks capacity to make the relevant decision, and that compliance or acquiescence does not amount to consent.*

---

[774] Featherstone et al, 2019, "*Routines of Resistance: an ethnography of the care of people living with dementia in acute hospital wards and its consequences.*" International Journal of Nursing Studies, 96, 53-60.

Even if framed more neutrally (as "assent" perhaps, rather than "consent"?) this seems to dangerously muddy those waters.

Personally, I am least comfortable with such "non-capacitous consent" taking someone outside the scope of Article 5 in an institutional setting. Equally, I am less comfortable with reliance on the private home as a "*No DoL*" trump card if the care arrangements there become coercive.

Putting the two approaches together feels safer ground: it would not be considered a deprivation of liberty if it were in their own home **and** P positively wants to be there?

This would need some degree of oversight; perhaps a visit by a social worker annually to check that, despite being under continuous supervision and control and not free to leave, it is genuinely their own home and P is positively content.

That might offer a principled basis to not inflict the full process of authorisation of a deprivation of liberty for Steven Neary, without abandoning all scrutiny for those "at home", and reducing the risk of projecting contentment onto those passively compliant in institutions.

But doesn't this just start to get over-complicated? Aren't there advantages to a one size fits all consistency (even if we have already carved out an exception for some medical treatment)?

This may all be academic for now. But if these arguments start to find favour with the courts, they will need a little more thought.

In reality, our definition of deprivation of liberty would be less fraught if we could move away from the binary cliff edge where meeting the definition or not makes a huge difference to the scrutiny and safeguards available. As the Law Commission proposed, something more gradual including consideration of those not yet regarded as deprived of liberty would take much of the angst out of this[775].

Something similar is under consideration in Scotland, where the Scottish Government felt that "deprivation of liberty" was "not a particularly helpful term", and suggesting a scheme of gradual guardianship, focussed on "significant restrictions on liberty" that could satisfy the demands of Article 5 without being explicitly tied solely to the idea of detention.

But as the Law Commission found[776], any such expansion would need the resources to make it real.

Resources

None of this makes sense without thinking about resources.

After his retirement, Lord Justice Munby said that the proper resourcing of any system to replace DoLS "*would be more significant and important than its structure*". [777]

It is not just a matter of effectively fully funding DoLS / the court to run the system we have now, put at £1.9bn in the LPS Impact Assessment[778]. There is also the issue of qualified and experienced staff to make it work.

More fundamentally, though, there is the strained resources of the health and social care system as a whole. It may be no coincidence that this issue has played out mostly in the austerity years since 2010. We would

[775] Scottish Government Adults with Incapacity (Scotland) Act 2000, Proposals for Reform. https://www.gov.scot/publications/adults-incapacity-scotland-act-2000-proposals-reform/

[776] See chapter 17 – these proposals were abandoned when opposed by the government due to the costs.

[777] "Dispatches from the front line: some current problems". Legal Action Group Community Care Law Conference, 2018.

[778] See chapter 16.

certainly see fewer deprivation of liberty cases in hospital, for example, if there were not such an appalling shortage of social care support available.

Imagine a world where people could be supported and encouraged to live where and how they want to with resource enough to do it. Would we still need a heated discussion about deprivation of liberty then?

The judiciary have been more ready, recently, to defy the tyranny of the single option being presented by public bodies when it simply cannot be described as being in the best interests of a vulnerable child, for example.

But as Lucy Series writes,

> *"The MCA and DoLS require the courts to stand "in the person's shoes" and choose between the options available to them; too often these choices are undesirable or unacceptable and substitute decision makers stand in ragged, pinching shoes."*[779]

Are we well served, then, when lack of resource (whether money or staff) means that someone does not get to live where they want to, or with the care package that they need or want, to respond by *identifying it as a deprivation of their liberty*, which brings only safeguards that are entirely toothless to tackle that underlying problem?[780]

I don't assume that resources will be more plentiful anytime soon, but it is hard to see that time and money is being well spent just now.

If I get the maths right, I reckon that if a DoLS referral is made for you today, you have around a 10 times great chance of dying before it is completed than you have of it being refused for failure to meet the

[779] Series 2022, p213.

[780] While I am howling at the moon, perhaps I can also wish for a world in which someone with a disability can just "go out", like anyone might, rather than "access the community". And perhaps, even in these straightened times, might we have a critical look at the poverty of ambition of the typical care plan for an older patient with dementia, compared to a younger patient with a learning disability?

qualifying criteria; more than *400 times* greater chance of dying than it being refused for not being in your best interests!

Is this really making enough of a difference, often enough, to be worth it?

If this all feels a little bleak right now, there are positive things we can do.

CHAPTER TWENTY

WHAT NOW?

Revising our approach to Article 5, moving the goalposts of those we include, would need new case law, if not legislation.

Reforming the way we deal with those cases, with a more streamlined process – LPS or something like it, in due course – seems unlikely to happen anytime soon.

And resourcing the system we have more generously might be equally optimistic.

But even without revision, reform or resources, it is in our hands to keep doing better with the tools we have.

Back to basics

A former regional DoLS lead, Lorraine Currie has been a stalwart of the DoLS system for many years, with a key role in streamlining the template forms in use, as well as in developing the ADASS guidance I mentioned earlier.

Her advice now is to get back to basics[781]. Look at what is *essential* in the DoLS process, do what we have to and no more. Some things, she says, are not required in the legislation, but have become custom and practice.

She gives examples that the BIA must record the name of every person consulted, but the Act does not say that they must consult them[782]. It

781 https://www.mentalcapacitylawandpolicy.org.uk/guest-post-by-lorraine-currie-i-wouldnt-start-from-here-a-blog-about-the-deprivation-of-liberty-safeguards/

782 For the purposes of DoLS, though of course s4 MCA sets out the need for consultation about the underlying best interests decisions.

does not say that both the mental health assessor and the BIA must visit the person, or specify the length and depth of any visit. There is nothing prescriptive about the signatory or authorisation role at the supervisory body.

Of course, we must also be mindful of the obligations of the underlying best interests decisions being made per the MCA, not just the DoLS stuff that overlays it, and in places it is good practice that has fleshed out the system. But, she writes, "*we simply do not have this luxury any longer when 41,000 people are dying without any protection being afforded for them, and at least 125,000 still wait*". (The figures have got worse since then[783]).

Currie went back to the legislation and extracted a helpful list of the things that actually must be done by each of the moving parts in the DoLS process – the managing authority, supervisory body, BIA and mental health assessor, and suggests that we use this to refocus our efforts. She has kindly agreed that I can reproduce it as Appendix 6.

I would add the same for applications to court for deprivation of liberty in the community, which must not be forgotten. Especially for those going through the *Re X* process, where we are used to making full blown applications to court, we must avoid the temptation to over engineer them. The court will judge whether the application meets the needs of Article 5, and doing more than that does no good for the people we are not getting round to.

Look beyond DoLS

We must stop treating the Deprivation of Liberty Safeguards as if they are the only game in town. As we have seen, they are only a part of the picture of the law about deprivation of liberty, and we should stop discussing the care homes and hospitals bit as if it is the only bit that matters, treating everything else as ancillary.

[783] See chapter 16 and Appendix 1.

I am much more often asked to give training on "DoLS" than on deprivation of liberty. But unless or until the law moves the goalposts, as imagined above, deprivation of liberty in the community matters just as much.

Remember that the obligation on the ICB to take steps (ie an application to court) to authorise a deprivation of liberty in the community for a package of care funded by continuing healthcare is set out in the National Framework for Continuing Healthcare[784], and does not depend on LPS coming into force.

And look beyond the deprivation of liberty

Equally, the deprivation of liberty – important as it is – is only one aspect of the person's care. We will get in less trouble if we think about the care planning more holistically, and give as much attention to Article 8 (right to respect for private and family life issues) rather than thinking only about Article 5.

Use the *Ferreira* exception

Among the piles of outstanding DoLS referrals are, no doubt, a number where there is a reasonable argument that it is not a deprivation of liberty due to the *Ferreira* carve out for some medical treatment[785].

While the precise extent of the exception is not yet clear, I think it is important that each hospital takes a view, with appropriate advice, on where it intends to draw the line, and sticks to it confidently, avoiding clogging the system up unnecessarily. I still see too many acute NHS trusts where this does not seem to have been included in their policy or in their practice.

[784] See chapter 14.

[785] See chapter 7.

Beware mission creep

Both for the sake of the individuals and the demands on the system, we must avoid the trap of getting drawn into using the tools to regulate deprivation of liberty just because we have them.

Lucy Series identifies the trend that laws introduced as purported safeguards around restrictive practices can have the counterproductive effect of legitimising and perpetuating them. Instead of trying harder to prevent the deprivation of liberty, we can be tempted to just identify and authorise it:

> *"History tells us that what begins as 'safeguards' for individual liberty can become the cutting edge of new forms of power"*[786].

There is an example in the recent case of *CC*[787], in which the local authority asked the court to authorise a deprivation of liberty for a 15 year-old girl where she would be under continuous supervision and control and not free to leave a placement on the basis that this was necessary to protect her from a risk of child sexual exploitation. She had no mental disorder, and felt effectively imprisoned against her will. The judge found that evidence of a real risk of CSE was flimsy at best, not least as the local authority were content for CC to have weekends away unsupervised, when surely any risk would have been at its highest. The judge formed the impression that the restrictions were not entirely necessary and may have been more for the convenience of the provider; no evidence was considered about other options that might have been available. This was no basis for making an order that allowed CC to be deprived of her liberty, and perhaps her care would have been approached differently if that application had not been possible.

---

786 Series, "Deprivation of Liberty in the Shadows of the Institution", Bristol University Press, 2022, p8.

787 [2023] EWHC 2179 (Fam)

"A Spotlight not a Padlock"

Likewise, the safeguards – whether DoLS or the court system – are safeguards, not tools of control. A spotlight not a padlock; to be used, to meet P's Article 5 rights, when the care that is appropriate, the least restrictive way to meet someone's best interests, necessary and proportionate to prevent harm, nonetheless amounts to a deprivation of their liberty.

So let's get away from the attitude, and the language – "*we DoLSed him*" – that suggests otherwise.

Keep it simple

Remember the point of all this: to ensure that there are appropriate safeguards and due process whenever an intervention in someone else's life, however well intentioned, reaches a certain level of intrusiveness.

Do not get too hung up on the complexities. For most of us, all we need to worry about is triggering that additional scrutiny when we recognise that there is *a risk of* a deprivation of liberty.

Build consideration of deprivation of liberty into care planning

LPS was designed to bring concern about whether there is a deprivation of liberty into the care planning itself, but there is nothing to stop us adopting this aspect of LPS thinking now.

Care planning should not happen without consideration of the individual's capacity to make their own decisions about the accommodation, care or treatment. In that assessment of capacity make sure that account is taken of the information about the (proposed) confinement[788].

---

788 *A PCT v LDV* [2013] EWHC 272; see chapter 9.

Care planning in someone's best interests where they lack capacity for the relevant decisions should explicitly consider not only whether the package is the least restrictive way to meet their best interests, but whether it might amount to a deprivation of liberty, and if so whether it is necessary and proportionate to prevent harm to that person.

Gathering the evidence to support this will be easier when this really has been done as we go, rather than trying to justify it when scrutinised afterwards.

Stop waiting for the cavalry

For some years, there would have been an understandable temptation to hang on until the LPS reforms made things easier. Perhaps, not to prioritise applications to court for deprivations of liberty in the community if an expanded scheme might soon provide an easier way. Maybe, not to refresh the MCA or DoLS policy or provide updated training if it was all going to change soon anyway. Those nettles have to be grasped now.

In the State of Care Report 2022/23, the CQC noted that the focus on training on deprivation of liberty had weakened while there was a prospect of the LPS coming soon, and that this needs to change[789].

Equally, we might now expect to see challenges brought to some of the significant problems that LPS would have addressed. Most obvious is the inconsistency of availability of non-means tested legal aid to s21A cases, but not to other litigation that authorises a deprivation of someone's liberty. Worse, perhaps, if your urgent authorisation has lapsed and a standard authorisation is not yet in place, there is no DoLS authorisation on which to hang a s21A case to get that legal aid.

[789] https://www.cqc.org.uk/publications/major-report/state-care/2022-2023/dols

Change what we can

The move to more positive language in LPS would have been welcome, but there is nothing stopping us from using the language of "*protecting*" P's liberty rather than "*depriving*" them or it. As Neil Allen observes[790], neither the terms "deprivation of liberty safeguards" nor "liberty protection safeguards" are in the actual legislation.

He also notes that the existing legislation:

- Allows use of "equivalent assessments"[791], relying on an assessment already done within the previous 12 months rather than repeating it afresh, perhaps more than is being widely used.

- Does not specify the authorisation role at the supervisory body, still less that every DoLS authorisations must be dealt with at the same senior level. Just as the courts initially heard deprivation of liberty cases only at High Court Judge level, they are now allocated among the wider and more junior judiciary according to their complexity. Might supervisory bodies broaden the pool of authorisers and triage in the same way?

- Allows for reviews, which are less onerous than authorisations. These could be used more, with BIAs including provision for an early or periodic review instead of recommending only a short authorisation, allowing more cases to be authorised for the maximum 12 months.

Proportionality and pragmatism

Even if we do not see the law change to take those in their own homes and / or those positively wishing to be in those care arrangements out of

---

790 https://lpslaw.co.uk/blog/files/coronation.php

791 MCA Schedule A1 paragraph 49.

our definition of deprivation of liberty[792], might we reasonably see those features as reassuring and indicative of needing a lower level of scrutiny?

Note that this is not the same thing as having a one size fits all process and deprioritising certain cases to the point where they are unlikely to be reviewed in any meaningful way at all. But just as we have the streamlined process for the community deprivation of liberty cases, can we reasonably apply a lighter touch for some DoLS cases?

Lorraine Currie argues that there are essentially two categories of case:

> *"those who need technical protection i.e. Article 5 requires it, but they're quite 'happy' there are no issues and no benefit arises from DoLS other than the safeguard of the safeguards. These should be shorter, simpler, checks on the arrangements. Then there are those who require substantive protection i.e. they are objecting, they never wanted to be in the place, they are heavily sedated, they are actively trying to leave etc. for these people DoLS often brings a substantive outcome; a return home, a care plan review with reduced restrictions, conditions set and so on.*
>
> *Until we feel comfortable drawing this line and practicing within the law in a pragmatic and proportionate way, I think DoLS will keep getting bigger."*[793]

Get the MCA right

Though deprivation of liberty can happen for those under 16 or who have capacity to make their own decisions, the MCA is the heartland of this; and getting the MCA wrong is almost always where things go off the rails for deprivation of liberty cases.

---

[792] See chapter 19.

[793] Private email correspondence, 20 October 2023.

This is why getting the policies and training up to date, implemented effectively and embedded, is so important.

The best way to avoid problems with deprivation of liberty issues is to get the MCA right:

- Focus on the decision that needs to be made, and the options actually available;
- Do not mistake a finding that someone lacks capacity for decisions about their care and residence to mean that they lack capacity for every other decision.
- Be wary of the "*protection imperative*" – Do not be too quick to find a lack of capacity where we want to intervene to keep someone safe, or to conclude that the safest option is the one that is in their best interests, properly understood more broadly.
- Remember that *what P wants matters*, whether or not they have capacity to make the decision. Proper weight must be put on their wishes and feelings, values and beliefs (and if we do move towards implementation of the UNCRPD we will need to be thinking about their "*will and preferences*").
- Best interests decision making should be collaborative and open-minded. The people to be involved are those who can best answer the question "*tell me about Bob?*", not exclusively those who may claim the closest family relationship. Be sceptical of those – whether professional or family – who insists that they alone know what's best.
- The Court of Protection should be used readily and promptly to resolve any doubt about capacity or about best interests, and not only when relationships and trust have already failed entirely.

It will help, no doubt, if we can get an updated MCA Code of Practice, if this is to be published sometime soon, perhaps once the LPS bits are stripped out. But I do not advise just waiting for this, while the timetable is uncertain and unreliable.

Push for reform

Wider reform may be off the table for now, but we don't have to like it.

The Welsh Government, for example, said it was:

> *"deeply disappointed with this decision not to proceed with implementation at this time. The right to liberty is one of our most fundamental human rights."*

The British Association of Social Workers added:

> *"Taking all this together gives the impression that the Government simply does not regard the everyday crisis situations that face many of the most vulnerable people, their families and the people who support them as worthy of energy and attention.... Tens of thousands of the most vulnerable people across England and Wales deserve better".*

Many other organisations have protested that this needs to be prioritised, and we can each lend our voice to this. For what it is worth, this is mine.

Look for the positives

In canvassing input for this book on social media, I was most surprised by the response when I asked people for the positives of the current system.

People said:

> *"helping people return home to where they wanted to live, without which their home would have been sold, leaving them with little option but to remain in a care home".*

"Advocacy under DoLS as one of the best rights protections … and self-funders who have no family or external oversight then having a voice in decision making…"

"as a BIA I was able to put into the conditions that a man with Korsakoff syndrome would have to have a functional skills assessment and rehabilitation programme by an Occupational Therapist, and when I reviewed him 6 months later he was able to move into a supportive living facility."

"Even if it's not fully understood, it has introduced new language that was not always used very often before, such as "least restrictive". Also it has helped people and their relatives to challenge and have access to the Court of Protection."

"The focus on autonomy and the switch to least restrictive has been transformative of attitudes and led to cultural change."

"I am immensely proud to have seen many wins for P. Most importantly for me is that P gets their voice heard, sometimes for the first time."

"Ensuring that P is legally detained; allowing professionals to focus on goals, ie discharge planning; ensuring that the person has advocacy support which is sometimes the crucial link to them getting legal advice. And in the event that a move from a care home is not possible, ensuring that small changes are made to make the person feel they have been listened to".

"It has curtailed arbitrary detention and paternalistic practice considerably."

"…recently enabled a self-funder to return home after 18 months in a care home, much to their relief"

"BIAs keep social care professionals on track with what is in the persons best interests rather than processes and budgets. DoLS provides the means for the person's voice to be heard, protects those who have no

family or friends to advocate for them and provides a quality check on care homes."

"Some years ago I went into a care home to assess someone placed by a LA when he lacked capacity but not re assessed. I found he was detained there but had regained capacity & I was able to arrange for him to go home the same day".

"Even when other residence options not feasible DoLS has been the catalyst for making liberating changes to care plans, either via conscientious BIA review/ conditions or legal scrutiny through CoP. More generally, DoLS has created the legal footing for human rights activism within health & social care, and has put safeguarding rights firmly on the agenda, alongside safeguarding from risks of harm".

"The potential power of conditions! During the covid pandemic & block on family visiting people in hospital, I assessed a lady with dementia who would not eat, largely I felt as she was missing her husband so badly. I recommended the condition he be allowed to come in to support her to eat at lunch time & they allowed this and he came in and she ate!"

"It gives P a voice. As a BIA I have been instrumental in starting the process for more than one P to go back to their own home".

This is not a story without heroes; not only the Enderby family who adopted HL in the Bournewood case[794], Mark and Steven Neary[795], and RF, whose efforts reunited his old friend CP with is cat Fluffy[796]; but the countless unnamed friends and families who care for, and fight for, those they love.

And I would also acknowledge the social workers, and clinicians, the IMCAs and RPRs, the BIAs and mental health assessors and even –

794 Chapter 2.

795 Chapter 3.

796 Chapter 15.

occasionally – lawyers whose commitment and everyday professional excellence sadly does not generate the headlines that bad news routinely does. There is a professional pride around many of these roles, taking seriously their roles as protectors of human rights or, in a term coined by Lucy Series, "empowerment entrepreneurs".

The judiciary dealing with these cases have by and large done so with great sensitivity and empathy; and the providers or care, NHS bodies and local authorities involved – who I am proud to act for – are overwhelmingly driven by doing the right thing for P.

And if anything good has come from the abortive (so far) attempts to introduce LPS, it is that attention has been drawn to the issues around deprivation of liberty again, and in particular the need to focus on the underlying care planning and getting the MCA right.

And finally – remember that this matters, and why

As I said at the start: this matters because this is the legal framework that protects us when other people, however well intentioned, start making decisions about where and how we live, often through to the end of our lives. What is more fundamental to our identity or our autonomy than that?

We have managed to develop a system that leaves hundreds of thousands of people without any meaningful safeguards, or deprived of their liberty unlawfully; organisations exposed to potential liabilities; huge amounts of time and money spent on a system that appears too often to yield little real benefit to those it is supposed to protect.

This matters, and we owe it to everyone involved to do better than this.

APPENDICES

APPENDIX 1

STARTLING STATISTICS[797]

85% of DoLS authorisations are for someone over the age of 65.

42% are for people over the age of 85.

1,700 pa – DoLS referrals pa by 2015/16 anticipated by the original DoLS impact assessment in 2008, settling down from around 5,000 pa on implementation, with a worst case scenario of 20,000 pa.

13,000 – DoLS applications received in 2013/14.

137,540 – DoLS applications received in 2014/15, the year after the Cheshire West Supreme Court judgment.

300,765 – DoLS applications received in 2022/23.

21 days – the legal timescale for completion of a DoLS referral.

19% – proportion of DoLS applications completed within 21 days in 2022/23.

156 days – the average time taken for completion of a DoLS referral in 2022/23.

126,050 – DoLS applications incomplete as at 31 March 2022.

39,810 – DoLS applications outstanding for more than 365 days as at 31 March 2022.

---

[797] Mostly drawn from – https://digital.nhs.uk/data-and-information/publications/statistical/mental-capacity-act-2005-deprivation-of-liberty-safeguards-assessments/2022-23 so relating to England only.

102,240 – DoLS applications refused in 2022/23 due to "change in circumstances" by the time they were assessed.

<2% – proportion of DoLS applications completed in 2022/23 refused for failing to meet one or more of the qualifying criteria (5,610 / 289,150).

<0.04% – proportion of DoLS applications completed in 2022/23 refused for not meeting the best interests qualifying requirement (115 / 289,150).

49,325 – people died while awaiting the outcome of a DoLS application in 2022/23.

53,000 – government estimate of the number of adults deprived of their liberty outside the scope of DoLS, for whom an application must be made to court.

6,265 – the total number of applications to the Court of Protection relating to deprivation of liberty in 2022, of which around a third are challenges to DoLS authorisations rather than applications to authorise a deprivation of liberty in the community.

6,600 – Department of Education estimate of the number of 16-17 year-olds for whom an application to authorise a deprivation of liberty is needed each year.

£1.92 billion – the *additional cost each year* to "*fully operationalise*" the current DoLS and Court of Protection system to authorise deprivations of liberty, according to the LPS Impact Assessment, March 2022.

APPENDIX 2

TIMELINE TO (NON) REFORM

13 March 2014	Parliamentary post legislative scrutiny committee on the MCA and DoLS reports that DoLS must be urgently replaced
19 March 2014	Cheshire West Supreme Court judgment
July 2015	Law Commission consultation on deprivation of liberty and interim proposals
May 2016	Law Commission interim report
March 2017	Law Commission final report and proposed draft legislation
March 2018	Government response to the Law Commission approach
July 2018	Mental Capacity (Amendment) Bill introduced outlining the Liberty Protection Safeguards

May 2019	Mental Capacity (Amendment) Act passed
March 2022	Publication of draft Code of Practice and consultation
July 2022	Consultation of draft Code of Practice closed
April 2023	Announcement that LPS will not be implemented before the next general election
Autumn 2023	Government response to the LPS consultation still outstanding

APPENDIX 3

A STATUTORY DEFINITION?

When the Mental Capacity (Amendment) Act 2019 enacting the LPS was on its way through Parliament, establishing the LPS system, there was a difference of opinion about a statutory definition of deprivation of liberty to trigger the new system's safeguards. No definition was included, initially, but in response to pressure from some quarters the government agreed to (in these terms) "give it a go"!

If that was not too reassuring, see what you think of this, which was the wording eventually proposed for a statutory definition:

> *(1) In this Act, references to deprivation of a person's liberty have the same meaning as in Article 5(1) of the Human Rights Convention and, accordingly, a person is not deprived of liberty in any of the circumstances described in subsections (2) to (4).*
>
> *(2) A person is not deprived of liberty in a particular place if the person is free to leave that place permanently.*
>
> *(3) A person is not deprived of liberty in a particular place if*
>
> > *a. The person is not subject to continuous supervision, and*
> >
> > *b. The person is free to leave the place temporarily (even if subject to supervision while outside that place).*
>
> *(4) A person is not deprived of liberty if*
>
> > *a. The arrangements alleged to give rise to the deprivation of liberty are put in place in order to give medical treatment for a physical illness or injury, and*

> *b. The same (or materially the same) arrangements would be put in place for any person receiving that treatment.*

All clear?!

This was not presented as any modification of the position based on existing case law, but just attempted, we were told, to faithfully capture the *Cheshire West* test, as modified by *Ferreira*.

I am not sure how well it captures the element of "control" from the acid test, alongside the supervision and not being free to leave, or whether the Court of Appeal in *Ferreira* would have recognised their exception as stretching to *any* medical treatment of a physical illness or injury.

But still, this is of largely academic interest only now, as it was abandoned for the more prosaic reason that this car crash of double negatives was widely considered more confusing than having no statutory definition at all.

On reflection, it was decided that the complex questions about the nature of deprivation of liberty to trigger the LPS system would best be left out of the legislation but would be explained in the Code of Practice in due course. A cynic might have felt that the difficult questions were simply being kicked down the road to ease the passage of the legislation through parliament.

APPENDIX 4

AMENDED MENTAL CAPACITY ACT S4B

<u>Current MCA s4B:</u>

4B Deprivation of liberty necessary for life-sustaining treatment etc

(1) If the following conditions are met, D is authorised to deprive P of his liberty while a decision as respects any relevant issue is sought from the court.

(2) The first condition is that there is a question about whether D is authorised to deprive P of his liberty under section 4A.

(3) The second condition is that the deprivation of liberty—

(a) is wholly or partly for the purpose of—

(i) giving P life-sustaining treatment, or

(ii) doing any vital act, or

(b) consists wholly or partly of—

(i) giving P life-sustaining treatment, or

(ii) doing any vital act.

(4) The third condition is that the deprivation of liberty is necessary in order to—

(a) give the life-sustaining treatment, or

(b) do the vital act.

(5) A vital act is any act which the person doing it reasonably believes to be necessary to prevent a serious deterioration in P's condition.

MCA s4B as amended by the Mental Capacity (Amendment) Act 2019

These amendments are NOT YET IN FORCE

(1) If Conditions 1 to 4 are met, D is authorised to take steps which deprive P of liberty.

(2) Condition 1 is that the steps—

(a) are wholly or partly for the purpose of giving P life-sustaining treatment or doing any vital act, or

(b) consist wholly or partly of giving P life-sustaining treatment or doing any vital act.

(3) A vital act is any act which the person doing it reasonably believes to be necessary to prevent a serious deterioration in P's condition.

(4) Condition 2 is that the steps are necessary in order to give the life-sustaining treatment or do the vital act.

(5) Condition 3 is that D reasonably believes that P lacks capacity to consent to D taking the steps.

(6) Condition 4 is that—

(a) subsection (7) applies, or

(b) there is an emergency.

(7) This subsection applies if—

(a) a decision relevant to whether D is authorised to deprive P of liberty is being sought from the court, or

(b) a responsible body is carrying out functions under Schedule AA1 [that's the LPS] with a view to determining whether to authorise arrangements that give rise to a deprivation of P's liberty.

(8) In subsection (7) it does not matter—

(a) whether the decision mentioned in paragraph (a) relates to the steps mentioned in subsection (1);

(b) whether the arrangements mentioned in paragraph (b) include those steps.

(9) There is an emergency if D reasonably believes that—

(a) there is an urgent need to take the steps mentioned in subsection (1) in order to give the life-sustaining treatment or do the vital act, and

(b) it is not reasonably practicable before taking those steps—

(i) to make an application for P to be detained under Part 2 of the Mental Health Act,

(ii) to make an application within subsection (7)(a), or

(iii) to secure that action within subsection (7)(b) is taken.

APPENDIX 5

MARK NEARY'S BLOG EXTRACT

From: https://markneary1dotcom1.wordpress.com/2017/03/18/the-day-cowley-became-a-gilded-cage/

18 March 2017.

> *"I have to say there is not one single moment of one single day as I observe Steven going about his business in his own home where it occurs to me that he might be being deprived of his liberty. Having been through the DoLS process when Steven was in the ATU, there isn't any comparison between his life then and his life now. The doors aren't alarmed. He isn't subjected to face down restraint (or any kind of restraint for that matter). He isn't given bucket loads of anti psychotics to make our job easier. He isn't prevented from going out for three months whilst we risk assess all the venues he goes to. He no longer lives an institutionalized life.*
>
> *So, do the deciding factors in Lady Hale's Acid Test apply to Steven in his Cowley home? Is he free to leave at any time? Is he under constant supervision? Immediately, I hit a problem because that is not the sort of language we use in his home. Steven's life isn't framed that way anymore. In the ATU, Steven was always trying to escape. In the six years since he's been home, he's never once attempted to escape. If he wants to go and get some Chewits, he'll say to me or the support worker, "Want to go to Jay's sweet shop to get some sweets". And off we go. I suppose the DoLS assessor will concentrate on the "we" in the previous sentence. Why is it "off we go" rather than "off he goes"? There are a number of reasons. Steven has poor road sense. Steven struggles with money, so would have difficulty paying for his Chewits. If a barking dog was to pass him along the street, Steven will become anxious and*

possibly kick the dog. That's why someone accompanies Steven to the shop. We don't see that as not being free to leave.

The second factor is "constant supervision". Steven needs someone with him 24/7. This is to support him with those things he cannot do and to prevent him from coming to harm if he becomes anxious. I've never once heard the support staff say that they are "supervising" Steven. It isn't the language of home life but it is the language of the institution. Steven has just put his Carry On Doctor DVD on. There are eight DVDs in the boxed set and he needed my help in selecting the right disc. As the menu is pictorial, Steven was able to select the correct movie from the drop down list. Was my input there supervision? Or helping? Now that Steven has settled into watching the film, I am typing this blog in my room and the support worker is doing the ironing in Steven's bedroom. Neither of us are directly supervising him.

Graham Enderby, who should know more about DoLS than most, said to me recently: "DoLs were meant to be about getting people back into their homes. Now they are about keeping people from their homes". He's spot on. And this ridiculous attempt to assess for a deprivation of liberty in one's own home has been shoehorned into legislation that wasn't written with that purpose.

I've no idea what is going to happen at the social worker's visit on Thursday. I've no idea of the questions that will be asked. I'm already feeling mightily resistant to Steven's life being reduced to something that it clearly isn't. To compound the nonsense of this, if the assessor decides that Steven is being deprived of his liberty in Cowley, the DoL can only be authorised by the Court of Protection. A supervisory body authorisation doesn't apply in Community DoLS cases. Just think of the time and the cost involved in that exercise. I imagine the social worker leaving on Thursday; Steven and I will get on with living our lives exactly as we were doing immediately before the visit. But a whole team of professionals will burst into action to follow through the bureaucratic process. Once again, another process that is nothing to do with Steven's life.

Roll on LPS. Perhaps a more sensible approach will be adopted[798]".

[798] We now know, of course, that at face value the definition of deprivation of liberty would not have changed under LPS, and so Steven might be expected to have still been regarded as needing an authorisation for this, albeit it might have been easier to do this through LPS than having to go to the Court of Protection, even under the *Re X* process.

APPENDIX 6

SCHEDULE A1 ESSENTIALS

With thanks to Lorraine Currie for her work and for sharing this.

What does Schedule A1 MCA actually require of each partner?

Schedule A1 MCA				
Managing Authority	Supervisory Body	General	Best Interests Assessor	Mental Health Assessor
Must request an authorisation if conditions are met	Must ensure all assessments are carried out by someone suitable and eligible. No definition of 'assessment' but regulations state who can carry out assessments.	What a request for a Standard Authorisation (SA) must include	Best Interests assessor (BIA) must consult the Managing Authority (MA)	Must consider how persons mental health will be affected and must notify BIA
Must keep a record of each request	Must keep a record of all requests	Regulations set time periods within which assessments must be carried out (21 days)	Must record the name of every interested person they have consulted	Must keep written copies of the assessment and give to Supervisory Body (SB)
Must give the BIA a copy of any assessments/care plans	Must give BIA copies of their needs assessment/care plan		Must have regard to Mental Health Assessors (MHA) conclusions	Must take account of any information provided by Relevant Persons Representative (RPR) and Independent Mental Capacity Advocate (IMCA)

Must notify SB if there is a change in place of detention	Can use equivalent assessments if less than 12 months old and there is no reason it is not still accurate but if using equivalent assessment Best Interests must take into account info by RPR, IMCA		Must have regard to needs assessments and care plans	
Must ensure the person is told about authorisation and understands effects and rights.	Must give authorisation if all assessments are positive and must not give if any are not positive. No instructions as to how this is carried out i.e., no concept of an Authoriser/signatory. If any assessments are negative they must tell any other assessor to cease their assessment.		Must state maximum authorisation period	
Must keep record of granted and not grated	Must decide the period no more than best interests assessor recommends		Must state if there's an unauthorised dol	
Must give an urgent if requirements are met and request a standard at the same time.	Must be in writing and state all following ….		Must consider if it is appropriate by review to vary conditions	
If give an urgent it must be up to 7 days in writing and state following …..	Must give copies as soon as practicable		Must keep written copies of the assessment and give to SB	
Must keep written record and inform interested persons.	Must have regard to BIA recommendation before setting conditions		Must take account of any information provided by RPR IMCA	
Must explain the effect and keep a record.	Must give notice authorisation ceased			

Must tell SB if the person ceases to meet eligibility	Must select assessors in response to third party requests, not if they wouldn't be eligible or appropriate.			
Must ensure any conditions on the authorisation are complied with	Must keep record of 3rd party requests and copies must be given and everyone notified everyone of outcome			
Third party request MA must supply all detail they would have	Must decide if to extend urgent and must give notice of decision			
	Must give notice urgent ceased to be in force			
	Must suspend and give notice and again when not suspended			
	Must carry out a review if requested by … Must give notice of the review, decide which grounds etc			
	Must vary or terminate following review and give notice/ written record			
	Must not select an assessor unless suitable, eligible and must not be same person for best interests and mental health			
	If using equivalent best interests assessment must consider, any representations from RPR/IMCA			
	Must appoint a representative as soon as practicable after authorisation and if a vacancy occurs during authorisation			

	The representative must not be appointed unless they can maintain contact with the person and represent and support them in relation to DoLS.			

BIBLIOGRAPHY

The best resource to find the case law referred to is:
https://www.bailii.org/databases.html

From there you can search for Court of Protection and High Court cases as well as Court of Appeal and House of Lords / Supreme Court judgments, using a key word search or the citation I have given.

Lucy Series – Deprivation of Liberty in the Shadows of the Institution; Bristol University Press, 2022. It is available open access as an e-book here:
https://bristoluniversitypressdigital.com/display/book/9781529212006/9781529212006.xml

Sarah Wise – "Inconvenient People: Lunacy, Liberty and the Mad Doctors in Victorian England", 2013.

Ben Troke – A Practical Guide to the Law of Medical Treatment Decisions, Law Brief Publishing, 2020 – for more on the MCA and capacity / consent / best interests decisions generally (and all proceeds to the Alzheimer's Society) –
http://www.lawbriefpublishing.com/product/medicaltreatmentdecisions

Many helpful resources, as well as always insightful commentary, are made available by 39 Essex Chambers –
https://www.39essex.com/information-hub/mental-capacity-resource-centre

And by Alex Ruck Keene KC (Hons) –
https://www.mentalcapacitylawandpolicy.org.uk/

Mark Neary – Get Steven Home, 2011 –
https://www.lulu.com/shop/mark-neary/get-steven-home/ebook/product-1dn2vww8.html?page=1&pageSize=4

Mark Neary – "There's Always Something or Other with Mr Neary", 2013 – https://www.lulu.com/shop/mark-neary/theres-always-something-or-other-with-mr-neary/paperback/product-1ggye6n8.html?q=neary&page=1&pageSize=4

Blog – https://markneary1dotcom1.wordpress.com/

Deprivation of Liberty Handbook, Second Edition – Aasya F Mughal and Steven Richards – https://www.bookswise.org.uk/deprivation-of-liberty-safeguards-d

Rachel Hubbard and Kevin Stone – "Best Interests Assessor Practice Handbook", Policy Press, 2018.

The Law Society produced guidance on identification of a deprivation of liberty in various settings in 2015, which is available here, and is currently being updated (to which I am pleased to be contributing) – https://www.lawsociety.org.uk/topics/private-client/deprivation-of-liberty-safeguards-a-practical-guide

MORE BOOKS BY LAW BRIEF PUBLISHING

A selection of our other titles available now:-

'A Practical Guide to the Independent School Standards – September 2023 Edition' by Sarah McKimm
'A Practical Guide to Estate Administration and Crypto Assets' by Richard Marshall
'A Practical Guide to Managing GDPR Data Subject Access Requests – Second Edition' by Patrick O'Kane
'A Practical Guide to Parental Alienation in Private and Public Law Children Cases' by Sam King QC & Frankie Shama
'Contested Heritage – Removing Art from Land and Historic Buildings' by Richard Harwood QC, Catherine Dobson, David Sawtell
'The Limits of Separate Legal Personality: When Those Running a Company Can Be Held Personally Liable for Losses Caused to Third Parties Outside of the Company' by Dr Mike Wilkinson
'A Practical Guide to Transgender Law' by Robin Moira White & Nicola Newbegin
'A Practical Guide to 'Stranded Spouses' in Family Law' by Mani Singh Basi
'A Practical Guide to Residential Freehold Conveyancing' by Lorraine Richardson
'A Practical Guide to Pensions on Divorce for Lawyers' by Bryan Scant
'A Practical Guide to Challenging Sham Marriage Allegations in Immigration Law' by Priya Solanki
'A Practical Guide to Digital Communications Evidence in Criminal Law' by Sam Willis
'A Practical Guide to Legal Rights in Scotland' by Sarah-Jane Macdonald
'A Practical Guide to New Build Conveyancing' by Paul Sams & Rebecca East
'A Practical Guide to Defending Barristers in Disciplinary Cases' by Marc Beaumont
'A Practical Guide to Inherited Wealth on Divorce' by Hayley Trim
'A Practical Guide to Practice Direction 12J and Domestic Abuse in Private Law Children Proceedings' by Rebecca Cross & Malvika Jaganmohan

'A Practical Guide to Confiscation and Restraint' by Narita Bahra QC, John Carl Townsend, David Winch
'A Practical Guide to the Law of Forests in Scotland' by Philip Buchan
'A Practical Guide to Health and Medical Cases in Immigration Law' by Rebecca Chapman & Miranda Butler
'A Practical Guide to Bad Character Evidence for Criminal Practitioners by Aparna Rao
'A Practical Guide to Extradition Law post-Brexit' by Myles Grandison et al
'A Practical Guide to Hoarding and Mental Health for Housing Lawyers' by Rachel Coyle
'A Practical Guide to Psychiatric Claims in Personal Injury – 2nd Edition' by Liam Ryan
'Stephens on Contractual Indemnities' by Richard Stephens
'A Practical Guide to the EU Succession Regulation' by Richard Frimston
'A Practical Guide to Solicitor and Client Costs – 2nd Edition' by Robin Dunne
'Constructive Dismissal – Practice Pointers and Principles' by Benjimin Burgher
'A Practical Guide to Religion and Belief Discrimination Claims in the Workplace' by Kashif Ali
'A Practical Guide to the Law of Medical Treatment Decisions' by Ben Troke
'Fundamental Dishonesty and QOCS in Personal Injury Proceedings: Law and Practice' by Jake Rowley
'A Practical Guide to the Law in Relation to School Exclusions' by Charlotte Hadfield & Alice de Coverley
'A Practical Guide to Divorce for the Silver Separators' by Karin Walker
'The Right to be Forgotten – The Law and Practical Issues' by Melissa Stock
'A Practical Guide to Planning Law and Rights of Way in National Parks, the Broads and AONBs' by James Maurici QC, James Neill et al
'A Practical Guide to Election Law' by Tom Tabori
'A Practical Guide to the Law in Relation to Surrogacy' by Andrew Powell
'A Practical Guide to Claims Arising from Fatal Accidents – 2nd Edition' by James Patience
'A Practical Guide to the Ownership of Employee Inventions – From Entitlement to Compensation' by James Tumbridge & Ashley Roughton
'A Practical Guide to Asbestos Claims' by Jonathan Owen & Gareth McAloon

'A Practical Guide to Stamp Duty Land Tax in England and Northern Ireland' by Suzanne O'Hara

'A Practical Guide to the Law of Farming Partnerships' by Philip Whitcomb

'Covid-19, Homeworking and the Law – The Essential Guide to Employment and GDPR Issues' by Forbes Solicitors

'Covid-19 and Criminal Law – The Essential Guide' by Ramya Nagesh

'Covid-19 and Family Law in England and Wales – The Essential Guide' by Safda Mahmood

'A Practical Guide to the Law of Unlawful Eviction and Harassment – 2nd Edition' by Stephanie Lovegrove

'Covid-19, Brexit and the Law of Commercial Leases – The Essential Guide' by Mark Shelton

'A Practical Guide to Costs in Personal Injury Claims – 2nd Edition' by Matthew Hoe

'A Practical Guide to the General Data Protection Regulation (GDPR) – 2nd Edition' by Keith Markham

'Ellis on Credit Hire – Sixth Edition' by Aidan Ellis & Tim Kevan

'A Practical Guide to Working with Litigants in Person and McKenzie Friends in Family Cases' by Stuart Barlow

'Protecting Unregistered Brands: A Practical Guide to the Law of Passing Off' by Lorna Brazell

'A Practical Guide to Secondary Liability and Joint Enterprise Post-Jogee' by Joanne Cecil & James Mehigan

'A Practical Guide to the Pre-Action RTA Claims Protocol for Personal Injury Lawyers' by Antonia Ford

'A Practical Guide to Neighbour Disputes and the Law' by Alexander Walsh

'A Practical Guide to Forfeiture of Leases' by Mark Shelton

'A Practical Guide to Coercive Control for Legal Practitioners and Victims' by Rachel Horman

'A Practical Guide to the Law of Driverless Cars – Second Edition' by Alex Glassbrook, Emma Northey & Scarlett Milligan

'A Practical Guide to TOLATA Claims' by Greg Williams

'A Practical Guide to Elderly Law – 2nd Edition' by Justin Patten

'A Practical Guide to Responding to Housing Disrepair and Unfitness Claims' by Iain Wightwick

'A Practical Guide to the Law of Bullying and Harassment in the Workplace' by Philip Hyland
'How to Be a Freelance Solicitor: A Practical Guide to the SRA-Regulated Freelance Solicitor Model' by Paul Bennett
'A Practical Guide to Prison Injury Claims' by Malcolm Johnson
'A Practical Guide to the Small Claims Track – 2nd Edition' by Dominic Bright
'A Practical Guide to Advising Clients at the Police Station' by Colin Stephen McKeown-Beaumont
'A Practical Guide to Antisocial Behaviour Injunctions' by Iain Wightwick
'Practical Mediation: A Guide for Mediators, Advocates, Advisers, Lawyers, and Students in Civil, Commercial, Business, Property, Workplace, and Employment Cases' by Jonathan Dingle with John Sephton
'The Mini-Pupillage Workbook' by David Boyle
'A Practical Guide to Crofting Law' by Brian Inkster
'A Practical Guide to the Law of Domain Names and Cybersquatting' by Andrew Clemson
'A Practical Guide to the Law of Gender Pay Gap Reporting' by Harini Iyengar
'NHS Whistleblowing and the Law' by Joseph England
'Employment Law and the Gig Economy' by Nigel Mackay & Annie Powell
'A Practical Guide to Noise Induced Hearing Loss (NIHL) Claims' by Andrew Mckie, Ian Skeate, Gareth McAloon
'An Introduction to Beauty Negligence Claims – A Practical Guide for the Personal Injury Practitioner' by Greg Almond
'Intercompany Agreements for Transfer Pricing Compliance' by Paul Sutton
'Zen and the Art of Mediation' by Martin Plowman
'A Practical Guide to the SRA Principles, Individual and Law Firm Codes of Conduct 2019 – What Every Law Firm Needs to Know' by Paul Bennett
'A Practical Guide to Adoption for Family Lawyers' by Graham Pegg
'A Practical Guide to Industrial Disease Claims' by Andrew Mckie & Ian Skeate
'A Practical Guide to Redundancy' by Philip Hyland
'A Practical Guide to Vicarious Liability' by Mariel Irvine
'A Practical Guide to Applications for Landlord's Consent and Variation of Leases' by Mark Shelton
'A Practical Guide to Relief from Sanctions Post-Mitchell and Denton' by Peter Causton

'A Practical Guide to Equity Release for Advisors' by Paul Sams
'A Practical Guide to Financial Services Claims' by Chris Hegarty
'The Law of Houses in Multiple Occupation: A Practical Guide to HMO Proceedings' by Julian Hunt
'Occupiers, Highways and Defective Premises Claims: A Practical Guide Post-Jackson – 2nd Edition' by Andrew Mckie
'A Practical Guide to Financial Ombudsman Service Claims' by Adam Temple & Robert Scrivenor
'A Practical Guide to Running Housing Disrepair and Cavity Wall Claims: 2nd Edition' by Andrew Mckie & Ian Skeate
'A Practical Guide to Holiday Sickness Claims – 2nd Edition' by Andrew Mckie & Ian Skeate
'Arguments and Tactics for Personal Injury and Clinical Negligence Claims' by Dorian Williams
'A Practical Guide to Drone Law' by Rufus Ballaster, Andrew Firman, Eleanor Clot
'A Practical Guide to Compliance for Personal Injury Firms Working With Claims Management Companies' by Paul Bennett
'RTA Allegations of Fraud in a Post-Jackson Era: The Handbook – 2nd Edition' by Andrew Mckie
'RTA Personal Injury Claims: A Practical Guide Post-Jackson' by Andrew Mckie
'On Experts: CPR35 for Lawyers and Experts' by David Boyle
'An Introduction to Personal Injury Law' by David Boyle

These books and more are available to order online direct from the publisher at www.lawbriefpublishing.com, where you can also read free sample chapters. For any queries, contact us on 0844 587 2383 or mail@lawbriefpublishing.com.

Our books are also usually in stock at www.amazon.co.uk with free next day delivery for Prime members, and at good legal bookshops such as Wildy & Sons.

We are regularly launching new books in our series of practical day-to-day practitioners' guides. Visit our website and join our free newsletter to be kept informed and to receive special offers, free chapters, etc.

You can also follow us on Twitter at www.twitter.com/lawbriefpub.

www.ingramcontent.com/pod-product-compliance
Lightning Source LLC
LaVergne TN
LVHW052213200926
848481LV00001B/94